TRADING ROLES

A book in the series

LATIN AMERICA OTHERWISE:

LANGUAGES, EMPIRES, NATIONS

Series editors:

Walter D. Mignolo, Duke University

Irene Silverblatt, Duke University

Sonia Saldívar-Hull, University of Texas at San Antonio

TRADING ROLES

Gender, Ethnicity, and the Urban Economy in

Colonial Potosí JANE E. MANGAN

DUKE UNIVERSITY PRESS Durham and London 2005

© 2005 Duke University Press

All rights reserved

Printed in the United States of America on acid-free paper ∞

Typeset in Carter and Cone Galliard

by Tseng Information Systems, Inc.

Library of Congress Cataloging-in-Publication Data

appear on the last printed page of this book.

To my darlings, Nicholas and Caroline

ABOUT THE SERIES

Latin America Otherwise: Languages, Empires, Nations is a critical series. It aims to explore the emergence and consequences of concepts used to define "Latin America" while at the same time exploring the broad interplay of political, economic, and cultural practices that have shaped Latin American worlds. Latin America, at the crossroads of competing imperial designs and local responses, has been construed as a geocultural and geopolitical entity since the nineteenth century. This series provides a starting point to redefine Latin America as a configuration of political, linguistic, cultural, and economic intersections that demands a continuous reappraisal of the role of the Americas in history, and of the ongoing process of globalization and the relocation of people and cultures that have characterized Latin America's experience. *Latin America Otherwise: Languages, Empires, Nations* is a forum that confronts established geocultural constructions, that rethinks area studies and disciplinary boundaries, that assesses convictions of the academy and of public policy, and that, correspondingly, demands that the practices through which we produce knowledge and understanding about and from Latin America be subject to rigorous and critical scrutiny.

We know much about Potosí's silver mines and their role in sustaining Spanish colonialism. We know surprisingly little, however, about the social matrix of production, trade, and consumption generated by seventeenth-century mining; we know little, in other words, about the quotidian practices of early capitalism in the Americas. Jane Mangan's extraordinary study provides us with the ethnographic vision we have long needed.

Spaniards, Indians, and Blacks, no longer producing their own subsistence, were forced to enter Potosí's expanding market economy. Mangan highlights the participation of women—especially women of indigenous descent—as well as the activities of other non-elites in this process. By focusing on the gendered and racial dimensions of economic practices, Mangan analyzes how mercantilism became a vehicle for the formation of social identities. By analytically divorcing the economy from its social fabric, her book makes us see what has been lost. *Trading Roles* is a fine-grained history of the social relations forging early capitalism and the modern world, relations that would irrevocably affect the lives of peoples in the Andes and throughout the globe.

CONTENTS

ACKNOWLEDGMENTS

I started my path to writing this book as a teenager on an exchange to Chile, gathered speed as a student of Leslie Offutt and Karen Stolley at Vassar College, took informative passes through Spain and Mexico, and finally, settled on Potosí while a graduate student of John TePaske at Duke University. This circuitous, transatlantic route is not unlike the routes traveled by silver pesos in the colonial era. It was a path characterized not by exchanges based on credit, but rather by ideas, words, and images from the sixteenth and seventeenth centuries mixed with conversations about history in the twentieth and twenty-first centuries.

Those ideas, words, and images came from the marvelous sources that I consulted for this project, all accessible thanks to extremely qualified archivists in Bolivia and Spain. My time in the Archivo y Biblioteca Nacional de Bolivia was both productive and pleasant thanks to the leadership of its then-director, René Arce Aguirre. Judith Teran, in particular, helped me on a daily basis by searching high and low for all the materials I requested. Also in Sucre, Joseph Barnadas, director, and Guillermo Calvo, archivist, provided assistance at the Archivo-Biblioteca Arquidiocesano "Monseñor Taborga." On my frequent research trips to Potosí, the staff of the chilly Archivo Histórico de Potosí, housed in the Casa Nacional de la Moneda, always welcomed me warmly with prompt and courteous assistance. Wilson Mendieta Pacheco, the then-director, graciously provided an electric heater next to my desk. Soraya Aramayo helped me sort through the offerings of the archive. Postdissertation research at the wonderful Archivo General de las Indias in Seville had a profound impact on my approach to several parts of the book. I finally understand why John TePaske lobbied so strongly for my trip there.

Over the past ten years, several groups invested in this study of Potosí's urban economy by providing funds to facilitate archival research and writing. At the dissertation stage, I am grateful for grants from the Andrew W. Mellon Foundation in the Duke Latin American Studies Program and the Duke Center for International Studies as well as for the Anne Firor Scott Award from Duke's Women's Studies Center. A Fulbright-Hays Doctoral Dissertation Research Abroad Fellowship generously funded a year in Bolivian archives. I was able to conduct critical research at the postdissertation stage in Spain thanks to a faculty enrichment grant from the Clark Fund at Harvard University. I am extremely grateful for a generous gift of time to revise the book, all made possible by a leave from Harvard as well as by a Harvard Faculty Research Grant from the David Rockefeller Center for Latin American Studies. Davidson College, my new home institution, supported the final stages of this project with a generous subsidy toward publication.

The conversations that influenced this book began during my graduate work at Duke University. The expertise of my advisor, John J. TePaske, complemented my desire to pursue questions of society and culture in a sector of trade that left so few economic traces since there were virtually no pesos to count. I am especially grateful for his urging to follow my own instincts. Because of this latitude, I have been able to develop my own identity as a historian. Also at Duke, John French and Danny James offered insights at various stages of the project. I count myself extremely lucky to have worked with Irene Silverblatt, for she always challenged my thinking about gender and power in the colonial Andes. Moreover, I met both Sarah Chambers and Nancy Hewitt during my studies at Duke. I am indebted to both for being very generous with their time, energy, and intellect, then and now. The project also benefited enormously at this earlier stage from the criticisms and support of fellow graduate students Jackie Glass Campbell, David Carter, Kirsten Delegard, Ginny Noble, and Rachel O'Toole. Their imprint on the project is still visible in certain places.

I am lucky to have had Valerie Millholland of Duke University Press start the process that turned my dissertation into this book. At every turn, Miriam Angress and Mark Mastromarino of Duke Press have offered advice in a cheerful manner. The readers for the manuscript provided important suggestions that helped to move the book along at a critical stage.

I have been fortunate to have the help and advice of many colleagues and friends along the way to finishing this book. I am indebted to three model colleagues, Ken Andrien, Kathryn Burns, and Ken Mills, for offering their thoughts on late drafts of the manuscript. Sarah Chambers, Jeremy Mumford, Bianca Premo, and Ana Romo read crucial portions of the manuscript in very timely fashion and provided key suggestions. Moreover, I wish to thank Andeanist colleagues who have both encouraged and critiqued this project, including Carlos Espinosa, Carlos Alberto González Sánchez, Karen Graubart, Luis Millones, and Sergio Serulnikov.

Much of the revision of this book took place while I was teaching at Harvard University. My senior colleagues John Coatsworth and Jack Womack offered practical and intellectual support for moving to the book from the dissertation. I am especially grateful to Joyce Chaplin for offering comments on an early draft in its entirety. Cathy Corman and Ruth Feldstein shared their wisdom and warm encouragement. José Mazzotti and Barbara Corbett were wonderful colleagues and neighbors. And, I quite enjoyed conversations with Tom Cummins and Gary Urton. I was lucky, indeed, to have the excellent help of Antoinette Sutto as a research assistant for two years. Kim Beauchesnes, Carrie Endries, and Jane Kim have also assisted me in various tasks associated with this book, help for which I am ever grateful. Patrick Florance and Rob Phocas deserve the credit for the maps. Finally, Susan Livingston helped me secure a quiet Hilles office for writing.

Good colleagues and generous funding make it plausible to complete a book; for me, family makes it possible. My sincere thanks to the greater Buckingham, Mangan, Phocas, and Tomasch families for the joy you bring. My husband, Rob, wins my greatest appreciation. You have always made my work as a historian your business so that both the challenges and the rewards of writing Latin American history are nestled into the life we share. Thank you also for making Nicholas and Caroline your concern as much as they are mine. In the midst of our world where trade exchanges and market values seem omnipresent, it is you three who remind me what is truly priceless.

Jane Mangan
Davidson, N.C.
September 2004

INTRODUCTION

In the words of an early seventeenth-century visitor, "He who has not seen Potosí, has not seen the Indies."[1] From its founding in 1545, this colonial Andean city captured Old World imaginations. The wealth produced by Potosí and its silver mines was an extremely captivating image in an era of colonial expansion. Moreover, the city's silver fortunes symbolized the enormous potential of colonial power. The mountain of silver loomed large in European portrayals of the city (see figure 1). For those Europeans who gained status through colonial rule, silver seemed easy to acquire. Nicolas del Benino told his audience that the quantity of silver was so great it "seemed almost a fable."[2] Visitors to the town were equally in awe of the luxury goods that crowded marketplaces and homes. When Spanish friar Diego de Ocaña wrote of a meal that he had consumed in Potosí it was so lavish he feared no one would believe him: "I write this with fear; but on a priest's word, I tell the truth."[3] This colonial scene was portrayed as so rich it defied European imagination. The tales that came from the silver city mixed reality with hyperbole. No one could discuss Potosí without resorting to myth.

When one takes into account the basic history of the city, this penchant for exaggeration is understandable. The population in the mining town reached one hundred thousand well before the close of the sixteenth century, rivaling European metropolises like Amsterdam and London. The fact that so many people came together, in such a short time span, in a severe location at thirteen thousand feet in the Bolivian highlands, was fuel for the imagination.

The growth of the mining city also sparked urban and regional economies that resisted characterization in European terms. Commerce in the city quickly became as remarkable as the silver. In Ocaña's view the marketplace of Potosí was not merely abundant, but "abundantísima."[4] To sustain Potosí's growing population, food trades multiplied. The majority of the inhabitants no longer produced food, alcohol, or even clothing for themselves as they had in rural communities but instead purchased these items from vendors and storeowners. What defied European imagination in these trading spaces was not simply the pace of commerce, but the products, the people, and the exchanges. Before the eyes of observers,

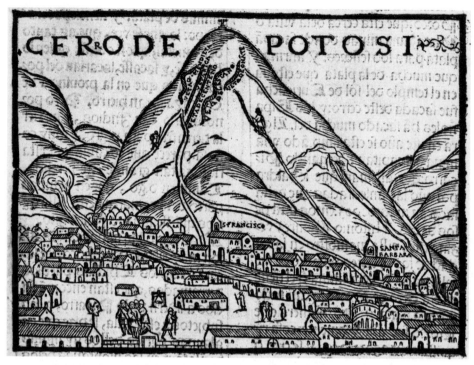

Figure 1. First engraving of the Villa of Potosí and its Cerro.
From Pedro Cieza de León, Crónica del Perú [1553].
By permission of the Houghton Library, Harvard University.

these sites hosted the creation of a colonial urban economy. In this book, I argue that the intersections of trade and urban society provided the context for negotiating colonial identity in Andean cities. Rooted in this characterization of trade is the notion that it can both create new social practices and serve as the key to upsetting existing social hierarchy (through profit for well-off Andean traders or loss for laboring Spaniards).

The majority of Potosí's population was indigenous, and this was reflected in urban markets. In 1550 the Spanish chronicler Pedro Cieza de León commented that "many Spaniards became rich in this mining town of Potosí having only two or three Indian women who contracted with them."[5] Again resorting to exaggeration, another visitor to the city reported the amount of native corn beer, *chicha*, consumed in the Villa was "an impossible thing to imagine."[6] The transition of chicha sales into an urban business dominated by women is emblematic of the intriguing market dynamics whereby indigenous products, suppliers, and vendors negotiated with Spaniards in the formation of Potosí's world of trade. These economic spaces became important sites where indigenous people and non-elite Spaniards influenced the development of colonial society.

This book invites readers into the markets, stores, and taverns of Potosí to witness the formation of colonial trading roles between the discovery of silver from 1545 to 1700, and the waning production of the late seventeenth century.[7] Though Potosí is often described as a market of every sort of luxury, petty trade, which provided food and alcohol for everyday subsistence, was predominant. "Petty" indicates the diminutive nature of the trade—small inventories, small capital, and small profits.[8] In this colonial society, places of trade were sites of economic exchange that simultaneously hosted cultural interactions. Thus economic transactions at the city and neighborhood level are repositories of a compelling colonial history.

Trading Roles constitutes, therefore, a social history of the city of Potosí with particular emphasis on people's interactions through trade. I call this work a social history of economic practice because it brings together lines of inquiry from the subfields of social and economic history. I use the term *social history of economic practice* to mean the study of how social factors shaped urban economies and daily economic practice shaped early urban history. By combining these approaches, this book addresses the significance of indigenous actors, women, and issues of identity (both gender and ethnic) in the urban economy. It compares men's and women's experiences in urban trade, as well as the distinct trade roles of Spanish and indigenous women. The study also brings together economy and material culture in an analysis of the very products and objects that dominated market and credit exchanges. My approach links analysis of people's roles in the economy to the changing meanings and values of certain goods in this colonial context.

Places of trade are unique in colonial Potosí because they captured the intersection of social and economic relationships that was key to the creation of a multiethnic colonial society. Despite Crown attempts to stabilize colonial identities, they were usually contested and shifting. The meeting of native Andeans, Spaniards, and Africans in places of commerce signifies that ethnic identity and cultural negotiation were built into this Potosí market from the start. Markets and stores reveal chains of buying, selling, and credit exchange that link neighbors, couples, relatives, and even strangers. These sites form a critical locus for activities of local resistance to Spanish rules about trade and social interaction.

By looking at economic transactions through a lens of social custom, ethnicity, and gender, this book brings into focus an urban economy where Spaniard and native Andean alike contested trading spots, products, and transactions, where family and kin ties sustained urban trade through the course of silver booms and declines, and where significant credit practices developed to mitigate the pressures of the market economy. Herein students of Latin American history gain an enriched understanding of how ordinary people experienced life in one of the most significant New World cities. Readers will also find this an important text for gender studies because it offers a rare comparison between men and women and among traders of different ethnic backgrounds. Finally, the study of Potosí's world of trade contributes to works on identity and colonial society by showing how trade was an activity (as trading places were sites) through which colonial Andeans negotiated their identities and the rules of their urban society. In particular, women and indigenous people were essential to the functioning of Potosí's urban economy. Indeed, they waged the very battles that determined how the local economy functioned, and by so doing they used trading roles both to create an urban economy and to establish unique urban entrepreneurial identities.

POTOSÍ IN ANDEAN HISTORY

History has made Potosí as infamous for its forced labor draft, known as the *mita*, as it was famous for its silver. The early modern Dutch engraver Theodor de Bry provided one of the most enduring visual images of the mine labor (figure 2). In contrast to pictures showing the grand Cerro Rico from the outside, de Bry's engraving opened up the view to indigenous workers laboring inside. For those who know Potosí's grand, conical shape, and the slope of the mine entrances, it would appear that de Bry, who had never seen Potosí, had it all wrong. His image became legendary, however, because it portrayed the Indians' victimization by the Spanish. In this aspect de Bry could not be accused of misrepresentation; the Spanish victimization of native Andeans through the mita is indisputable. De Bry's striking image of Potosí is still used routinely to illustrate the exploitation of native peoples by Spanish colonizers.

Had de Bry's European contemporaries been able to turn their view 180 degrees from the mines and face the town center of Potosí, an equally compelling, if less well-known, scene would have appeared. Sixteenth-century Potosí resident Luis Capoche described it as follows: "Next to the plaza principal of this Villa is the Plaza del Metal. . . . This plaza

Figure 2. Engraving of the labor of the Cerro Rico, Potosí, by Theodor de Bry,
Collectiones peregrinationum [1590]. *By permission of the Houghton Library,*
Harvard University.

has many stores, where a great deal of coca, which is the trade and business of the people from Cuzco, is sold; the baskets of coca are placed at
the doors where many Indian women trade it for ore or silver . . . and it
seems to me that there must be four hundred to five hundred people who
come with ore to sell."[9] Capoche's view of the bustling marketplace highlights three major areas where Andean historians have modified a de Bry-
like image of Indians as victims of Spanish colonization: the complexity
of the indigenous experience; Andean engagement with the economy;
and Andean initiative in silver mining and refining.[10] Social historians of
the region have exposed the complex levels of difference in the colonial
indigenous experience. Economic historians have revealed that highland
native Andean groups, like the Lupaqas and the Carangas, made a business trading coca, foodstuffs, and llamas. Finally, historians of mining and
labor have shown how Indians stole silver to sell for their profit (and thus
boosted the brisk exchange in the marketplace). Andean historians do not

claim, nor do I suggest here, that indigenous men and women did not suffer under Spanish rule, but rather that the history of the Andes shows that they were not merely victims in the colonial experience.

Less than two decades after Spanish conquest, Cieza de León referred to women engaged in the aggressive pursuit of market profits. Native participation in the market economy has been an intriguing subject for Andean historians because economic exchange in native Andean cultures was distinct from early modern European modes of exchange. The theory of exchange through vertical archipelagos has long dominated thought on pre-Columbian markets in the Andes. According to this theory, native Andeans traded staples not through markets, but among kin groups that were spread up and down various ecological zones, from the warm lowlands to the cool highlands.[11] Because the exchanges took place within the kin-based unit, known as the *ayllu*, no commercial market existed for trade. The relative ease with which native Andeans adapted to commercial trade and markets has led to some debate about the extent to which trade might have occurred outside the ayllu.[12] Some scholars have suggested that the Inca ruler restricted trade that had taken place in the highlands prior to Inca conquest.[13] These ideas notwithstanding, the abrupt adaptation to markets and to selling products and labor has mystified historians who have confronted indigenous initiative in the colonial economy time and again. Native Andeans adapted preconquest modes of production and supply, and they also created new practices so as to meet economic challenges spurred by colonial exploitation.

Take the case of the baskets of coca for sale in the doorways of the Plaza del Metal (known also as the Gato de las Indias, or market of the Indian women). The path of this coca to Potosí reveals markets *within* the Andes, colonial subjects as economic actors within markets informed by a multitude of economic and social relations. While the impact of Potosí's silver in the world economy was widely recognized, Carlos Sempat Assadourian focused on its role in the regional economy—that is, on how coca crowded the market that Capoche observed. Assadourian brought innovation to the study of economic history in the Andes by taking an approach that privileged geographical space and acknowledged the creation of a new mining economy.[14] In this mercantile economy he found that goods circulated on major trade routes, all of which headed toward Potosí. Remarkably, native Andean *trajinantes*, or transport traders, were responsible for much of this circulation of goods.[15]

Admittedly, trade in coca, silver, and other products took place in a new setting. The social contexts of exchanges and the cultural practices

that gave meaning to economic exchanges underwent important processes of change as the colonial era continued. A pathbreaking collection
on Andean markets, *Ethnicity, Markets, and Migration*, complemented
Assadourian's work by explicitly focusing on social agency. The volume
challenges "lingering assumptions about the destructive or assimilative
powers of global market forces in Andean history, without falling into
the trap of . . . implicitly celebrating Andean commercial ingenuity."[16]
Native Andeans who engaged in the market economy did not buy into
Spanish culture in wholesale fashion. Most market transactions had economic goals, while the use of profits was aimed toward community or kin
survival. Yet when indigenous communities adapted the colonial market
economy to their advantage, these economic engagements had complex
consequences for native ayllus.[17]

As historians uncovered the various means of economic engagement
by native Andeans, they revealed evidence of social differentiation.[18] On
the heels of these studies, it became impossible to speak of a single or
common indigenous experience in the colonial era. The potential for economic gain and social power within the colonial world was distinct for
kurakas, the native elites, in comparison to the non-elite members of their
ayllus.[19] Furthermore, ayllus in different geographic locations experienced colonization at different tempos and with differing degrees of exploitation. Native Andeans had preconquest subgroups with distinct ethnic identities, and, with increasing migration to cities, they created new,
postconquest identities as strategies for survival. As Thierry Saignes's
work argues persuasively, not all migrants to cities abandoned ayllu at-
tachments.[20] Still, these distinctions suggest that economic integration
and ethnic identity must be considered in tandem.

The evidence of differentiation in the indigenous experience is profound in Potosí. Potosí was not an ordinary colonial city. It did not have
a preconquest urban center as the basis for its colonial development.[21]
Its concentration of mita laborers and proximity to silver contributed
to an accelerated transition to the colonial economy.[22] One sees ample
native initiative and agency in the urban economy and even, though it
seems almost physically impossible, within the mines themselves. Many
of these enterprising Indians were *yanaconas*, nonayllu Indians responsible to Spanish masters. They dominated the refining sector and enjoyed
elevated economic status in comparison with indigenous mine laborers.[23]
Further, historians have shown that the very miners depicted by de Bry
were not equal. As Peter Bakewell has shown, the mine labor draft existed
in tandem with wage labor, paid to skilled workers known as *mingayos*.[24]

This was not the plan of the Crown, but rather a scenario that came to exist because of labor needs and indigenous demands. Much of the ore for sale in the Plaza del Metal moved from the mines to the market because mine laborers endeavored to keep mine owners' profits for themselves. This tradition of miners appropriating ore in the sixteenth century progressed by the eighteenth century to entrepreneurial groups of unofficial miners overrunning the mines on weekends.[25] If, taken as a whole, recent scholarship on Andean trade has highlighted the critical importance of indigenous adaptation to colonial rule, that community's overwhelming exploitation by the colonial system was never far from view. And in the case of Potosí, the combination of silver riches and forced labor brings together indigenous initiative and indigenous suffering in a dramatic way. Thus the very site of the mita, the most dramatic symbol of Spanish exploitation, proved home to a history of native perseverance and innovation.

The image of indigenous vendors overwhelming the physical space of the Plaza del Metal reveals the complexity of an urban economy where Spanish officials met the Aymara landscape. This study embraces that complexity and in the process dramatically shifts our view of Potosí in Andean history. First, a history of Potosí's world of trade moves the study of indigenous economic activity from a regional plane to a local one where Indians compete with both Spanish regulation and thousands of laboring (poor) Spaniards. The example of Potosí's urban economy tells us much about how indigenous individuals entered the cash economy (especially as merchants instead of consumers) and complements work on ayllu economic strategies for tribute.[26] I contend that elite indigenous families who became well established in sixteenth-century trade passed on their gains and status to subsequent generations, some of which remained dominant through the end of the seventeenth century.

In addition, seeing the urban economy as the central window onto colonial Potosí brings laboring men and women of distinct ethnic backgrounds into the same visual field. Indigenous participation in Potosí's markets raises a whole new set of questions, because the city had a great variety of indigenous peoples, tens of thousands of Spaniards and other Europeans, as well as mestizos and Africans.[27] Urban traders fused Andean and Spanish customs into a set of market practices and assumptions that constituted "colonial urban trade." By comparing trade practices and roles of native Andeans, Africans, and Spaniards, this work uncovers urban credit networks that permeated the lives of Potosinos of all social groups.[28]

Finally, this history shifts our view of Potosí from the mines to the market. For a city much dominated by the shadow of mine labor, the shift provides a full picture of the complex economic and social interactions in trading spaces. It expands our understanding of how people experienced life in this silver metropolis. This change of scenery also places women at the forefront of inquiry by focusing on urban markets, instead of on the male-dominated mines or the long-distance trade mechanisms that supplied the city.[29]

Inasmuch as this book offers a new history of Potosí, it has important lessons for other Spanish American cities about how women and men of different ethnic backgrounds influenced a growing colonial economy. The development of trading roles in Potosí began earlier than in most other cities and occurred in a more intense fashion. But the study here offers a structure that can be used to consider urban trade in other sites. In addition, the Potosinos who migrated away from the city in the mid- to late seventeenth century carried with them their trading roles.

WOMEN AND URBAN ECONOMY

In the same era that Capoche observed the market plaza, Cuzco native Catalina Palla marketed bread and coca on credit to indigenous residents of Potosí.[30] The mother of several children with Spanish men, Palla dressed in finely woven native textiles known as *cumbi*. Engaged in urban economic and social exchanges that included both native Andeans and Spaniards, Palla was representative of an urban marketeer. Anyone who has visited or read of the Andes is familiar with the image of market women, usually dressed in layered skirts and wearing the bowler hats of the Bolivian highlands.[31] Indeed, market women are an important topic for anthropologists and ethnographers interested in Latin America's informal economy.[32] These women dominate the market plazas and street stalls of cities and towns to sell food, drink, and other goods in ways that link them historically to colonial traders like Palla. The image of Latin American market women is archetypal, but the history of their role in the development of the urban economy has not been detailed or clarified.

These female traders won the attention (and sometimes ire) of merchants, dealers, and officials in the sixteenth and seventeenth centuries, and they also became a magnet for historians of the Andes. The women drew scholars into a debate as to whether urban Andean women either enjoyed a degree of autonomy or suffered isolation from kin networks that accentuated the trials of gender and racial discrimination. Some scholars depicted these women as bold merchants fighting against the colonial system for handsome individual gain. Others saw them as industrious workers in a system that sapped family and community resources and left them scrambling to provide for their subsistence.

Elinor Burkett first argued for the significant economic role of indigenous women in her study of colonial Arequipa. These women provisioned Andean cities and in the process amassed property and used the colonial judicial system to defend their interests. For Burkett, this picture evoked the modern image of the "chola" who was "aggressive economically and socially."[33] Noting an absence of indigenous male wills or judicial claims in sixteenth-century Arequipa, Burkett concluded that urban Andean women gained under colonialism, while urban Andean men lost ground.[34]

Writing in the mid-1980s, about ten years after Burkett, Irene Silverblatt applied gender analysis to indigenous women's rural experience under colonial rule in Peru.[35] She argued that the gender expectations of Spanish colonials made colonialism a more difficult experience for Andean women, particularly peasant women. For Silverblatt, Andean women suffered more than men did. They did not suffer passively, however: she also found that women more vigorously resisted the intrusions of Spanish culture. The conclusions of Burkett and Silverblatt provided very different pictures of women's experience in the colonial Andes, and the questions raised by their distinctions opened the path to gender studies in the Andes.

In her case study of Potosí, Brooke Larson emphasized how women's kin ties to male miners gave them access to silver and allowed them to dominate local markets. Larson qualified this picture by cautioning that Potosí presented a unique chance for indigenous women to gain control of production and that even there the women who profited were a minority.[36] Another grim picture of life for urban domestics came from Luis Miguel Glave's analysis of a 1684 census of La Paz.[37] These women generally worked as the single servant in a household, lost links to family and ayllu through early (and sometimes forced) migration to the cities. The Paceñas, or women from La Paz, seemed trapped and open to none of the networking that Burkett's Arequipeñas had enjoyed. In addition, a well-known critique by Ann Zulawski challenged Burkett's rosy characterization of native women's experience and faulted her lack of focus on class or on kin economic strategies. Looking at women from Oruro, La Paz, and Charcas, Zulawski found great similarity in the experiences of indigenous men and women: "the masses of people, both men and women, as they entered the market economy began at the bottom rungs of the social ladder and most stayed there."[38] Overall, the historiography that treats the socioeconomic status of Andean women favors urban women, and it qualifies the independence of indigenous women in cities.

This book adds to this debate, but not by coming down on one side or the other, that is, by offering either the grim or rosy picture of urban Indian women. Rather, it highlights the *range* of experiences for indigenous women in Potosí. While some like Bartolina brewed chicha for the Spaniard Francisca Nieto for pitiful wages, others ran their own businesses.[39] The booming silver economy and the city's large population made room for female entrepreneurs like Leonor Sasytoma who sold articles of clothing and adornment to urban Indians like Martín Copi.[40] Thus, I insist, we find women who suffer, manage, and thrive; and only by treating this complexity can we understand how the urban economy functioned as a whole.

Using the world of trade as a window onto women's *and* men's socioeconomic experiences in colonial cities, I treat gender, ethnicity, and class together in my analysis, and thus allow several characterizations of urban Andean women to coexist in one scenario. Instead of isolating one group of women within the urban setting, indigenous women come into a single frame of analysis with laboring Spanish and African women. Comparison exposes both the female networks and the divides that operated in the urban society. In addition to comparing ethnic identity, I look for men alongside women in the urban economy to determine what was gendered about the world of trade. Men's situation in Potosí, as owners of stores and taverns, as creditors, as customers, and as enforcers of Spanish regulations, reveals hierarchies as well as connections between women traders and male kin. Indeed, men and women were linked not only in social relationships through marriage and family but through daily trade exchanges.

The new history of women's trade activities presented here speaks forcefully to the debates on gender in the Andes and elsewhere in colonial Latin America. Some of the indicators of women's advantage appear in Potosí, supporting Burkett's argument: wills notarized in urban areas by indigenous people were overwhelmingly those of women; extension of credit through loan and pawn was more common among indigenous women than indigenous men.[41] When petty merchant María Vargas dictated her will to a notary she revealed that an indigenous woman named Ursula visited her to pawn no fewer than four small silver plates, two medium silver plates, one silver salt cellar, and one silver pitcher, all for the sum of fifty-three pesos.[42] Yet in addition to these signs of lively economic participation by women, destitute indigenous women like those Glave and Zulawski highlight also surface (as do mestiza counterparts to these indigenous women). Moreover, instead of an absolute dominance of the urban scene by indigenous women, indigenous men in Potosí appeared as important economic actors in the roles of silver refiners (especially yanaconas) and leaders of mita contingents.[43]

The book also speaks to general debates in women's history about how women, indigenous and Spanish, experienced patriarchal power in the Spanish colonial world.[44] Potosí brings together male privilege with rich trading spaces dominated by women, exemplifying how agency and ruling hierarchies mingled in the markets. Students of Latin American history are now well-versed in the ways women contested gender norms espoused by the Church or by colonial rulers, as well as the responses of indigenous women and families to Spanish rule.[45] Here I shift the view of women from studies of the home, church, and family to place women's actions in a new context where we can see how they influenced the economic and social practices of urban trade, and earned respectable sums in the process. Women appear not merely as traders of cultural influence in the colonial context, but as economic actors.[46] This city, while governed by colonial and patriarchal institutions, needed women traders. Female grocers, barkeeps, marketers, and creditors therefore played dominant roles.[47]

The attention to women's roles in trade helps this book speak to studies about women and economic activity in the early Americas and Europe. Women have been credited with a dominant role in the production and sale of alcohol in other early modern and colonial settings.[48] In the case of chicha in Potosí we see a similar phenomenon, though the regulation of chicha is more fraught with tension than that of other alcoholic beverages because of its indigenous identity. Moreover, rather than seeing a pattern of women losing control of alcohol trades to men, a hierarchy emerges in which Spanish women are owners of taverns, and indigenous women are producers of alcohol. In the case of credit transactions, prior discussions of women and credit have centered on the practice of pawning as a response to capitalism and industrialism. Patterns in Potosí show the practice emerged in a mercantile economy as well.[49]

And, finally, Potosí's women traders prompt a reconsideration of when and how female identity became linked to sites of Andean commerce. The emphasis on women's emergence on the market scene and the urban economy in the nineteenth and twentieth centuries has hidden the remarkable influence of women in the sixteenth century, precisely the era when practices of the urban economy were developing.[50] Potosí's female residents were part of the urban economic landscape from the 1550s forward. Women traders in colonial Potosí dominated specific sites of commerce, the sale of certain products, and credit exchange at the low to middling rung of the urban economy. Their activities in neighborhood trade networks suggest that we must think about markets (as well as stores and taverns) as sites of gendered cultural production in the early colonial era.

URBAN IDENTITY AND TRADING ROLES

This history of urban trade in Potosí points to the creation of an unwritten code, a set of behaviors and guidelines, that came to govern trade in the colonial city. I have traced how Potosinos developed this code, in reality a set of trading roles, through two ongoing sets of interactions: the negotiations (and sometimes battles) between vendors and Spanish officials and the exchanges between vendors and customers.

First, the attempts to regulate and legitimize trade that occupied vendors and the town council added another dimension to the role traders played in the colonial city. The transactions of trade had cultural as well as economic significance. Andean scholars have considered peasant markets as arenas for contests over hegemony.[51] Potosí's trading places were no different. The town council consistently integrated social and economic goals into its policing of petty trade. It monitored prices of subsistence foods and payment of the sales tax, or *alcabala*, to the Crown.[52] And, it specified who might sell what products and where, especially with regard to race and social position. The town council regulations reveal that the urban marketplace was subject to the scrutiny of Spanish law. Yet given the vast quantity of unofficial trading operations in both unminted silver and food and drink, the sites of petty trade emerge not as arenas controlled by Spanish rulers but as loci of colonial cultural production. In these distinctly colonial spaces, ordinary people negotiated the encounter of dominant Spanish laws and norms of trade with the needs of the local population as well as with Andean customs.

Second, the acts of buying and selling that took place between vendors and their customers constituted the most common medium through which male and female Potosinos of various ethnic and class backgrounds interacted, often on a daily basis. And, as such, this commerce played a crucial role in the development of trade practices and the colonial culture of the city. In city-center markets, especially, Spanish men and women bought goods from indigenous and African vendors. The increased interpersonal contact brought an exchange of food as well, so that indigenous market women began to offer bread as well as corn and potatoes, and Spanish women opened up taverns to sell chicha. In addition to products, the city's buyers and sellers also negotiated the means of exchange so that people came to rely on new credit strategies like pawning and loans. Over time these practices assumed shared values in the colonial market, and people understood, for instance, the unwritten rules governing petty pawn transactions or the going price of chicha.

Most petty traders in early colonial Potosí showed a good degree of entrepreneurial spirit. The ability to earn a profit was the major motivation to enter trade. Indeed, they viewed their trades as petty enterprises, and proudly defended what they earned through their "industrias" and their "tratos y granjerías." This trade was part of an economy, however, where each transaction, be it for a basket of coca leaves or a single cup of chicha, carried both economic and social meaning. Thus, notions of economic function based on tenets of capitalism cannot be applied neatly to this context.[53] Given what we know of ayllu survival strategies, we must always interrogate economic exchanges with questions about identity and motive.[54]

Part of the tale here, then, is how different ethnic backgrounds influenced the creation of commonly held trading practices. The intricate exchange webs among vendors of all races indicate that a strict focus on indigenous residents or even a dichotomous Spanish-Indian view of the city denies the ethnic complexity of the Potosí experience. While indigenous women and men appeared to dominate petty trade, the most successful indigenous vendors were those who fostered connections with men and women of their own neighborhoods as well as with African vendors and Spanish customers. Non-Indians participated as vendors, too. The most prominent example is that of Spanish women.

Indigenous influence on the products and practices of these markets was clearly strong, but it met with the affects of European monetary units and trade regulations. From the Spanish point of view, ethnic identity emerged as a category by which to classify, tax, and punish vendors in the urban economy. The corollary to this, however, was that vendors used the urban economy as a site from which to assert their identities. Indigenous women came to be associated with certain sectors and spaces of the urban economy, beginning with the coca in the Plaza del Metal and expanding to coca, wax, and textile trades in latter decades. These colonial vendors were not unlike the chola market women of the nineteenth century, who used their prominence in trading ventures to consolidate a powerful identity in Bolivian national discourse.[55] As in the republican era, the identity of colonial petty traders was marked heavily by both gender and ethnicity.

Ethnic identity in the colonial era bears some discussion. While Spanish discourse did differentiate between races, passing laws about Spaniards, Indians, and Africans, distinct ethnic categories within racial groups figure significantly in the period under discussion here—hence my use of the term *ethnicity* rather than *race*. Of course, using these labels to discuss historical actors is problematic for a variety of reasons. *Indian*, a term I employ in the text, is a European label that connotes no specific native Andean reference, but rather Spanish legal significance for sixteenth- and seventeenth-century Peru. Even the term *native Andeans* lumps together peoples who had numerous preconquest ethnic identities; one common in Potosí was the Lupacas, who are frequently silenced in the colonial texts.[56] In addition to these concerns, the category of *Spaniard* is equally inaccurate. Historians, argues Elizabeth Kuznesof, too often ignore the mixed ancestry of *criollo* Spaniards. While those born in Spain might have had claims to blood purity, or *limpieza de sangre*, some 20 to 40 percent of Spaniards born in the sixteenth-century empire had Indian or African blood but assumed Spanish identity all the same.[57] Labels like *mestizo/a*, *mulatto/a*, and *criollo/a* as used in colonial discourse were not only categories which were socially constructed, they were defined on the basis of much more than ancestry or phenotype. Colonial Potosinos considered kin ties, dress, occupation, and language when evaluating their own identity and that of others.[58] Throughout the book, then, I refer to ethnicity to discuss these categories in play in colonial Potosí.

Colonial documents themselves reveal inconsistencies and complexities with regard to labels of identity. The will of grocer María Benítez identified her, at different points, as "mestiza" and "india."[59] These complexities, and in some cases errors, do not imply that the labels have no value for colonial studies. On the contrary, I study their usage in the texts and also employ them frequently in writing. Scholars must not read such labels as an absolute designation of ancestry; rather, they should consider when these labels are used in colonial documents, who uses them, and what significance is attached. For instance, officials used labels, but so did common people, especially in witness testimony. The labels they used might conflict with the notary's designation (or with other neighbors'), but people did grasp these labels and use them to identify the people with whom they lived and worked in Potosí. These discrepancies in how individuals labeled themselves and each other reveal the dramatic shifts of ethnic and racial categories in the sixteenth century, when people came together from Andean, European, and African backgrounds. And, if Spanish designations marked people's legal status in urban society, Potosí's residents used markers of ethnicity to situate themselves whether they pursued large profits or petty credit in the urban economy.

SOURCES AND ORGANIZATION

Studying women and indigenous people in the economic realm presents a challenge because many Spanish trade regulations discriminated against them, and thus they do not always appear in places where one reads about taxes or economic transactions. While market women are persistent characters in colonial *historias* of Potosí, they appear in few official lists of Potosí merchants or long-distance traders. When these women surface, they are generally nuisances from the Spanish perspective. Scholars of late colonial Potosí find that Indians and mestizos encountered a double discrimination: in markets and in the documents of the era that ignored their roles as merchants.[60] Even the term *merchant* was reserved for Spaniards and not readily bestowed on anyone else. While Indians and women played a major role—not only in silver trading and refining but also in provisioning the burgeoning city—their actions are portrayed as marginal, tangential, illicit, and secondary to a very Spanish and male colonial economy.

If many of the participants in this Andean urban economy, such as an indigenous woman contracting to sell chicha; a female African baker suing a store owner over unpaid debts; and two Spanish fishmongers, brothers, receiving new inventory from their supplier, do not appear in official tax records, they do come into view in judicial cases, town council records, royal decrees, and notary records. Important details of quotidian trade emerge from criminal cases, where witnesses portrayed the goings-on in general stores or taverns as they recalled crimes. Town council regulations reflected the desires of the Spanish elite to control production and sale of food and alcohol as well as the location of sites of trade, but these regulations were generally produced as a response to trading practices that had developed in Potosí and thus reveal as much about everyday practices as they do about elite efforts at social control. More references to the numbers of pesos that exchanged hands in these sites of petty trade would be desirable. Like the fleeting nature of these small-scale transactions, however, the records tend to reveal fewer peso amounts than notarial records reveal for large sales of merchandise.

The words of individual traders, especially non-Spaniards but also la-

boring Spaniards, are rarely available to historians without the filter of a notary or some other official or scribe. Thankfully, in the course of reviewing documents that bear the heavy hand of a notary, the individual interests and preferences of people can emerge from time to time. María
Poco, a widowed coca trader, made a point of emphasizing the independence of her trade ventures, saying she had used "my money," and not any from her husband, to purchase a house and store.[61] Generally, however, these sources offer an official, Spanish record of people's actions.

Certain shifts in practice become apparent when reading thousands of actions in this body of material from 1570 to 1700. I gathered a sample of notarial records for approximately every five years during this period. Most of the notarial records, by their nature, give a snapshot of a particular window in time. Wills, for instance, offer static information on one stage in a person's life. Certain pieces of evidence contained in wills do reveal, however, life changes such as basic family history (marriage, birth, death) and property acquisitions. Notarial documents, though fixed in time, can also reveal dynamic loan and pawn transactions. When these individual transactions are analyzed in bulk they offer a portrait of economic activity over the colonial era.

Notarial documents like wills do have a bias. The men and women who went before the notaries had some degree of privilege in colonial society. After all, most people had neither the property nor the money to make their way into such elements of the historical record. Yet Potosí's central role in the colonial world and the innumerable debates about its mita labor offer sources on the commoner's experience of the city's economy, both from the perspective of kurakas, colonial officials, and the poor seeking wage labor contracts. The character of relevant sources from before 1570 also bears mention. Since Potosí proper did not have an active town council or permanent notaries until several decades after its formation in 1545, royal decrees and published descriptions of Potosí by colonial authors are the predominant windows to the very early formation of the urban economy.

This book opens then, in an era of bounty with the 1545 founding of the Cerro Rico silver mines, and it closes at the end of the seventeenth century, when Potosí's economy collapsed with the decline in silver production. The rise and fall of the silver mines is seen here through the perspective of the world of trade and serves as the backdrop for a thematic exploration of the spaces, products, credit transactions, and gender roles in the urban economy. From 1545 to the late sixteenth century, the city witnessed a dramatic course of silver production, economic exchange and population growth. Chapter 1 focuses on the first half-century of Potosí's history, when its coins traveled to Europe and Asia and made the city famous around the world. From 1545 to the 1570s, the population that came together in Potosí created a dynamic urban economy that hastened the indigenous population's transition to the market economy. From the mid-1570s to 1600, Toledan ordinances on mine labor and silver production further augmented the city's population and hastened the decline of indigenous dominance in the local economy. Through these decades of growth and change the city came to host a variety of traders and customers. During this time one could find in Potosí Indians and Spaniards rich and poor and everything in between.

Following this discussion of the growth of Potosí's urban economy, the book moves into four chapters which draw on overlapping evidence in notarial, judicial, and town council records in order to discuss places of trade, marketplace items, credit practices, and women as entrepreneurs. Each chapter has at its core a chronological emphasis on the 1600 to 1650 period, the zenith of Potosí's population.

The day-to-day operations that established this world of trade emerge as the focus of chapters 2 and 3. Battles erupted between the town council and vendors over sites of trade and product distribution as food trades expanded to meet the needs of the growing, multiethnic population. If indigenous networks for supplying goods like coca helped Indians in the marketplace of Potosí, Spanish regulations about the sale of alcohol and official groceries did not. In chapter 2, the places of petty trade emerge not merely as locations of economic activity, but also as sites of social identity and magnets for political struggles over that identity. The chapter charts the growth of venues of trade spawned by an enterprising group of Potosinos and a clamoring clientele, while Spanish officials attempted to sanction only the venues and practices of trade that they deemed appropriate.

One significant concern about locales of commerce was the goods that each sold. Evidence of booming trade as a force of cultural change emerges in chapter 3 with a comparative analysis of the consumption, production, and regulation of two local products: bread, originally a Spanish product, and chicha, originally an indigenous one. Within a short time, Potosinos of every background consumed chicha, so Spanish vendors, many of them women, capitalized on its sale. The larger population welcomed wheat bread as well, and it became a daily purchase for most city residents. Store and bakery owners profited from African slave labor and exploited indigenous laborers who needed pesos for the cash economy. As both products became widespread in the market in Potosí, producers and vendors became conspicuous targets for town council regulations.

The following two chapters treat two major elements of the book's argument on urban economy. The fundamental role of credit in petty trade transactions in this economy is immediately apparent in chapter 4. Store-owners and vendors acted as de facto bankers for their neighborhoods. When confronted with urgent and severe economic demands of urban living, people had to adapt to new forms of economic transactions in silver-rich Potosí. Because of its proximity to mining and refining operations, raw silver and coins saturated Potosí's economy to a far greater degree than that of other colonial cities. The majority non-elite population relied on mechanisms of credit like pawning and loans, not on pieces of silver, to fund life's expenses. Material culture played a significant role in this colonial economy; goods once linked specifically to indigenous or Spanish culture gained a market value so that they could be exchanged across ethnic lines for credit or cash.

Chapter 5 focuses on the predominance of women as economic actors. It considers how and why they reached this position by carefully analyzing the marital status and kin structures of women traders. Women who, regardless of marital status or ethnic identity, had well-positioned families in Potosí or strong ties to *cofradías* (lay religious organizations) had good chances for economic success in the urban economy. This economy needed women traders as sources of goods and of petty credit; thus, despite official discouragement of women in certain economic positions, they found male support to engage in trade.

As a bookend to the concentrated focus of chapter 1 on the 1545–1600 period, the final chapter focuses on the latter part of the seventeenth century and highlights changes in urban trade in the midst of decline in Potosí's silver production. At this time, the town council turned its interest from taxing and policing petty vendors to dwindling coffers and a shrinking population. Even with the decline in silver production in the late seventeenth century, Potosí's rules of petty trade underwent little modification because this sector of society valued social connections as much as silver. Traders and clients developed customs that relied on new instruments of credit as well as traditional ties with neighbors and kin. Despite the economic advantages enjoyed by Spanish competitors, strong socio-economic networks helped propel indigenous and a few African vendors, women prime among them, to successful careers in petty business as they wielded critical influence on the roles of trade in the urban economy. Contractions in the larger economy made for consolidation of urban resources among fewer people, but the rules of petty trade were well-established and Spaniards could not displace Indian and African competitors from the colonial trading practices they had helped create.

A brief glimpse into the future in the conclusion confirms that colonial trading practices had helped to define certain identities within the urban economy, especially those of indigenous women traders, that would prove to be legacies to the republican era. Resourceful men and women in Bolivia, and all over Latin America, carve out economic spaces in the informal economy, dodging laws and national regulations. Their creativity to respond to onerous economic demands by ruling peoples has a history—a history that is as much about coercion as it is about resistance, as much about society as it is about economics. In the changing colonial world of the mining metropolis, daily trade reveals how urban residents responded to the challenges of Potosí's mines and Spanish rule with trading roles that reflected both tradition and creative adaptation.

"THE LARGEST POPULATION
AND THE MOST COMMERCE"

The Genesis of Potosí's Urban Economy

Potosí was discovered by two native Andeans transporting food from Cochabamba to the mines of Porco, or so claimed one early seventeenth-
century source. These men, *guayradores* who smelted silver, traveled a
route that took them past the foot of the Cerro Rico. At precisely this
point in the journey one of their freight llamas strayed from the rest.
The man known as Guallpa chased the llama up the slopes of the Cerro
only to stumble onto a huge outcropping of silver. He discretely replaced
the llama's load of food with silver and rejoined his companion. For several months Guallpa returned to the Cerro, took the ore, and refined it
for himself. His fellow guayradores in Porco became suspicious because,
suddenly, he was eating and dressing better than they were. Where, they
asked, do you find such rich ore?[1]

Accounts of discovery have a way of blending events and myths. This
tale contradicts others in the precise details, but it reveals the dominant
themes of Potosí's dynamic sixteenth-century history. Silver and sustenance were the twin engines of Potosí's economy from its 1545 founding;
native laborers were its fuel. Thus it is supremely fitting that this recounting of Potosí's discovery has at its core two native Andeans transporting
commercial goods from the breadbasket region of Cochabamba to silver
mines at Porco (see map 1). Other hints of Potosí's sixteenth-century history also emerge here. These men were experts in the art of refining silver.
And, with a bit of skill and calculation, Guallpa obtained higher profits
than other native Andeans.

But the silver riches bred discontent. Guallpa revealed his secret to a
friend, and the two argued over how long they could disguise the source
of their material comforts. In the words of El Inca Garcilaso de la Vega,
since "its wealth was so great that they *could not or would not* conceal
it from their masters, they then revealed it."[2] The masters, *encomenderos*
named Villaroel and Quixada, traveled to the site with fellow Spaniards.
Then, having confirmed the existence of silver, they undertook the legal
acts necessary to found the *asiento de minas* on 16 April 1545.[3] In the end,

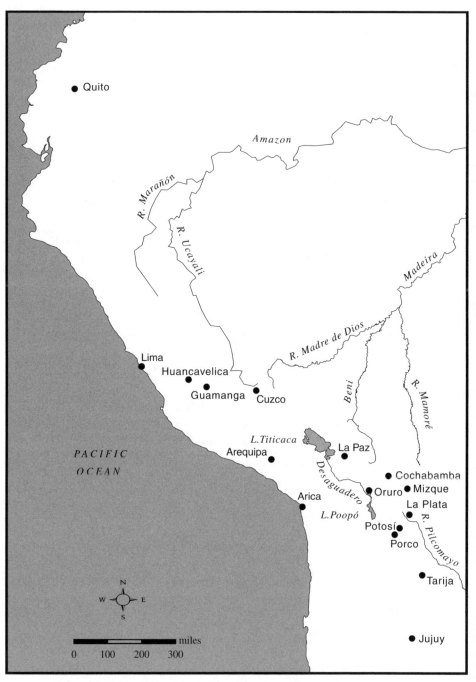

Map 1. Map of South America highlighting relevant preconquest and colonial sites.

the tale of discovery plays out ominously for native Andeans, as the economic advantage passes to Spanish masters.

The period between Guallpa's discovery and the late sixteenth-century Spanish domination of silver refining is the subject of this opening chapter. Two major themes emerge in this development of the urban economy. First, the history of the initial decades stands out because the city's mines and markets offered opportunities for both Indians and Spaniards to earn profits. Thus, in Potosí's incipient urban economy one can read complex tales of benefit for a small sector of the indigenous population, which would become increasingly differentiated. Second, these economic developments reveal a history of both men's and women's activities in the urban economy. The urban economy complements our understanding of male mine laborers by adding a view of women's activity to the evolution of the city.

The silver refining expertise of yanaconas like Guallpa gave them a clear economic advantage in the first decades after Potosí's founding. Indigenous elites, known as *kurakas*, and later indigenous labor draft leaders (*capitanes de mita*) had opportunities to provision Potosí's growing market and to profit from such exchanges. At the same time indigenous women emerged as critical leaders in urban trade. While monetary gain is clearly a motive, many of these individuals also enacted economic strategies for the benefit and with the assistance of their *ayllus*, the basic kin unit in the Andes which comprised numerous household groupings related through endogamous lineage. The nature of Potosí's economy changed between 1545 and 1600. Barter and supply based on Andean modes of production characterized it in the first decades, but by the 1570s and that decade's Toledan reforms, cash-based exchanges and supply influenced by Spanish economic regulations were increasingly common. During the late sixteenth century, after Toledo's tenure, the population shifted to include more Spaniards, and even Spanish women, who would compete with native Andeans for mining, refining, and trade profits. By this point only certain elements within the indigenous population had the ability to benefit from Potosí's economy. This interval of Potosí's history provides clues to the economic and social negotiations, as well as the trade and personal relationships, that contributed to the growth of its unique urban economy.

Do not take the silver from this mountain. It is for other masters.
—Arzáns de Orsúa y Vela, *Historia de la Villa Imperial de Potosí*

None of the many tellings of Potosí's discovery mention preconquest mining at Potosí, and most ignore possible Inca or local knowledge of the silver located there. The closest settlement to Potosí was Cantumarca, a native community located almost two miles to the west of the Cerro Rico. This village revealed no evidence of having carried out preconquest mining at Potosí. Yet it is difficult to conclude that native Andeans had *no* knowledge of the silver at Potosí, since Inca laborers worked the silver mines at Porco, some twenty-two miles to the southwest.[4] Both mountains of silver sat at the very extremes of Collasuyu, the southeastern quadrant of Tawantinsuyu, as the Incas called their empire. This land was home to ancient Aymara kingdoms invaded by Inca expansionists during the fifteenth-century reigns of Tupac Inca Yupanqui and Pachakuti.[5] Inca rule was not peaceful for the Cantumarca: groups of Guarani soldiers attacked during the reign of Guayna Capac. The Inca responded to their displays of strength by sending several thousand royal soldiers from Cuzco to the town of Cantumarca. After a battle that left thousands of Guarani dead, Guayna Capac entered the town to receive praise from local peoples. Spanish legend had it that on this trip Guayna Capac spied the Cerro Rico from afar and ordered his men to reconnoiter the site. They arrived but refrained from mining after a voice coming from inside the mountain ordered them, "Do not take the silver from this mountain. It is for other masters."[6] As the colonizers tell the story, the mountain of silver was destined to glorify Spain.

In contrast to this European version, Inca history reveals a very productive center of silver mining at nearby Porco. Here Guayna Capac kept yanaconas busy mining silver. The yanaconas were a group of Inca subjects who performed a variety of services for the Inca ruler in places throughout his empire. Yanaconas did not belong to a specific ayllu. Instead, they were loyal retainers of the Inca, from whom they received special honors and status for their service.[7] The yanaconas at Porco became expert in retrieving ore and refining it by *guayra*, a native process that used clay ovens (hence the name *guayradores*).

The demand for silver from Porco or other mines in the Inca period was not monetary. Silver artisanry, both religious and ornamental, adorned the palaces of the Inca in and around Cuzco, but silver was neither made into coin nor used as a method of payment. Exchange took place within ayllu structures using "vertical archipelagos," whereby people traded staples among kin groups spread over various ecological zones.[8] Llama caravans carried goods from one zone to the next on trips that might last for several days. In spite of the distance, inhabitants at each stop were related to the travelers through kin ties. This trade did not occur within a commercial market, but rather was compatible with the general framework of reciprocity that governed native life in the ayllu. A decidedly not-for-profit ethos governed the relationships among these households; the Andean community was thus one in which, as Steve Stern has noted, "social mobility had a collective rather than individualized flavor."[9] Reciprocity, not capitalist motive, reigned in all facets of life—be it work, religion, or trade. This ethos would be challenged in Potosí's urban market, though it would not be eradicated.

Thus, no evidence suggests that markets met in the vicinity of Potosí prior to conquest, and certainly no preconquest Upper Peruvian market could rival what was to come after 1532. The rhythms of economic and social life began important processes of change after the Spanish wrested control of the Andean heartland from the Incas. By the late 1530s, Spaniards under the leadership of Francisco Pizarro had moved into the region surrounding Potosí. In 1539 they founded the city of La Plata in the site known as Chuquisaca, some 150 miles away from the Cerro Rico.[10] The encomenderos in the region of Chuquisaca wasted no time in sending laborers to mine at Porco for their benefit. These miners, of course, were the community from which Guallpa came. Some of the Porco miners were yanaconas who had mined for the Inca and they began to use their expertise for new Spanish masters.[11] In return for their service to Spaniards, be it in mining or other tasks, the yanacona Indians received a reputation for being more loyal than other native Andeans. A 1541 royal *cédula* exempted them from tribute and mita service to the Crown.[12] Many Porco yanaconas had fallen under the control of Gonzalo Pizarro during his rebellion against Spain. Even during the years of the rebellion and civil war in the Andes, economic development and Spanish exploitation of indigenous labor continued apace. Thus, when the mines of Potosí officially opened on 16 April 1545, the experienced mine workers from Porco lost no time.[13] In roundabout fashion Guallpa had answered the queries of his fellow smelters; off they went, along with the better part of the Spanish male population of La Plata, to the rich ore of the Cerro Rico.

In many parts of Peru silver mines have been, and are still, found, though none like those of Potosí. . . . It stands on a plain and is shaped like a sugar loaf: it is one league round at the base and a quarter of a league at the top. The top of the hill is round. It is beautiful to see, for it stands alone, and nature decked it so that it might be as famous in the world as it now is.

—*Garcilaso de la Vega, 535*

Potosí's mountain drew people to create a silver industry; the silver drew still more people to trade. With the end of Spanish civil conflict in the Andes, Potosí became a destination for those who lived beyond Porco and La Plata. When news of the silver bonanza reached the Crown, word spread throughout Europe and a global market emerged for Potosí silver.

Imagine the route traveled by Guallpa and his llamas as the thoroughfare for thousands of people and thousands of pack animals. The year of 1549 marked the first great rush to the mines by ayllu Indians, known in Quechua as *hatunruna*. Some traveled to the city to engage in market transactions with the goal of earning tribute payments for their ayllu. Others came at the behest of their Spanish masters, the encomenderos, who were eager to profit from the silver rush. Many workers brought their families with them, and the presence of women in Potosí was as fundamental to the shaping of the marketplace as men were to the shaping of the mines. As many as twenty-five thousand men and women marched along the roads to Potosí by 1550. On their journey they climbed higher and higher, to nearly thirteen thousand feet, in a climate so cold it "hurt the temples."[14] In addition to chilly temperatures, the months of December through April threatened lightning, thunder, snow, and hailstorms, while the rest of the year brought furious winds known as Tomahavi.[15] Despite the forbidding environment, the population surged to seventy-nine thousand by 1565.[16]

Picture then the Cerro Rico, climbed not by a single man chasing a single llama, but by hundreds of mineworkers and hundreds of llamas. The men were burdened on the ascent by the combination of thinning air and the weight of the tools of their trade: candles, coca, and ladders made from animal hides. They endured lengthy periods of forced labor deep inside the furnace of the earth only to emerge to Potosí's infamous chill. On the return down the mountain to family and friends, the miners were weighed down by the silver they managed to secret away for their own profit. Llamas dotted the slopes of the Cerro, too, their climb surely less onerous than their descent with bags of ore destined for Potosí's refineries and official Crown markets.

And, finally, envision the marketplace, filled not with the contents of a single *trajín* of llamas, but by hundreds of women and men and the cargo of hundreds of llama caravans. To new arrivals, the bustling marketplace could only have seemed like pandemonium. From the very year the mines opened, colonial forces conspired to bring workers to Potosí to earn for their encomenderos or for their ayllus' tribute; either way, the mines drew them into the colonial economy. These scenes of the crowded roads, mines, and marketplace were unlikely visions for a town perched thirteen thousand feet in the Andes, in the midst of highland plains known for bitter cold winds and parched earth. But the scenes had begun to unfold. In the space of a few years Potosí boasted the "largest population, and the most commerce, in all of Peru."[17]

The first hints of urban settlement one encountered on approaching the town were not the Spanish buildings or patterned streets but the *rancherías*, indigenous neighborhoods characterized by *buhíos*, modest round dwellings constructed of adobe and straw. The first ranchería grew up at the very foot of the Cerro Rico, logically enough given its proximity to the mines. With the growth of the city's population, rancherías came to circle central Potosí on all sides. Moving past the rancherías toward the center of town, the houses became larger and more elaborate, with the grandest residences located in view of the main plaza. Early evidence shows that shelter in the mining settlement was built from large stones found on the mining site, using local agave branches as roof beams. Bills of sale suggest that at least by 1549 residents constructed more permanent buildings. Property records indicate that by 1559 *casas de morada*, a more refined dwelling, lined some streets in the town center, including the Calle de los Mercaderes.[18] The main parish church and government buildings, the *cabildo* or town council hall, the Caja Real or Treasury Office, and the Casa de la Moneda or Mint, were symbols of Spanish dominance that ringed the main plaza, the geographic center of town.[19]

Places of trade became quickly established in the new mining town. Markets sprouted in specific spots, and stayed there over decades, cultivated by daily custom. The northwest corner of the main square fed into the largest market plaza of Potosí, the *kjato* or *gato* in Spanish, often referred to as the Gato de las Indias.[20] Buyers and sellers met there every day of the week. In the 1550s, popular products included maize, *chuño*, coca, *ají*, and clothing.[21] In addition to the main market in the Spanish center of town, "the Indians have many others, and in particular one they call 'del

Figure 3. "Vendedora y otros tipos populares (Potosí)." In Mercado, 96.
By permission of the Archivo y Biblioteca Nacionales de Bolivia.

carbón' where they sell all types of food and unrefined silver."[22] The Plaza del Carbón offered hens, eggs, and lard in addition to charcoal, while other plazas specialized in the sale of flour, barley, wood, ore, llama dung (for fuel), and even the corn beer starter, known in Quechua as *muk'u*.[23]

It was in these plazas that women's roles in the city came into relief.[24] Even though no one owned any particular selling spot, market vendors returned day after day to a precise location and gradually fixed custom geographically (see figure 3).[25] In these spots, market women vied for the most appetizing display as they arranged pears in careful columns or potatoes in miniature pyramids. They called out to passersby, showed off their wares, and tempted customers with samples. Those selling coca or bread knew that the keen demand for their items made presentation less important; they kept their goods in large, practical baskets. The scent of freshly baked Spanish bread mixed with the aroma of dried coca leaves and the trailing odor of midday meals being fried by African women. The urban street markets were a cacophony of negotiations in Spanish, Aymara, and Quechua; a mosaic filled with the colors and patterns of foods, people, and clothing; a whirlwind of barter and exchange. The scene at the market could become all the more chaotic when the Tomahavi winds blew in June, July, and August. For their comfort, the indias "had some sticks fashioned into sunshades . . . weighed down with a great weight of clothes," but when the wind came it "lifted them so high that they were lost from sight."[26]

Despite the adverse weather, these indoor and outdoor sites of commerce moved enormous quantities of merchandise, with estimates of daily trade volume as high as sixty thousand silver pesos for 1549.[27] In the early years, indigenous staples like corn, chuño, *oca*, and quinoa constituted a large part of the food trades. Baskets of dried pepper (*ají*), a mainstay of native Andean cooking, sat alongside the coca baskets. Production in the Andes became geared toward the market at Potosí.[28] The availability of wheat grew in the 1550s. By the 1560s enterprising Indians and Spaniards shipped corn to the highland metropolis in the form of flour instead of grain to simplify the process of making the traditional Andean corn brew *chicha*.[29] Vendors in the marketplace also sold the necessities for work in the mines. Indigenous merchants operated wax stores (*cererías*) to sell candles for mine labor, four for one real.[30] Firewood, charcoal, and llama dung had two crucial purposes in Potosí: to keep fires burning for the smelters and to warm homes on days so cold that "one cannot live except behind the fires."[31] Cloth and ready-made clothing filled the market. Corregidor Diego Pacheco boasted, not without reason, that in addition to these staples, Potosinos could purchase "everything else that the land yields in this kingdom."[32] Indeed, indigenous laborers like the Guaquis could eat a better variety of foods in Potosí than they did at home.[33]

Claims such as those of Pacheco and the Guaquis proved to outsiders that Potosí could support its enormous population. It was no secret that Potosí would never yield food the way it did silver; yet the bounty at the markets gave the impression that Potosí occupied a fertile agricultural valley. This illusion was the result of the trajín, a well-organized system whereby indigenous transport workers, called *trajinantes*, placed goods on the backs of llamas, tethered hundreds of the animals together in train-like configurations, and guided them on treks to Potosí.[34] Though the trajín was not official tribute labor, the Crown, with a keen interest in ensuring supplies to Potosí, made the provincial Spanish magistrates, *corregidores de indios*, intervene to ensure workers for the trajines.[35] Some transport workers labored under contract with indigenous and Spanish merchants.[36] These were lengthy endeavors; the return trip between Cuzco and Potosí lasted four months. Moreover, they did not always lead to economic gain for the freighters, as the merchants did not pay a wage for the return home. So it was that llamas journeyed forth from Potosí laden with its only export, silver, and returned to the city burdened with the necessities of life, like food, drink, and clothing.

By the late sixteenth century, Potosí's need for staples had worn grooves into the Andean hills and valleys with the constant comings and goings of trajines. Indigenous and Spanish trade arrangements powered circuits of exchange that had become routine.[37] Tarija sent hams, tongue, pork loin, and bacon, prized as the best cured meat in Peru. Paria produced similar meats as well as cheeses.[38] Game birds like partridges, as well as hens and *vizcachas*, Andean hares, came from nearby. For Friday meals, fish came salted from Arica or fresh from the lakes in the Chucuito region. Fruit was abundant; pears arrived from Chuquisaca, raisins from Arequipa, apples from Cuzco, and the market stocked fresh grapes for six months out of the year. Fruit preserves survived the journey from Cuzco, La Paz, or Chuquisaca. Wine, an indispensable part of the Spanish diet, "always came with the fleets."[39] In addition, Peruvian production from vineyards near Arequipa and in the province of Pilaya y Paspaya blossomed, and most Potosí merchants offered a choice between domestic and imported wines.[40] Grains from the fertile Cochabamba valley and from Tomina provided for bread and chicha.

Even more remarkable than this selection of goods was the extent to which the market priced items never before "for sale." Of the 1550s and 1560s, Brooke Larson comments that, "Telescoped into two decades was the transformation of basic subsistence goods, traditionally exchanged outside the domain of the market, into commodities that fetched inflationary monetary prices."[41] The trade of coca leaf is exemplary of economic changes in this era because it shows the transformation of a product with highly ritual significance into one with commercial purpose. Native Andeans used coca leaves in ritual offerings to deities and, according to some sources, the Inca elite limited its circulation.[42] Thus, while the dried leaves of the coca bush had been commonly consumed in preconquest society, they had never been available in the abundance seen in the Potosí markets. Production increased throughout the region. Spaniards sent laborers to work scores of new coca fields in low-lying valleys of the Yungas and Cuzco regions.[43] Both street vendors and shops dealt in the native antidote to the high altitude. Indigenous miners became famous consumers, as they relied on the juices of the leaves to help ameliorate the effects of exertion at high altitude.[44]

While coca remained a product associated with indigenous culture, its beneficial effects were not lost on the most practical of Spaniards, some of whom adopted the "vile" habit.[45] Garcilaso de la Vega told of a poor

Spanish man caught with a mouthful of coca leaves by another Spaniard. The man rationalized his actions by his need to carry a daughter piggyback through the highland terrain. If most Spaniards in the 1550s and 1560s disdained the associations of chewing coca leaves, they did not ignore the benefits of selling them. Coca sold for as much as eighteen pesos per basket in 1549, and although it would plunge to between four and five pesos per basket by the 1560s and 1570s, it was always inflated in the Potosí market, where the proximity to silver raised prices.[46]

The increased coca production and its consumption by indigenous laborers reveal how market demands for Potosí pulled native Andeans into the colonial economy. To the approval of the Crown, Potosí gave many non-Spaniards a first introduction to a cash economy. In these first decades, however, the cash economy had a heavy dose of barter. Indigenous people traded widely with coca.[47] Miguel Choloyla earned coca, corn, and llamas for his work in the carpentry shop of Juan Carrasco.[48] Inés Taquima, a single woman from Misque, labored for Diego de Gómara as a servant. Her wages spoke eloquently to her indigenous identity, since she took a portion of her pay in cloth, specifically the *chumbe*, a wide wool belt that was wound around the waist two or more times to give shape to the woman's *acsu*, or dress.[49]

The urban economy of early Potosí was distinguished by indigenous dominance in three major activities: refining silver, trading unminted silver, and exchanging subsistence goods in markets. Native Andeans achieved a temporary monopoly on silver refining prior to the promotion of mercury-based amalgamation by Toledo in the late 1570s. In the 1550s and 1560s, since indigenous men and women ran the most efficient refineries in town—the guayras—Spanish titleholders had to pass through them to obtain their silver.[50] Indigenous miners as well as women who combed the tailings for good ore also made use of indigenous smelters. The guayras kept busy. One observer romanticized the Potosí landscape in that era: "It was a pretty sight in those days to see eight, ten, twelve, or fifteen thousand little [clay] furnaces blazing away on the hillsides."[51] Fifteen thousand may have been hyperbole, but six thousand was not. Miner Luis Capoche counted 6,497 guayras in operation in Potosí prior to 1585.[52]

Between the 1550s and the 1570s the guayra method of refining silver was dominant, and native Andeans profited individually from the sale of services to the Spanish mine owners. In particular, it was the yanaconas (and not ayllu Indians assigned to serve Spanish encomenderos) who dominated the guayra refining. Thanks to their expertise in smelting local ore at high altitude, they "diverted a substantial share of Potosí's riches into Indian hands."[53] As Garcilaso de la Vega noted, the Spaniards "sought to remedy this state of affairs and to keep the metal to themselves by making their own foundries and employing the Indians by the day."[54] Much as they tried, the Spaniards could not perfect an alternative system. They devised great bellows to blow into ovens like wind and contrived mills rigged with sails. In the end they "gave up these devices and went on following the system invented by the Indians."[55] It is no exaggeration to say that the early economic dynamics of silver allowed Andeans to participate in the market economy and amass respectable sums. One guayra named Isabel was able to donate three bars of silver worth 629 pesos to her son Francisco.[56]

The indigenous monopoly on refining silver matched up handily with the indigenous appropriation of and trade (or *rescate*) in unrefined silver ore. While Spaniards owned virtually all mine claims, indigenous miners acquired ore for themselves, in a practice that was tolerated as a necessary evil.[57] To obtain the silver, some miners worked the mines from Saturday evening until Monday morning for their own benefit.[58] Others smuggled out silver during the workweek. Indigenous women played a primary role in rescate. They carried food to their mineworker husbands on Wednesdays and returned home with whatever ore their husbands had been able to put aside.[59] Whether carried out by miners or their female relatives, the illicit silver followed the well-trodden path down the side of the mountain to the indigenous smelters and from there entered the Potosí economy in the main market plaza.

Colonial Peruvians recognized, according to José de Acosta, "that for a long time the silver called 'ordinary' was used, which was not stamped or set aside. . . . This was all the silver that circulated among the Indians and much of the Spaniards' silver, a practice that, as I saw, had lasted until my time."[60] In theory, the Crown required refiners to register all silver produced from the Cerro Rico so that it could take its share, one fifth or the *quinto*. Yet the rescate signified that a large amount of silver taken from the mines was never minted into coin, and never subject to the Crown tax. Though some objected to the rescate trade, others acknowledged that at least some of the stolen ore represented wages deserved by workers. They questioned the logic of depriving indigenous laborers of this means to supplement inadequate pay.[61] Despite official and unofficial concern, Spaniards never impeded the trade in unstamped silver.

The Gato, initially known as the Plaza del Metal, was famous as the best site to trade. The ore trading was a sight to behold.[62] Four hundred to five hundred people arrived to sell ore to those who refined it, mainly guayradores. The busiest market days were Thursdays, Fridays, and Saturdays, when people gathered from seven o'clock in the morning. Near the town council offices, Indians, both men and women, crowded together to sell ore. Despite their numbers, they maintained a semblance of order by grouping according to the quality of their product. Numerous coca stores lined this plaza. The sales of the plaza spilled over into the Coca Street, where indigenous women sold coca from baskets in exchange for silver or for ore. The town council restricted access to the trading plaza. Indigenous guayradores had the option to purchase ore first. Spaniards, or more specifically, the yanaconas who worked for Spaniards, were not to enter the market until ten o'clock. Indigenous access to ore and skill with the guayras made the Gato a space of vibrant indigenous economic activity.

Trading of subsistence goods in Potosí's markets was the third economic activity with significant indigenous participation in pre-Toledan Potosí. Native Andeans supplied this market sometimes by force, other times through their own initiative. Between 1548 and 1551, the earliest years of the Potosí market, the Sakaka Indians from Charcas paid tribute to their encomendero don Alonso de Montemayor in a scheme that illustrates how native ayllus were forced into economic activity at Potosí.[63] Though the Sakakas paid silver to Montemayor, a significant amount of their tribute was payable in goods that had a valuable market in Potosí. The Sakakas provided the encomendero with maize, chuño, llamas, and cloth, and delivered these goods to an agent of Montemayor's in Potosí.[64]

Indians also found ways to act as merchants in Potosí. Priest Cristóbal Díaz de los Santos observed that indigenous residents of Potosí engaged freely in trade. Nowhere outside of Potosí, he exclaimed, were there "such great benefits for the said indios and yanaconas as in this said Villa because together they bring things to the tianguez [market] in this Villa. . . . from everything they make money."[65] Certainly profit was a major draw of Potosí. The city drew encomienda Indians in the 1550s because "mining provided them with the tribute that their encomenderos demanded, and . . . this tribute was difficult to produce elsewhere."[66] Kurakas made trade agreements with European merchants and then drew on Andean modes of production to supply them with goods.[67] Further, non-encomienda Indians from the royal province of Chucuito found Potosí's mines and markets to be instrumental for meeting annual tribute payments to the Crown. Beginning in the 1550s, some five hundred indigenous males left Chucuito yearly for mine labor in Potosí, from which they earned thirty thousand pesos for tribute payments.[68]

Indigenous men and women also became increasingly important consumers in the Potosí market. Given the relative ease with which silver was mined, mine workers obtained sufficient quantities to trade in the busy markets for food, clothing, and supplies. Only a few years after Potosí's founding, Pedro Cieza de León pointed out that indigenous women engaged in commerce as their primary occupation.[69] Much of what they sold was aimed at indigenous buyers. Upon arrival of goods to Potosí, the women purchased the items in smaller quantities and resold them, often at inflated prices, in the various trading sites about the city. If men were predominant in tasks related to silver production, women played a critical role in Potosí markets from the 1550s on. Given the absence of markets in this region prior to conquest, the enthusiasm and speed with which these Andean women embarked on trading careers is remarkable. While independent female traders emerged in the late sixteenth century, women who worked in Potosí's markets in the 1550s generally did so at the behest of kurakas and in support of their ayllu community.

The kurakas, along with Spanish leaders, sometimes expressed frustration at the way Potosí's silver and market profits influenced indigenous men and their families to extend their stays in Potosí. In the 1560s *licenciado* Juan de Matienzo, then *oidor* of the Audiencia (high court) of La Plata, reported to the Spanish Crown that kurakas did not want their ayllu members to go to Potosí. As Matienzo portrayed the situation, the ayllu Indians "have freedom and earn money and deal with Spaniards who teach them, and if under force they do give some [Indians] to live in Potosí, they make sure that they stay for a very short time and soon send others, new ones so that they remain as their subjects and do not learn to know to complain, or become rich."[70] Both Matienzo and the kurakas may have exaggerated the situation.[71] A related claim by native Andean elites was that indigenous women left kin behind for the chance, by no means guaranteed, to gain economic advantage through relationships to Spanish men or by freeing themselves from sharing the burden of mita and tribute with indigenous men.[72] Both complaints, however exaggerated, reveal that native Andeans in Potosí reckoned with the cash economy at a basic level earlier than most of their rural counterparts.[73] Moreover, the draw of that economy had significant implications for native society at home and in the city.

In the 1550s and 1560s both yanacona and hatunruna mine laborers reaped benefits from their work that far outweighed what laborers would earn after 1570. The earliest yanacona mine workers had to relinquish two marks of silver per week to their masters, yet they were able to keep comfortable sums for themselves.[74] Still, the earnings of some came at the expense of others. Differentiation among the indigenous Potosinos was clear to observers even in the 1550s. In a well-known letter to the Council of the Indies, Fray Domingo de Santo Tomás highlighted this differentiation. He noted that the Crown's informants, presumably men like Polo de Ondegardo, "trick many people into thinking that these mines are advantageous for the Indians because they see that some Indians . . . are well-placed and happy, and they do not see that these Indians, ones called yanaconas, are few in comparison with the many who perish."[75] The levels of well-being among the indigenous population of Potosí became even more differentiated in the decades following Fray Domingo's remarks. Further, the city's economic opportunities turned into problems because Spaniards and kurakas each wanted productive labor from the same group of indigenous workers. Or, even worse, the workers abandoned ayllu obligations for wage labor opportunities in Potosí.

When miners found themselves expending more and more labor and being rewarded with less and less metal, the market dropped into a depression. Indeed, actual mining (digging deep into the mountain to follow veins of silver) only began in earnest in the mid-1550s. The late 1560s, in particular, brought an economic downturn because miners had depleted the easily accessible veins, known as surface ores. Silver production during the first ten years may have seemed tremendous for those (both Spaniard and native Andean) who profited from it, and for those who felt the effects of the silver on the regional economy. In retrospect, however, the output was low in comparison to Potosí's production from the 1570s to the 1710s; overall output from the first cycle of the 1550s to 1570s was low and in decline.[76]

Luis Capoche, a mine owner who lobbied the Crown to supply laborers for Potosí, claimed that by 1572 Potosí was "'almost abandoned, the buildings in disrepair, and the residents empty-pocketed.'"[77] Catastrophic floods, sparked by intense hailstorms, in both 1567 and 1570 seemed emblematic of the city's misfortune.[78] Though silver was still traded in the Gato, it must have seemed like a ghost market for those who had witnessed the early days of silver bounty. Capoche alleged that those traders who still attempted to operate in Potosí had turned away from incipient capitalist forms of trading and back to preconquest forms of barter.[79] The downturn may have been particularly hard for indigenous residents. An indigenous woman named Beatriz sold rights to half of the mines she owned to a Spaniard, Vasco Valverde, in 1559 because she did not have any miners to work them.[80] Her case points to an era when it became more difficult for indigenous hands to retrieve significant profits. It serves more generally to highlight the problem that confronted the Crown in the 1560s. Potosí's dwindling profits meant fewer incentives for indigenous laborers to come to the region; fewer laborers meant shrinking urban and regional economies. In 1568, precisely when it seemed to some that these silver mines had given their full yield, Francisco de Toledo received orders to sail to Peru as the new viceroy.

"THE LARGEST TOWN IN THE REALM"
TOLEDO'S POTOSÍ

Upon his arrival in Peru in 1569, Toledo undertook a five-year *visita* of his jurisdiction. He carried with him on this journey the burdens of an ambitious ruler. King Philip II had charged Toledo with reviving silver production and increasing indigenous economic participation through-out the viceroyalty. During the course of his visita, Toledo penned decrees to expand the *reducciones*, or forced resettlements. By moving the indige-nous population into Spanish-designated areas, Toledo planned to maxi-mize Crown control over indigenous labor, tribute collection, and social and religious instruction. Further, while some native communities had al-ready been paying Crown tribute in pesos, Toledo moved to require all tribute in specie.[81] These changes added social and economic burdens to native communities whose traditional modes of production had been dis-rupted. Many fought the attempts to remove them from their homelands by taking leave of the reducciones. Ironically, this flight often fulfilled the Crown's goal of pulling them into the economy through wage labor, though not precisely on Crown terms. The overall intent of Toledo's re-forms is clear: to emphasize Crown control over taxes, settlement, and labor as opposed to local control, either indigenous or Spanish.

In the case of Potosí, Toledo's initiatives restored its status as Peru's largest economic center and "the largest town in the realm."[82] Happily for mine owners like Luis Capoche, Toledo's pass through the region in 1572 and the discovery of mercury at Huancavelica, Peru, shifted the dynamic of silver production in favor of European mineowners.[83] The viceroy pro-moted innovations in silver refining that progressively ate away native profits from refining, as well as related indigenous dominance in rescate and markets. Specifically, Toledo accelerated silver production through the creation of the Ribera, a large refining and processing complex, which spread up and down both sides of a stream running through town. With mercury available from a Peruvian source, Toledo could promote mercury amalgamation. The emphasis on mercury amalgamation as the preferred method for refining silver curtailed the indigenous monopoly on the traditional guayra method. Moreover, silver production soared as the new technology processed two decades of tailings that had been too low-grade for the guayra refineries. Potosí would register its highest yearly rate for the production of silver in 1592. So began what historian Peter Bakewell has termed a "decas mirabilis for Potosí . . . that took a hundred and twenty [years] to subside."[84] This miracle in production would come at a cost of increasing hierarchy among native participants in the market economy.

Mercury amalgamation was one part of the equation; mita was the other. Toledo restructured the de facto labor draft to provide an adequate number of indigenous workers for the mines. The first Toledan mita of 1572 totaled 9,500 men and this number increased in 1575 and 1578.[85] To serve the draft, native peoples arrived from a total of sixteen provinces between Potosí and Cuzco and as far away as Guamanga.[86] The corregidor de indios then made an official count of the workers in his jurisdiction, or *corregimiento*, and sent them on their journey to Potosí. Typically *mitayos*, the mita laborers, and their families drew on traditional Andean modes of production to outfit themselves for this journey. Their long llama caravans, with provisions like ají, chuño, and *charqui* (dried llama meat), rivaled commercial endeavors. But in large part the mitayos' supplies were not sold upon arrival to Potosí because the goods, including the llamas, met consumption needs.[87] In fact, the number of llamas slaughtered for food so alarmed the Potosí town council that they feared a scarcity for transport purposes.[88]

Viceroy Toledo's plan to summon men to fill the mita quotas had important structural links to Andean society. Toledo appointed six native men as *capitanes generales de mita*, regional leaders or liaisons between local Indian kurakas and Spanish officials.[89] These leaders came from regional divisions that approximated the preconquest, not Spanish, divisions in the region between Potosí and Cuzco (see map 2).[90] The capitán general commanded those men elected to serve as *capitanes enteradores de mita*. The enteradores were responsible for gathering men from a localized area, usually made up of several ayllus. The position of capitán connoted status, though it was often a difficult task to convince men to serve in the onerous Potosí labor draft. At times enteradores had to call in favors in order to supply the appointed number of workers, or they had to make payments in pesos to compensate for missing workers.[91]

It was also possible, however, for the men who served as capitán gen-

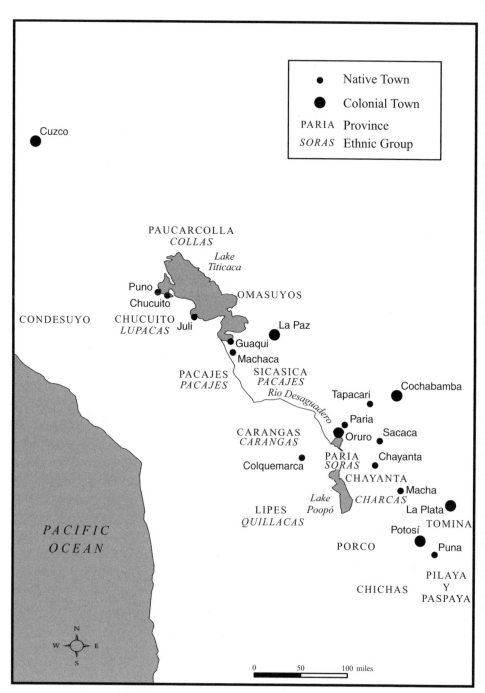

Map 2. Communities from Cuzco to Potosí included in the Toledan mita.

Legend:
- Native Town
- Colonial Town
- PARIA Province
- *SORAS* Ethnic Group

Cuzco

PAUCARCOLLA
COLLAS

Lake Titicaca

Puno
Chucuito
CHUCUITO
LUPACAS Juli

OMASUYOS

La Paz

Guaqui
Machaca

CONDESUYO

PACAJES
PACAJES

SICASICA
PACAJES

Río Desaguadero

Tapacari
Cochabamba

Paria
Sacaca

CARANGAS
CARANGAS

Oruro
Chayanta

Colquemarca

PARIA
SORAS

CHAYANTA

Macha

Lake Poopó

LIPES
QUILLACAS

CHARCAS

La Plata

TOMINA

Potosí

PORCO

Puna

CHICHAS

PILAYA
Y
PASPAYA

PACIFIC
OCEAN

N
W E
S

0   50   100 miles

eral or capitán enterador to profit in the Potosí market. Native enteradores, like all indigenous merchants, enjoyed an exemption from taxes on their cargo—generally corn, coca, and textiles. The Crown charged a sales tax, or *alcabala*, on many food products and imported luxury goods. Since the Crown required native Andeans to pay tribute, though, it freed them from the alcabalas on goods that originated in their home communities. Generally, the Spanish assumed that enteradores transported homegrown goods necessary for subsistence in the city. Yet some goods, like coca, were destined for the marketplace. The enterador operated on an axis between the barter economy, still at work in the rural community, and the cash economy, dominant in Potosí. He had the power to command community resources and to trade them within Potosí. A few capitanes became legendary as they carried out extensive commercial transactions and used Spanish representatives to handle their Potosí affairs.[92]

Mitayos lived in the rancherías, indigenous neighborhoods bordering town limits. Six rancherías developed prior to the 1570s; with the growth of the indigenous population in Potosí, Toledo added an additional eight rancherías in the interest of religious conversion and labor control.[93] The rancherías were born of Spanish labor demands and sustained by urban networks with rural and ethnic bases. Ayllu members settled together in huts adorned, according to Spanish observers, with little more than animal pelts and chicha jugs.[94] Some Spaniards, like Matienzo, argued for housing mitayos from one region together, because it would be easier for employers to gather them up in one stop and, presumably, they would be more productive if laboring together.[95] Keeping ayllu members together also appealed to some kurakas; don Juan Colque went so far as to ask viceroy Toledo to order that any Indians who came to Potosí for commercial endeavors be ordered to live "with those of their *natural* and pueblos."[96]

The Toledan plan called for all mitayos to assemble on Mondays before the corregidor of Potosí, who would assign them to one of three tasks: mining silver, refining silver, or building new refineries. The workweek was generally Tuesday to Saturday, as Monday was taken up with gathering and assigning workers, and Sunday, the day of rest, was often spent waiting for payment. Toledo envisioned a system where indigenous mine laborers would be paid in the manner most valuable to them. He ordered in 1573 that workers were to be paid in ore that they might refine or sell as they wished in the Gato. Toledo's plan called for only half of the mitayos gathered in Potosí to be working at any one time, so in theory the off-duty mitayos could profit from commercial activities and silver refining. To this end, Toledo left numerous guayras in operation, and he set up workshops to teach amalgamation to Indians. The guayra business of native Andeans declined, however, and Indians never gained a foothold in Spanish-dominated mercury-driven amalgamation. By the late 1570s Toledo recognized that native Andeans had no position to use ore in the amalgamation sector, and he pushed for cash wages.[97] In 1578 he ordered workers to be paid three and one-half reales daily wage in coin. Potosí's new mint, ordered built by Toledo in 1572, guaranteed that coin would be more accessible.[98] Thus, Toledo's rules on cash wages moved the ranchería population toward more cash-based transactions.

Residents of the ranchería, meanwhile, contended with an expanding population. In the words of José de Acosta, the city had a magnetic appeal: "The power of silver, desire for which draws all other things to itself, has populated that mountain with the largest number of inhabitants in all those realms."[99] The city's emerging economy needed more workers than the mita could provide, and Potosí welcomed many nonmitayo Indians and mestizos with wage labor opportunities. Antón de Miranda earned his living as a shopkeeper in the city during the 1590s.[100] Miranda, who identified himself as an *indio ynga*, likely benefited from his elite or even royal standing among the Inca dynasty. Ties to the Inca elite carried weight because Spanish rulers fostered alliances with indigenous leaders. Yanaconas continued to be an important presence in the city. In 1582 Toledo appointed don Pedro Cusipaucar, originally from Cuzco, to serve as the capitán of all yanaconas.[101] Other migrants to the city had fewer ties. One mestiza newcomer, María Carrillo, had no master nor kin and "wandered about the ranchería, lost" until she found the means to support herself as a domestic servant for Juan Barba and his wife.[102] Indeed, for those who could not establish connections with fellow newcomers from their native communities, the size and diversity of the urban population proved problematic. The residents of Potosí, perhaps as many as 120,000 during the 1570s, continued to grow to an estimated 160,000 by the turn of the century.[103]

The Spanish sector of Potosí was growing and changing, too. The birth of the first Spanish baby allegedly occurred in 1584.[104] This signified a major change from the practice of sending Spanish women to warmer climes, and lower altitudes, for childbirth and child rearing. In addition to an increase in Peruvian-born Spaniards, or *criollos*, in the town, European migration swelled in response to transatlantic tales of silver riches. Spaniards and other Europeans, such as Italians and Portuguese, tried their hands at the business of mines. Not everyone, however, had the financial backing to profit in mining. Furthermore, many could not secure employment in the refining industry or commerce. In 1581 the Crown wrote the judges of the Audiencia in La Plata to warn that the presence of many foreigners in the Villa Imperial could be "inconvenient."[105] The Crown surmised that many had left Europe without permission, and it requested a report detailing names, nations, and occupations of all foreigners in the Villa. The answers to this query must have been disconcerting: by 1589 the Crown warned city leaders to "throw out . . . the idle ones."[106] Potosí also hosted many soldiers, mestizo and criollo, who had fought in Spanish battles of expansion into what is today Paraguay. Generally unhappy with what they considered meager financial rewards for their efforts, these soldiers added a degree of violence and instability to the city's population.[107] The Crown was eager to flood Potosí with able-bodied indigenous workers. It was not willing to entertain European guests and soldiers who drained the city of productive energy.

Another demographic possibility the Crown seemed unwilling to consider was the integration of African men and women into the mining sector or the rancherías of Potosí. In truth, the Crown was not altogether clear about how the growing population of Africans fit into its plan for the mining city. A small population of free people of African descent lived in the town by the late sixteenth century, but by and large Africans in Potosí were slaves. African slaves arrived in Potosí after a lengthy journey, usually from Angola or Congo to Brazil and then down the coast to Buenos Aires and across a land route to Potosí. Francisco, a thirty-five-year-old African from the Wolof region, entered the town in 1572 a few weeks after Viceroy Toledo and went into the service of a Spaniard, Catalina Hernández.[108] Criollo slaves came from various parts of the Spanish Empire, like twelve-year-old *negro* Domingo, who was born in Lima before moving to Potosí to serve the shoemaker Sancho Antón.[109] Africans in Potosí fulfilled roles of servant, artisan, and street vendor, as they did in other urban areas.

While indigenous and African workers overlapped in the artisan trades and as marketplace vendors, they did not overlap in the mines. The switch to mercury amalgamation and the decline of indigenous guayra smelting in the 1570s and 1580s led to the use of slaves in some refineries, but slave labor was never seriously entertained as a replacement for the mita. Mine owners lobbied to maintain their access to inexpensive mita labor by discounting the option of slave labor. The Spaniards alleged that in addition to not being skilled miners, Africans were not suited to Potosí's high altitude, nor could they survive on the market mainstays such as corn, coca, and other indigenous staples that "are not appropriate for slaves."[110]

The mine owners' strategic manipulation of the facts worked to protect the mita, but such rhetoric did not isolate Africans from Potosí's economy. Men and women of African descent adapted as well as Europeans to Potosí's altitude, and they engaged readily as vendors *and* consumers in markets, where they crossed paths with indigenous traders. When Luisa de Villalobos, a free *morena*, wanted to buy a pair of shoes from Sancho Antón's shop, she pawned a piece of unminted silver.[111] Judging from Villalobos's wardrobe, which included an acsu, the dress of indigenous women, as well as the *sayas* (pleated skirts) and *jubones* (tight blouses) worn by Spanish women, this was not the only illicit silver to which she had access.[112] Villalobos likely visited the Indian-dominated *rescate* plaza and enjoyed the possibilities of trade opened up by proximity to the mines. Some Africans even had opportunities in the mining sector. In 1577, Antona, a free African, received ten *varas* (approximately twenty-eight feet) of a mine shaft from Andrés Vela, who declined to specify the reason for his gift.[113] Leaving aside the intriguing question of why Vela gave Antona this gift, let us ask what he expected her to do with it. Did she have the resources to work the mine? Maybe he simply planned that she would sell the mine shares. On the other hand, perhaps she possessed the resources to hire laborers. This situation would be exceptional but for the fact that she lived in Potosí on the verge of its greatest annual production of silver. The socioeconomic status of African Potosinos raised enough eyebrows to warrant a 1589 ordinance from viceroy Toledo forbidding *negros* or *mulatos* from having yanaconas or other Indians work for them.[114] Some apparently had the means to hire the laborers; Toledo hoped to ensure that the privilege would remain out of their reach.

The growth in Toledan-era Potosí brought together Spaniards, Africans, and native Andeans in a rapidly changing urban context. From an official perspective, all these urban dwellers had distinct rights and obligations under colonial rule linked to their social identity as *indios*, *negros*, or *españoles*. Official regulations of trade always emphasized the identity of vendors and customers, yet the determination of ethnic identity in colonial society was a subjective process in which phenotype, language, dress, and social networks all played roles. Moreover, numerous examples in Potosí's notarial records show that ethnic identity was not fixed.[115] The world of trade exhibited a high volume of economic transactions between buyers and sellers across ethnic lines—a pattern that increased sharply with the city's expansion as the seventeenth century dawned.

Once Toledo enacted reforms in Potosí, silver production grew, the number of laborers increased, the demands of the urban economy extended, and the urban population rose. The regularization of the mita, whereby the state designated which ayllus had to provide how many mitayos, proved a critical turn for the history of the mining city. Cash wages allowed these urban indigenous workers to purchase goods in what had grown to be a phenomenal metropolitan economy. Native Andeans participated in a market where more and more of the profits went to Spaniards. If Toledan reforms were successful in increasing state control of the economy, the by-product was resistance to that control. It was possible to see Toledo's reforms unraveling by the late sixteenth century. The numbers of reporting mitayos never met the quotas. Mita captains had to make payments for those laborers who failed to show. Mine owners used those payments to hire wage laborers known as mingayos, or, by the early seventeenth century, they merely put those payments into their pockets rather than hire additional laborers.[116] People simply devised ways to avoid the mita, to avoid taxes, and to transact business with illicit silver.

The fact that people took extreme measures to avoid Toledan mita regulations did not signify, however, that people avoided Potosí. In fact, the city was growing. A 1611 census registered 160,000 inhabitants, including 76,000 Indians, 43,000 Europeans, 35,000 creoles, including *mestizos*, and 6,000 negros and mulatos.[117] The sizeable indigenous population was something of a conundrum since mita officials were always trying to locate male Andean laborers. Following Crown policy, the indigenous population of Potosí would never have reached 76,000 but would have comprised only mitayos and a small sector of yanaconas. Moreover, each mitayo would spend the majority of his life in his home community, serving one turn at the mita every seven years. In reality, the initiatives and choices of the mitayo population (staying on after one's mita turn had ended, fleeing to escape mita labor, or venturing to the city as a wage laborer) created the character of the urban population. Many indigenous people who did not owe a turn at the mita migrated to Potosí in search of economic opportunity, so that by the early seventeenth century thousands of indigenous residents in the rancherías were not mitayos.

Potosí's economy, just like its population, reflected native initiative, collective and individual, in addition to Spanish decrees. In the Toledan

era, the Potosí economy witnessed strengthened governmental interven-
tion, both at the local (cabildo) and the viceregal levels. At the same time,
native Andean ayllus faced further threats to their ability to sustain themselves. When Toledo drew increased numbers of tribute laborers to Potosí,
he pulled even more productive laborers from the ayllu's force. Furthermore, his promotion of mercury amalgamation cut the profits of guayra
entrepreneurs. A regionwide epidemic in the 1590s added to the burden.
At each pass a smaller native Andean population, with narrowing economic options, remained to shoulder the onus of mita service in Potosí
and cash tribute payments.

Surprisingly, the urban picture offers suggestive examples of indigenous profit that remind us of the extreme differentiation among urban
Indians. Some ayllus made their forced marches to Potosí work to their
economic benefit into the seventeenth century. Don Diego Chambilla,
an early seventeenth-century mita captain from Lupaqa, used his control over ayllu resources to gather llamas, ají, and *avasca* (native cotton)
cloth.[118] He delivered the goods to a Spanish attorney named Mateos,
who sold them and raised pesos for Chambilla. If Chambilla did not have
enough men from his Lupaqa ayllu to meet the quota, he could pay the
corregidor to hire wage laborers. Chambilla was fortunate in his ability
to garner trade profits from his ayllu's goods, since by the early seventeenth century Spanish hacienda owners dominated bulk trade to Potosí.
In addition to trade, some individuals grew wealthy through silver profits
outside the largely defunct guayra sector. Spanish friar Diego de Ocaña
told of one indigenous Potosino who made his wealth as a *mercader de
plata* (silver merchant), transforming silver into bars and coin. His wealth
was "always in his house, in front of his eyes. He has one room full of
silver, in one section the bars, another the *piñas*, and in another, in some
jugs, the reales."[119]

And, finally, indigenous women made profits in the marketplace. The
dynamic market begs for the integration of women, marketplaces, and
native initiative into the familiar Potosí narrative of men, mines, and coercion. Women had dominated local trade from the 1550s on, and those
with kin ties to the indigenous elite maintained their formidable roles into
the seventeenth century. In fact, don Diego Chambilla's agent Mateos
negotiated the sale of Chambilla's products to aggressive indigenous
women marketers. Mateos charged that these merchant women were
"well-known *gateras* and they have resisted me ferociously and as I see it
they leave with it [the goods] and go somewhere else [to sell]. . . . they are

bold hucksters."[120] The activities of female kin in the "best supplied plaza in all of Peru," represented a key strategy for native Andeans seeking to meet colonial economic demands.[121]

CONCLUSION

At the turn of the sixteenth century, Spanish observers of Potosí marveled at the city's commerce. When Fray Ocaña traveled through in 1600 he boasted of the feast to celebrate San Francisco. "They gave us," he exclaimed, "a meal that in Madrid could not have been more plentiful."[122] José de Acosta focused his gaze on European goods, and rightly so, since the availability of wines, luxury cloths, and fine jewels was remarkable given Potosí's isolated location. "Silver," wrote Acosta, "has made [Potosí] so rich in every sort of foodstuff and luxury, that nothing can be desired that is not found there in abundance. . . . Its marketplaces are full of fruit, preserves, luxuries, marvelous wines, silks, and adornments, as much as in any other place."[123] As much as it might impress a Spanish audience, this European selection of goods was not the lifeblood of Potosí's markets. Brooke Larson, discussing the city's effect on the Cochabamba region, has argued that "Potosí's greatest commercial power rested not with exotic luxury goods from Europe, but with its capacity to attract the staples of life."[124]

The urban economy thrived on the daily transactions of subsistence goods. In the early morning light, a mitayo on his way to work the claims of the Cerro purchased the necessities for his trade: candles and coca leaves from a vendor on the street, like Isabel Ycica.[125] By mid-morning, elite Spaniards sent servants out to shop for the day's meals. Women of indigenous or African descent dominated this servant category, such as Elena, the Chiriguana servant of Juan Pérez, or Ana, a *mulata* woman, who served Sebastián de Palencia.[126] Servants purchased dry goods from the *pulpería*, or general store, of a local shop owner like Gabriel Velez. They bought wheat bread from a street vendor, probably an indigenous woman like Isabel Cayo.[127] Market vendors sold fruits like figs, vegetables and greens, as well as jugs of milk and cream. Juan Rojas, a *mulato* swordmaker, sought lunch from the African women who dominated a stretch of the main plaza to cook stews of fish, beef, or vizcachas.[128] Male traders, like Francisco de la Cavallería and his brother Gerónimo, who dealt in fish and sardines, sold the main ingredients for these meals.[129] By late afternoon, an indigenous woman might search out some grain in the Placuela

Segunda del Mayz or the Placuela de la Harina to start a batch of chicha.[130] Men, like the Andean elites don Francisco Martínez Ayra, don Francisco Yana, and don Francisco Turumayo, who delivered corn flour to Spaniard Felipe de Torres, dominated bulk trade.[131] At the end of the day, a Spaniard might stop in a tavern for a few glasses of wine. Customers chose between Spanish and domestic vintages, the former brought to town by merchants like Lope Rodríguez Salgudo, who sold 270 bottles of good white wine from Spain, at ten pesos apiece, to Diego Bravo.[132] To finish off the evening, a traveling merchant like Rodríguez could dine at one of thirty "restaurants" and settle in for the evening at an inn like the Tambo de los Melones.[133]

The exchanges in these trading sites reveal the degree to which material culture from both indigenous and Spanish traditions influenced the developing colonial urban culture. The interaction of people in this marketplace is equally telling. Trade brought together people from a wide variety of backgrounds. Spanish attempts to categorize people into discrete groupings fell apart in the larger marketplace of Potosí because interactions among groups were not only necessary but part of everyday life. Trade also joined male and female labor. The urban economy of Potosí reveals a contrast between male figures like the enteradores and the trajineros and the female figure of the market seller. By focusing on women's urban role, the familiar vision of male migrations to Potosí is revised. Colonial migrations to Potosí appear to transplant native Andean society with gendered, complementary forms of labor. These distinct male and female roles are most evident in the urban system of trade.

A glimpse at daily trading places in Potosí reveals both a variety of venues *and* a measure of permanence. Unlike other boom and bust mining towns, Potosí grew into a city that was as much a site of major cultural and economic transformation as it was a mining town. Spaniards pushed for the development of Potosí because they sought its silver, and they attempted to command profits from the urban market as well. When mita laborers swelled the city's population, contentious negotiations about trade broke out among consumers, vendors, and Spanish officials. Places of trade and the products sold at each emerge in the following two chapters as points of friction over the control of economic and social transactions in the Villa Imperial. Spanish elites could marvel at the luxury products in Potosí's stores; they could imbibe the familiarity of Castilian wine. Yet equally familiar in this urban economy were profiteering mita captains and their marketing female kin selling baskets of ají or providing Spanish tavern owners with jugs of chicha. None of these people or products was native to Potosí proper, which had been but an empty hillside that beckoned to Guallpa's llama in 1545. By 1600, the site was home to a unique colonial economy that recognized markers of ethnic identity and cultural distinction, but ultimately honored initiative and profit from native Andean and Spaniard alike.

MAKING ROOM TO SELL

Location, Regulation, and the Properties of Urban Trade

2

The town crier, Benito de Camudio, made his way through the streets of Potosí at ten o'clock one April morning, calling out the latest message from the town council. In the main plaza, walking past the African street cooks and in front of the luxury merchandise stores, he read aloud the new rules for the location of *pulperías*, the colonial general or corner stores. At its April 1589 meeting the council tackled a growing problem—the random establishment of general stores all about town and in rancherías. Convinced of the social and economic offenses encouraged by too many stores, the council outlined its first systematic attempt to restrict places of trade. The council defined a limited area in which the stores could operate: "from the corner of the store of La Merced in the upper part of the block of the said monastery straight ahead to the store of Francisco Ortís," and so on.[1] This border circled downtown Potosí and excluded aspiring retailers from the outlying rancherías. Further, the council limited the number of stores to twenty-four and designated nineteen men and five women, all Spaniards, to be the official *pulperos* and *pulperas*, or storekeepers, of Potosí. "Juan Antonio . . . Gabriel Velez . . . Isabel Ximénez . . .": the town crier sang out the names of the newly appointed official traders of the town.[2]

This decree signaled official resolve to define the role of the pulpería in Potosí. In theory, the council ensured that pulperías and markets made basic provisions available to city residents. Council control of these stores was part of a larger Spanish plan for the colonial economy; a plan whereby Spanish officials enacted production quotas on native goods to ensure markets for peninsular imports, fixed prices to keep subsistence goods affordable, and imposed taxes (on stores and products) to steer a percentage of profits to the Crown. Pulperías in Potosí, as in many other colonial cities, were not all made in the mold the council imagined. Away from the center of sixteenth-century Potosí, settlement became less orderly, the houses notably humble, the residents increasingly impoverished

Figure 4. Planta general de la Villa de Potosí.
Courtesy of The Hispanic Society of America, New York.

(see figure 4). Pulperías adjusted their inventories and their exchanges ac-
cordingly. Well-stocked pulperías sat on the main plaza.[3] Pulperías located
near or in the rancherías offered a more limited variety of dry goods, and
stocked smaller portions, if any, of luxury items. The locations of stores
constituted a code for the type of trader who operated there, the activities they or their customers carried on, and the type of scrutiny they were
likely to face from colonial officials. More troubling to the council was not
that pulperías in the rancherías lacked flour, sugar, or spices, but rather
that the majority of them were not merely dry goods distributors. Indeed
the 1589 decree came to pass after a series of complaints about the alleged
sale of wine to indigenous people who paid with stolen clothes and silver.[4]
Pulperías sold alcohol to indigenous peoples. They bought items from
middlemen, often called *regatones*, which drove up prices. Further, pulperos accepted numerous items as payment. Products potentially stolen
during any stage of silver production like azogue, pellas, and piñas were

valuable currency in the Potosí economy.[5] All these practices ran counter to Spanish ordinances.

Thus when colonial officials tried to assume control of pulperías it was a step toward larger control of the urban economy. Pulperías that sold low quality goods at exaggerated prices or sold goods in exchange for contraband items were the embodiment of numerous illicit trading practices the council hoped to stop. To the town council, then, it seemed logical to limit the number and location of pulperías in order to reduce the perceived drunkenness and pilfering of town inhabitants.[6] This chapter begins with a detailed analysis of the motivations for regulation of pulperías. We will also review the history of pulpería regulation to find efforts at both control and resistance. Taken together, the city's pulperías represented a significant piece of the urban economy. They were well connected to both large-scale rural merchants and small-scale urban ones for their supplies. Town council attempts to ordain grocers and decree store locations faced a difficult battle, as those in business were likely to oppose any council rulings that infringed on their enterprises.

To satisfy the diverse palates of more than one hundred thousand potential customers, Potosí boasted numerous venues for petty trade, both in- and out-of-doors. Indoor trading sites included the pulperías, taverns called *chicherías*, and inns called *tambos*. The second section of this chapter analyzes ownership and rental of these properties. The examples that emerge from property records clearly show that men and women operated pulperías and other stores in ways that did not coincide with town council regulations. The owners of these sites entered council debates in order to protect the rents they garnered from stores and taverns. While town council regulations and rulings were effective in some instances, as we will discuss in section three, the overall picture from Potosí shows that actors in the local economy typically bested the authors of colonial policy.

Town neighbors skillfully used the ordinances when their properties or businesses were threatened. Two case studies that illustrate how trading locations emerged as points of dispute about social and economic power constitute the final section of this chapter. They demonstrate with great detail how Camudio's reading of the 1589 ruling was not a final performance of Spanish rule in the urban economy, but rather the opening act in a production of policy by property owners, grocers, tavern keeps, and residents alike.

Potosinos understood all too well that their personal wealth and their status as a villa imperial could disappear with waning silver production. Thus town council members advised the Crown about the goings-on in the silver mines and lobbied to retain the mita system, abolish the sales tax (*alcabala*), and urge merchants to ship goods to the city.[7] The councilmen governed along with two magistrates (*alcaldes ordinarios*), one chief constable (*aguacil mayor*), and, as a direct consequence of Potosí's silver industry, a corregidor of the mines, two judges for mine cases, a chief magistrate of the mint, and officials of the royal treasury.[8] While these local officials had silver first and foremost among their concerns, it was also their duty to ensure that the city was provisioned and consumers protected against fraud and other criminal activities in stores and markets. And, in the case of consumption of alcohol by laboring Indians as well as the exchange of illicit silver or stolen property, the lofty goal of keeping the silver mines operating intersected neatly with the more mundane matters like the sale of food and alcohol. This convergence of duties prompted the 1589 pulpería regulations.

By controlling the location and number of stores as well as the identity of those who ran them, the council hoped to control alcohol sales, barter with stolen goods, and pricing of food staples. Spaniards never failed to comment on the natives' perceived habit of drinking excessively. The fact that pulperías made wine available at every imaginable corner, from the main plaza to the edge of the Cerro Rico, fueled elite complaints.[9] The first prohibitions on the sale of alcohol to indigenous men and women and to Africans date from the Toledan era. Indians and Africans were also forbidden to own taverns.[10] If the council could limit the places that dispensed alcohol to twenty-four (and twenty-four respectable Spaniards, at that), it reasoned that this would discourage illicit sales.

The Toledan restriction on non-Spanish pulperos fit with concerns that pulperías acted as transfer points for stolen goods, including the trade in contraband silver that Spanish mine owners had debated since the 1540s. On city streets people traded widely with the unrefined or unminted silver, but pulperos who accepted the silver in their stores fostered an exchange that ran counter to council policy. Other stolen items, including clothing, supported an urban black market trade that threatened elite merchants. In the seventeenth century, the council made explicit links between exchanges involving stolen goods and the ethnic identity of grocers and customers. When Ana de Saldana opened her store in 1659, for instance, she agreed not to accept unrefined silver, silverware, or any other pawns from *indios*, *negros*, or *mulatos*.[11] Pulperos commonly received material goods through their barter and credit economy with customers, but the council warned Saldana that barter and pawn with non-Spanish customers would earn her a fifty-peso fine. In 1650, when constables found the mulato pulpero Bernardo de Estrada in possession of goods allegedly stolen from Potosí surgeon Alonso de Ribas, that was all the proof the council needed to reaffirm the Toledan-era ban on pulperos of African descent. "Experience has shown," the council lectured, "that many dangers and inconveniences result from *negros*, *negras*, *mulatos*, *mulatas*, *zambahigos*, and other people of this quality who have or are allowed to have pulperías."[12] Despite numerous examples to the contrary, the council did not trust non-Spaniards to buy and sell goods through licit channels.

Finally, council members believed that limitations on the number and identity of grocers would allow them to control the prices of goods. The town council was duty bound to promote reasonable prices, and it did not want prices to reflect the desires of grain-producing encomenderos or urban regatones. It required pulperos to make a declaration of all goods both Spanish and native for sale in their establishments so that contraband trade could be monitored.[13] When too many middlemen entered into the trade process, the prices fixed by the town council went unheeded. Viceroy don Fernando de Torres y Portugal blamed inflated prices on "powerful persons" who brought food and sustenance goods from regions bordering Potosí like Cochabamba, Tomina, and Mizque and then sold them to regatones.[14] These regatones, urban vendors, proved obstacles to the council's attempts to control supply and pricing.

More often than not, indigenous women appeared as the culprits within the city limits. In 1615 one council member charged that "in this Villa there is a great quantity of regatones of partridges and chickens and roosters, and however many enter this republic, they cut them off and buy going out to the roads, to obtain them outside only then turn and resell them."[15] The market women purchased partridges outside the city at eight or nine reales and then sold them for two pesos (sixteen reales); they bought chickens for four or five reales and sold them for eight. In the 1620s, Mateos, the Potosí dealer for indigenous merchant don Diego Chambillas complained that women vendors had gone into business for themselves and were "bold regatonas."[16] Town council members echoed Mateo's frustration; they fixed prices on everything from flour to wine to barley and warned time and again against the regatones.[17] Given their illicit nature, price hikes by third parties are rarely seen in documents. But council complaints about the regatones' practices hint at the complex relationships between rural suppliers and urban vendors, especially female ones, whom the town council failed to control.

These motivations, then, prompted the council to devote its agenda to pulperías at least thirty-one times between 1589 and 1635. Between the 1590s and the 1610s, the viceroy in Lima and the Crown in Spain applauded the council's moves for strict control of the stores. In 1590, the Viceroy don García Hurtado de Mendoza ordered the council to renew its limit of pulpero licenses to twenty-four in light of the many "vagrants" who hoped to make their living through the trade.[18] In 1597, señor Renglón repeated the lament that excessive numbers of pulperías cluttered the rancherías "and from this came much danger to this republic."[19] In 1618, three years following a council reprieve on pulpería limits, the viceroy reiterated the prohibition on pulperías in the rancherías and ordered that the council revoke any licenses granted after 1615, all in the name of preventing the sale of wine to Indians.[20]

Despite continued rulings between 1589 and the 1630s, the limitations never achieved full-scale compliance. When Captain Juan Ortiz de Zárate toured the city in 1592 he found not twenty-four but more than one hundred stores in operation.[21] Though the transfer of stolen goods and the sale of alcohol to non-Spaniards constituted longstanding issues of Spanish concern, they appeared on council or Crown agendas with more urgency in some years than others. Three explanations for this flexibility emerge: bureaucratic battles between the *real audiencia* (or high court) and the council, priorities for tax revenue, and bribes.

The tensions between colonial administrative bodies erupted in nearby La Plata. There the members of the Real Audiencia of Charcas sided with Potosí pulperos who were not awarded one of the initial twenty-four licenses.[22] As early as 1591, the pulpero pretenders traveled to La Plata to plead their case. Much to the chagrin of Potosí councilmen, the audiencia awarded licenses to open new shops. Again, in 1593, the audiencia judges wrote the Potosí council urging them to revisit their 1589 rulings and increase their quotas.[23] This challenge to the ruling of the Potosí council is not altogether surprising. Potosí and La Plata had an intertwined history of governance because La Plata ruled Potosí from the latter's founding until 1561.[24] Given the dominance of mining interests on the new Potosí council, it often clashed with the heavily encomendero-based La Plata government. Eventually, the merchants and petty traders of Potosí used the adverse relationship between the local council and the audiencia to further personal interests.

In the second instance, the council periodically rescinded mandates for control to increase tax collection instead of regulating alcohol sales and illicit barter. To some, these seemed ills to be remedied through restrictions; to others the numerous pulperías bespoke not ills but economic expansion and taxation opportunities. For example, rumblings began in 1599 about the dwindling of the city coffers and the limited revenues that could be collected in the form of pulpería taxes. In 1615, don Joan de Sandoval y Guzmán spelled out the situation in plain language. "The income has fallen into a great slump," he announced, "for having taken the pulperías out of the rancherías and outskirts, many pulperos have fled so that today one third less [tax] is collected than usual."[25] His arguments convinced the council to put aside its concerns about alcohol consumption and trafficking in illegal goods and completely reverse its policy, allowing a higher number of pulperías to operate legally in an attempt to generate additional taxes.[26]

The taxation of pulperías remained a council priority until the 1630s. At this point the Crown, ever seeking new ways to raise revenue, claimed a share of pulpería taxes. In accordance with a 1631 royal cédula on the *composición de pulperías,* the Potosí council would control, and benefit from the taxation of, twenty pulperías (known henceforth as *pulperías de ordenanza*). The remainder of Potosí's many pulperías paid taxes to the Crown, and thus earned royal protection as *pulperías de composición.* Potosí's stores were of particular profit to the Crown because Potosí's pulperos paid forty pesos in comparison to either thirty or thirty five pesos for all other cities in Peru. This cédula prompted an intriguing set of tensions because the Crown siphoned tax revenue from the town council. The Crown suggested that royal officials could designate these stores as pulperias de ordenanza or "you can allow the cabildos to name them if it seems better not to innovate where there is a custom."[27] Once designated, however, the Crown ordered that the cabildo had no right to inspect them, tax them, or otherwise interfere in their operation unless a case of "notorious excess" arose.

When the Potosí town council considered the matter of the composición in late 1633 and early 1634, council members settled on reserving twenty-six pulperías for the jurisdiction of the council. Those remaining would belong to the Crown. Councilmen Diego de Mayuelo and Sebastián de la Torre announced great displeasure at the impending reduction in council income. In this era, de la Torre served as the council's main inspector of pulperías. He estimated he had been taxing nearly 130 stores in recent years. Now, he charged, "even though they [the Crown] have left twenty-six pulperías of 130 that ordinarily operate, they are so tenuous and poor" that profits stood to suffer "grave danger."[28] De la Torre eventually took his grievance to the real audiencia. The council challenged the Crown's ruling by naming twenty-six instead of twenty pulperías for its own inspectors. Then, in 1636, the *procurador general* wrote on behalf of the council to negotiate a certain number of inspections per year for the council's benefit.[29] Despite these negotiations, the Crown continued to dominate taxation of the pulperías through the seventeenth century.[30]

Both before and after the Crown's 1631 move for the lion's share of pulpería taxes, local officials made money from storeowners and operators. What goes unspoken throughout the debates inspired first by the 1589 ruling and then by the 1631 cédula is the third major contributing factor to the failure of pulpería limitations: bribery. Officials collected taxes during *visitas*, or inspections, of the stores. In this context, the word *visita* often implied acceptance of bribes. When members of the council visited a store they had an opportunity to earn extra money. Evidence strongly suggests that for a price people could open up stores where they chose, whether licensed or not. The forces of corruption help to explain the sheer number of stores during a decade when both council and viceroy denounced the excessive quantity of pulperías.[31] In a tax roll from 1599, councilmen registered ninety-three stores as having paid some amount of tax. Similar tax rolls from 1600 and 1601 registered a dramatic decline, falling to forty-eight stores and thirty-six stores respectively, but they nonetheless exceeded council mandates. By the 1620s, the going rate to open a pulpería was a one-thousand-peso bribe.[32] In 1623 priest Juan de Alfaro accused then-corregidor Felipe Manrique of selling pulpería licenses *in the rancherías*.[33] Three decades later, in the aftermath of the royal composición, councilman de la Torre cited 130 stores paying a tax to the council. To discourage this corruption, the Crown's 1631 cédula specifically prohibited council members from inspecting pulperías de composición. It is noteworthy that during the 1630s debate over who should receive pulpería taxes, neither Crown nor council remarked on the total number of pulperías in the city. The Crown reiterated its ruling banning pulperías from the rancherías, but it never suggested restricting the number of stores. The dramatic increase in Potosí's population between 1589 and 1630 (an estimated rise roughly from 100,000 to 160,000) reveals one reason for the shift in regulation. Potosí could support more stores and had more residents making a living through trade.

The majority of extant ordinances on pulperías discuss the physical limits announced by Camudio in 1589, yet Spanish officials theoretically aimed to regulate the identity of pulperos (their ethnicity, gender, and place of origin) as well. Few ordinances or petitions refer to the council's stated goal of restricting pulpería licenses to married Spanish men— no *estranjeros* allowed—in the company of their wives.[34] In this way the Crown reserved the licenses for mature Spanish men who settled in Potosí with family. The marriage requirement suggested a desire for some evidence of stability, but it also showed the Crown's desire to offer these commercial posts to men who needed to provide for a family. Though the Crown reserved the twenty-four spots for male heads of households, five single women figured among the initial twenty-four pulperos appointed in 1589: Isabel Ximénez, Catalina de Cavallos, Beatriz Rodríguez, Ana Muñoz, and Luisa Hurtada.[35] Women continued to populate official tax lists of pulperías in the seventeenth century. Further evidence of women's involvement is that men and women received equal punishments for infractions involving pulperías, as well as in all issues of quality, price, or supply.[36] The Potosí town council ignored the gender component of the cédula from the start. By the seventeenth century, it also ignored the "Spanish" stipulation since grocers of indigenous and African descent came to appear on official tax lists.[37]

The council's rulings on pulperías represented a quintessential Spanish perspective. Following its logic, closing down the stores in the "Indian" neighborhoods and choosing responsible Spaniards to run the twenty-four legitimate pulperías in the urban zone would force Indians to stop drinking wine and ensure that they could not pay for items with suspect goods. The council eased the workload of inspection teams by designating a select number of official pulperías. Nonetheless, it embraced a fallacy when it assumed that Indians never drank in pulperías outside their rancherías or that Spanish storeowners would heed rules better than indigenous or African pulperos. Moreover, their specific attention to wine consumption, not chicha, missed the additional quantities of alcohol imbibed by residents. These rulings most likely placed legitimate stores and licenses in the hands of Spanish men and women with some ties to the council. What these rulings tell us, however, is more about whom the officials wanted to run the pulperías than who actually did. Evidence in addition to the official tax lists shows that men and women of a variety of ethnic backgrounds ran pulperías throughout the history of the town.

The repeated rulings and persistent policing that punctuate the regulatory history show that participants in the urban economy, whether they ran stores or market stalls, viewed official decrees as just one of the factors involved in negotiating the urban economy. Thousands upon thousands of people found themselves in Potosí at the behest of the Crown. Once there they needed to use cash or credit to eat and drink. They primarily obeyed social customs of trade and consumption that served to benefit themselves or their families and neighbors, and adjusted to council announcements by Camudio and other criers as they saw fit. The Crown and council both wanted a large population of workers in Potosí; and they wanted ample supplies of subsistence goods to keep the population satisfied. To fulfill these desires, however, the economy that developed moved beyond Spanish parameters and used its own agency to determine the value, mode, and location of economic transactions.

SETTING UP SHOP IN A "PARTE COMODA"

Beatriz de Soto earned income to support herself and her children from the rental of her pulpería. When she could not meet tax payments on the store, Potosí officials closed it down. "I am a woman and a poor widow and laden with children," she pleaded unsuccessfully to the council in November 1609, "I do not have other wealth with which to support myself or my children except the rent from the said pulpería."[38] In addition to emphasizing her identity as a woman, widow, and mother, Soto appealed to the council's concern for physical location of pulperías, arguing that her store, located next to Our Lady of Copacabana church, sat in a "parte comoda," or convenient area, of Potosí. (To locate Soto's store and other sites of commerce, use the list in the appendix in conjunction with map 3.) In this spot, it served the crowds of Spaniards who passed by each day. Despite Soto's eagerness to emphasize her legitimate location, most places of petty trade have a history distinct from the theoretical pulpería zone. This history of pulperías, chicherías, and, to a lesser extent, tambos emerges in notarial documents on ownership and rental of properties and suggests that the geography of urban trade imagined by the town council in Camudio's 1589 declaration was generally disregarded by those who ran the businesses.

People passed a pulpería in almost every block in town. The prime location was a corner. The main part of a pulpería was its front room, where the storekeeper displayed goods and transacted business. Many also contained a *trastienda* (back room) or an *alto* (second-story loft), where shopkeepers lived or stored inventory. Some pulperías concentrated on selling food; others focused on wine.[39] In those that promised food, a

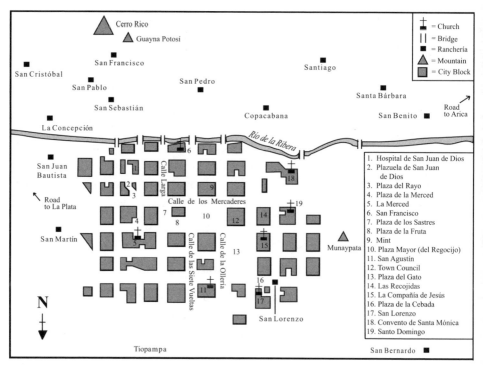

Map 3. Map of Potosí market plazas, churches, indigenous rancherías, and major landmarks.

canvas awning extended on wooden supports to shade any items spilling out the doorway. Stepping inside the pulpería from the street, the customer encountered a display of staples such as wine, bread, flour, sugar, and soap, kept behind a counter or stacked on shelves lining the walls. Beyond such staples, however, some carried higher-priced food items such as figs, raisins, olives, and spices like cumin, aniseed, saffron, cinnamon, or pepper.[40] A marble countertop gleamed in some stores, while more humble wooden ones served in other establishments. Several earthen jugs lined the counters; large ones contained wine and small ones held honey. Oil and vinegar sat close at hand in cruets with stoppers. Store assistants, often women, used standard scoops and weights to measure out wine, vinegar, oil, and honey.[41] In pulperías that more closely resembled taverns, proprietors served wine by the glass (and sometimes chicha), and men congregated inside to drink a few rounds while they played cards or conversed.[42]

Grocers could rent pulperías well equipped for business. In the summer of 1659, Potosí native Ursula Sisa rented her pulpería to Francisca de la Reynaga for the next year. Reynaga had at her disposal a counter with its drawer and key, two large and two small wooden shelves, two poles with canvas for an outside awning, and nine "well-worn" wooden crates to display food.[43] A statue of the Virgin of Bethlehem watched over the store. Magdalena Hernández rented her pulpería not just with these items, but also with account books, numerous jugs, measuring cups and scoops, and a hanging sign.[44]

The most popular establishments devoted to alcohol were not pulperías but chicherías. These served the corn brew along with small snacks, but they offered little in the way of food staples. Some *chicheras* found they could open a business behind their homes in a *buhío*, a simple, straw-covered hut with no more than a few stools and clay cups.[45] Other chicherías offered a more roomy setting. In one typical Potosí chichería a hinged door led to a rectangular room, stretching some nineteen feet deep with a front wall thirty-eight feet wide. The room was covered by a thatched roof and divided in half by an adobe counter.[46] The earthen vessels, such as jugs and vats, which lined the walls of these Andean saloons, signaled their identity for passersby.[47]

Tambos offered food, drink, and a place to rest. Travelers seeking lodging chose among numerous Potosí inns including the Tambo de los Melones, Santo Domingo, Mencia, San Agustín, and Carangas.[48] Prospective Spanish lodgers found the Tambo de Mencia at the intersection of Santo Domingo Street and the Jesuit convent. Owned by the convent of Santo Domingo, it exemplified an urban tambo.[49] Rather than one single building, it was really a compound consisting of upstairs and downstairs rooms, a store, a tavern, a large courtyard, and a corral.[50] In addition to these inns, several houses of gambling and prostitution catered to locals and visitors alike.[51]

The location of properties determined the amount owners could charge for rent and, often, what type of customers the store would serve. In 1615 a pulpería on Tailor's Street, in the city center, rented for 400 pesos annually.[52] Yet a pulpería with its storeroom in the indigenous San Pedro parish was worth only 200 pesos in rent.[53] In contrast to stores or taverns, tambo owners rented their inns for lengthy periods, as many as three to six years, and charged anywhere between 550 to 1250 pesos per year.[54] The shifting faces and uses identified with these properties show that urban peoples innovated to work around Spanish rules on urban trade. Further, the value of rental properties gave owners an important incentive to lobby the town council about regulation on trade.

Given the importance of renting these places of petty business, the town council's pulpería and chichería restrictions often ran counter to the interests of property owners. When pulperías or other establishments closed, individual property owners stood to lose their source of income. When rental incomes dropped precipitously, the Church, as a major property owner, started lobbying council members to have pulperías reopened, even those that sold wine to Indians.[55] A longtime foe of alleged drinking sprees by the native population, the clergy nonetheless took its business investments very seriously. The council was not immune to such complaints. In 1651, when the viceroy ordered the council to maintain its prohibition against pulperías in the rancherías, the council lobbied the king for one pulpería in each of the twelve rancherías so that church-owned stores might reopen.[56] Eight years later, in the aftermath of an October 1659 decision to close thirty-five chicherías, the council showed its willingness to change mandates on public welfare in the face of negative economic repercussions. By April 1660, the council had given many taverns the chance to reopen because the owners, primarily convents or poor people, depended on the rent generated by the chicherías. The council acknowledged that its initial actions were "to the detriment of the community."[57] In the midst of this decade of debate people like the indigenous couple Juan Quispe and Juana de la Cruz paid 120 pesos to sublet the chichería of the Tambo de los Melones from doña Ana Quintanilla.[58] The business of selling food and drink continued apace despite council rulings.

Doña Quintanilla had rented the Tambo de los Melones from the convent of San Agustín and, indeed, most urban stores and taverns fell into the hands of churches or Spanish men.[59] The church extended its reach into urban real estate through bequests of houses, stores, and taverns in the wills of indigenous and Spanish parishioners of varying economic levels.[60] Men dominated as tenants of these rental properties: they rented 179 of the properties; women, 41; and married couples, 9 (see table 1). These numbers reveal that men were the majority of both owners and renters of the spaces of urban trade.

Women also owned and rented pulperías as well as other food venues. While women rented only 5 of 78 tiendas (6 percent), they rented 36 of 151 (24 percent) properties strictly related to food and drink (see table 1). Thus, when the rental figures for stores are divided between *tiendas* (stores commonly rented to serve as shops for artisans and tradespeople) and stores used for dispensing food or alcohol (pulperías, chicherías, *pastelerías*, tambos, coca stores, and bakeries), the percentage of women renters increases dramatically.[61] Women represented almost one-quarter of those renting properties linked specifically to the production and trade of food

TABLE 1: *Ownership and Rental of Properties by Gender, 1570–1700*

Store Type	Owner			Renter		
	Women	Men	Couples	Women	Men	Couples
Food and drink properties						
Pulpería (N=116)	19	94	3	25	87	4
Chichería (N=14)	2	12	0	4	8	2
Pulpería and Chichería						
(N=6)	1	5	0	2	4	0
Tambo (N=6)	0	6	0	2	4	0
Coca store (N=2)	0	2	0	1	1	0
Bakery (N=4)	2	2	0	2	2	0
Pastelería (N=3)	1	1	1	0	3	0
Total (N=151)	25	122	4	36	109	6
Tienda (N=78)	11	65	2	5	70	3
Total (N=229)	36	187	6	41	179	9

Source: AHP-CNM.EN, 1570–1700, extant volumes for every fifth year.

Note: Figures include information from both rental agreements (N=183) and subleasing (*traspaso*) agreements (N=46), for a total of 229 owners and 229 renters.

and alcohol. These examples indicate that the portrayal of women's involvement in petty trade needs to be expanded from vending in outdoor markets to include running stores as well.

Furthermore, women made contributions to these petty businesses beyond the roles of official owner or renter. Men could sign rental agreements for properties that they owned or operated along with their wives, without including the women in formal paperwork.[62] It was also common practice for many renters not to run their stores. Women, especially indigenous or African ones, labored behind the counters of most Potosí stores. The Spaniard Eugenio López managed a store in Potosí selling corn flour, coca, and charqui products to indigenous customers. He did not operate the store on a daily basis but rather hired an indigenous woman, Isabel Sica, to conduct transactions with clients. The arrangement between López and Sica was representative of a common practice in Potosí, whereby Spanish men owned or rented properties for petty trade, but did not engage in the daily practice of trade itself.[63]

Colonial economic forces compelled women like Sica to seek these labor arrangements, and they occasioned women's impact on the customs of the urban economy. In the above example of López and Sica, an indigenous woman sold native products to customers who were probably indigenous like herself. The profits that López extracted at the end of the day were as important as the cultural definitions of exchange that Sica and her customers developed throughout the day.[64] In fact, people who frequented the store might not have known López at all. The indigenous woman Joana Sánchez corroborated the significance of a woman's daily presence behind the counter of the store in her witness testimony for a 1618 property lawsuit. Sánchez swore that the complainant Costanca Almendras was the true owner of a house and an adjacent pulpería. She explained her conviction by adding that she had seen Almendras in the store "many days, selling bread and wine and other pulpería goods."[65] Though Almendras may not, in fact, have owned the property, her physical presence in the daily trade operations signified to neighbors that she was in control.

The history of rental properties reveals how property changed hands, between men and women and across ethnic lines. Since pulperos were obliged to seek reapproval each year, there was no guarantee of a lengthy stay in a trade that entailed startup costs, like renting a store and stocking it with food and wine.[66] If a renter decided to move off the property, he or she located someone to take it over for the remaining time on the lease, and the parties signed an agreement before a notary. At the beginning of the seventeenth century, the tambo of Santo Domingo, facing the tower of the church of the same name, changed hands from Joan Suárez de Carbajal to Amador de Albarez Vegalado, both Spaniards. Then, Francisco Moreno and his wife María Gerónima, probably a *mulato* or mestizo couple, took over the tambo.[67] By 1630, Diego Martín Vello had had his fill of running the worn-down property and turned the rest of his lease over to Juan Guijado Vorregas.[68] The indigenous woman Sicilia Flores was yet another operator who attempted to manage the inn and its various stores from 1681 on.[69]

In addition to changing hands from year to year, the usage of Potosí properties also changed over time. What had once been licensed pulperías in the early 1650s housed, within the space of a few years, a *barbería*, a chichería, a merchant's store, a shoe store, a carpenter, a silversmith, and a tailor.[70] In one case, a site in San Sebastián parish turned, over a fifty-year stretch, from an empty plot of land to a compound with a family dwelling, pulpería, and chichería.[71] Though it never became a particularly desirable piece of property, it did serve the needs of Spanish, indigenous, and African neighbors in Potosí, in particular the six women and three men who used it to launch their participation in petty trade.

Though Beatriz de Soto hinted to the council that the most desirable stores, including her own, were located in a "parte comoda," small businesses turned marginal profits in a variety of spots in the city. Some were legal and in well-traveled sites; others operated clandestinely in alleyways. The particulars of property agreements related to urban trade reveal that the urban economy in Potosí differentiated significantly by gender: men owned and rented most properties of urban trade, women (particularly non-elite women) operated them. The frequent makeovers of these urban stores reflect the instability that characterized the lot of grocery and tavern operators. Additionally, property records show distinct examples of Potosinos' setting up shop in defiance of council rulings on trade.

PLEADING PROPRIETORS BEFORE
THE POWER OF THE COUNCIL

In contrast to these petty traders who informally ignored council rules, the owners and operators of groceries and taverns who officially challenged the council met with only mixed success. In the 1589 ruling that approved twenty-four official pulperos, the council demanded that each grocer find a guarantor, offer surety, and pay a monetary duty fee to obtain his or her license. Without the money to purchase the right to operate officially, pulperos found that the council stood by some of its rules. In November 1609, Roque de la Paz confirmed that he could not afford to pay the remaining twenty pesos he owed on his taxes. Despite his entreaties to the council, they did not grant him leniency.[72] While some storeowners like Paz came to resolve tax problems, others came to ask for permission to operate stores. The town council did not greet all petitioners with equal sympathy. When petty merchants approached town officials to gain permission to run their businesses, the type of business, the location proposed, and the ability to pay taxes affected the receptiveness of council members. Yet a merchant's identity within Andean urban society also reflected the way individuals chose to draft a petition. Ultimately, ethnicity, and to a lesser extent sex, shaped their presentations to the council. However presented, the requests came from individuals trying to maximize their own or their family's success and profit in the urban economy.

Lorenzo Layme, a native of Chucuito, lived off income from a chichería in the indigenous San Sebastián neighborhood when he became too old to work in the mines.[73] As part of a series of ongoing regulations of stores and taverns in Potosí, the council outlawed chicherías in March 1635, citing the "injuries, deaths, and inconveniences" that occurred when the drinking and gathering in the taverns turned to physical outbursts or sexual liaisons.[74] Faced with being shut down permanently, Layme approached the council in April 1635 seeking legitimate recognition for his chicha tavern, alternately called a pulpería by the council. He had heard the town crier proclaim the Crown's order that no one could run a chichería in Potosí, but Layme explained his was not the type of chichería the council feared. He rented a house where he kept four jugs of chicha and sold the drink in a well-controlled atmosphere. In his house, he argued, "there are not nor do I consent to drinking binges."[75]

Layme's case reveals that he had operated the chichería for a significant period without a license. Storekeepers and tavern owners did not generally approach town leaders for permission to operate until threatened with closure.[76] Indeed, the return business that earned them their living was a more important source of daily approval. In the aftermath of the March ruling, when council members instructed inspectors to search out small-scale operators and shut them down, Layme chose to take his case to the council rather than close quietly or retreat into a clandestine operation paying bribes to the appropriate officials. Layme was singular in a town where mainly women served as chicheras.[77] He cited over forty years of work in the Potosí mita as evidence of his service to the Crown and proof that he deserved the chichería. Furthermore, Layme said, at more than eighty years of age, he had no other means to support himself and his four children. If forced to close, he threatened, he had no other choice but to beg alms.[78] One supposes that council members expected Layme's four, presumably adult, children to support him in his advanced age. In the end, Layme left without satisfaction: members unanimously denied his proposal for a license to reopen the tavern.

A very few petty merchants tried to gain the legal right to open a pulpería by pleading their case in advance before the council. While not the norm, these examples reveal what the council liked to hear before offering its approval. In 1647, don Pedro Benítez de la Vega brought an interesting proposal to the table. In exchange for cleaning up a dung heap that offended both eyes and noses of neighbors, Benítez wanted permission to open a pulpería in its place. The dung heap, located in the Ollería next to the San Agustín tambo, was "very prejudicial and damaging to the Republic and the neighborhood because of the filth, stench, and mud" that accompanied it.[79] Benítez's offer seemed to make sense as a public service. In March of that same year, the council scribe, señor Osorio, took Benítez to the dung heap and gave him rights to the property where he had already begun "cleaning and renovating a large part with which he is touching up and decorating the neighborhood."[80] In Osorio's words, this was a "special" service to the community. Then Osorio gave Benítez permission to build and open a pulpería in sight of the former dung heap. The council's acquiescence in the matter came easily because Benítez had chosen to champion a spot located squarely inside the council limits for pulperías and inside the "Spanish" sector of the town. Furthermore, Osorio ascertained that the new store would not impinge on any other store-keepers, because there were no other pulperías in the blocks leading to and from the location. This claim is dubious; three pulperías were open for business in the alleyways of San Agustín in the mid-1630s.[81] Any secret deals between the two remain a mystery but at the very least Osorio must have considered the council's chance to gain a forty-peso annual tax from Benítez. His novel compact with Osorio and other council members allowed Benítez to operate or rent his pulpería fully within the lines of council law.[82]

Given the council's legislative history on pulperías and chicherías, it is perhaps predictable that Benítez, a Spaniard, won his case to open up a grocery inside the official limits. Equally plausible is the case of Layme, an Indian and former mitayo, who did not gain permission to maintain his chicha business. Rules such as the 1589 limits on pulperías served as a prelude to so many examples of exceptions that they appear as mere pieces of paper. To those whom they affected, for better or for worse, they had tangible historical consequences. These cases serve as a reminder that council rulings, while brazenly abused by both entrepreneurs and officials seeking bribes, were effective from time to time.

"TO THE DETRIMENT OF . . . MY PULPERÍA"
ORDINARY RESIDENTS, THE COUNCIL, AND THE FATE OF TWO PULPERÍAS

Town council rulings spoke to the needs and desires of certain Potosí residents in two exemplary cases about the location and operation of pulperías. City inhabitants and business competitors cared passionately about the location of certain stores, and they employed the council ordinances on the pulpería zone to support their arguments.[83] Their examples show how ordinary residents interpreted the concerns of the town council—official limits for pulperías, fears about indigenous drinking, the identity of owners and operators. These themes, then, were not merely the stuff of council meetings but part of the social and economic weave of this colonial society. Entrepreneurs and neighbors did not necessarily share the views of the town council, but they did understood how sites of urban trade, especially ones that sold alcohol, acted as flashpoints for local power.

One indigenous woman, María Sissa, called for some neighborhood redevelopment in the hopes of running a pulpero out of business when she made an initial appearance before the Potosí council on 31 August 1635.[84] A native of Potosí with yanacona status, she lived in San Lorenzo, or Munaypata, with her family. She came to the council aiming to clean up her corner of that neighborhood. Bordering her home, she complained, was a useless alley (*callejonsillo*) that served only as a dung heap and "hideaway of thieves and other such undesirables."[85] Sissa wanted to protect her home and her neighborhood from the sorts of people who entered this unkempt alleyway and from the crimes, particularly theft, that such wanderers brought with them. Though walls surrounded her house, Sissa feared that thieves easily could climb over and threaten her family's home. On this, her first action in the matter, she asked that a representative of the council come personally to verify her assessment of the problem, and then close off the alley.

Such entreaties held the council's attention with their accounts of no-good thieves. Aldermen Joan Gutiérrez de Paredes and Diego Rodríguez de Figueroa went to survey the scene. The town leaders decided to donate the alleyway to Sissa. She offered thirty pesos for the site, but the council rejected her offer citing her limited resources and the expense she would incur in order to enclose the area with a wall.[86] On 24 November 1635, María Sissa stood in the alleyway in Munaypata along with don Pablo Vázquez Cusi Ynga, the capitán general of the yanaconas in Potosí, who had taken up Sissa's cause. Don Vázquez was a powerful, if controversial, figure in Potosí politics who had unseated the reigning captain don Francisco Cusi Paucar in 1632 thanks to the scheme of a Spanish official.[87] In the presence of the scribe Pedro de Barona de Maldonado and three other witnesses, Sissa took possession of the alleyway and agreed to close it off and make it part of her property.[88] No protests interrupted this simple ceremony.

If Sissa emerged from this first act as a neighborhood champion, trying to protect family and property for the Munaypata residents, she later played the role of uppity troublemaker in this unfolding drama. For many of the people who lived on or near the infamous alleyway, it was nothing more than a regular thoroughfare; for others, it was a path to their businesses. Neighbors' subsequent responses to Sissa's actions clearly illuminate the role of neighborhood politics in the urban economy.

The neighbors expressed their reaction more formally six weeks later, on 11 January 1636, when Francisco Chamorro, a pulpero, along with four other neighbors, appealed the council's decision to close the street.[89] All five of the objectors, two men and three women, identified themselves as Munaypata residents who wanted to speak up for the many indigenous mine laborers and Spaniards who lived in the area with their families and used this alleyway. They mentioned their married status to lend respectability to their appeal. Previously the council considered only Sissa's opinion, along with their own best interests, when they gave her the property and agreed to close off the street. Ostensibly, Sissa was bettering the area much as don Pedro Benítez de la Vega had done when he built a pulpería in a former dung heap. In this case, Sissa would not have the last word. How, the appeal asked, could the council commit such a violent offense without listening to the opinions of others?

The narrow alleyway and dung heap of Sissa's petition assumed a different identity in the appeal, becoming a "Royal street that led from the center of Monaipata [Munaypata] to the refineries of the Ribera and to neighborhoods and trade across the whole district of Monaipata."[90] Further, the cast of characters who peopled the street was respectable: married Spaniards and mitayos. According to the four petitioners, these people found themselves barricaded in their houses at the behest of María Sissa. The once pleasant walk to the main plaza and cathedral now involved a circuitous route through Potosí's city streets, several blocks out of the way. Yet perhaps the more serious complaints stemmed from the lost value or income from rental properties and a pulpería located in the disputed passageway. Francisco Chamorro had run a fully licensed pulpería in the alleyway on which he had paid, in previous years, the forty-peso tax demanded by the Crown. Closing off the street spelled the end of his business and the end of his means to pay the forty-peso tax.[91] Of significance here, however, is the fact that in 1634 Chamorro had elected to make his establishment a pulpería de composición and pay his forty-peso tax to the Crown, not to the council.[92] The council lost no money by impinging on the business of a royal pulpería, and council members still smarting from the 1631 ruling may have felt justified in their actions. Chamorro's image as a respectable businessman lost force as Sissa forged ahead in the conflict.

Following the group protest, Sissa returned to the fight through the voice of don Pablo Vázquez. Many reasons existed to uphold the council's earlier actions, but at the very least, Vázquez demanded, Sissa should receive compensation for the materials and labor involved in closing off the area. In his reply, Vázquez quickly cast aspersions on Sissa's main complainant. Francisco Chamorro, he assured the council, had spearheaded the cause to reopen the alley because he stood to lose business in his pulpería. Sissa may not have intended to hurt Chamorro per se, but she probably identified his business as contributing to the atmosphere she disliked in her neighborhood. One also wonders if Sissa herself had aspirations to operate a tavern or store from her home (a common practice) and hoped to use her suit to wipe out competition from Chamorro. In this case, the physical location of Chamorro's pulpería (that is, within official limits or not) never became an issue. While the site of the store in the San Lorenzo ranchería had been off limits to pulperías in 1589, Spanish residents of Potosí had moved into the area in the seventeenth century. Instead, Vázquez made his case about alcohol, laboring Indians, and illicit pawn activity. He argued that, Sissa's actions aside, Chamorro's store deserved to be shut down since he cheated mita Indians and sold them bad Peruvian wine. He also accused Chamorro of accepting any sort of pawn objects, like silver dress pins (*topos*) and clothing, as payment in violation of pulpería ordinances that forbid pulperos to accept pawns from non-Spaniards. The accusations against Chamorro registered on two levels with council members; not only did he inflict personal ruin upon unsuspecting Indians, who in their eyes did not know enough to control their drinking, he also threatened the operation of the mita labor draft at the Cerro Rico silver mines by encouraging the profligacy of indigenous peoples.[93]

Further, as Vázquez reminded the council, the alley in question did not hold the city status of a "royal" street. Moving to the facts, he described the closed street as very narrow, barely six feet in width, and twenty-eight feet in length.[94] He called attempts to portray it otherwise as "sinister." Its appeal as a neighborhood thoroughfare declined even further during the rainy season when the alleyway became, in Vázquez's words, "a total swamp and puddle with water more than two feet high where not even a mule could pass."[95]

Vázquez charged on in his tirade against the appellants. He alleged that the location of the street assured that it would serve as a hiding place for thieves who lay in wait and spied on unsuspecting indigenous men and women strolling the path to go drinking at Chamorro's pulpería, or worse —on their merry way home after drinking. On that street, charged Vázquez, "it is notorious that dead Indians are found."[96] He stopped short of linking Chamorro to a conspiracy with the thieves, and left that inductive leap to the suspicious and crime-obsessed council members.

Vázquez's ire is perhaps best explained by his role in the colonial world.

As a captain of the yanaconas, he defended María Sissa in her attempts to clean up her end of the neighborhood for herself and her family. When he linked her opponents to the sale of alcohol to Indians, it strengthened the council's resolve to keep the alley blocked off. Sissa's position, and by extension Vázquez's argument, that the alley ruined the neighborhood won the support of the council largely because the location of a pulpería in the ranchería of Munaypata, a predominantly indigenous section of the city, defied earlier council rulings. The ruling of the council on the case of the blocked alleyway became an official pronouncement, an attempt to shape the urban economy according to societal priorities. In this hierarchy of needs, a productive and dependable labor force ranked above tax revenue from a marginal pulpería. Made in the same year that the council outlawed chicherías, the assertion that Chamorro's pulpería contributed to the degradation of native peoples held sway.

Yet those indigenous men or women who drank at Chamorro's pulpería did not participate in a life of socializing and drinking solely at the behest of an eager businessman. They found a tavern owner located in an inconspicuous spot in the ranchería, presumably outside Spanish earshot. He accepted their goods as pawn for food and drink. To Vázquez, the sale of wine in exchange for pawn goods represented an injustice by Chamorro against the Indians, although Vázquez also provided evidence of indigenous desire for such places: "Everyday the Indians secretly went down it [the alleyway] to drink in the said pulpería two blocks away, and especially Monday mornings, hiding themselves from the miners and overseers of the Cerro and from the Señor Corregidor who kicks them out [of the pulpería]."[97] According to Vázquez, if they succeeded in hiding from their overseers, the Indians spent the whole day drinking in the taverns with their wives, missing work, and spending all the money they earned in one week of mita labor, which amounted to a pitiful sum. Whether owned by indigenous women or Spanish men like Chamorro, the taverns formed part of the social world of a Potosí ranchería and at times formed the basis for an underground economy. Alcohol consumption went hand in hand with socializing, forming a sense of community for men forced into the mines by the Spanish Crown, and offering a badly needed emotional respite from toil in the silver mines. The social environment that Chamorro sponsored did not please don Pablo Vázquez, who used the inherent paternalism in Spanish law to fight for indigenous people like the yanacona María Sissa, who shared his social status and goals. But charges of drinking and pawn, however much they rankled, would not have prevailed without Vázquez's power. Vázquez's tight links with Spanish rulers

—recall his rise to power through the ouster of a third-generation indigenous leader—clearly strengthened Sissa's case. Although this matter consumed the council with unusual intensity, don Pablo Vázquez finally won his case at their 1 February meeting.

A pulpería lay at the heart of yet another neighborhood skirmish, this one involving three separate parties—two Spanish individuals and one indigenous group. The licentiate Domingo Rodríguez de Quiroga went to the court in 1644 to protest the activities of Diego de Padilla Solórzano who was renovating a nearby pulpería on the border of the San Sebastián parish.[98] Rodríguez argued that he purchased a home and attached pulpería from Matías García de la Vega located in the Arquillos, behind the refinery of Bartolomé de Uzeda. He opened the pulpería with an official license granted locally by don Francisco Sarmiento de Sotomayor, the corregidor and justicia mayor of Potosí. The store fell within the council's limits and served a neighborhood of Spaniards. The pulpero had operated the store without incident until he discovered Padilla renovating the corner pulpería up the street. Rodríguez argued that Padilla's work was in vain: despite the proximity, Padilla's planned store sat in the ranchería of the Callapas Indians, an area outside official limits. "The said house that he intends to open will not be within limits but in the Indian ranchería," Rodríguez argued to the council.[99] Citing the government's prohibitions against any outsiders of Spanish or African descent trespassing in indigenous neighborhoods, Rodríguez stated that Padilla had to be shut down. Rodríguez was interested not only in the civic good, but in the consequences of this new pulpería for him personally: he expressed his concerns to the council about "the noteworthy damages to me and my income" from the competition of another store.[100]

Unimpressed by Rodríguez's extensive arguments, Padilla countered with his own petition. Padilla waved before the court a provision from the Real Audiencia (high court) of Charcas supplying witness testimony that his home had functioned as a pulpería for some sixty years. He assured the court that the pulpería sat within the given limits, on a public and royal street with sizable Spanish commerce. He argued that despite his opponent's claims to the contrary, neither the 1605 nor 1624 council rulings on the limits for pulperías had closed this store down.[101]

Padilla also noted, no doubt with some satisfaction, that he had already won a lawsuit that ruled his store was within legal limits. Shortly after Padilla purchased the building from the absentee owner, he visited the property along with council representatives and community officials to engage in a ritual act of taking possession of the land. During the process, a group of Pacajes Indians from Callapa, headed by their kuraka don Diego Alanora, brought the process to a halt.[102] They intervened and offered two petitions that stated their objection to the purchase of the house and lot by Padilla and asked him not to disturb their possession of the land. Padilla soon landed in court with the Pacajes, who claimed he was taking property that lay within the borders of their ranchería and that therefore belonged to them. In a 1642 ruling by the real audiencia in the initial suit, Padilla prevailed over the indigenous complainants.[103] He returned to the property to undertake a second act of possession, during which one of his companions ejected a group of indigenous inhabitants along with their personal effects from a small hut adjacent to the lot. The initial phase of the battle had ended, but the indigenous men and women were not content to watch quietly as Padilla set up shop.

When Rodríguez launched his complaint, the Pacajes Indians found yet another legal opening to make their protest. They were joined by other Pacajes from Callapas, many of whom were mitayos, and the larger group presented their complaints through an indigenous defender, the *protector de naturales*, who represented the parish of San Sebastián. He argued that the lot lay within his jurisdiction and reminded the court that Spanish law prohibited Spaniards, mestizos, Africans, and mulatos from residing in rancherías. He further argued that Viceroy don Francisco de Toledo had granted the property in question to the Callapas in the 1570s to provide a place for them to live while they performed mita service. The attack on their property, the protector argued, was "in grievous detriment to the smooth operation of the mita and to the detriment of the royal fifth [the Crown's take of silver]."[104] He decried that the court held the wishes of one man more important than those of forty-nine mitayos and concluded that the actions of the court would only encourage indigenous men to abandon their mita assignments and migrate elsewhere. He even ventured that in the wake of their loss to Padilla in the original lawsuit, the indigenous inhabitants had been left homeless.

His representation of these native groups did not prevent the protector from employing negative stereotypes about them to arouse Spanish fears of a lazy indigenous population. In language that reflected earlier council rulings and viceregal provisions, the protector argued that opening another pulpería would cause "danger and harm to my clients because of the dangers and inconveniences that happen to the Indians when wine is sold in the ranchería. It gives [the Indians] the opportunity to drink and get drunk and keeps them from climbing up the Cerro [to work]."[105]

As Padilla phrased his aim, he simply wanted to restore the ramshackle structure and emulate the one woman, Ana de Funes, who ran a *licensed* pulpería on the spot. This site and its buildings, however, had hosted numerous characters in a chaotic series of turnovers. In 1590 Joan Muyo and Joan Balas, yanacona Indians, sold the property to Ana de Funes, alternately referred to as a Spaniard or a mulata.[106] Funes had plans to enter into petty trade. She built a pulpería on the property and obtained a license from don Rafael Ortiz de Sotomayor to open the business. In the early seventeenth century, María de Tena purchased the pulpería with the legal acknowledgment of her second husband, Diego Rodríguez Cabanillas. There they maintained a home and the pulpería, which Tena ran until moving to Lima in 1617. The property remained in her name, and she appointed two men, Rodrigo Salguero and Simon Hidalgo, to manage it in her absence. The property sat idle for a few years, which one witness blamed on disruption caused by a 1619 epidemic; the urban skirmishes between the *vicuñas* and the *vascongados* from 1622 to 1625 is another possible factor. Finally, Salguero and Hidalgo drummed up interest in the property and rented the pulpería to Isabel de Torres for four years, to Marcos de Riba de Neyra and Simón Rodríguez for an unspecified time period, and finally to Ana de Contreras for two years.[107] After Contreras left, the property fell into decay, heavy rains caved in its roof, and thieves carried away its wooden doors and windows.

Next, in 1630, Gonzalo Hernández Paniagua contracted to buy the property for 450 pesos from María de Tena, who was still in Lima and now widowed for the second time. Though he carried out no renovations, his contemporaries contended that he rented the run-down property. A married Spanish woman, Bernavala Gutiérrez, did rent a shack that was still standing adjacent to the main structure. From 1640 to 1642 she ran a chichería out of the shack, hiring two indigenous women to make chicha and staff the ramshackle tavern from day to day. Rent alone did not earn sufficient profits for Hernández to pay his debts on the property in full. Thus, at his death, the executors of his will auctioned the property to Diego Padilla for a mere 250 pesos with the proceeds going to Tena. After the sale, Padilla took possession of the property when he allegedly ejected a group of chicha-drinking Indians along with bottles and jugs from a small hut (*guasesillo*) adjacent to the main structure. This move not only symbolized his taking ownership, but also reinforced his claim to run a legitimate petty business in contrast to the existing shady tavern.

Padilla's petition tried to downplay the chichería stage of the house's history, since chicherías had been outlawed since 1635. Instead, he reminded the town fathers that they stood to benefit from the forty-peso annual tax that would come with reopening the store. Further, his petition attacked Rodríguez's motives, asserting that the property was never part of the Callapas's ranchería and that Rodríguez used the false argument to "obstruct my justice. Because he sees me poor and blind he has always opposed me to take away this small means from the said house and pulpería and prevent me altogether from the support of myself and of my wife and three children who are suffering extreme necessities of hunger and nakedness."[108] An unsympathetic Rodríguez countered Padilla's pleas, arguing that playing to poverty and the needs of his three children was sinister. Even if the extreme need was true, Rodríguez quarreled, there was no reason to "remedy nor feed [his wife and children] at my cost and to the detriment of me and my pulpería."[109] Despite a council ruling that Padilla be denied a license, the final extant ruling from the real audiencia proclaimed that Padilla's store sat within the ordained limits.[110] The competition to Rodríguez's establishment, the displacement of mita Indians, and the potential threat to mita labor did not prevail in the final analysis. Still, the legal ordeal represented a threat as well as a considerable expenditure of time and money to Padilla. With neighbors like María Sissa to police alcohol consumption and illicit pawn or ones like Rodríguez to patrol pulpería limits, who needed council inspectors?

CONCLUSION

When the town council set the 1589 limits for the location of stores, it aimed to curtail illegal practices facilitated by the high number of stores outside the purview of Spanish officials. In theory, the restriction of pulperías to a limited zone, a very Spanish zone at that, allowed for easy inspection. Thus at a very basic level, the council attempted to gain official Spanish control over people and trade. The general tenor of policies about trade revealed royal concern with any threat to silver production. Mine laborers and other indigenous migrants to the town needed supplies of good quality food at fair prices and limited chances to consume alcohol. Grocers had to be trained not to accept silver items (or any unrefined silver) in exchange for goods or pesos. The official right to run a store was reserved for Spanish male heads of households who paid taxes, and in some cases bribes, for their grocers' licenses.

The forces at work in Potosí's economy, however, clashed with these regulatory ideals in every way imaginable. Potosinos of varied ethnic and class backgrounds made room to sell in spaces across their city. Some operated their businesses in accordance with, and others in spite of, town council ordinances. Real estate records show that stores existed all over Potosí and operated without official consent.[111] Moreover, owners or those who ran pulperías were a varied cast. Laboring Spaniards who did not gain access to silver riches in Potosí often turned to trade to make a living, and they drew in wives and children along with them. Indigenous men and women figured as owners and operators of both official and unofficial stores, and by the mid-seventeenth century, Potosinos of African descent ran stores as well. Frequently, indigenous women and African slaves conducted daily business from the stores. Few complied with council and Crown rules that limited commercial opportunities for many residents.

Regulations about the urban economy, and the debates that accompanied them, shifted over time as the city grew and its population changed. In the late sixteenth century, when the council first aimed to control pulperías, it did so in the context of a rapidly expanding urban population and burgeoning silver production. Rules about the identity of grocers and the locations of stores were fueled by discourses that linked indigenous mineworkers to trafficking in stolen goods and heavy alcohol consumption, both practices that worked against official Spanish interest. In the first decades of the 1600s, changes in regulations reflect the increasing diversity of the city's population. Many non-Spaniards now ran pulperías. Rather than debate the validity of these shops or their operators, Spanish officials focused on profits to be earned through taxation. Furthermore, beginning in the 1630s, these issues of monies to be gained from storeowners were tied to jurisdictional issues between the Crown and the council. In the period of the 1630s and 1640s, of course, the discourses about problematic behavior by indigenous residents in illicit pulperías were still employed, but not by the council. At this point, individuals like María Sissa or Diego de Padilla used them to defend their own interests. And, finally, as silver production slipped into its long decline around the mid-seventeenth century, council anxieties about the urban population produced regulatory efforts at social control of Africans and mixed-race castas in the city's taverns.

Here we have seen how many voices from the first half of the seventeenth century entered the debates over rules of trade in colonial Potosí: a weary Spanish widow trying to rent out her store, a righteous indigenous vendor demanding that he be allowed to sell where he was situated, and a vociferous Spanish bureaucrat bemoaning the numerous bars mucking up the center of the city. In cases for or against the operation of pulperías, the council heard of illegal pawn and illicit drinking from

María Sissa, of declining tax revenues from Church property owners, and of needy families from men like Diego de Padilla. These cases reveal that by the 1600s, the 1589 attempts to create twenty-four well-situated pulperías were both ineffective and insufficient. Individual merchants used the council regulations to challenge and drive off economic competitors. Merchants and even property owners also manipulated forces outside the town council, namely, powerful mining interests and the La Plata audiencia, to their benefit. While the town council tried to sustain and control Potosí's lifeblood of mine labor through trade regulations, urban traders adapted their economic activities in response to food supplies and business interests. Increasingly, the voices that urged limitation of the pulperías fell quiet. By the end of the sixteenth century, well more than twenty-four stores paid a tax, and many likely paid a bribe as well, to ensure they could keep their doors open.

Like the growth in numbers of stores, what pulperías sold and how they sold it was also markedly different from what Spanish council members had foreseen. In both cases, this difference was the result of local influence. The pulpería in 1600s Potosí was quite foreign to a visiting Spaniard. Pulperos, as Fray Diego de Ocaña defined them for his Iberian readers, "are men who have stores where they sell wine and jugs of chicha."[112] This definition fits well with the momentum to relax quotas on pulperías in exchange for increased tax revenue. It was a tacit acknowledgement that Potosí pulpería transactions moved goods, money, and people in ways that Spanish officials could not, and sometimes did not want to, control.

LIGHT ON THE CHICHA,
HEAVY ON THE BREAD
The Colonial Market for Brewing and Baking

3

In 1604, the news spread through Potosí slowly as the new smell that wafted up from the steaming chicha cauldrons, trailed into taverns and flour warehouses, and, finally, deposited its noxious message at the seat of municipal power: chicha brewers were making their traditional corn brew with wheat flour. From as early as 1565, the city of Potosí tried to restrict imports of corn flour in an effort to limit indigenous consumption of chicha. Some years brought more success than others. In 1604, however, it was clear that Crown officials' and council members' best efforts to control the supply of corn flour to Potosí had backfired. Innovative chicha brewers responded to the restricted supply by simply changing their recipe. This creative adaptation of indigenous tradition to new Spanish rules thwarted attempts to control indigenous drinking and threatened a quintessentially European product—wheat bread. Overwhelmed by the news that wheat flour was being diverted to chicha, Spanish town council officials revoked the corn restrictions rather than continue to lose the main ingredient in their bread.[1]

In their parallel climbs to the top of the colonial Potosí market, chicha and bread often appeared in town council minutes, but rarely as concurrently as in 1604. Underweight bread and massive consumption of chicha were the principal food offenses that the town council aimed to amend, but their tactics to regulate production and sale of the two products diverged sharply. The council encouraged the production of bread, deemed a vital victual in the Spanish colonies, as a service to the republic; it aided bakeries with labor subsidies and attacked bakers only when their loaves failed to measure up to the standard weight. When the members turned to a discussion of chicha, in contrast, it was to ward off a threat to the colonies and a potential drain on human resources. Despite continual attempts to control both products, the overall results were disappointing. When indigenous brewers had difficulty procuring corn flour, they turned to wheat, thus making supplies scarce for the production of bread. As was the case with Crown and cabildo ordinances on the locations of pulperías, Spanish officials competed with landowners, merchants, vendors, and consumers over the regulation of marketplace products.

These same players also negotiated the very significance of items like bread and chicha. Bread was originally a Spanish product, chicha an indigenous one. Just as language, clothing, and religion served as crucial markers among groups of people, so did food and drink. In the sixteenth century, elite observers like the Potosí town council labored to keep firm such cultural demarcations. The categorization of foods along ethnic lines, in both council minutes and modern histories, hid the parallel transformation of these two products into mainstream colonial fare. By the 1570s, indigenous brewers found Spaniards and Africans buying their chicha; by the early seventeenth century, Spanish bakers sold wheat bread to African servants and indigenous workers. Side-by-side analysis of the production and retail of the two products reveals the full gender and ethnic complexity of this colonial urban economy. In Potosí one finds that mulata women sold chicha, indigenous men baked bread, indigenous women sold it, and Spanish women operated petty businesses in both products to earn a living.

And, thousands upon thousands of Potosinos purchased the two items. In 1603 bread and chicha ranked as the highest selling food and drink items in Potosí. Twenty-eight bakeries sold an estimated 1,210,900 pesos' worth of bread per year. The chicha industry supplied 600,000 bottles per year worth 1,024,000 pesos. In comparison, wine, which sold at up to 10 pesos a bottle, was only a 500,000-peso industry, and potatoes, a staple of the indigenous diet, were a 120,000-peso industry.[2] Apart from having high volume sales in common, both bread and chicha offered nutritional value with wheat and corn flour as their bases. Both shared the distinction of being highly regulated by the town council. The two goods had contrasting modes of production—chicha remained a small-scale industry, whereas bread was generally produced by large bakeries with forced labor and organized bakers' guilds. Yet both products were locally made comestibles—as opposed to goods like coca, fruit, or wine that were imported from outside the city—and thus allow for in-depth study of the creation of urban industries.

This chapter traces the rise of chicha as a colonial industry in Potosí, from the 1560s to the 1660s, and considers the drink's regulation, production, and consumption. A like analysis of bread follows, with attention to town council rules, product demand, and bakery labor. As these trades expanded to satisfy the demands of an emerging colonial palate, the process of production reflected marked disparity in Potosí society. Bakeries relied on forced labor of both native Andeans and African slaves. Chicha production soared in part because many cash-poor indigenous women secured advances from Spanish tavern owners who sold the corn brew. In terms of consumption, chicha and bread shed their labels as indigenous and Spanish products to emerge as distinctly colonial comestibles.

"ALL THIS FLOUR, THE INDIANS OF POTOSÍ USE FOR DRINK"
REGULATING CORN FLOUR

When sixteenth-century mill owners began to produce new mill-ground corn flour, the effects of this practice became the center of debate about alcohol in the colonial market. In 1565 the corregidor of Potosí, Gaspar de Saldana, blamed "the invention" of corn flour for a dangerous increase in chicha consumption by indigenous residents of the city. The best way to remedy the situation was, in his opinion, to prohibit "corn flour[,] because without it they have to grind the corn to make the said *acua* [chicha] and they cannot grind more than that which is necessary and moderate like they did before the said flour was made."[3] Others would comment on chicha's moral, physical, and social ill effects. But Saldana's overwhelming preoccupation was that drinking caused a "great impediment . . . to the labor of the mines, which was the reason they [Indians] were brought here, because most of the time that they are supposed to work in the said labor they are occupied in the said *borracheras*."[4] Keeping laborers sober and fit for grueling workdays at the mines was at odds with the economic and social incentives for alcohol consumption.[5] Moreover, royal officials and priests alike bemoaned the "grave dangers"—namely, spiritual and sexual offenses—committed by chicha drinkers who were "capable of dancing and drinking for nights and days."[6] By prohibiting corn flour, Saldana hoped to save Potosí's mitayos from themselves and keep them fit for mine labor.

The council's desire to limit chicha by controlling the supply of corn was not unusual, since the council oversaw all provisioning for the city. The council made the rules for the sale of corn, once putting an embargo on corn flour and at other times mandating that sacks of flour be divided to promote small-scale sales.[7] When its attempt to ban corn flour failed, the council could do no better than attempt to reduce corn flour's sale.[8] Ordinances on the sale and provision of corn flour exhibited a flexibility that reflected the elite's economic and social needs. By the mid-seventeenth century, town council members would turn from interventions in the production of chicha to tirades on chicherías, the prime distributors of the brew. Yet Saldana and his colleagues targeted not chicha consumption but control of its main ingredient.

Royal officials in the audiencia and in Potosí had discussed a corn flour embargo prior to 1565, but they were opposed by landowners in Charcas, who feared profit losses. In 1565, Saldana prepared a report to convince the Crown and the real audiencia to ignore "inconveniences to the particular good of those owners of chacaras [small farms] and haciendas" and prohibit the delivery of corn flour to Potosí.[9] Saldana's report emphasized the intoxicating effect of chicha and downplayed the nutrients offered by its corn base. To fend off criticism that the prohibition would harm the diet of indigenous residents of Potosí, Saldana called forward four kurakas as informants. Don Phelipe of Condesuyo; don Geronimo, ynca of Cuzco; don Phelipe of Tapacari; and don Diego of Macha alleged that the prohibition would not deprive anyone of sustenance because indigenous Potosinos used corn flour only for the production of acua.[10] Testimony from numerous priests and friars reflected not on physical well-being, but on the social ills and idolatrous acts that prohibition was sure to prevent. One of the witnesses, Fray Alonso Trueno of Santo Domingo, claimed to have lived in the Villa for fifteen years. He dated the arrival of the corn in flour form to 1557, and he swore that were the flour prohibited, "the better part of the said drinking binges and the said dangers and inconveniences would cease." Prior to corn flour besting corn grain in the marketplace, Trueno asserted, "there were not great drinking binges."[11] For Saldana, Trueno, and the others testifying that chicha hindered both missionary work and mining, the arrival of corn flour in 1557 marked the beginning of an upswing in alcohol consumption that threatened Spanish control of Potosí. These men hoped that the 1565 ban on corn flour would free them from the chicha regulation issue, but the work had only begun.

Between 1565 and 1604, policies on the prohibition of corn flour emerged, flip-flopped, and then waned. In Lima in 1572, Viceroy Toledo pondered what he had seen on his tour of Potosí and, of like mind with Saldana, ordered that corn be brought to the highland city only in the form of grain and not ground as flour.[12] This would theoretically slow the pace of production. Toledo also floated the idea of establishing exclusive chicha-dispensing sites in the rancherías, though this never become a concrete project.[13] Rulings in 1582 and 1586 upheld the prohibition on flour and barred wealthy mill owners (Indians as well as Spaniards) and their mestizo and indigenous workers from grinding the corn into flour or selling to merchants who carted it to Potosí.[14] The 1586 ruling came directly from Viceroy don Fernando de Torres y Portugal, count of Villar.

He lamented that indigenous women needed corn grain to make the gruel *mote*, and that chicha instead was the predominant use: "[because] corn . . . is brought to the said Villa in flour and not in grain the result is little corn and many occasions of drunkenness among the Indian inhabitants and even other bigger dangers like idolatry, incest, and other monstrous and weighty sins in offense of God our Lord."[15] He blamed the *justicias* of Potosí for ignoring the previous viceregal ordinances that had prohibited the sale of corn in Potosí. With such a prohibition, rural landowners, millers, and urban traders lost business. Increasingly, however, these economic interests would win out.

Severe droughts in 1590 and 1591 aggravated concerns about food supply and prices and led to easing of the corn policy. Prohibitions penalized only poor indigenous traders and consumers, not the "powerful persons who carry out this business," according to Viceroy Marques de Cañete don García Hurtado de Mendoza. He ordered that "whatever persons, Spaniards as well as Indians, can trade freely with corn flour, the former for business and the latter for their drinks."[16] In this era, indigenous women, wives of indigenous flour traders, won permission from Corregidor don Pedro de Lodena to sell corn flour in small quantities at council-mandated prices.[17] Writing to the Potosí council in 1596, Secretary Juan de Losa promoted the corn prohibition one more time.[18] Within a few years, however, the council again lamented the policy's failure. The council claimed that when prohibitions by Viceroys Toledo, Enríquez, Velasco, and Marqués de Cañete had made corn flour scarce in the Villa, some Indians had responded by purchasing wheat flour for their brew. Council members in 1604 recognized that the use of wheat to brew chicha was counter to their goals for bread production. Moreover, they acknowledged the dietary significance of chicha in the rancherías and urged the free trafficking of corn flour to avoid the "dangers caused among the Indians for lack of corn flour for their drinks."[19] By 1604 corn flour prohibition had lost its staunch defenders.

The regulations on corn flour reveal administrative responses to the emergence of a colonial business in chicha.[20] This shift was most visible between the 1565 attempt at a corn embargo and the 1604 scare over the scarcity of wheat. The transformation encompassed a variety of economic and social processes visible through changes in supply, production, and consumption. During the late 1550s, when mining and agricultural elements of colonial Charcas were at odds over local governance of Potosí, Spanish hacienda owners promoted a market for chicha production by sending ground flour to Potosí. Growers from the valleys of Cochabamba,

Pitantora, and Fronteras de Tomina supplied the corn. The corn flour came into the city on the backs of llamas, and the trajinantes delivered it to one of numerous *canchas* in the city. At these canchas, enclosures that consisted of a few rooms used to store the grain, distributors generally sold their grain or flour wholesale. The flooding of the market with the flour mimicked the tremendous shipments of coca to Potosí. With chicha, new production and consumption patterns shaped colonial meanings of a preconquest staple.

The new availability of corn flour affected the ancient task of brewing chicha. Chicheras concocted the popular drink from fermented grains, typically corn, although other grains like quinoa or wheat could be used when corn was not available.[21] To make chicha, brewers soaked grains of maize in water for several days until they began to sprout. Then they ground the sprouted grains, called *viñapu*, boiled them in the water in which they had soaked, and transferred the mixture to large vessels for fermentation. These great earthen vats were known as *urpus* in Quechua, spelled *virqquis* or *birques* in colonial Spanish, and often identified by colonial observers as *tinajas*, the Spanish version of a large clay container. The grinding of the corn grains happened in one of two ways. Brewers might grind them by hand and wet them with water to form a paste known as *muk'u*. In the more traditional method, the chichera ground the grains by chewing them in her mouth, a manner that, for Spaniards like José de Acosta, "provokes disgust even to hear about it."[22] The brewer left the corn paste to soak for ten days, then cooked it and returned it to a large vat to soak in more water. After a process of repeated grinding, straining, and soaking, the brew was ready for sale.

In the early seventeenth century, a segment of Potosinos still produced chicha in the traditional manner. The city had a plaza devoted to the sale of muk'u. Fray Lizarraga noted that six- and seven-year-old children of mita mine workers earned money by chewing corn to make the leaven for chicha.[23] However, in Potosí, individuals masticating the grain or grinding it by hand competed with millers grinding the corn.

When Potosí chicheras abandoned traditional production by using mill-ground corn for their chicha, they made a different product, perhaps less intoxicating or less flavorful. Whatever changes resulted, demand did nothing but rise. When visiting the Fronteras de Tomina in 1600, Fray Diego de Ocaña marveled at the six hundred thousand cargas of corn destined for Potosí. He surmised of shipments from Cochabamba, Pitantora, Tomina, and other valleys that "all this flour, the Indians of Potosí use for drink."[24] From Ocaña's observation, Potosí buyers would have no problem earning profits to pay for the flour. He reported that sales of wine and chicha at the turn of the century amounted to three hundred thousand pesos per week. Of this voluminous trade Ocaña minced no words: "This is the most notable thing that I can say of Potosí."[25]

The language Ocaña chose is of note. Saldana's 1565 report dated itself in its consistent use of the Quechua *acua* to refer to corn beer. Ocaña, thirty-five years later, wrote of *chicha*. The latter term, an Arawak word the Spanish applied generically to most indigenous alcohol they encountered, is predominant in colonial materials from the 1570s on.[26] As for its production, Ocaña did not even mention corn grain or the grinding process, saying chicha was made "from corn flour; they put it in water and boil it and in five days they drink it."[27] Ocaña simplified, to be sure. Yet even in this brevity, change is evident. As residents of Potosí altered or substituted for the main ingredient, maize, as they exaggerated quantities of their drink and called it by a different name, chicha began its expansion as a colonial industry. By the time the town council relaxed its prohibition of corn flour in 1604, the production of chicha constituted a major informal industry. What Saldana and others had witnessed in 1565 was the beginning of this important colonial business.

"MAIZE SERVES THE INDIANS NOT ONLY AS BREAD, BUT ALSO AS WINE"
CHICHA AS COLONIAL BUSINESS

As a drink of great significance in the preconquest era, chicha had been regulated prior to colonial times. Because of chicha's association with rituals of the Inca calendar, some colonial sources claimed the ruling elite controlled its consumption.[28] The Inca did oversee production of chicha, in particular through the *aclla*, select women chosen to live in communal settings and serve the Inca.[29] In addition to spinning and weaving fine cloth, the aclla brewed chicha. Maize beer fulfilled a nutritional role in Andean life, but the aclla's production of fine chicha destined for imperial consumption (by people and by deities) reminds us that the drink fulfilled both political and spiritual functions.[30] At both the Inca and the ayllu level, drinking chicha from the vessels produced solely for that purpose — the *queros* or *aquillas* — was the high point, the act that gave life to rituals. Each quero had a twin, and both needed to be used in Inca ritual in order to fulfill its meaning.[31] In colonial times chicha held on to its ritual significance for some of those who brewed and consumed it. Ritual offering of chicha by kurakas conveyed power and responsibility. When a Spanish inspector to the north coast forbid kurakas from providing chicha to the Indians in their ayllu, one kuraka exclaimed that his Indians would no longer work because it was through the chicha that they gained respect.[32] In the highlands, chicha toasts marked the beginning and end of journeys to ensure a safe return for those conducting ayllu labor or carrying goods to urban markets.[33] With the fall of the Inca state apparatus that regulated chicha, the corn brew lost its status as a drink that the ruling class revered. Instead, it became the subject of Spanish regulation that focused on suspect associations: drinking binges and idolatry. This section details the roles of Potosinos in production and consumption of chicha to show that as the meaning of the drink underwent change, so too did the identity and social status of chicha brewers and the motivations to brew chicha.

Generally, town council members and priests perceived chicha as a native Andean drink. And chicha did play a central role in ayllu celebrations that touched all the senses. Ocaña recalled that "at all hours of the night one hears the drums [*tamboriles*] of the rancherías; and as they dance around in circles they keep drinking, both the men and the women, until they finish the *botijas* of chicha."[34] But while thousands of native Andeans did brew, sell, and consume chicha, it appealed to a much broader segment of colonial society.

Because chicha was a readily available and cheap alternative to wine, the laboring city residents of Spanish and African descent crowded chicherías to consume it. In 1603 Potosinos enjoyed some 1.6 million bottles of the maize beer per year—"such an enormous quantity of chicha . . . that it seems an impossible thing to imagine," according to one mystified observer.[35] Some have questioned the accuracy of the 1603 figures, but Carlos Sempat Assadourian argues that the exact figures matter less than the overall picture of Potosí as consuming more chicha than wine.[36] Chicha sold in these quantities because the uses of chicha diversified in colonial life. Even in the early colonial period, residents in large urban areas like Potosí relied on ready-made food and drink.[37] Mitayos drank chicha and chewed coca while waiting for their assignments each Monday.[38] Urban residents, both men and women, gathered on a daily basis to enjoy chicha at local taverns.[39] In addition to many indigenous chicheras, Madalena, an African slave, brewed chicha and sold it in the plaza in 1623. A free mulata named Dominga operated a chichería in the 1650s, as did Salvador de los Ríos, a free mulato, in 1681. In 1690, the Spaniard Pedro Velásquez Rodero offered chicha to his thirsty pulpería customers.[40] To the dismay of bureaucrats and clergymen, these sites offered chicha to laboring Spaniards and mixed-race *castas*.[41]

In the Andes during the sixteenth and seventeenth centuries, a more diverse group of people sold and consumed chicha than do so today. The widespread consumption of chicha reflected the tradition of Potosí's large indigenous population and the changing palate of African and Spanish colonials. It also signaled the mechanisms put into play as a result of colonial economic pressures. Many Spanish tavern owners found it easy to secure supplies of chicha at low cost from indigenous brewers who were in debt. On the basis of this unequal partnership between vendors and brewers, chicha became a significant industry.

The profile of chicha producers in Potosí was less diverse than that of drinkers because it included few men. As was customary in preconquest times, women brewed and men drank. This gendered identity was not without exception, but it was imbued with strong pre-Columbian hues. As recounted by the chronicler Betanzos, chicha drinking played a ritual role when elite Incas visited each other. If women went out to visit, they carried with them a full urpu. If men went calling, however, the host provided the chicha.[42] In colonial highland cities, indigenous women also dominated the making of chicha, and they delivered it not as visitors but as vendors. Women, alone or in pairs, produced enough chicha to satisfy the thirsts of thousands of Potosinos. Men owned and rented chicherías, but, in resemblance to pulpería arrangements described earlier, men rarely participated in the day-to-day business of selling the chicha.[43] Just as women dominated street markets and daily sales from pulperías, they also staked out the task of making chicha and the business of selling it as their entrepreneurial ground.[44]

Tight controls on the distribution of flour led to the development of a putting-out system, where established vendors provided flour to chicha brewers (chicheras), who paid off their debt in liquid installments. Chicheras found it difficult to manage an outlay for large amounts of flour without access to cash or credit, especially with Spanish merchants. Chicheras with diverse trade interests counted on enough capital to make their own arrangements for buying flour wholesale. In the mid-seventeenth century, Juana Lorenzo Hernández stockpiled thirty *costales* of corn flour for chicha.[45] Other indigenous residents of Potosí had access to flour from their native villages, either from their own lands or from relatives', or through ties to nearby villages. Antón de Miranda and María Alcapuco stored 150 fanegas of corn in the village of Pocoma for use in their late sixteenth-century Potosí chichería.[46] Most indigenous women, however, did not have easy access to flour and a hierarchy emerged between the tavern operators (native elite and Spanish) and brewers (non-elite natives) in the chicha industry.

Women who relied on chicha for their livelihood worked surrounded by sacks of corn and any number of the special containers earmarked for producing chicha. They stored and transported large quantities of the drink in birques. The brew sat around taverns and homes in smaller two-handled jugs known as *cántaros*. Women served the brew in handleless jugs known as botijas. Indigenous women, the chicheras, not the Spanish tavern operators, prized such equipment. Doña Juana Cayala's large inventory of chicha containers included eight birques, seven cántaros, and fourteen botijas.[47] Impressed with the proportion of chicha vessels to other objects in the interior of indigenous homes, Jesuit priest Bernabé Cobo observed that "to make, store and drink chicha, they have more implements and containers than for their food."[48]

Chicha containers figured as important property in the wills of some indigenous women, but they were absent from the wills of Spanish tavern operators, who contracted with native indigenous women to obtain chicha. In their wills, these women did not subsume containers into a generic category of "other household items" but rather gave them their own clauses, with specific identification of their use for chicha and sometimes instructions for their destination after the owner's death.[49] These items, wooden and adobe containers of various sizes, were significant to brewers who owned few material goods. They were also important to successful traders like Juana Lorenzo Hernández, who counted brewing containers along with a house, numerous pieces of clothing, and 686 pesos in reales in her 1658 will.[50] The chicheras carefully enumerated the vats and jugs because they measured the value of the birques and cántaros in both cultural and economic terms.

The significance of the containers cannot be understood fully without mention of the role of the urpu in Inca times. The urpu was the most common ceramic vessel used for holding chicha and as such was frequently drawn into the ceremonial space of rituals. Yet female brewers valued the urpu not just because of its intimate link to chicha, but also because of its gendered significance. In an Inca male initiation ceremony, boys received a pair of drinking cups—the queros—while girls stood by with chicha-filled urpus to serve them.[51] The urpus were women's objects.

Though brewing chicha remained the work of indigenous women, numerous Spanish women entered into the once Andean domain of selling it. Spanish women made contracts or, in the language of the day, "sent out" to have chicha made.[52] No one ever identified these female vendors as *chicheras*, a term seemingly reserved for the native Andean producers. While not predominant as brewers, Spanish women played a major role as distributors of chicha at least by the early seventeenth century. Few Spanish women migrated to Potosí in the 1550s or 1560s because of the widespread opinion that European women should be spared the harsh climate, especially if pregnant. By the 1580s, however, Potosí's renown brought Spanish women to the city in growing numbers.[53] They established themselves as tavern operators, work at odds with social expectations in the colonial world, both in terms of the nature of their work and the product they sold (not wine or brandy but chicha).

In colonial Potosí, then, not all Spanish women lived up to standards. The Spanish women who sold chicha did not inhabit the same sector of Potosí society as elite *españolas* who donned the luxurious silks for sale in the merchandise stores around the downtown plaza. Spanish chicha vendors arrived in Potosí alone or with husbands who were unsuccessful in the silver mines. They labored to earn the sole income for their families or to supplement the income of other family members. Petty trade in food, alcohol, sewing, or doing laundry were the most typical opportunities for women to earn wages. The petty entrepreneurial initiatives of these women highlight important degrees of differentiation among the city's Spanish residents. In Potosí, at least, Spanish women performed jobs associated with women of indigenous or African descent. In addition, their identity within colonial Potosino society reminds us of the unfixed nature of racial labels in this late sixteenth- and seventeenth-century urban context: many individual chicha vendors were referred to alternately as *española* and *mestiza* or *española* and *mulata*.

Spanish women's entrance into the chicha business capitalized on the overwhelming demand in a town that had one of the greatest concentrations of chicha drinkers in the New World. As newcomers, Spanish women who had an eye for enterprise noticed the steady clamor for chicha. This trade could not have grown, however, without the new thirst for cash among indigenous women. Both rural and urban indigenous women entered into contracts with Spanish women and provided them with ready-made, authentic chicha. In this way, the native women earned cash needed for tribute or other payments as they were drawn increasingly into an economy based on the peso. Luis Miguel Glave has noted a similar pattern for 1660s Cuzco.[54] In Potosí, the widow Madalena Piqllana, a native of the village of Santiago de Guasi, made chicha for the Spaniard doña Petronila Camargo to repay a debt of seventy pesos.[55] Doña Camargo credited her five reales for each batch of chicha, one real of which went toward food for Piqllana and not to the seventy-peso debt.

Indigenous chicheras and Spanish vendors often went to the trouble of having these business transactions notarized. While indigenous women, particularly those with vested interests in petty trade, were no strangers to the colonial judicial system, it would appear that most of these dealings were notarized at the behest of the chicha vendors and not the chicheras. In many cases, indigenous women received cash prior to the signing or arrangement of a chicha contract. Thus, the chicheras were in a subordinate position to the Spanish women, who were ensured by the notarized contracts that the indigenous women—or, in some cases, their guarantors—would be responsible for repayment. If an indigenous woman had accepted a loan beforehand, her skill in brewing chicha was perhaps the most valuable thing other than cash that she had to offer a Spanish woman. Despite the potential for exploitation of the brewers, some indigenous women approached Spanish women asking to make such contracts as a way to rescue themselves from debt to a third party. In the mid-seventeenth century, María Cangua and Juana de Torres, a mother and daughter, took a loan from María de la Barrera and had no means to repay the debt. They "asked and begged" Graviela de Toro to pay de la Barrera the eighty-two pesos and four reales, and then repaid her by brewing chicha.[56]

Vendors also made arrangements with indigenous women to brew chicha through informal oral agreements. The evidence of these informal arrangements, stretching from 1615 to 1700, suggests that chicha business relationships were widespread.[57] Some vendors kept tally of the debts or agreements and listed them in their wills. Doña Luisa Pardo, a married Spanish woman and mother of a four-year-old boy and a newborn girl, received chicha from María, a Pacora woman, who owed Pardo a remaining forty pesos on a debt.[58] Pardo, who feared death after her daughter's difficult birth, listed the debt in a hastily drafted will. She allowed her husband, Luis de Padilla, the latitude to lower the forty-peso debt in recognition of the service María had provided.

The most common arrangement for chicha production was between an Indian chichera and a Spanish vendor, but some native Andean women controlled enough capital to pay others to produce their chicha. Like their Spanish counterparts, these tavern operators advanced money to brewers. Such was the case of María Lorensa Gonsaga, who paid a forty-five peso debt for María Uscana to secure her release from jail. In return, Uscana agreed to be at Gonsaga's beck and call to make *and* sell chicha for her.[59]

Gonsaga's ability to loan, in effect, forty-five pesos to Uscana and then retain her services in a chicha business reminds us that individual indigenous women could and did compete with Spanish women in the petty trade sector of the urban economy. Indigenous women who had the resources to hire brewers to serve them counted on support from elite family connections dating from before the colonial period, or in some instances from a close connection to a Spanish man. As with the important socioeconomic distinctions between Spanish chicha vendors and nonlaboring Spanish women, indigenous women in Potosí had a range of experiences that favored strong business resources in some, led others to seek credit, and even, as in the case of Uscana, landed some in jail because of debt.

Chicheras and chicha vendors did not negotiate the exact amount of chicha expected with each delivery, which suggests that standard quantities existed in the trade. In the chicha contracts, the payment of five reales per chicha delivery was a consistent price for the seventeenth century.[60] The precise number of servings in each jug is not designated, but the price of the jug's contents as a whole serves as an approximate guide to the amount of profit garnered by the chicha vendors who contracted with chicheras to brew the alcohol. In 1600 each botija of chicha sold for one peso. Each sack of corn, valued at five pesos in 1603, produced seventeen botijas of chicha (another source cites a yield of thirty-two botijas).[61] Assuming a brewer delivered at least seventeen botijas of chicha per trip, the vendor could clear a profit of eleven pesos and three reales. The profit margin may have differed depending on whether brewers started their process with corn grain or corn flour. The chicha contracts rarely specify if the brewer was to use corn grain or corn flour. Flour clearly grew in popularity by the seventeenth century. Tavern owner María de Guzmán, for example, supplied flour to her indigenous brewers Antonia and Francisca.[62]

In any number of instances, chicha appears as a widely accepted commodity for indigenous women to offer and a useful currency for Spanish women to accept because it turned a ready profit. In fact, Spanish or indigenous women who took deliveries of chicha as repayment for debts may not have been full-time vendors or operated full-time taverns. Instead, they may have worked as petty traders from time to time and hammered out the chicha agreements as the best way to collect money owed them by indigenous women. Casual commerce in chicha on the streets of Potosí or from the front doors or windows of homes could bring an infusion of reales into a household economy. The chicha entrepreneurs who realized the greatest profits, however, ran taverns or pulperías and continuously employed chicheras. In the late seventeenth century, doña Juana de Urquizo, a single woman and mother, had no fewer than five indigenous women supplying her with chicha for her business.[63]

Selling chicha could provide the means for subsistence, but it could also impugn the character of the vendor. When Costanca de Almendras went to court in the early seventeenth century to defend a pulpería she claimed as her property, her trade became evidence of her downtrodden situation. She presented herself as a Spaniard, although various acquaintances referred to her as a mulata, and others said she sometimes dressed as an indigenous woman. Her ambiguous ethnic identity cast a long shadow over her character in the eyes of some observers. To nurture such suspicions, the complainant, Bartolomé Manuel, produced witnesses who claimed that Almendras was so destitute that she had stooped to selling chicha.[64] Almendras was able to present witnesses in her defense who claimed that she lived in a pulpería and had one of her indigenous servants selling chicha for her, thus explaining the damaging misconception that she herself dressed in native clothing and sold chicha. Nonetheless, Manuel's tactics revealed the implicit cultural links between the chicha trade and a life of desperation; he won the case. Specifically, the ethnic and class associations of chicha production, sale, and consumption could have negative consequences in legal or regulatory clashes.

No matter what perceptions Spanish elites had of chicha vendors and chicheras, many women clearly gained an edge by participating in the urban economy through this activity. Doña María Pacheco Altamirano, a Spanish woman who contracted with chicheras and ran a small business at the Carata refinery, "commonly went about very lustrous in different dresses."[65] In fact, one local claimed that she was the only woman in the small town with Spanish-style dresses. Catalina de Goycos moved to Potosí in 1637 with her husband Diego Gutiérrez. Once in the mining city, Goycos, termed a "very hard worker" by one acquaintance, turned to petty trade to earn a living.[66] She contracted with indigenous brewers for chicha, which she sold. From time to time, she took on sewing projects to earn extra money. Though her husband worked for the mine owner Francisco de Yzaguire, it was the work of *both* husband and wife that allowed the couple to acquire a home, a slave named Sisilia, and a string of pearls. In this case, making and selling chicha led to the accumulation of valuables and was thus judged as the business of a hardworking woman whose finances were on the rise, in contrast to the destitute Almendras whose fortunes had dwindled.

The most successful chicha vendors trafficked in chicha along with other goods. Spanish women like Goycos took in sewing or sold wine or bread in addition to selling corn brew. The mestiza María de Guzmán profited from the ownership of both a pulpería and a chichería.[67] Indigenous women who worked as vendors, either making or contracting to have chicha made for them, offered it from their stores or huts in addition to running enterprises in other crucial indigenous items. Madalena Carbayache catered to the high demand for coca leaves in addition to selling chicha. Juana Lorenzo Hernández, who lived in the Tío section of Potosí, sold coca and ají (chili peppers) along with chicha.[68] Indigenous women branched out into products demanded by indigenous ranchería residents, while Spanish women varied their offerings to suit their clientele and urban neighbors.

In addition to giving women a means for subsistence, or even a means to prosper, selling chicha also offered them a critical measure of autonomy. Women could determine when and where they worked, combining petty trade with domestic tasks. Moreover, counter to town council descriptions, not all chicherías were dens of debauchery where customers at the bar hoisted drinks throughout the night and patrons in dark corners committed offenses against God. On some nights the widow Jasinta Sisa, an indigenous woman from the Jujuy, was asleep in her home by eleven o'clock, a moderate hour for a barkeep.[69] If a chicha vendor was in need of money, however, she might open her house at any hour when a knock on the door alerted her to late-night revelers casting about in search of alcohol. The trade was not without risk—male-on-male violence generally occurred at or near chicherías or pulperías and might put women in harm's way. Still, chicherías also could be "safe havens," since women were far less susceptible to violence inflicted by men in a public and social place surrounded by companions than in a private home.[70]

Chicherías dotted the city of Potosí, from the central plaza out to the ends of the rancherías. Generally, chicherías in the indigenous neighborhoods were housed in *buhíos*, thatched-roof adobe structures, better described as chicha huts, adjacent to a main house or in the patio or backyard. María Payco, an indigenous property owner, maintained three buhíos for selling chicha.[71] In contrast to buhíos, chicha taverns were street-front stores, often complete with a counter to serve customers, and connected to larger dwellings.[72] The street with the biggest concentration of chicherías in Potosí, located adjacent to the central Plaza del Gato, was christened Chicha Street. Other clusters of the taverns were found about town. When María de Segovia rented a "store to make and sell chicha" near the bridge by the convent of San Francisco, her neighbors on both sides ran identical establishments.[73] The large number of chicherías suggests that they were gathering sites that provided an intimate social atmo-sphere combining aspects of home and public life.

While Potosí chicherías had the warm allure of conviviality for many, others saw them as pockets of urban blight. In 1659 the mayor Francisco de Gamboa reported to the council that chicherías near the central plaza of Potosí annoyed and harmed neighbors.[74] The council agreed, claiming that the taverns were well-known for "the crimes committed in and around them by negros and mulatos as well as indias, mulatas, and others in the offense of God."[75] Elite Spaniards like Gamboa associated chicherías with illegal forms of economic exchange, illicit sexual behavior and violent crimes, including murder. In their view, chicha taverns were sites that gave limited autonomy to native Andeans and Africans, and thus acted as places where the fabric of colonial society came undone.

Clearly, the council would have been happy if all the chicherías in town had been shuttered, but councilmen ranked some as more offensive than others. By the middle of the seventeenth century, the council honed its scrutiny of chicherías to the thirty-five in the town center where indios, negros, mulatos, and other persons carried on, in the view of some residents, in a criminal manner, offending God and the neighborhood. The first extant council ruling that banned all chicherías was proposed at the behest of Diego Villa de Figueroa, who alleged that runaway slaves, both male and female, congregated in the many Potosí chicherías.[76] Although Villa's colleagues on the council seconded his idea, it had little permanent effect. Francisco de Gamboa ordered them closed anew in 1659.

These initiatives to close city-center chicherías reflected a shift in council emphasis. In 1565 officials bemoaned drunken Indians, but by the seventeenth century they most feared drinking and socializing of the mixed race urban plebe. Town council records indicate that as the seventeenth century wore on, the council's interest in corn flour supplies as a chicha concern had all but disappeared. Instead of attempting to halt the supply of corn flour to the city, which could entail lost revenue for both Spaniards and Indians involved in growing, milling, and distributing flour wholesale, the council members now tried to curtail demand by closing up consumption sites. All the extant council rulings related to chicha from 1635 through 1681 focused on the excessive numbers of chicherías in Potosí and initiated ordinances to close them down.[77] The changing emphasis in regulation acknowledged both the inability to prevent chicha production (highlighted best by the 1604 discussion of wheat-based chicha), the profitability of the chicha business for flour traders and chicha producers, and the shifting demographics of Potosí. These late seventeenth-

century Spanish rulers cast a blind eye toward the chicherías in the rancherías and instead focused on social interactions among the mixed-race
clientele, whose nighttime camaraderie threatened the comfort of urban
elites.

The varied ethnic identity of customers was emblematic of the colonial following that chicha enjoyed. In addition to indigenous brewing and
consumption, Spanish and African men and women quenched their thirst
with chicha, and Spanish and African women capitalized on its popularity
to enter petty enterprise. When Potosinos raised mugs of chicha together,
they enjoyed the fruits of an enterprise that women brewers and vendors built through transactions with landowners, millers, transporters,
and tavern owners. With the rise of chicha as an urban industry, Acosta's
observation that "maize serves the Indians not only as bread, but also as
wine" was due for revision.[78] By the seventeenth century, corn beer was
a "wine" for a multiethnic urban population, enjoying a customer base as
diverse as that of wheat bread.

"LIGHTWEIGHT BREAD WITH BAD AND MOTH-EATEN FLOUR"
PROMOTING GOOD BREAD

Wheat flour and bread appear frequently in town council minutes by
the 1590s, approximately three decades after Saldana's chicha report. In
contrast to chicha, the regulation of wheat flour and bread was marked
by debate not over excessive consumption but over scarcity of grain, poor
quality product, and pricing. Wheat flour and bread were cultural signi-
fiers to royal officials. The Potosí town council viewed it as both its prerogative and its duty to regulate the sale of bread in the Villa Imperial. The
council filled its agenda with mandates to control its weight and quality so
that each baker offered customers good quality loaves at a reasonable cost.
At given intervals, council members inspected each bakery, approved its
weights, and checked its bread prior to distribution and sale.[79] But if plentiful quantities of good quality bread bolstered Spanish culture for some,
for others the significance was more economic. The council's common
complaint over "lightweight bread with bad and moth-eaten flour" suggests that it fought a tough battle against grain producers, suppliers, and
bakers bent on profiteering.[80]

Council members controlled the price of bread by pegging it to the
shifting price of wheat flour. Thus, the eyes and ears of the council focused
on prices, with members asking about harvest conditions and the arrival
of shipments.[81] Prices of agricultural commodities were exceedingly high

in March 1592, when a *fanega* of wheat flour sold for twenty to twenty-one pesos and more despite the council's order to set the price of one fanega of wheat flour at fifteen pesos.[82] Such price-fixing helped bakers temporarily, but it was not successful at lowering prices to what the council considered a fair price. Bakers often responded by baking smaller loaves. In May of that same year, the council complained about the widespread sale of underweight bread, warning the perpetrators that one-real bread should weigh twelve ounces, no exceptions.[83] Prices fluctuated throughout the colonial period, often within a matter of months, so that one-real bread had been fixed at sixteen ounces in July 1593, a weight that, with a drop in flour prices, rose to twenty ounces in August 1593.[84] The fluctuations between 1592 and 1593 were not unusual for Potosí—the council returned to the issue of bread time and again throughout the coming century.

While the council rhetoric on bread was mild in comparison to its obsession with chicha drinking, the council's punishments for those who broke the bread rules were more stringent.[85] When 1607 brought plentiful harvests, flour prices dropped. The council noted this on January 27 and ordered bakers to make one-real loaves weighing twenty ounces and half-real loaves weighing ten ounces. If inspectors or constables found underweight bread, the council would fine bakers and vendors thirty pesos. At the first offense, they lost all their bread to the poor housed in the jail, hospital, and convents, and they spent ten days behind bars. On the second offense, the punishment doubled, and the council took away their licenses as bakers or pulperos.[86] In other years, the council showed less patience, threatening bakers and pulperos with a six-month suspension from their trade for the first offense and a two-year banishment from Potosí for the second. The council made clear that its mandates applied to all people, male and female, involved in the production and sale of bread. Ordinances consistently referred to "panaderos y panaderas" and "pulperos y pulperas." The specificity regarding gender is striking; no one took any chances by using the non–gender specific Spanish words *panadero* or *pulpero* to refer to women as well as men. This specificity may indicate the intention by the council to prosecute whoever disobeyed, both large- (mostly male) and small-scale (mostly female) operators. It also suggests that women played enough of a role to warn bakers of both sexes. The council offered no special treatment for female bakers or vendors; they were assessed fines and given jail time just like men.

If the council held bakers responsible for their actions, the bakers in turn made demands of the town council. Bakers generally asked the council to raise bread prices, while reminding the members of the costs of flour, wood, salt, and labor.[87] Bakers also asked the council to check the accuracy of pricing through *ensayes*, or tests where council representatives witnessed the baking of bread from start to finish, weighing both ingredients and final product. The bakers hoped the ensaye would lead to a price adjustment in their favor. The council, however, initiated tests with the goal of lowering prices. These checks required the cooperation of council members, flour distributors, and bakers. On 6 July 1594, Francisco Cortés and Cristóbal Bustamante, two bakers who requested a test, accompanied the council's "faithful executors" to the house of a flour vendor, identified only as Isabel, negra. Once in Isabel's house, they weighed a fanega of clean wheat flour that totaled 151 pounds and six ounces. They placed the flour in a clean sack and headed off to the house of the baker Joana Silvera. Silvera ordered her workers, indigenous men and women, to prepare the dough and knead it. After baking, the finished loaves weighed nine ounces.[88] In other instances, pressure from bakers may have initiated a price change without an ensaye.[89]

The bakers never called themselves a guild, but they acted as one when they appeared before the council as a group. In 1634, when they decided that high flour prices jeopardized their profits, the bakers sent Martín de Soles forward as their representative to the council. The Potosí town council did not record their individual names and instead called them the "panaderos," so it is impossible to determine who comprised the group. Both men and women likely approached the council, given that the panaderos who went before the La Plata town council in the early 1700s were seven men and three women, all Spanish.[90] These ad hoc bakery guilds contrasted with the female-dominated chicha industry, where no such unified groups stood before Spanish institutions to ask for consideration on the price or availability of corn flour. Soles pled his case at two council meetings on 22 October and 24 November, but the council ignored his arguments both times. He argued that although the council priced bread based on a nine-peso-per-fanega price of wheat, by November 1634 this cost had risen to eleven or twelve pesos per fanega. The 1634 group seemed to have found Soles an earnest, if unsuccessful, leader.[91]

Through their de facto guild, Potosí bakers gained a measure of power that bread vendors did not enjoy. The vendors, who did not represent themselves before the council, were perhaps most vulnerable to charges of violating council rules on bakery practices. When Gerónimo del Salto, *fiel executor* of the council, caught an indigenous woman selling underweight bread, he sent *her* off to jail, and not her supplier.[92] Was she the only one with underweight bread or was she singled out by Salto as an example?

According to the council, vendors and the bakers who supplied them were equally to blame for the sale of faulty bread. In this case, however, Salto used the arrest to put pressure on the Spanish bakery owner producing the bread. The female vendor confessed to Salto that her bread was from the bakery of licenciate Diego Pacheco, *presbítero*. Pacheco soon showed up to complain angrily to the council. He upset the members present when "he gave everyone a lot of grief saying disturbing words to the discredit and denial of justice."[93] When he demanded just treatment, the council warned him that a man in his position had no right to run a bakery on his property. Still, no one punished the Spaniard Pacheco, whereas the indigenous woman whom he contracted to sell his bread found herself facing arrest. Pacheco felt the sting of the accusation that he baked substandard bread and stormed the chambers of the town council demanding justice. In contrast, a Spanish official had arrested the bread vendor on the street, in front of customers and fellow marketeers, and no one deemed her protestations, if any, significant enough to be recorded.

The treatment of the indigenous vendor by Salto gives a vivid image of the social gap between vendors and bakers. And she was not alone. Council officers frequently used spot checks of indigenous women vendors as the initial step in their tracking of guilty bakers. In 1678, a report to the council charged that wheat flour had dropped in price and that bakers needed to give more weight per real. The council decided to attack the problem of the low-quality, low-weight bread by visiting "bendedoras," female vendors, in the plaza.[94] The indigenous women who sold bread in the plaza gave the names of their suppliers in the face of threats by Spanish officials. But the frequency of complaints about poor quality bread suggests that Spanish officials rarely used these confessions to fine errant bakers. As much as the town council wanted to control the cost and quality of bread, it needed the bakers to sustain production of wheat bread for reasons of both cultural significance and consumer satisfaction.

"IT HAS NOT BEEN DISCOVERED THAT THEY HAD ANY SORT OF WHEAT"
BRINGING BREAD TO THE ANDEAN MARKET

Few sixteenth-century arrivals to Peru from Spain shared José de Acosta's opinion that "maize is not inferior to wheat in its strength and power of sustenance."[95] Wheat was not native to the Americas and the absence of this European staple compounded Spaniards' sensation that they lived beyond the reach of civilization. As the author Garcilaso de la Vega reminisced, "in 1547 there was still no wheaten bread in Cuzco . . . for I remember that the bishop of the city, don Fray Juan Solano, a Dominican and native of Antequera, was received in my father's house . . . and my mother fed them on maize bread."[96] The implication in the memory of the young Garcilaso was that the maize had indeed been an inferior substitute for wheat, especially when breaking bread with the bishop. In the very early years of the colony, the Spanish imported wheat from Spain and the meager amounts that survived the sea journey rarely met the high demand. By the 1570s, Potosí could count on wheat shipments from the fertile valley regions of Peru like Cochabamba and Chuquisaca. Though Garcilaso could recall a time without wheat bread, Africans, mestizos, and indigenous peoples who lived in colonial towns and cities soon joined Spaniards in their consumption of wheat bread. At that same time, Africans and urban Indians also moved into the production and sale of bread, in both forced and voluntary labor.[97] Bread thus created an important colonial enterprise and transformed the Andean marketplace.

One important sign that wheat bread ceased to be an item consumed only by Spaniards was the hierarchy of breads that came into being over the course of the seventeenth century. People began to distinguish breads by their quality, reflecting a growing consumption of wheat bread, albeit of a lesser quality, by the indigenous population. In the 1590s, the Potosí council set weight standards for one-real and half-real pieces of bread. During the 1610s, they differentiated between the coarse flour used to make *pan baco* (yellowish brown bread) and the higher quality flour that bakers used for *pan blanco* (white bread). By 1650, the bread known as "three-fer" (three pieces sold for one real) dominated sales in the main plaza and in the fruit market.[98] This poor quality bread, made from coarse flour, was baked for poor Spaniards, Africans, and Indians. By the latter part of the seventeenth century, bakeries were producing three classes of breads, table bread, "three-fer," and *molletes*. The indigenous population and servants ate molletes, the cheapest and lowest quality of the three breads.[99]

Despite the growing consumption of bread by non-Spaniards, in times of shortage it was Spaniards who received priority. A grave wheat flour shortage in the early seventeenth century prompted the council to limit the sale of wheat bread in the rancherías. In 1602 the council showed its ethnic bias by ordering bakers not to sell wheat bread in the rancherías, and in 1610 it repeated the order in a more detailed fashion.[100] The council thus gave Spanish and mestizo customers in the center of town access to the limited supplies of bread.

The perceived political value of a steady supply of wheat bread translated into labor support for bakery owners from local and Crown leaders. Thus, colonial bakeries became bread "factories" or quasi-prisons, staffed with a free or cheap supply of non-Spanish workers. In Potosí bakers used hired or coerced indigenous workers and African slaves of both sexes to prepare flour and knead and shape dough. The bakers, who tended to the baking ovens and endured continuous smoke and heat from the fires, were generally male. Apart from the participation of women as owners and laborers and the reliance on indigenous labor, the descriptions from bakeries elsewhere in the Spanish Americas are similar.[101] Rampant abuses included providing inadequate food and clothing for workers, using outright physical violence, maintaining workers in shackles, and luring them into a form of debt peonage.

In one such arrangement, groups of Indians came into Potosí to work in bakeries to fulfill mita labor obligations imposed by the Spanish state, which paralleled the labor draft that brought men to the mines of the Cerro Rico.[102] On 16 August 1603, Viceroy Luis de Velasco ordered 140 Indians from the province of Lipes to be sent to Potosí bakeries. The higher court reinforced the legitimacy of the Lipes arrangement on 14 July 1655. The terms of the Lipes Indians' employment in the bakeries included daily payment and four months' leave to return home to plant fields and visit wives and children. Despite such contract stipulations, miserable labor conditions characterized the bakeries of the era. According to Peter Bakewell, the situation of the Lipes bakery laborers was one of the few examples of debt peonage in colonial Potosí. Even the objection of the Potosí corregidor, who suggested that bakers purchase African slaves to do the work, did not end the labor cycle. The Lipes Indians' corregidor continued to send people to the city's bakers. Once in the city, the bakers lent Lipes natives amounts they could never repay on the meager salary the bakers were obliged to pay them.[103] Some natives also found themselves looking for bakery work in exchange for cash. In June 1590, Domingo Guanare made a contract with don Juan Pérez Galarca to serve for one year as his panadero in exchange for food and a 120-peso salary—a sizeable sum in comparison to the Lipes workers.[104]

In addition to the indigenous labor supplied by Spanish officials, some bakers purchased African slaves to make their bread. Juan López Vallejo counted on the manpower of four African slaves for his bakery.[105] Slaves represented a substantial capital outlay that most bakers hoped to avoid. Each of López's slaves cost six hundred pesos. Given the high initial price of slave labor in comparison to the paltry wages paid to indigenous workers, bakers preferred to hire them over buying slaves. But mining, agricultural, and public work sectors proved a greater draw for indigenous labor. In the end, bakers arranged a compromise with colonial officials and Spanish slaveholders whereby the bakery owners imprisoned African slaves as laborers in bakeries when their owners wished to punish them.

The agreement served both slaveholders and bakers: the self-contained urban compounds proved generally secure; moreover, the atmosphere amid the hot ovens proved a terrifying prison. Ultimately, urban bakeries relied on African slaves for a large percentage of their labor force. Slaveholders, both male and female, commonly sent slaves they wished to punish to work in bakeries, labor for which the masters charged only a real or two per day; they were primarily interested in having bakery owners "rehabilitate" their slaves. As if grueling work in the hot and smoky atmosphere was not punishment enough, most slaves, whether male or female, were shackled while inside.[106]

Africans used both legal and illicit means to protest the use of bakeries as institutions of social control. In 1670 in La Plata, Francisco Díaz went to court to protest when his wife, the mulata María Atienzo, was sent to a bakery and placed in shackles.[107] In Potosí, two slaves reacted to their imprisonment in the bakery of don Juan de Balda by planning an escape. Joseph de Llanos, a creole slave of Captain don Santiago de Ortega, sat in Balda's bakery by order of his owner for having run away.[108] Joseph de Llanos shared the prison with Vicente, a slave owned by the Jesuits. On 14 April 1707, Vicente confided to Joseph that his wife, an indigenous woman named Juana, had brought him a file when she came to visit and that he was filing down his shackles in order to escape through the roof. While Vicente escaped, Joseph, who had less time with the file, had to surrender under the weight of his iron chains.

A network of deliverymen and vendors supplied the bread to urban consumers. Non-elite Spanish men called *repartidores* oversaw the distribution of freshly baked bread to indigenous or mulato men, known as *petaqueros*, who loaded large sacks and delivered bread to the male and female vendors at other sites in town, like pulperías or the town plaza. Many bakers used indigenous men to deliver their bread.[109] Juan de Soliz y Ulloa, a seventeenth-century baker in Potosí, used Sebastián Picón as his distributor.[110] Picón in turn hired indigenous and mulato deliverymen to work his bread route for him. On occasion Spanish men occupied themselves by delivering bread. The Potosí baker doña Isabel de la Bandera recruited her husband to deliver bread to her pulpero customers.[111] These workers delivered to individual vendors about town, many of whom were indigenous men and women who sold bread to pay off debts they had acquired as they were drawn into the cash economy. The indigenous couple Francisco and Francisca contracted with Martín de Tineo for Francisca to sell bread for two years to pay a 102-peso debt on six baskets of coca.[112] Other vendors set up sites in the plazas or street markets in Potosí.

Support for labor and a supply of needy vendors meant bakery owners reaped healthy profits. Consider the success of María de Vargas, a *peninsular* who ran a bakery in the early seventeenth century.[113] In 1619 this Spanish widow supplied bread to thirteen pulperías, the convent of Santo Domingo, and the royal mint—the Casa de la Moneda. The relationship of these thirteen pulperos to Vargas was long-standing. When they drew up their accounts in July 1619, the pulperos, the convent, and the mint owed Vargas for bread and rolls worth 1,944 patacones and 6,810 pesos.[114] These accounts were profitable for Vargas, who was able to secure 5,000 patacones' worth of flour on credit from Francisco Olmos. The money owed her by customers covered her debts and left a surplus of 3,269 pesos, not an extraordinary profit in silver-rich Potosí, but not an insubstantial sum either.[115] Vargas's experience points to women's ownership and success in bakery endeavors. Of the eighty-two bakeries identified in Potosí from 1570 to 1700, men owned fifty-four; women owned twenty-five; and couples, three. The bakeries run by women were not merely small-scale operations.

In fact, ethnicity may have been more important than gender in ownership of a large bakery. Very few non-Spaniards operated large bakeries, in sharp contrast to the number of non-Spaniards who ran pulperías or chicherías.[116] Non-Spanish bakers could not count on Spanish officials for labor support (by Indians or Africans). Equally critical was ability to raise substantial amounts of capital for bulk flour, money to which non-Spaniards did not often have access. The canchas in Potosí distributed flour in bulk to bakers. Distributor Felipe de Torres purchased flour from three native elites, the *principales* don Francisco Martínez Ayra, don Francisco Yana, and don Francisco Turumayo.[117] Once in Potosí, both Spanish and indigenous traders sold flour to bakers in wholesale quantities, often on credit. Doña Isabel de la Bandera managed to obtain 2200 pesos' worth of flour on credit from Juan de Soliz.[118] Bakery owners needed to cultivate numerous business relationships to obtain the supplies that kept their ovens running.

Bakers who operated small-scale operations had less chance of obtaining bulk flour, much like chicheras, and bought their flour from pulperos rather than wholesalers. Leonor Rodríguez, a free African described as a "negra morena," worked as a baker in nearby La Plata.[119] Unlike the Spaniard Vargas, Rodríguez supplied no more than a few pulperos at a time with bread, biscuits, pies, and pastries. The pulpero Miguel Jorge contracted with her for baked goods in 1592. In contrast to large bakers, Rodríguez took flour from Miguel Jorge in exchange for the finished products she later supplied to him. She charged him enough to profit over what she paid for the raw materials. Most of Rodríguez's earnings were tied up in money the pulpero owed her.

Leonor Rodríguez and the bakery owner doña María de Vargas stood at opposite ends of a spectrum, exemplifying differences between large- and small-scale bakeries. Vargas and other large owners received their raw ingredients from large distributors, who expected them to pay (eventually if not immediately) in pesos.[120] Vargas, a Spaniard, delegated hard labor tasks to indigenous and slave workers. Further, large bakeries like hers used distributors and deliverymen to sell bread throughout the city each day. Large bakeries had a tendency to produce the institutional forms of bread mandated by town councils, such as bread in one real and half real pieces. Judging by the variety of goods Rodríguez baked, including breads, pastries, pies and biscuits, she had both the freedom and the need to diversify. Rodríguez worked on a supply and demand basis with individual pulperos, soliciting goods as needed, paying a higher price than did large bakeries as a penalty for her small purchasing power.[121] Instead of dealing in coins, Rodríguez paid the pulperos with a finished product for them to sell in their stores. She was, moreover, the principal laborer in her operation, although she may have recruited a helper if demand ran high. Most of the time a petty baker like Rodríguez was the boss, financier, baker, and deliverywoman.

Rodríguez engaged in activities very similar to other women involved in petty production for the marketplace. Her status as a free African allowed her to choose her work and guaranteed she could keep her own wages. She enjoyed more autonomy than she would have as a domestic, or even as a worker in a large bakery. With this autonomy, however, came more responsibilities such as collecting from pulperos like Miguel Jorge. In her claim against Miguel Jorge, she explained that, since she was unable to read or write, she had to rely on the pulpero's word that a receipt showing a debt he owed her was true. Her trust had limits, however: she made sure there was a witness to her side of the story, her friend María Sánchez, a sixty-year old free morena, who witnessed the transactions with Miguel Jorge.[122] Rodríguez's lack of confidence in her immediate business colleagues contrasted with the solidarity of large-scale bakers like Vargas, who often petitioned the town council as a guild. Another critical difference between the two women was Vargas's status as an official baker. Recognition by the town council meant that Vargas paid taxes to the town each year. But it also guaranteed her labor support and eased her road to economic success. Working in a large-scale cottage industry, relying on inexpensive and slave labor, and distributing products widely throughout town, Vargas was able to garner enough earnings to dower her daughters handsomely.

The support of bakers like Vargas was no frivolous subsidy. Even after the cultivation of wheat on Andean soil became prevalent, bread maintained its special status as a dietary designator of Spanish civilization. This was especially clear in the minds of town council members, who assiduously promoted its production and sale through labor assistance to large bakeries, consistent price-fixing, and quality checks. By their reckoning, "well-baked and seasoned" bread should be made available to the general population for the lowest price possible. This was an obligation of the rulers—and by extension the king—to the subjects of the Crown. Wheat bread on the table not only tasted good, it was a symbolic reproduction of Spain in the colonies.

CONCLUSION

In Inca times the production of chicha was a service to the state performed by the women of the aclla, but by colonial times it was bakers who served the colonial state through the production of bread. The regulation of these two products, one a vice and the other a virtue, illuminated both elite and popular perceptions of colonial Potosí culture via food and drink. The rulings of the town council on bread and chicha not only legitimized the former while demonizing the latter, they also revealed official conceptualization of space in Potosí. As I argued in chapter 2, the very ordinances stipulating where vendors could operate revealed the council members' distinctive perceptions of ethnicity. The council tried to outlaw pulperías (viewed as Spanish establishments) in the indigenous rancherías; it tried to rid the Spanish town center of chicherías frequented by Indians and Africans. In the minds of sixteenth-century council members, Potosí consisted of two concentric circles, the innermost circle was the Spanish world, where wheat bread but not chicha was sold and consumed; the outermost circle was the Indian circle where one found chicha but not bread. By the seventeenth century, cultural and labor developments that drove the colonial brewing and baking industries had collapsed the simplicity of these imaginary circles into overlapping and ever-shifting rings of social and economic activity.

Trading patterns show that despite the rules, a non-indigenous laboring audience had emerged for chicha by the 1570s, and urban Africans and Indians began to consume bread by the early 1600s. That these products proved transcultural says much about the social transformation that had occurred. Yet herein we also find important tales about profit and coercion in the developing urban economy. Profit motives nourished people's changing habits and tastes. Profit-seeking grain and flour producers aimed production toward the Potosí market for chicha and bread. By the final decades of the 1500s, the need for pesos prompted native Andeans to sell bread, a product unknown to the Andes before the 1550s. In the 1600s, baking bread became a form of tribute to the Crown. In the case of chicha, its rapid growth as a colonial industry in the last decades of the 1600s had an impact on the economic situation of both indigenous women and Spanish women. The former began to produce chicha for the latter as laboring Spanish women sought income through taverns that specialized in chicha, not Iberian wine.

Despite changes in who consumed and sold these products, certain constants remained. Of the two trades, bakers had more social prestige and generally made greater profits—in the thousands of pesos in comparison to the hundreds of pesos for chicha vendors. The disparities in earnings are explained by regulation and production. Chicha was never encouraged by elite Spaniards, who tried to suppress it with ordinances against the importation of corn. In contrast, the town council consistently promoted bread with labor support and provisions to secure adequate wheat flour. Moreover, the organization of production and sales for chicha remained less hierarchical than for bread; no wholesale chicha producers emerged in the sixteenth and seventeenth centuries. These factors helped bakers reap far greater financial profits than chicha vendors and chichería operators.

Both gender and ethnicity factored into the economic opportunities afforded by the two types of enterprises. The trades involving food and alcohol provided a crucial outlet for women's energies and a measure of financial stability. For bakeries, ethnicity mattered more than gender in terms of the hierarchy of labor. Spanish women and men together formed a cohort of financially successful bakery owners; indigenous and African men and women endured low wages and miserable working conditions as the producers and vendors of bread. For chicha, however, gender mattered. Few men emerged as key players in the chicha industry. Spanish and indigenous women dominated as vendors and tavern owners who used chicha as a means to profit from petty enterprise. Ethnic identity emerged as a strong factor in the lower levels of the chicha industry, too, as indigenous women dominated the labor-intensive and poorly paid work of brewing. In both the bread and chicha industries, however, the profits of a diverse but small sector of owner/operators came from the exploitation of indigenous brewers and Indian and African bakery laborers.

The potential to earn higher profits through baking resulted from consistent Spanish town council support in the period studied here, and it reflected the cultural superiority of bread in the urban market. The economic and cultural gap between the two industries emerges in great relief in the example of doña Isabel de la Bandera. In 1609 doña Isabel and her husband, Lucas de Aguirre, became involved in a bitter court battle with a creditor over two thousand pesos. Though Aguirre did maintenance work on the reservoirs outside Potosí, it was de la Bandera who sustained the family through urban trade. "If the said doña Isabel de la Bandera were not such a hardworking woman," claimed friend and witness Andres Bravo, "and did not have, as she does, some businesses, they [de la Bandera and Aguirre] would die of hunger."[123] Only when de la Bandera failed in her business as a baker did she turn to small ventures like sewing and running a chichería to support her family.[124]

De la Bandera's case ties up the threads of this chapter by highlighting its three main themes: Potosí's unique development as a city affected demand for food and drink, necessitated strict regulation of that food and drink, and structured new kinds of labor and economic agreements that fueled both brewing and baking. Each theme reveals important shifts between the sixteenth and seventeenth centuries.

First, the growth and diversity of Potosí's population prompted changes in consumption patterns over time. Bread was not in demand by indigenous consumers in the mid-sixteenth century, but it fast became a priority item for Spanish elites and royal officials. The extreme geographical isolation of Potosí made the production of bread all the more symbolic for Spaniards. By the seventeenth century, royal officials authorized the use of Lipes natives to ensure bread production for a growing non-Spanish laboring population. Akin to the mining mita, such labor drafts brought indigenous men and women into Potosí's economy not merely as laborers but as consumers, too. As for chicha's popularity, we must acknowledge that Potosí's population was predominantly indigenous, owing in large part to the mita labor force. This accounts for growing chicha consumption as early as the 1560s and the subsequent changes

to its production (specifically the use of milled-ground corn) to suit an
urban lifestyle. But by the early seventeenth century, Potosí also had a
large Spanish population of some sixty thousand men and women, including creoles and mestizos. This population was much larger than could
be sustained by the mines or large-scale merchant activities. Thus, Potosí
was home to thousands of poor, laboring Spaniards. The mass market for
chicha became an attractive option for Spaniards like Isabel de la Bandera.
The Spanish engagement with the chicha trade is a distinctly colonial phenomenon and contrasts sharply with the lack of Spanish involvement in
the republican era, for example.[125]

Second, the history of Potosí's chicha and its bread reveals that a variety of efforts at social control permeated these local industries. Sixteenth-century attempts to regulate chicha production show Spanish officials eager to limit native drinking. By the seventeenth century, however,
the new generation of council members focused their ire on mixed-race
taverns in the city center. In the case of bread, the most systematic accounts of social control stem from the widespread confinement of African slaves in bakeries as punishment. In the seventeenth century, however,
the demand for bread had grown sufficiently to encourage the Crown to
force Lipes natives into abusive tribute assignments in Potosí bakeries. In
effect, bakeries became agents of social control in the colonial order when
bread became part of the diet of all Potosinos, in a manifestation of the
new colonial culture.

In this new culture where Africans and native Andeans could be indentured or imprisoned in bakeries, it is ironic that one also finds both native
Andeans and Africans drinking chicha—and, to the disappointment of the
town council, keeping company at the tavern. Council efforts, like those
of Villa de Figueroa or Francisco de Gamboa, to close chicha taverns reflected great unease about the congregation of Indians with mulatos and
negros. It is also ironic that ordinances which aimed to close these gathering spots were neutralized by Spanish policies themselves. For instance,
bringing the Lipes natives into an urban setting, especially inside bakeries, no doubt put them in close contact with Africans. In the main, ordinances restricting interethnic socializing were undone by labor schemes
and profit motives in the colonial economy.

Third and finally, the development of the chicha and bread industries
suggests that both producers and consumers relied heavily on credit negotiations (the subject of the following chapter). Men and women sought
credit in Potosí as bakers, brewers, and consumers. Owners of bakeries
and chicherías sought credit for bulk flour purchases. Consumers' need for

pesos to pay debt or tribute pulled in laborers to produce bread or chicha. Credit was interwoven into labor structures for the baking and brewing industries, too. Indigenous men and women went to work for Spaniards, often after signing contracts that created a form of debt peonage. Such labor contracts revolved around economic concepts new to some Potosinos. Both the chicha contracts and the Lipes Indians' lengthy tenure in bakeries point to the strong pull of the peso in the urban colonial economy.

Profits from chicha and bread worked in tandem with the changing social makeup of the population to influence the colonial identity of these two products. Both would come to have strong economic value in the colonial market. By the first decades of the 1600s, this economic power gave opportunities to women, like Spanish bakers and indigenous chichería owners, that they would not have enjoyed otherwise. What remained constant, however, was that the rise of these two colonial industries neither made chicha and bread equal in the eyes of the town council nor limited the exploitation of indigenous and African Potosinos who produced the goods.

THE WORLD OF CREDIT
IN THE CITY OF SILVER

4

"An india *colla* named Urcomo who lives in Santo Domingo parish," declared Catalina Palla in her 1572 will, "owes me three pesos and two reales for coca and bread that I sold her."[1] The native Cuzqueña went on to list debts of between two and a half to twelve pesos to indias named Aguallo, Tocta, and Quicana and an indio named Diego, all for bread and coca that she had sold them. Pulpero Juan Bautista Jinobel, who, like Palla, was an urban trader in Potosí during the late 1560s and early 1570s, also claimed similar petty debts. Numerous Spanish men, including García Hernández, owed him a few pesos each for items such as wine and cloth. Likewise Bautista noted that "an indio named Martín, whom my servant Teresa knows, owes me five pesos for things he took from my store."[2] Palla and Jinobel traded in different spaces in Potosí—spaces linked to distinct products and clientele. Palla recalled geographical identity (colla region) and place of residence (Santo Domingo) to locate her debtors. Jinobel drew on the assistance of his servant Teresa. What the two had in common, however, is telling of how urban trade functioned in Potosí. Both traders offered their goods to customers on credit.

From at least as early as the 1570s, Potosí's residents counted on credit for everyday purchases. Credit was a crucial response to the specifically urban pressures of the emerging market economy. As the examples of Palla and Bautista suggest, market vendors, storekeepers, and tavern owners played an important part in the dissemination of these practices. The potential sites where people could seek credit were numerous. Market vendors sold goods in the Gato de las Indias and tens of other small plazas about town. The combined total of official and unofficial stores operating in Potosí well exceeded one hundred. Furthermore, taverns could easily have equaled the total of pulperías since at least thirty-five operated in the city center alone. The credit transactions at these sites of trade involved men *and* women of indigenous, Spanish, and African backgrounds. The sum of their activities constituted a busy banking network that existed alongside the more traditional lending of religious institutions.

The non-elite, and often non-Spanish, element in this web of credit raised a red flag for political and church leaders. In chapters 2 and 3, we saw the town council's priorities: controlling the location of stores and the products for sale. Officials made attempts to ban pulperías from indigenous neighborhoods, and they set rules for the appropriate locations, hours, and prices to sell chicha and bread. The method of payment for these products in stores or markets was also a matter of concern to the council. Credit transactions at the petty level sparked fears about the exchange of mercury, silver ore, or piñas. In addition to the items associated with the silver trade, the town council feared that storeowners accepted stolen goods. The fretting escalated when indigenous purchases of alcohol entered the picture. Complaints about Indians' spending on alcohol were ubiquitous in the writings of Spanish observers.[3] An even greater worry for them was that Indians were purchasing alcohol with stolen goods, since this indicated that the Spaniards had failed to educate, in moral and religious terms, their indigenous charges. Official grumbling and regulation notwithstanding, credit practices could not be confined to the councilmen's narrow vision. Loans and pawns for petty sums spread widely throughout the food and drink sector of urban economy.

Uncovering credit practices within the realm of urban trade adds a new dimension to common notions about colonial credit by placing stores, and not churches or convents, at the center of inquiry. The pawn and loan transactions in small commercial establishments formed a set of secular credit institutions that paralleled the religious ones of the colonial world. People sought credit throughout the Spanish Empire, but the ability to obtain it depended on one's position in colonial society. The role of ecclesiastical institutions, the Holy Office of the Inquisition, and regular, as well as male and female monastic, orders as providers of credit is well known.[4] In some regions of the empire the *caja de censos de indios*, an emergency fund built up by contributions from indigenous communities, became an unintended credit source for elites when the Spanish administrators of these funds extended them to people outside the indigenous community. In cities, merchant communities also established credit institutions that did not pass through ecclesiastical channels. Furthermore, individuals who could afford the services of a notary might enter into a loan agreement by signing a *carta de obligación*, or promissory note. The common thread in these credit options is the elite status of those making the deals. Non-elites, indigenous peoples, and women had restricted access to these sources of credit. It is not altogether surprising, then, that the sectors of society excluded from the traditional credit mechanisms would create their own.[5] If participants in the middling to higher levels of the urban economy used creditors (*fiadores*) to gain access to pesos, the use of *prendas* (pawned items) was more common among, though not restricted to, the lower classes. In Potosí these alternative channels of obtaining credit formed through links to local petty trade.

Both men and women provided credit in the city's places of trade. Given women's dominance in marketing food and alcohol, they were much more likely to emerge as prominent creditors in this sector of the economy than they were at any other site in the city.[6] And, while men gave credit in their role as pulperos or bread distributors, women gave credit from pulperías, chicherías, and street market operations that sold bread, coca, fruit, and clothing.[7] Women's role in this web of credit transactions is remarkable. They acted not only as credit seekers, as is the case in many historical contexts, but as moneylenders and pawnbrokers.[8]

This chapter analyzes the dynamic role of small credit exchanges in the sector of urban trade. It begins with a discussion of the tremendous economic changes that the metropolis presented for most migrants. When forced to pay pesos and inflated prices for services, people were creative about how to find sources of money. That creativity drove changes in urban trading practices. Urban transactions in the sixteenth century contained elements of barter or exchange of one type of goods for another. Coca was commonly used to pay for all types of purchases, even appearing in notarized real estate transactions.[9] Over time, however, new exchanges took root as stores and markets, the places that people frequented for petty economic transactions, became neighborhood banks.

After a discussion of this transformation in urban trade transactions, the chapter continues with an analysis of the economic and social function of first loan practices and then pawn. Securing small loans or credit in the amount of a few pesos became commonplace at least by the late sixteenth century and probably earlier, though records are not extant. To gain credit, people needed to have either a good reputation or a material object of sufficient worth to guarantee payment. Thus, pawn soon emerged as an alternative to loans. Examples of pawn transactions are scarce, though present, for the late sixteenth century, and they grow in frequency over the course of the seventeenth century. Throughout the period, pawn is a practice favored more by women than men. As was the case with barter, goods played an important role in pawn transactions. In theory, pawn was not an exchange of one type of goods for another, but rather a *temporary* placement of one's goods with a storeowner to obtain cash, credit, or merchandise. In reality, however, people risked alienation of culturally valuable objects in order to obtain the monetary value of those objects in the urban market. Because these credit transactions took place in a particular social and economic context, the chapter concludes with analysis of overall patterns of loan and pawn with regard to gender and ethnicity. The distinctions in practice between men and women, or among Indians, Spaniards, and others reveal that credit practices had both economic and social implications. Gender and ethnic identity influenced the way Potosinos engaged with new urban credit practices.

"SO MUCH WAS THE SILVER"
THE RISE OF CREDIT PRACTICES

A certain irony surrounded the reliance on credit in sixteenth- and seventeenth-century Potosí because the amount of silver taken from its mines was, in the minds of some observers, almost unimaginable. "So much was the silver that circulated in that town," marveled one commentator, "that to say so seemed almost a fable, and to think it, almost a dream."[10] The economy of the town was saturated with raw silver and coinage in comparison to other colonial cities: the silver mines injected unrefined silver into the market, the royal mint stamped out coins, and dozens of silversmiths produced innumerable pieces of valuable wrought silver. Tons of silver sat around the city in various forms, yet mechanisms of distribution favored local elites and royal coffers. Thus, the economic practices of the majority non-elite population relied on credit, not pieces of silver, to fund life's expenses. Potosinos counted on vendors for more than a piece of bread or a mug of chicha; their proximity to the world of trade made vendors ready bankers.

The urban poor used tactics like pawn and loans to pay for their daily needs because life in Potosí presented new economic demands. Those who were new to the city found that items like clothes, which rural residents likely produced or obtained through barter, had to be purchased. Average food expenses for a mitayo in 1596 totaled twenty-six pesos per month, higher than the ten-peso salary set by royal ordinances.[11] Those urban residents who sought to rent stores or dwellings found rent was payable in pesos, often on a monthly basis. Throughout Potosí, merchants named prices in Spanish coin—pesos or reales, the derivative of pesos. By setting food and alcohol prices in reales, even street vendors responded to and augmented the Spanish push toward a cash economy in the colonial period.[12] A slave selling chicha for her master in the town plaza was expected to bring home a three-peso-per-day profit. Workers increasingly entered labor agreements as a means to pay debts accrued in Potosí. Pedro Cabautista contracted out his slave Elvira to work for Gerónimo Leto for ten pesos a month so that Elvira could pay back her creditors.[13] In a similar fashion, many chicha brewers found Spanish vendors to pay off their debts in exchange for labor. These changes signified that money or access to credit was vital not only to purchase substantial items like property or bulk merchandise, but for the very provisions of daily life.

Masters usually paid workers cash, clothing, and food, a combination that reflected the early stage in the transition to a cash-based economy. When the indigenous couple Isabel Guayro and Pedro Azque made a contract (or *asiento*) with Joan de Guzmán for Guayro to sell food in Guzmán's store, it stipulated that Guayro was to receive sixteen pesos per year, two dresses, twelve sacks of corn, and one silver *tomyn* per week for the purchase of meat.[14] Most Potosinos earned some money through labor and employment, but not enough to pay costs for tribute, cash substitutes for male relatives' turn at the mita, property upkeep, or daily responsibilities. Moreover, payment took place, at the most, once a month and more commonly only at the end of a year of service. In the meantime, cash flow problems meant people made purchases on credit even for basic staples like bread.[15]

People looking for loans in the city were not only experiencing the rise of a cash economy, they were also negotiating how to form economic relationships in a new urban setting. In many cases, they had to leave an item behind to ensure that moneylenders would reap some return. Thus pawnbroking increased with the population of cities like Potosí, which drew indigenous people out of agricultural communities where an oral promise to repay a debt was as good as a silver platter. Isabel del Benino, an indigenous female property owner in Potosí, moved home to the valley of Anti to sell farm animals and products in later life. In this rural setting, she knew her customers well. Her 1601 will, for example, listed sixteen debtors, none of whom had been required to leave goods with her as security.[16] In the relatively anonymous and transitory world of a new city like Potosí, however, people used pawning to expand their economic networks.

In some ways these new urban practices drew on previous traditions. Pawn was akin to barter because it drew value from material culture, and with the work of silversmiths, pawn transactions involving silver plates and silver candlesticks were innumerable in Potosí. Loans to indigenous men and women often took the form of advances on years of labor. Cultural factors also influenced Potosí's economic strategies. Loans of pesos or goods on credit were often based on kin ties. Pawn prices and conditions proved better for close friends or family. This new peso economy did not diminish patron-client ties; masters and servants exploited such connections to gain money or goods. Moreover, the very nature of the items that people chose to pawn, the goods that they felt compelled to buy on credit, and the places where they went to carry out those transactions reflected their identity in the community.

Colonial pawn had an unsavory reputation. Elite leaders in colonial Potosí claimed that thieves used pawn to turn the spoils of a crime into cash or store goods. After one robbery, for instance, thieves were found in a chicha tavern drinking on credit they received from the woman chicha vendor for items they had stolen that very night.[17] Slave owners, in particular, feared that their household servants would steal from them and run off to pawnshops to reap a profit. Official instructions to new petty grocers (*pulperos*) forbade them to accept pawned goods, especially from African or indigenous customers.[18] If robbery victims or town council elites equated pawn with trafficking in stolen goods, however, the majority of Potosinos felt otherwise.

Customers frequently pawned personal belongings to obtain goods on credit from storeowners. The mestiza María de Orduña owed a peso to the pulpera Francisca Martín, for which she left a single silver spoon in hock. Diego Quispe left two brown cloaks of Quito cloth as a deposit for nine pesos' worth of goods from Paredes's pulpería in the ranchería. Grocer Elvira Sánchez advanced two bottles of wine and a four-peso pot of butter to Salomé Méndez on a pledge of two small silver plates, weighing one pound apiece.[19] Whether they carried silver or clothing to the corner store, and whether they pawned it in search of pesos or *pan*, pawn was a way in which Potosinos who did not have enough cash could make ends meet—at least for the time being.

In some instances people used this alternative world of credit to help with daily purchases, but in other cases urban traders themselves sought significant sums—loans of up to several hundred pesos or start-up loans for businesses.[20] When the indigenous woman Juana Colquema established herself in the world of trade, she had a generous creditor. Her initial grant for the startup of her wax store came from another woman with the same name but a slightly different spelling, Joana Colquema, who offered her five hundred pesos to "work with to seek her livelihood." Juana Colquema repaid the debt, but the lender asked her to make five wax statues of the baby Jesus as a payment of interest.[21] She continued to seek creditors during a career in which she operated a chichería, a wax business, and a coca store simultaneously. Juan Loyola acted as a guarantor for an installment of 165 pesos' worth of coca and Captain Sebastián de Cassa did the same for wax valued at 387 pesos. Some creditors who provided start-up funds required material goods as a deposit for the extension of pesos. Doña Lorenca de Salas y Rivera borrowed 112 pesos from Cristóbal Gutiérrez de Bivar when she first established her corner pulpería on Gerónimo del Salto Street.[22] Those 112 pesos helped to provide furnishings for the store and provisions to set up an inventory. In recognition of her promise to pay Gutiérrez, Salas y Rivera gave him various silver items, including two large candlesticks, a salt cellar, two plates, and two large drinking vessels.

Other storeowners devised more complex schemes involving material goods to solve their credit problems. Costanca de Almendras confided to Joana Sánchez, a native of Cochabamba, that she needed money to help pay for the houses and pulpería she had recently purchased.[23] She asked Sánchez to buy some goods—a European-style woman's shirt for sixty pesos, a *lliclla* (shawl) lined with taffeta for thirty pesos, a *nanaca* (head covering) for twenty pesos, and a large vat of preserves for seventy pesos. Almendras then resold the clothes and preserves to others at a profit. Though Almendras and Sánchez dealt in clothing and preserves, not chickens and barley, their scheme had parallels to the price-hiking regatones frequently bemoaned by the town council. Such methods as this ploy by Almendras to raise extra cash were not illegal per se, but the town council liked to think that decisions about who could overcharge customers and in what circumstances were its prerogative.

More generally, street vendors and tavern keepers also needed credit to buy stock. María Benítez purchased bottles of wine on credit for her store at the corner of the Church of San Pedro.[24] Chichería proprietors also looked for outside credit.[25] Obtaining stock for stores on credit was a fundamental concern for owners and managers of pulperías. Some storeowners solicited goods to sell on consignment, which for them required no immediate outlay of cash. Pulpera María de Guzmán sold honey in her store on consignment for Francisco Rodríguez, who lived on the southeastern frontier of Peru. Other pulperos took basic items like bread on credit. Twelve grocers bought bread on credit from bakery owner María Vargas. Their debts ranged from a low of 200 pesos owed by Beatriz Sudino to a high of 960 pesos owed by Francisco Pacheco.[26] Given the large sums outstanding, however, Vargas probably acted as a guarantor or backer to some of the pulperías in addition to advancing them bread. When Diego Chambilla sold goods to Potosí merchants in the 1620s, he accepted cash and pawn items or gave credit.[27] Although credit appears to have been the favorite, Chambilla's example suggests that Potosí traders used a range of payment options as they stocked their stores and market stalls.

Coca vendors relied heavily on creditors to obtain their inventory.[28] Isabel Cotaqui, married to a church sacristan, did not have the capital she needed to operate a coca business.[29] Cotaqui turned to doña Isabel Pacheco and became a distributor for her. Pacheco provided as many as twenty-six baskets of coca to Cotaqui. She would hand over the coca, however, only after obtaining numerous items to guarantee payment. In all, Cotaqui offered over thirty pieces of indigenous clothing, six silver pieces, various household items, and thirty pesos in reales to guarantee future payment in full of 360 pesos to Pacheco.[30] In similar fashion, the aforementioned doña Sevastiana Cusi Paucar extended one hundred pesos' worth of coca leaves for the *coquera* Petrona.[31] In contrast to the Cotaqui-Pacheco arrangement, Cusi Paucar did not demand goods as collateral. Cusi Paucar might have recognized kin or social ties linking her to Petrona that the Spaniard Pacheco did not share with Cotaqui. The broader similarity in the two examples is equally important here: in both instances indigenous women who did not have the pesos to buy coca stock for their stores turned to women higher in the urban hierarchy of trade. Though vendors and storeowners often functioned as bank-like institutions for their neighborhood, providing modest amounts of credit, they occupied a middling position in the larger urban economy that forced them to seek credit to establish and maintain their businesses.

In this new world order, everyone needed cash—for food, for clothes, for rent. The quest for currency forced residents into wage labor in bakeries, refineries, or the households of the elite. The wages of labor, however, did not meet Potosinos' need for specie, especially since many employers insisted on paying their workers largely in goods. Cash-starved in a city of silver, Potosinos were forced to put the city's network of pulperías, chicherías, and street vendors to double use. With proprietors who doubled as moneylenders and pawnbrokers, these establishments supplied the city's residents with the cash and credit essential for survival in an urban economy as well as bread for their tables. For the majority of Potosinos, their social networks and household goods could be mined for currency like the surrounding mountains for silver ore. Potosinos mined these resources on a regular basis, beseeching the neighborhood pulpera for cash, demanding that vendors advance them loaves of bread, or putting their nicest outfits in hock to pay the rent. These complex transactions, which made use of several layers of exchange, allowed the economy of this booming metropolis to function.

"FOR THE LOVE OF GOD FORGIVE ME"

MAKING LOANS AND COLLECTING DEBT

In July of 1700, the indigenous widow María Mullo, a Potosí store-owner, drew up her will with the knowledge that she could not pay all her outstanding debts. Among them she listed twenty-five pesos owed to her former master (*amo*), don Juan de Velasco (deceased), and his wife doña Lorensa de Quiroga. "For the love of God," she wrote, directing her plea to the wife, "forgive me [this debt] as my *amo* don Juan de Velasco already forgave me in life."[32] Like Mullo, many Potosinos included in their wills brief clauses that attempted to square even the smallest of debts. The mestiza Juana de Medina remembered a four-peso debt she owed to Francisca, a fruit vendor.[33] A person's word was bond on debts and loans in a community where most lenders did not keep scrupulous written notes, and all clients had to depend on local reputation to guarantee repayment.

When two people agreed on loans for large sums of money, they often went before a notary to record the terms of payment and repayment. Scribes noted the precise type of currency because coins were difficult to obtain; a loan made in peso coins was expected to be repaid in peso coins and not in reales. But in Potosí the majority of the loans were not agreed to in the presence of a scribe or a Crown official. Despite the unofficial nature of these loans, most people aimed to meet the terms of any agreement, whether written or oral.

Social networks, critical for obtaining and collecting on loans, also had to be cited when begging forgiveness of debts, as María Mullo's will reveals. While it is not known if doña Quiroga erased Mullo's debt, some testators did exonerate debtors in their wills. Spaniard Mariana de Oriola erased the many months of debt that her cousin Pasqual de Armona had incurred while renting (and never paying for) a room from her. Her generosity did not extend indefinitely, however. Oriola added that Armona would be forgiven the rent provided that he did not continue to reside in the dwelling after her passing.[34]

Wills from the late sixteenth and seventeenth centuries reveal much about moneylending practices during this period.[35] Loans were transacted often, in many neighborhoods of Potosí, and their collective presence in the history of the town shows the extent to which people needed pesos for daily urban life. Men and women lent out sums of hard-earned pesos to neighbors and friends in need. In a gesture of support, Juana de Mansilla loaned six hundred pesos to her daughter doña Isabel de Tamayo.[36] In some exceptional instances, loans took the form of objects to be pawned. Doña Juana de Gamboa, for instance, loaned a 2.5-pound silver salt cellar to doña Ignacia Rodríguez for Rodríguez to pawn.[37] Vendors or pulperos might list numerous loan transactions as well, like Juana Colquema, who listed a combination of twenty-two debts she owed or was owed. Many petty loans in Potosí were an extension of credit by storeowners. Doña Damiana Bohórquez bought food on credit from the shop of Matheo, a pulpero in the Tambo de Mencia, as well as from the store of his competitor across the street.[38]

If we consider lenders according to gender exclusively, women appear to have made more petty loans than men (see table 7 in the appendix). Women were lenders in 303 cases; men in 172; and couples in 24. Men borrowed money in 274 cases; women in 203; and couples in 23. Given the high incidence of women lenders, it comes as no surprise that both men and women approached women as lenders more often than men. Women chose female lenders for 125 loans and male lenders for 71. Men borrowed from women 196 times for money or goods, and went to other men only 89 times. In the case of Potosí, men were more than twice as likely to approach women as men for petty loans. This predominance of women could be explained by their extensive role in places of petty trade, where they functioned by offering small peso amounts of credit to customers. In addition, however, they may have had more trouble collecting than did men, and thus they listed the small debts more often in their wills.

Despite laws that privileged men in financial transactions, women used each other for banking purposes like loans and savings. When doña Juana Sisa wanted to buy property in Potosí in 1633, she made an agreement with Juana Payco to purchase the home for her. Sisa trusted Payco with three hundred pesos but Payco never had time to complete a purchase, since she died six months after their agreement. Sisa made a claim on Payco's estate to recover the money.[39] Women also used each other to safeguard large sums of money. Isabel Poco, for instance, turned to María Poco (perhaps a relative) to guard the sum of 108 pesos corrientes.[40] Luisa de Villalobos, a free black, entrusted a sum of one hundred pesos to the morena María Fula in Lima before Villalobos moved to Potosí. Villalobos kept funds for the slave Catalina, who entrusted her with four pesos of eight and two pesos corrientes. And Villalobos loaned Jorge Cocana thirty-four pesos, money she handed over in front of Francisco Martín and demanded in front of María de Herrera and another slave. Her use of witnesses for the transactions suggests a need to back up her claims about money—a move that a male lender might not have to make.[41]

The record of these debts, from a century when the majority of the population was economically active, but not literate, prompts very practical questions about how people recorded economic transactions and followed them to their completion. The manner of recording and remembering the amounts owed and to whom they were payable varied widely, but for small sums most creditors and debtors relied on their memories instead of on written accounts. The records of Sebastián Picón, the bread deliveryman in the previous chapter, help to reconstruct the categories that traders used to remember customers.[42] When Picón came around with fresh bread, no one pulled out coins to pay him; they instead relied on credit. By his accounting, customers owed him a total of 644 pesos. Picón delivered to a cross-section of Potosí society, men and women, Spanish and non-Spanish, and to individuals and stores. Most of his deliveries were small, probably made several times throughout the week. Clients did not pay him with each delivery, nor did they allow large debts to accumulate over months. Street vendors bought bread from distributors like Picón before selling the goods in their traditional plaza spots. Stores like pulperías that dealt in modest amounts of bread bought from him rather than journey to an outdoor market or the bakery itself. His practice of providing the bread on credit to numerous customers highlights the crucial role of credit for even the most modest of purchases.

In an attempt to dig out from under a mountain of debt, Picón relinquished papers to a Spanish court that mapped out his delivery route. On his path, he stopped at the home of a military captain, a count, a fireworks maker, a tailor, a silversmith, a barber, a blacksmith, and an African domestic slave. He visited at least seven stores that sold his bread; deliveries to what he listed as "corners" may have been additional stores since corners were very common locations for pulperías in colonial towns. In addition to businesses, twenty-one individual men and fourteen women bought his bread. Significantly, he listed clients by location, and very few by name.

More than forty clients owed him money for bread.[43] Three clients each owed two reales, the lowest debt: a certain Potes, the mother of the Herrera family, and the small store in front of the false door of the Merced church. In 1694, two reales bought approximately 48 ounces of good quality table bread or 120 ounces of low quality rolls (molletes).[44] The Count of Belarios topped Picón's client list with his twenty-peso debt for three weeks' worth of bread. The count's debt was unusually high.

Overall, thirty-two of the debts fell under five pesos and eleven above the five-peso range.

Given his haphazard style of identifying his bread buyers, how did Picón remember which customers owed what amounts? The distributor
was on a first-name basis with a Madalena who ran the small store below the house of Bachiller Andújar. And, when knocking on the door at the *cancha de las tejas* for a three-peso debt, he greeted doña Josepha Zerro by her full name. For the most part, however, his identification of clients often appeared careless, like his record of "an old lady on the corner of the slaughterhouse" and "the mulata Bainasa next to the Nuns," who each owed him one peso and two reales.[45] Likewise, the *cancha de bolas* owed six pesos, but from whom he collected them we do not know. He mentioned "the pulpería of Jerusalem" and "the small store in front of the false door of the Merced church," but not their owners. Picón must have made numerous deliveries of bread to the woman at "the broken door behind San Sebastián," who owed him eight pesos. But, to Picón, she was nameless—"the mestiza who sold bread in the Plazuela Chacón." Despite the glaring absence of a name to identify each debt, a standard practice for literate post-Enlightenment accountants, Picon's record-keeping shows that he used physical cues to prod his memory and guide him to his debtors. His notes recall that in colonial Potosí, he did not need a name to identify a person—location, trade, physical appearance, and dress by themselves created a conspicuous identity.

Picón did not state the race of most clients, although he did identify two mulato clients, one negro, and one mestiza. Many of his clients' names appear to be Spanish, though these names did not indicate race since many native Andeans and Africans assumed or were "given" Spanish names. Further, his use of the titles *don* and *doña* with certain names indicated elevated social status. What may be more telling is that Picón chose to use racial terms for several clients, but never used *español* or *española* in his record-keeping. The absence of a racial indication for the rest of his customers suggests that culturally speaking they were like him—criollos.

As a middleman in a business where most of his clients and fellow deliverymen were likely illiterate, Picón was not unusual in his vague manner of identification. In fact, the more specific Picón's references were, the less he may have known the client. Judging by Petrona Beltrán's record of a 350-peso debt to a flour vendor in Potosí, of whom she could only remember his small build and light hair, even bakery owners did not always keep specific records.[46] Storeowner María de Guzmán could not remember the name of one man who supplied her with honey; nor did she remember what type or amount of grain she had sold to Juan de Paredes y Herrera. To help jog her memory, however, Guzmán did have a "libro de quenta," and all indications from her will suggest that she made notes in it to record store business.[47]

Picón's and Guzmán's use of written language to record customers' debts set them apart from the majority of participants in the food and alcohol trades in colonial Potosí. It bears mention that for native Andeans the *quipu* (or *khipu*) may have factored into the bookkeeping without books that permeated markets and stores of the Andes. The production of the quipu, a device which used pieces of colored wool woven into strands and knots to record data such as population figures and crop production, meant that native Andeans were familiar with keeping records without using written words.[48] Making and using the quipu appear to have been limited to a small sector of the population. The majority of people could not decode it, though sixteenth-century kurakas may have used the quipu to keep track of shipments to the Potosí market.[49]

Most people relied on social ties to locate debtors and hold them accountable. Lifelong friends and neighbors knew the particulars of credit exchanges. Leonor Sasytoma claimed that her sister María knew the pulpero to whom she owed money; María would identify him to make the payment. Other traders who had the means to hire servants often relied on them to remember the names of customers and debtors. María Poco, an indigenous vendor who enjoyed elevated socioeconomic status, relied on her servant, Leonor, to collect her debts. When she dictated her will, she ordered that Leonor retrieve money for seven baskets of coca delivered to the Conde Indians, ten pesos from Luis Muñoz, and six pesos from an individual known only to Poco and Leonor. In turn, Poco granted the proceeds from these three collection trips to Leonor "on account of the service she has provided."[50] Leonor clearly fostered social networks that eased the process of collecting money, the value of which Poco likely recognized above and beyond the task itself. The Spaniard Juana de Urquiza emphasized social pressures to force payment when she hired one indigenous man, don Pasqual Fernández Colque, to collect a one hundred-peso debt from another, Juan Ramos.[51] When storeowners hired servants and when testators chose their executors, they took into account their ability to force payment on loans or pawns.

If collecting on debts required particular strategies in urban Potosí, so did paying them. Some borrowed from relatives, taking on a new debt—perhaps in a closer social net—to pay an old one. As a response to economic pressures in Potosí, the practice of auction (*remate*) of goods in the aftermath of someone's passing became a quite common way to pay off debts. When a woman named Dorotea lay dying in the Royal Hospital in Potosí, she called on María de Guzmán, a woman she trusted for both emotional and economic assistance. Guzmán received Dorotea's belongings—a wool bedspread, a few pounds of worked silver, and other items—and auctioned them off for two hundred pesos to pay debtors. The remainder of the profits was to benefit Dorotea's grandchildren, Miguel Fernández and Thomasa.[52] Executors sold all remains, even everyday goods, in a process that functioned much like a modern estate sale with items going to the highest bidder. Instead of passing on symbolic clothing, jewelry, or other goods, people in debt hoped for strangers to buy the goods as a means to earn pesos.

People needed pesos for daily urban life, and when they lacked the actual pieces of silver, they sought them through credit transactions. Loan transactions occurred often and in many neighborhoods throughout Potosí. The variety of loan transactions shows that both large- and small-scale economic transactions, from the purchase of twenty baskets of coca to the sale of pieces of bread, hinged on credit. Most of these petty loans were not notarized. People lent to familiar and unfamiliar customers. They used cues like place of residence (physical location in the city), ethnic identity, and gender to remember and collect, or they called on relatives and servants to assist them. While some examples emphasize the difficulty in collecting on debts, most testators made attempts to pay even the small peso debts they owed to pulperos or market vendors. People repaid debts as best they could because extensive debt tore away at the social fibers of an individual's credit network. Loans continued to be common as Potosí grew toward its peak population of 160,000 people; but with this demographic expansion, creditors increasingly sought to guarantee the reputation of their customers through a valuable material object.

"I HAVE NOT WANTED TO SELL THEM BECAUSE THEY WERE MY MOTHER'S"
PAWN AND THE INTERPLAY OF MATERIAL CULTURE AND COLONIAL ECONOMY

In Potosí many credit advances were distinct from loans because people left material goods to cover debts until they could repay them. Ana de Cabrera, a mestiza, made up her will while awaiting the birth of a child. She had pawned to a storeowner named Almendras a new *acsu* (dress) that she had never worn along with two large silver *topos* (dress pins)

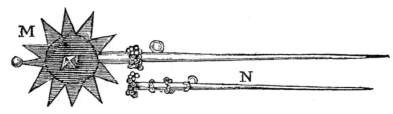

Figure 5. Illustration of topos from The Gentleman's Magazine and Historical Chronicle (1752). By permission of the Houghton Library, Harvard University.

adorned with bells and chains (figure 5). Cabrera ordered her executors to pay the twenty pesos she owed on the pawned items so as to collect them from the shop next to San Agustín and return them to her estate. She especially wanted to have the dress pins in the possession of her family. Though she had been offered as much as fourteen pesos for them in the past, Cabrera remarked, "I have not wanted to sell them because they were my mother's."[53] Embedded in the details of Cabrera's pawning experience is the shifting role of material culture in the urban economy. Her act of hocking cherished dress pins reveals the intense pressures on Potosí residents to acquire cash in the urban economy. Moreover, it shows how material objects, indigenous as well as Spanish, acquired market value. Such pawn transactions wove together economic practice and material goods with the fibers of individual credit networks.

The vast majority of non-elites used pawn as a practical economic strategy to pay for their basic needs. But it operated at all levels of society, with elites pawning goods only occasionally and under the most private of circumstances, and non-elites pawning often and in public places like stores and taverns. Even dowries to Spanish women sometimes listed pawned goods as assets.[54]

The practice of pawn in colonial Potosí looked different than it does today. No pawnshops lined the streets of the town. Pulperías and chicherías functioned as part-store, part-pawnshop because the owners or managers had access to pesos, and, unlike street vendors, they had space to store the goods left in hock.[55] Francisca Nieto, a pulpera and chicha vendor who lived in the pulpería adjacent to the parish of San Cristóbal, took a lliclla on pawn for five pesos.[56] The pulpería of Juan Martínez Flores and his wife Angela de Mendoza, a well-situated store on a corner of the plaza in La Plata, held numerous pawn items on its shelves. In their 1680 inventory, the couple listed 9.5 pounds' worth of silver, including six unmatched plates. They had also given credit on clothing, new and used, a handkerchief, and a sword and dagger set.[57] For the majority of Potosinos, credit could be found in any number of household items, from the platters that sat on the table to the religious paintings that lined the walls, to precious jewelry and the clothes on someone's back.

The inability to recover pawned goods was a sign of severe financial trouble, especially among working Spaniards. The married couple doña Isabel de la Bandera and Lucas de Aguirre was in financial ruin, in the eyes of one acquaintance, when they "barely had enough [money] to get some pawned goods out of pawn."[58] People who pawned objects expected to recover them. Few viewed a trip to the pawnbroker as a final parting with a dress or a silver pitcher; rather, they saw it as a deposit of their goods in safe hands until they could reclaim them.

A pawn might be retrieved soon after its deposit. Francisco de Aguirre and a friend made a trip to María de Guzmán's store to pawn a shot-gun (*escopeta*) and a fancy doublet (*coleto*) of Spanish suede trimmed with gilded lace and green ribbon. Guzmán offered the two men one hundred pesos for both items. Apparently, Aguirre missed the shotgun more than he anticipated. He soon returned with thirty pesos to recover the weapon, though he did leave his doublet behind. On the other hand, a pawned item might begin to collect dust on the storeowner's shelves. Doña Mariana Pérez borrowed one hundred pesos on a worn bedspread, a small silver pot, and a pair of earrings with blue stones and did not return in twenty years to reclaim the items. While this is an extreme example, it is notable that Guzmán listed it in her will and ordered under no uncertain terms that the one hundred pesos be collected and the pawned goods returned to Pérez.[59] Vendors did not expect to be left holding others' possessions.

Storeowners who acted as moneylenders surely preferred to make a profit from a pawn transaction. A differential between the amount of credit extended and the reclaim value of an item or an out-and-out inter-est charge would seem to be the most obvious avenue for storeowners to make money on these exchanges. If such a practice were commonplace, it is well hidden in the record—much as historians of elite credit mecha-nisms have spoken of interest charges being hidden in the censos.[60] At the lower level of the credit world, haggling over the pick-up or return of pawned goods is a good indicator that interest charges were common-place. In one example, doña Juana González bought a new bedspread of high-quality *cumbi* cloth in 1674 for 120 pesos. Shortly thereafter, she went to the nearby city of La Plata, where she pawned it to Felipe de Arcienaga for the amount of forty pesos. In 1676, González believed that she had paid off this debt to Arcienaga after loaning him the labor of an indige-nous bread baker named Pablo. When Arcienaga handed her a bedcover

TABLE 2: *Popular Pawn Items Mentioned in Notarial Records, 1570–1700*

Category	Percentage of Total
Silver (N=65)	34
Clothing (N=56)	29
Jewelry (N=26)	13
Religious (N=19)	10
Household (N=18)	9
Other (N=9)	5
Total (N=193)	100

Source: AHP–CNM.EN.

that she barely recognized, González accused him of subjecting her pawn item to considerable wear and tear.[61] Arcienaga responded to her claim with the counter-assertion that the bedspread was in this condition when he first received it. Moreover, González still owed him forty pesos. In González's view, the 120-peso value of the bedspread diminished greatly by Arcienaga's careless possession, and she stood to lose more money on the deal than the initial forty pesos she had been granted as its pawn value. González's complaint revealed an unwritten rule that persons who accepted pawned goods implicitly agreed to protect and preserve them. Arcienaga, on the other hand, felt entitled to profit or interest for the extension of credit.

The overwhelming majority of Potosinos in search of credit carried their silver and clothing to pawnbrokers (see table 2). Those increasingly desperate put their jewelry in hock, holding on to their religious and household pieces until they had no other options. Potosinos first pawned silver and clothing because they brought value from the pawnbroker, yet were common enough that many households could spare a few items and still take care of basic needs. As one might expect, the sizeable mining operation and numerous silversmiths who plied their craft nearby made silver goods plentiful in Potosí, perhaps more than in other urban areas of Spanish America. No household would founder without silver plates or candlesticks, which brought prestige even in the silver-rich city. Don Alonso de Lisana gave up the use of a large silver pitcher when he pawned it to doña María de Sala, but the two hundred pesos he received in return no doubt assuaged any sense of loss until he could recover the item.[62]

Clothing was also expendable, though more vital than silver items. In addition to the clothing that they regularly wore, Potosinos often inherited clothes from friends and family, so it was not uncommon for people to own extra clothing. Given the hours of labor involved in the production of cloth and garments, individual pieces might bring a high price. People in search of pesos literally might pawn the shirt off their backs; they could also hock their most valuable cloak or cast off a number of used pieces of clothing that they rarely wore. In 1572, Martín Copi pawned two acsus and one lliclla (the pieces of an indigenous woman's outfit) and two *camysetas* (the Spanish name for the *unku*, a pre-Columbian version of the poncho) to Leonor Sasytoma. All of this indigenous clothing brought ten pesos. Doña Catalina de Arraya had two pieces of clothing, a yellow *basquiña* (a skirt worn by wealthy Spanish women) trimmed with silver and a green velvet *faldellina* (pleated Spanish skirt), which she pawned to Juan Esteban de Billamonte for 120 pesos.[63]

Less common items left in pawn include jewelry, religious pieces, and household items. Few people had jewelry on hand to pawn, since only the most elite of Potosí owned gold and precious stones. Martín del Desaca pawned a nine-strand pearl necklace to María de Vargas for one thousand pesos. Other pieces of jewelry brought more modest returns, like the two pairs of gold and pearl earrings that doña Inés de Bargas Machuca pawned to Juan de Chaveasca for thirty pesos, or the diminutive pearl necklace for which Petrona del Castillo offered the mestiza Mariana de Oriola a mere fourteen pesos.[64] Religious items were more common than jewelry since they adorned the walls or altars of most homes in Potosí. Doña Alfonsa Díaz pawned an altarpiece (*retablo*) of the Virgin to Andrés Cintero for twenty-six pesos. Indigenous women also owned religious art and relics. Doña Pasquala Sumbi pawned an engraving of the Resurrection of Christ with an ebony frame to doña Ana María de Monrroz for one hundred pesos.[65] Household items used as pawns ranged from pieces of furniture to practical tools. An indigenous fruit seller took her two wooden stools to the mestiza doña María Rencifo and walked away with eight pesos, while doña Juana Romero gained forty-eight pesos from an old desk that she pawned to fellow Spaniard doña Ana de Estrada.[66]

Items that men and women chose to pawn offer clues about their social status and their economic strategies. A noteworthy gender distinction exists between what items women and men took to the pawnbroker, as women favored silver and religious items more so than men. Forty-two percent of women used silver goods (forty-seven pawn transactions), in comparison to 36 percent of men (eighteen); while 14 percent of women pawned religious items (sixteen pawn transactions), compared to only 6 percent of men (three pawn transactions). Women's wills confirmed the tendency of women to collect wealth in clothing and silver apart from their dowries. Even married women had economic power over clothing and silver if these goods had been part of their dowry.[67] Women could pawn more easily those items they controlled independently.

The amount of cash or credit a pawnbroker would give in exchange for an item depended on its condition and market value, as well as the relationship between the broker and the client. Spanish men and women offered pawn values into the hundreds of pesos. Indigenous women offered pawn values from 4 pesos to a high of 105 pesos, while *mestiza* women offered less—between 8 and 25. Indigenous men, who rarely acted as pawnbrokers, set the value no higher than fifteen pesos. Given the incredible variety of goods that people presented to Potosí pawnbrokers, from a bolt of green cloth to a silver engraving of the Cerro Rico, it is difficult to determine the relative value of given items over time. The pawn sample reveals, for example, that one set of sheets brought twenty-five pesos in 1640 and a different set brought only six pesos in 1670. Were the 1640 sheets made of high-quality, embroidered cloth? Did the 1670 set have holes from years of use? Did one customer make a better argument for the value of her sheets than the other? Or did the pawnbrokers, a mestiza woman in 1640 and a Spanish woman in 1670, offer the amounts based on the desperation of the client? Doña Damiana Bohórquez pawned a two-sided mirror to doña Gabriela de Rojas for the small sum of ten reales. A señor Solórzano, however, was able to pawn a nondescript mirror for twenty pesos' worth of services from mestiza washerwoman Lucía de Baños.[68] María Josepha de Herrera obtained 215 pesos from pulpera María Guzmán, and in pawn she left a few pieces of worked silver valued at only 100 pesos.[69] In all likelihood, the value assigned to any item by a pawnbroker depended as much on the relationship between the customer and the broker as it did on any intrinsic value.

SOCIAL IDENTITY AND PATTERNS OF LOAN AND PAWN

Social networks provided important connections to promote the extension of credit. How did clients choose lenders and vice versa? Gaspar Chayna approached Ana Chuqui Cani when he sought to make a deal, and she advanced him twenty pesos on two pairs of silver *tembladeras* (cups).[70] Their exchange was not merely a business transaction, it was an exchange underwritten by two important social factors. First, Chayna was a migrant to Potosí from Paucar Colla on the shores of Lake Titicaca, the same region where Chuqui Cani had been born. A second critical point beyond Chayna's birthplace was that he was a kuraka (chieftain). This position of

esteem might have obligated Chuqui Cani to make the deal; to her benefit, however, his influential position as a kuraka signified that he was a
good risk in terms of repayment. By the time of their exchange in the late
seventeenth century, overcrowding in many Potosí neighborhoods meant
that migrants to Potosí were no longer guaranteed easy settlement with
others from their home community. Though Chuqui Cani had been born
in Paucar Colla she did not reside in Potosí's ranchería of Santa Bárbara,
home to mitayos from Paucar Colla. Rather she lived in the ranchería of
San Lorenzo, a parish contiguous with the Spanish center of town. These
changed residence patterns did not limit the use of kin ties to find work,
housing, and, significantly, sources of credit. It was no coincidence that
Gaspar Chayna called on Chuqui Cani with two pairs of tembladeras.
Nonetheless, her location near the central market plaza brought her into
contact with people from different places. Chuqui Cani gave credit and
loans to a kuraka of the Cachas, who tended to live in San Pedro parish;
a second in command of the Indians from Chaqui, found in San Pablo
parish; and an *yndio fiscal* from the parish of Copacabana. All three of these
men lived on the opposite side of the Ribera at some distance from San
Lorenzo, a sure sign of the busy webs of exchange that criss-crossed the
city daily. But, wherever they lived, all three held positions of esteem like
Gaspar Chayna.[71] Chuqui Cani liked to deal with clients of status.

Much as in the case of Gaspar Chayna, one can see close ties in Spanish credit transactions. Even though Spaniards enjoyed elevated social
and legal status in the colonial world, many laboring Spaniards in Potosí engaged heavily in pawn and loan to satisfy economic needs.[72] In one
particularly convoluted exchange, doña Juana de Figueroa approached a
doña Melchora to pawn a silver candlestick. Doña Melchora offered her
four pesos with the candlestick as deposit, yet some time later she pawned
it to Juana's sister, doña María de Baldivieso.[73] These examples hint at
the complex social cues, like blood relationships, kin networks, neighborhood reputations, and master-servant obligations, that provided a context
for all economic negotiations.

Gender and ethnicity also proved important in these transactions. Gender defined work roles as well as social and economic practice during the
early colonial era. Though societies in early modern Europe and preconquest America had distinct gender norms, each nonetheless used gender
as a basis for differentiation, and this continued in colonial Potosí. Ethnic
identity proved a revealing factor for colonial Potosí because indigenous
and European backgrounds influenced the way people handled economic
transactions as well as their socioeconomic status in the colonial world.

Generally speaking men and women of various backgrounds commonly interacted through credit transactions (see the ethnic and gender breakdown in tables 7 and 8 in the appendix). On closer analysis, however, three significant trends emerge. First, although everyone sought credit, people found the most opportunities for credit with those of like ethnic background. Second, Spanish men acted as lenders in more credit transactions than Spanish women, while indigenous women played the role of lender in significantly more transactions than indigenous men. Third, women favored pawn as a means to seek credit, while men tended to use loan transactions to gain credit. The discussion below and tables 3 and 4 detail these trends.

In the first trend, taking into account the ethnic identity of credit seekers and credit holders, the number of Spanish-Spanish and indigenous-indigenous transactions is higher than the total of Spanish-indigenous transactions. This may be explained not solely on the basis of racial distinctions but as a practical effort by people to foster ties with stores and vendors in their immediate vicinity, in their parishes or neighborhoods. People used these connections first when seeking credit. These predominant patterns notwithstanding, the numerous cross-ethnic exchanges make it clear that people did create social networks across ethnic, neighborhood, or class lines for certain economic exchanges. These leaps outside of the financial community of their closest kin and friends could be desirable and possible because of their jobs or because of their business aspirations.

Considering the entire sample of loan transactions, the second pattern that emerges is a remarkable gendered distinction between indigenous and Spanish practitioners. Since men enjoyed a generally higher economic status than women in colonial Latin American society, it would be reasonable to assume that men would be the most common lenders and women would be the most in need of credit. And, indeed, Spanish men were the most common lenders to Spanish men and women, yet indigenous women emerged as the most common lenders for both indigenous men and women (see table 4). In the case of Spanish women, they approached Spanish men for loans more than any other gender or ethnicity of moneylender—thirty-nine transactions compared to twenty-nine with other Spanish women, three with indigenous women, and two with indigenous men (see table 4). Spanish men chose other Spanish men to lend them cash on sixty-two occasions and turned to Spanish women in fifty-one instances. While males were the most common lenders for the Spanish community, this same pattern did not emerge in the indige-

TABLE 3: *Number of Credit Transactions, by Ethnicity and Gender,*

	Spanish		Indigenous	
1570–1700	Men	Women	Men	Women
Loans				
Made	151	119	39	149
Sought	144	74	111	97
Pawns				
Brokered	64	49	3	21
Sought	33	70	15	19

Source: AHP–CNM.EN, 1570–1700, extant volumes for every fifth year.

nous community. Instead, indigenous women looking for loans over-whelmingly chose other indigenous women over other potential lenders —in fifty-three transactions compared to twenty-two loans from Spanish women, eleven loans from Spanish men, and only four loans from indigenous men. In contrast, indigenous men chose their counterparts as lenders in only eighteen cases, but they went to indigenous woman to ask for loans in sixty-five cases. As brokers of pawn and moneylenders, indigenous women trailed Spanish men only slightly in terms of number of lending transactions in the urban economy.

The lending activities of indigenous men are strikingly minimal. In urban areas, indigenous women, like Ana Chuqui Cani above, stood as pillars of the credit arena for the men and women of their communities. Indigenous men who sought pawns overwhelmingly chose indigenous women as their brokers.[74] This information could be read to support the argument that indigenous women benefited from urban society at the expense or to the detriment of indigenous men.[75] However, the main reason that indigenous women in Potosí made more small-scale loans and pawns than indigenous men was because they dominated marketeering and petty trade and thereby controlled the urban resources and spaces necessary to function as pawnbrokers and moneylenders. Spanish men, on the other hand, made loans from their position as pulperos. Thus, while looking at the role of stores and markets in providing small-scale credit to urban residents, it makes sense that indigenous men (by and large not urban storeowners or marketeers) are relatively invisible. Women manned, so to speak, an important portion of trade sites and thus engaged more heavily in the extension of credit.

Additional reasons exist as to why indigenous men do not appear in great numbers in records of urban pawn and loan. Indigenous men

TABLE 4: *Number of Borrowers and Lenders, by Gender and Ethnicity, 1570–1700*

	Lenders			
	Men		Women	
Borrowers	Spanish	Indigenous	Spanish	Indigenous
Men				
Spanish	62	3	51	17
Indigenous	6	18	11	65
Women				
Spanish	39	2	29	3
Indigenous	11	4	22	53

Source: AHP–CNM.EN, 1570–1700, extant volumes for every fifth year.

worked primarily in the mines or long-distance trade (*trajín*).[76] In both cases, they were important participants in the economy; as mineworkers they had silver nuggets to trade and as *trajinantes* they arrived at the city laden with trade goods. In neither instance, however, were they called upon for petty loans. And in many cases they were working collectively, perhaps even negotiating their labor responsibilities and payment through a kuraka who ensured their contributions to ayllu tribute. Men's activities are apparent not so much in wills but in work contracts (for urban work and rural to urban transport), large-scale debt obligations, and lawsuits about mining or other labor. When their wills do surface in the record, they reflect accumulation not in urban enterprises but in rural wealth comprised of animals and land.[77] In her study of urban women's socioeconomic status, Ann Zulawski argued that the distinct roles for indigenous men and women in urban areas could represent household or kin economic strategies.[78] Certainly connections between male long-distance traders and female urban marketeers may have operated among members of the same ayllu.

Females of the numerically smaller ethnic groups like mestizos or Africans may have had similar investments in the urban economy in a way that their male counterparts did not. The sample size precludes definitive pronouncements about patterns of loan and pawn, but no male Africans or mestizos appear in the sample. For African participants in this world of credit, the sample includes three female African pawn clients, who took their items to Spaniards (two males and one female). African women, free or slave, called on Spanish bosses or masters close to their living and working spaces for loans rather than turning to indigenous residents of the city.

The paucity of Africans in credit transactions speaks to the underground character of many of the exchanges. One compelling reason for Africans to keep pawn transactions out of the written records was that they were suspected of stealing from Spanish employers. Individual wills suggest that Africans were involved in cash and credit practices similar to those of Spaniards, mestizos, and native Andeans.[79]

For mestizos, the extent to which the category of *español* was used by and for men and women of mixed indigenous and Spanish descent obscures the picture of their activity. However, the individual examples suggest that some mestiza women lived among Spanish neighbors, while others, called "mestiza en habitos de india," lived in indigenous neighborhoods, spoke predominantly Quechua, and dressed in "Indian habit," wearing native shawls and dresses. Thus, individual mestiza storeowners fostered networks with Spanish clients if they operated near the town center and indigenous clients if they lived in the rancherías. Mestiza clients preferred Spanish brokers (in nine of ten transactions). Some mestiza brokers like María Guzmán, however, divided their business between indigenous and Spanish customers. Thus, they brokered economic transactions in both city center and ranchería, negating a rigid ethnic divide.

The third major trend that emerges in these transactions is that women were especially likely to use pawn to stretch credit networks. Overall, more loans appear in the sample, but when people chose to engage in pawn, more of them were women. When the activities of indigenous women and Spanish women are combined, women pawned items for cash or credit approximately twice as often as men did (102 transactions by females compared to 48 by males). Moreover, women appeared slightly more active than men as pawnbrokers (83 transactions compared to 67).[80] Thus, if we consider all pawn transactions on the basis of gender, women played a more critical role than did men both as brokers and as clients. Several factors could have influenced the tendency of women to seek money through pawn—the exchange of material goods—and to accept such items as collateral for credit. Female brokers may have felt more comfortable making loans when they received a pawn item in exchange because it guaranteed at least some return without having to rely on colonial bureaucratic channels, which could favor males. Also, Spanish women were the most likely group to use pawning as a way to access money. Their reliance on material objects to gain cash or credit can be explained through their wealth in material items. In most marriages, women controlled clothing, silver, and jewelry because they brought these items into the marriage through their dowries. Thus, when women needed pesos, they transformed their material wealth into a form of money that they could use in the urban economy. Female clients may have had greater need to engage in pawn on a frequent basis than did men, who enjoyed a relatively superior economic status in colonial society. Further, society's expectation that women were responsible for purchasing and providing food for men signified that women needed to make arrangements for buying food, on credit if need be, more often than did men.

Women of all backgrounds showed ample reason to engage in pawn to gain pesos. Yet indigenous women appeared to act as pawn brokers with more frequency than Spanish or mestiza women. Indigenous women counted on each other for credit for daily purchases and for larger sums for urban enterprise.[81] Spanish women, however, relied heavily on Spanish men to broker pawn transactions. They turned to each other next, crossing racial lines in increasingly smaller numbers. In contrast, indigenous women crossed racial lines before gender; they turned most often to each other for pawns and then to Spanish women. How can we explain this ethnic-based gender distinction? That Spanish women turned to Spanish men for loans (both with and without the guarantee of pawn items) suggests that they sought assistance from male relatives and acquaintances who, given their superior economic status in colonial society, were willing to provide credit. When indigenous women chose each other and then Spanish women, they were making use of trade networks a step or two lower than those inhabited by Spanish men—shabbier stores, perhaps, and smaller inventories. The generally elevated economic status of Spanish women, though, is evident in the practice of indigenous women asking Spanish women for credit on pawns more often than the reverse (see table 4). Here we also see that all women crossed neighborhood and kin boundaries to create economic networks that stretched up and down the social hierarchy. In fact, in urban credit exchanges clients, as well as the cultural identity of the items they pawned, crossed borders.

CONCLUSION

Though many customers entered the stores of the mestiza María de Guzmán without a peso in their pockets, Guzmán gave them food, drink, and, sometimes, cash.[82] The assortment of goods on Guzmán's shelves told the story of what she received in return. Juan de Ybarra, a young carpenter, traded in his tools for five bottles of wine valued at thirty-seven and one-half pesos. An indigenous woman named Bárbara, who was a vendor in the plaza, pawned two trunks filled with indigenous clothing in exchange for one hundred pesos. Juan de Quiñones walked into her store with a clavichord and left with fifty-two pesos. Serving equally as banker and grocer, Guzmán extended cash loans and gave goods from the store on pawn items. The exchanges from Guzmán's late seventeenth-century shop reveal that during the century of Potosí's waning silver production, the city's world of petty credit became more complex.

Buying staples on credit was common as early as the 1570s. Vendors also provided small peso loans in this era. These practices coexisted with barter exchanges of, say, coca leaves for potatoes, textiles, or even a house. Pawning an item for cash or credit was less common in the sixteenth century, but with the growth of Potosí's population, material goods as pledges helped to cement economic transactions. The increased use of pawn in the seventeenth century, when Potosí's silver production was fast declining, suggests that more people needed to pawn their belongings in order to pay for basic living costs. But equally important, as the city grew, credit seekers reinforced their ability to repay a peso debt with an object. The demand for pesos to transact urban trade promoted and shaped the activities of loan and pawn.

While the use of loans and pawns proliferated, not everyone practiced these strategies equally. Both indigenous and Spanish Potosinos pawned goods, but indigenous residents did so less than their Spanish neighbors. This discrepancy may indicate that, overall, they owned fewer goods, or that they found it harder to give up objects that held substantial cultural value. In addition, some indigenous laborers in the city may have used the promise of labor as a backup for a loan when they had few material possessions to spare. Loans were very popular with all groups. Spanish women sought money more often than did their male counterparts. In terms of moneylending, though, Spanish men and women appear to have been almost equally active. Indigenous women, on the other hand, were much more active as lenders in the world of credit than their male counterparts. Kin ties could prove particularly important here as women extended credit to men from their native ayllus. Unlike Spanish men and women, Potosí's indigenous residents practiced a gender division of labor that gave women more access to urban money. Many families and kin communities pooled economic resources across gender lines, using women's presence in the urban marketplace to complement men's work in mines or transport.

Spanish men who ran pulperías proved an important source of loans and goods on credit, but women's significant presence in this world of petty credit is remarkable. The extent to which women bought and sold goods, and sought and proffered credit, reveals colonial women's day-to-day engagement with the urban economy. Much of their participation involved petty sums and pawn transactions. A convergence of factors pushed women to engage in pawn and serve as pawnbrokers. Few official channels were open to women who sought credit. Through pawn, they could decide when to let go of material possessions in order to gain items of first necessity for running their household. The ability of so many female pawnbrokers to extend credit reflects their ubiquity in the urban economy. Their apparent preference for offering credit in exchange for a pawned item suggests that they, more than male counterparts, sought guarantees for repayment. Women's loans and credit schemes were not limited to insignificant amounts of money. When Juana Colquema made a loan of five hundred pesos, a significant sum for colonial Potosí, this indicated that women traders, just like men, had the chance to become large-scale creditors, a role rarely highlighted for women in other colonial cities. Moreover, as an example of a highly successful trader, she exemplifies the pronounced role of native Andean women as sources of credit in the urban marketplace. Through these credit transactions, women exercised an important degree of economic independence, both as traders and as financial agents of the home.

In addition to the innovations in the way people handled the high prices and cash demands of Potosí's urban economy, colonial credit practices register changes in how people viewed objects of cultural or personal importance. Some indigenous women bequeathed articles of clothing, especially the finely woven *cumbi* cloth, to female relatives.[83] Yet many testators began to request that their belongings be sold at auction in order to obtain cash to pay debts or to leave something to their children deemed more valuable than a shawl. Of particular note is the extent to which indigenous textiles and silver became objects one could pawn with either Spanish or indigenous pawnbrokers. In the second half of the seventeenth century, Salvador de Vega served both indigenous and Spanish clients as a pulpero and a pawnbroker. In his possession he held four llicllas (shawls), two nanacas (head coverings), and two acsus (dresses).[84] Since Vega had married Spanish women (three different ones) and named no indigenous or mestiza relatives, the mention of the clothing is intriguing. It is highly likely that he obtained these pieces of traditional indigenous women's dress as pawns. For Vega the goods were foreign to the possessions of his household. The clothing held some significance as a marker of indigenous identity for whomever left the items behind. Yet it also held a cash value in the economy where Vega lived and traded.

A similar example of how the market linked Spanish and indigenous cultures is that of Ursula Poco, who pawned a pair of ritual silver drinking vessels (aquillas) to a Spanish flour vendor for nine pesos.[85] Far from being relics of a distant pre-Columbian past, these aquillas were probably new. Potosí artisans produced aquillas decorated with a new style of European-inspired images. Despite their colonial production, the commercial value of the aquillas was linked to pre-Columbian tradition: they had a pawn market value only in pairs, the way native Andeans used them in ritual.[86] This market value made for a new kind of ritual. Instead of a female drawing chicha from her urpu to fill a chieftain's aquillas, Poco handed over the silver drinking cups to obtain nine silver pesos from a Spaniard. Corn beer was completely absent in this colonial transaction; money was present in its place.

The business at Potosí's sites of urban trade revealed the rule of the city's economy: money mattered. People learned a heightened sense of cash value. Through loans and pawn exchanges in corner stores, they adapted creative measures to obtain the pesos they needed. Credit practices show the financial decisions of urban residents as they struggled for subsistence or sought to invest in petty business, but their financial decisions were embedded in a context that reveals information beyond economic practice.

Credit practices grew and changed in response to the city's history. Credit negotiations, from Potosí's period of massive population growth through its decline, reflected and responded to the bounty of silver ore and objects, the dominant cultural influence of the indigenous community, cash-poor laborers, and the presence of women in the urban economy. Patterns show physical and social boundaries in the city were based on ethnicity and gender. Social markers—elite or non-elite status, ethnic identity, and gender—affected how people made money and how they used it. In addition, legal distinctions based on ethnicity had a measurable impact on people's daily lives. But while these social and legal factors were in place, the boundaries they created could be porous under the right circumstances. With a good introduction, a winning proposal, or the right pawn object, people crossed those boundaries to gain credit. Moreover, as we see in Vega's llicllas or Poco's aquillas, Potosí's residents came together to agree on the value of objects from different cultures. Along with sites of trade and products of trade, the credit practices of Potosinos reflected the colonial culture of this urban economy.

ENTERPRISING WOMEN
Female Traders in the Urban Economy

5

Once people arrived in Potosí, they discovered that items like food, drink, and clothes, which rural residents likely produced or obtained through barter, had to be purchased. Vendors like Leonor Sasytoma ran the urban enterprises that supplied these goods. As the population swelled in the late 1500s, Sasytoma found she could earn her living by selling native Andean clothing to urban Indians.[1] Sasytoma sold all the basic components of indigenous female dress, known by their Quechua names: *acsus* (dresses) and *llicllas* (shawls), cinched at the waist with *chumbes* (belts) and fastened at the shoulders with decorated gold or silver *topos* (dress pins). She also did a brisk business in numerous smaller pieces of clothing for both men and women: coca pouches (*chuspas*); sleeves (*mangas*); head coverings called *vinchas* and *llautus*; and sandal-like footwear known as *joxotas*.[2] This clothing, while traditional in form, was often produced with European fabrics new to the Andes. Moreover, the manner in which people obtained the clothes—paying pesos, buying on credit or in exchange for pawn items—represented new types of exchanges. As Sasytoma took advantage of opportunities presented by the city, she exemplified the integral role of women in the colonial urban economy.

The history of trade in the city reveals the preeminent role of men, especially Spanish men, as owners of pulperías and bakeries. In other corners of the city, however, a different history emerges. It is one that highlights women's dominance in several sectors of trade, especially the sale of food in street markets, raw silver, and chicha. Sasytoma's activities reveal how indigenous women had also cornered the urban market on clothing, especially Andean-produced *ropa de la tierra*.[3] In addition to these sectors associated with female vendors, some women gained success as grocers and bakers. Women's niches—and roles—generally varied along ethnic lines. Indigenous women dominated street trade and stores specializing in coca and wax. These women often had links between their business endeavors and male kin involved in long-distance trade. African women, selling for themselves or for their owners, had their corner of the economy in the sale of cooked meals. Spanish women rarely engaged in street trade except as customers. The goods they did sell were primarily foodstuffs, sundry items, and alcohol.

The extent to which women were engaged throughout the urban economy is made all the more interesting because women's activities within social and economic realms were more narrowly conceived than were men's.[4] This chapter opens with a discussion of how legal status, as determined by marriage, influenced women traders' identity before Spanish institutions. Historians who have looked at petty trade in other parts of Spanish America have always been able to locate women as street vendors and in modest enterprises like pulperías.[5] Potosí was no different. Women dominated open-air markets, and they comprised a minority in the ranks of official grocers who paid taxes to the town council. Yet while market women represented themselves in city business, most women who worked as official grocers were represented by their husbands.

Although gender-based legal and political rules limited women's opportunities, women found places to make profits, and women traders have left substantial information about how they operated their urban enterprises. In general, they nurtured credit networks with women for petty loans and with men for larger extensions of credit. Religious institutions and family or kin ties served as organizing principles for traders' social and economic networks. The bulk of this chapter offers detailed analyses of these findings. The chapter sections categorize the women according to marital status and discuss the role of male support in trade endeavors of married, widowed, and single women. Given the significant legal distinctions made among married, widowed, and single women, far too little attention has been given to the relative significance of marriage for Spanish, indigenous, or African women.[6] The evidence from Potosí refutes some common wisdom about marital status. Married women were no more restricted in terms of trade than single counterparts. Further, most widows did not have the financial independence to engage more easily in trade than married counterparts. And, finally, single women became successful traders. Marriage made a difference in many women's options, resources, and strategies, but it did not emerge as the most important factor explaining financial success. One's family of birth, or inherited status and resources, appear as more critical factors in terms of economic success.

The significance—to the women themselves and to the city—of their participation in urban economy is discussed in the concluding section of this chapter. Many women gained measurable financial success through their urban enterprises. A comparison of these success stories confirms that their particular roles and strategies in the urban economy varied according to ethnicity. Yet a woman's degree of financial success within those roles was linked more to social and financial networks than it was to ethnic identity or marital status. Women made money in Potosí because they supplied goods and credit to an urban population that needed them. They had the chance to play this role because they received support from fellow female traders as well as male relatives or creditors. From its beginnings in the 1550s, the market in Potosí had been home to women who exerted economic and social power through trade. These enterprising women have extraordinary stories. When told together, they reveal that women's presence in Potosí's economy was remarkably ordinary.

"Y SU MUGER"
FEMALE IDENTITY AND LEGAL RECOGNITION IN THE URBAN ECONOMY

In February 1628, the Spanish widow doña Juana de Funes made a successful bid to the Potosí town council to open a tambo.[7] Funes was fortunate to be a propertied widow with the means to open an inn. She also enjoyed, as a widow, access to the town council without male representation. With the opening of her inn, situated some ten miles outside of Potosí on the road to La Plata, the widow Funes entered into the ranks of official taxpaying merchants. Unlike Funes, many women never had their roles in the urban economy clearly recorded. One reason for this is marriage; husbands' names could mask their wives' work on the official documents. Census or tax information tended to give priority to males, listing for example "Francisco López y su muger" or perhaps listing a man and ignoring his wife's role completely.[8] Women emerged only as the silent or at least anonymous partners in business, producing goods for sale or filling shelves, tasks so common they left no lasting impression. In addition to marriage, ethnic identity was linked to both trade restrictions and tax exemptions which obscured, in particular, indigenous women's economic activities. These examples point to the important role of gender and ethnicity in law, taxation, and official recognition within the urban economy.

Political bodies created legal constraints on women's economic roles. The town council in Potosí, for instance, aimed to restrict the trade of *pulpero* to men who were married or at least over forty.[9] The town rulers reserved these positions for married men who needed to provide for families. Their ruling also implied that married couples would run respectable stores and prevent purchases of wine or chicha from turning the pulpería into a noisy tavern, a development considered more likely if young men or single women were the proprietors. When the town council tax scribes recorded the grocers of Potosí, men dominated the lists of those who paid taxes to operate their businesses. A few women conducted enough business to earn the right for their names to be listed independently, along with the amount of tax they paid. Yet the women made up small percentages of those listed as grocers. For the years 1599, 1600, and 1601, percentages for female grocers ranged from a low of 10 percent to a high of 24 percent (see table 9 in the appendix).[10] The gender breakdown for bakers, a position not earmarked for males, was similar during the same years—women made up 9 percent to 22 percent (table 9 in the appendix). In contrast to grocers, however, no husbands represented female bakers on the tax rolls.

Husbands could represent female grocers in front of the council. For example, Diego de Penranda paid twenty pesos in 1599, but in the following two years his name appeared on the list again when he paid ten pesos "for his wife."[11] Had she been running the store in 1599 and her occupation gone unrecognized? Or did she take over the responsibilities in 1600? Given her two consecutive listings as the grocer, it is likely that she was a pulpera all along. In addition to Penranda, four men were listed along with their wives in the 1601 tax records. Alonso Nieto was not a pulpero, but he paid the twenty-five-peso tax for the store run by his wife. Francisco Gallegos did likewise for the fifty-peso tax on his wife's store. The two other times that husband and wife appeared together, they ran stores as couples: Joan Perupe and his wife owed twenty pesos, and Joan Abolena and his wife Francisca Guillen, sixty pesos.[12] Remarkably, Guillen was the only female represented by her husband who was listed by name and not merely through the generic "y su muger." Perhaps Guillen physically paid the taxes along with her husband, and at her or her husband's insistence had her name added to the record.

The tax records of the town council reveal that other women obtained independent listings on the records, without male representation. One reasonable explanation is that the women listed independently were widows. Widows enjoyed more freedom to represent themselves in legal transactions without having to seek permission from a male guardian. This might have been the case with Francisca Martínez, who ran a pulpería in the Juego de la Pelota, or Catalina Vásquez, whose store sat in the Plaza of Merlo. The appearance of the pulpera Elvira Angulo as a taxpayer from 1599 to 1601 offers a possible clue. Recall the appointment of Francisco de Angulo as one of the town's official pulperos in 1589—Elvira

Angulo might have been his widow.[13] If her widow status enabled her to become an official taxpaying pulpero, the other women listed might have been in the same situation. In this instance, widows enjoyed more independence in economic activities than married women. Most women were recognized solely through the identities of their husbands. The absence of these women's names from the town council rolls did not lessen their visibility in the community as grocers. But the practice of using husbands as representatives corresponded to the legal and social expectations of the era whereby a husband was responsible for his wife's actions.

Both wives and daughters enjoyed this type of male representation. With the representations came partial protection of women's property from an abuse of power by male guardians—especially the husband. All legitimate children, whether male or female, received equal shares of the inheritance. Thus, daughters stood to inherit along with sons.[14] Any such inheritance or any dowry that a woman received from her parents or guardians always remained her property. Her husband could borrow money from her for ventures that would benefit both of them, but under law he was required to repay it. Couples made a distinction between wealth accumulated during the marriage and that which they brought to the marriage. At the time of a husband's death, the wife received half of the couple's joint earnings, her dowry (if the husband had used it), and all property that was her own.

Even though the general spirit of legal codes restricted women as independent agents, many women in Potosí engaged in legal and economic activities on their own. Some had permission from husbands, others had been separated from or abandoned by husbands, and still others, particularly indigenous women, petitioned the court of their own accord, regardless of the law. Town council quotas for married, male pulperos attempted to limit unmarried women in legitimate trade in pulperías. From the standpoint of town council regulation or Spanish law, traders who were not married, Spanish, and male should have been excluded from licit trade. Yet married Spanish women could be official pulperas through their husbands, as could Spanish widows.

The instances of these official female grocers were few compared to those of men. Thus, despite the exceptions, the reality was that more women operated stores that sat, physically or otherwise, outside the visual borders of the men who sat on the town council. The overall percentage of women grocers in Potosí was higher than tax records show. References to female pulperas in civil and criminal testimony were quite common and represented a higher percentage than seen in property and tax records (53 percent, or 36 of the total number of 68 references, compared to 24 percent, or 98 of 402 references). Examples include Spaniards, Indians, mestizas, and mulatas. Consider the case of the pulpería that Diego de Padilla tried to renovate against the wishes of a fellow pulpero. Extensive witness testimony from Spaniards and Indians alike recreated a list of people who ran the store from the late sixteenth century to 1644. Of ten people linked to that store as owners and operators, five were women. These women, including Spaniards, Indians, and one mulata, contrast with percentages from the council tax records for female pulperas. Such a case reveals that women had more opportunity to operate their businesses in locations like that of Padilla's store (bordering the ranchería of the Callapas) which were not inhabited by elite Spaniards. When the town council attempted to establish a pulpería border around the urban center, it is likely that women ran many of the pulperías outside the ring of legitimacy.[15]

Looking outside pulperías, we find that many indigenous women opted to enter into different types of businesses. They found means, other than official recognition from the Crown or the cabildo as merchants, to become urban traders. Recall that Spanish laws did not require indigenous men and women to pay sales tax, the *alcabala*, on goods considered native products. So it was that many Spanish pulperos paid the alcabala, while many indigenous merchants who might sell the same products did not pay.[16] They could sell regionally produced clothing (*ropa de la tierra*) or goods like coca, chuño, charqui, and maize without paying a tax. Town council tax rolls from the turn of the seventeenth century listed no women as merchants of clothes, coca, and other goods. The women who dominated these trades were usually indigenous. Thus their absence from the tax rolls tells as much about ethnic identity and tax exemption as it does about marital status and women's trade opportunities.

In addition to the evidence from the tax rolls, the presence in the seventeenth century of women known as *mestizas vestidas de india* (or *mestiza en abitos de india*) further confirms the links between identity and trade dominance. Wearing indigenous dress and speaking in Quechua or Aymara, especially for those who were conversant in Spanish as well, suggests motivations for one's identity that were both economic and social. Women who engaged in the urban economy drew on indigenous identity for the right to claim exemptions from alcabalas, but also because the urban economy was the domain of indigenous women. While women in Spanish dress might run chicherías, they did not engage in large-scale market transactions of subsistence goods, coca, clothing, or wax. Women who made a conscious decision to don indigenous dress, to speak in Quechua, and to live in the rancherías did not create a piecemeal identity that made them into "Indians" at work so as to go duty-free only to then become mestizas or Spaniards when they closed up shop. This is not meant to deny instances of racial drift in Potosí. Yet these market women appear to have had a day-in, day-out identity which signified more than economic advantage in the colonial system; it bespoke their intent to privilege indigenous customs over Spanish ones in the urban colonial world.

Female traders needed male representation depending on their location and goals within the urban economy. Having a husband's representation determined neither how much a woman could achieve through trade nor the significance of those activities. Women's presence as official grocers hints at the need for married women to be active in Potosí's economy. It further suggests that families sanctioned the activity, especially husbands who stood in for their wives on tax rolls. Many other women traded in markets, taverns, and illicit stores, where they represented themselves, whether married or not. The numerous advances of credit that people arranged in legal or extralegal fashion meant that women could fund their ventures by manipulating familiar sources—inheritance, dowry, and credit from friends and family. In the end, married Spanish women had the best chance of finding a role in male-dominated niches of the urban economy. Yet given the multitude of places and products involved in Potosí daily trades, women found places to trade whether or not they had a husband to stand behind them.

"WORKING WITH MY WIFE"
MARRIED TRADERS WORKING TOGETHER

In 1670 Antonio de Carrión, a native of Guanico, married doña Francisca Gómez de Peralta, a native of Oruro. The newlyweds quickly started a business together. That same year they notarized an 8,603-peso dowry that Gómez brought to the marriage. By the time they appeared before Potosí notary Pedro Bellido, however, the couple had already halved the total dowry. They invested four thousand pesos in the purchase of a bakery in the Villa, where Carrión noted he was already "working with my wife."[17] As a widower twenty-four years later, Carrión visited a notary public once again. By this time Carrión had moved the business, resettling in houses adjacent to property he inherited from his wife. He recorded this property in his will, describing *his* bakery in detail, but he gave no indication of doña Gómez's prior participation in the trade with him.[18] By

1694, his wife's former activities had fallen into the margins of his will, masking both her economic and physical input. Yet in 1670, their use of the dowry to buy a bakery indicated a true working partnership, of money and labor, at the outset of the couple's married life.

The example of Carrión and Gómez is representative of the experience historians have traditionally envisioned for women involved in the urban economy—a woman assists her husband in running a small business, and he represents both of them before the law. Most historians of the early modern period recognize the family as an economic unit whose members operated together in what has been called a "household economy." This model posits that men and women were called upon for certain tasks that, when carried out in a complementary fashion, helped to make the whole household function at or above a subsistence level.[19] When men ran stores, for instance, women helped with the daily sales. Thus, both the husband and wife owned and worked in the store, although men were the recognized owners. Potosí's urban economy did host such household enterprises, but many couples who participated in Potosí's urban economy did not follow this example. In the case of indigenous couples, as we see in the following section, wives were generally active in trade, while husbands took on other ventures. Most couples who worked together in petty urban businesses were Spanish.

The husband and wife Francisco Feijo and Juana de la Pérez opened a pulpería together in Potosí in the early 1600s.[20] De la Pérez did not have a generous dowry, nor did Feijo bring substantial wealth to the marriage, and thus the couple went into debt for seven hundred pesos to buy the original equipment for the store. The money bought weights and measures as well as inventory, including wine, cheese, and soap. Both husband and wife entered into a loan agreement with Juan de Medina Bonal, so that their joint efforts in the store involved both labor and economic obligation.

Some couples jointly invested their energies and their finances into businesses but maintained distinct gendered daily duties. In the late seventeenth century, doña Michaela de León and her carpenter husband Juan Alfonso Robledo operated a pulpería in the plaza of the Hospital of San Juan de Dios.[21] León claimed that it was her husband Robledo who kept track of all the debts "in his head" and was responsible for collecting them. However, since he operated his carpenter's shop down the street from the pulpería, it was likely León who ran the store. The proximity of the two businesses suggests the couple cooperated closely. Their example provides enough detail to visualize a family economy where an intricate web of credit existed between customers and suppliers for the two shops.

While León had Robledo's assistance in keeping track of the accounts for the store, she did not have much financial backing from him for the business. He brought no wealth to their marriage. León owned the two stores, property left to her after the death of her first husband, Marco Sánchez de la Cruz. De la Cruz had been a *barbero*, a trade he pursued in the store that Robledo turned into a carpenter's shop. Neither of the two, however, made great financial gains from their enterprises. León had no estate apart from the family's home and stores to list in her will since they had earned enough "only to have nourished and supported our children and ourselves."[22] Moreover, despite her use of the honorific *doña* when addressing or referring to her three daughters, the family lived in cramped quarters, the back room and loft of their stores.

León maintained her trade as a pulpera throughout marriage to two men, drawing on the first for the property she owned and on the second to keep track of her debts. She probably tended to the store over the years, calling on her husbands when she needed help, while they carried out their respective trades. She may have been aided by one of her four children, aged nineteen months to thirteen years in 1700. Her choice of trade allowed her to control her work schedule and made her answerable only to her husband and her customers, not an employer.

In some marriage partnerships, husbands followed in the established trade of their wives.[23] Doña Isabel de la Bandera was a baker long before meeting and marrying her husband, Lucas de Aguirre. Aguirre worked in a seasonal job on the reservoirs outside Potosí. Likely a maintenance position on the man-made lakes that provided water for the silver refinery process, this job was low-level manual labor and provided only a small income. After the two married, however, she did not stop her bakery to help Aguirre with his endeavors. Instead, Bandera continued to sell bread. Bandera's apparent dominance in their household economy emerged in a 1604 civil suit over a flour debt to Juan de Solís.[24] She maintained a bakery in her home on the street of the captain Rodrigo de Esquivel, where she bought large quantities of flour from distributors, and hired indigenous workers to prepare dough and bake bread.[25] Her husband not only gave his consent to this operation, but he also helped by delivering bread to her pulpero clients.[26] Above all else, it was practical for her husband, a man of little fortune, to assist her in that business.[27] Sticking to her bakery, Bandera was both bread maker and breadwinner. Friends admitted that she sustained the family.[28] Here the usual pattern of women helping husbands in their trade is reversed; in the historical record the work of Bandera, the woman, predominates, while the role of Aguirre, her husband, comes to light only as an incidental matter.

The Bandera example suggests that not only were there unnamed wives who tended stores and sold goods, but at least some of the time it was women, and not their husbands, who initiated petty business. This may have been more typical in urban areas, particularly those with boom economic cycles, like the mining town of Potosí. Consider that Spanish men who lived in or came to Potosí were apt to try their fortunes at mining or intracolonial trade. Without good credit, neither of these ventures could succeed. Females of all races in Potosí looked to baking, cooking, and serving food and drink to supplement incomes. Those with good fortune might come to own a moderate-sized bakery and hire laborers, as did the exceptional Bandera. New husbands who failed in mining endeavors might find, as Aguirre did, that marriage brought not just a wife but a new trade.[29]

"TO SEEK HER LIVELIHOOD"
MARRIED WOMEN, INDEPENDENT TRADERS

In contrast to the above examples, some married women operated their businesses independently of their husbands. Yet even when husband and wife did not labor in the same pursuit, marriage could provide economic and legal benefits that bolstered women's gains in the urban economy. In theory, married women were entitled to financial or material support from their husbands. And many husbands who could provide such support to women's shops or businesses were happy to do so. But marriage in colonial Potosí definitely offered women different protections or benefits depending on the social and economic status of their husbands.

The merchant doña María Osorio, a Spaniard born in Seville, linked her enterprise to Sergeant Juan Bicente de Morales when she married him in 1637.[30] She ran a clothing store where she dealt in quantities of thousands of pesos. Osorio received credit using her husband's name for the purchase of costly bolts of imported cloth and elaborate pieces of clothing. She attained a degree of wealth that allowed her to live in some luxury, in contrast to most of the other women considered in this chapter. She owned three African slaves and numerous pieces of valuable pearl and gold jewelry. Morales's exact position in Potosí is unclear, but his title undoubtedly translated into some status. Osorio capitalized on his name and her energy in the first three years of their marriage to produce a busy clothing store that she portrayed as her, not the couple's, enterprise.

When María Benítez married Juan Osorio (no relation to doña María Osorio in the preceding paragraph), both parties brought goods to the marriage.[31] During their marriage, they purchased a second home together from which Benítez ran a pulpería. The house and attached store, located in the San Pedro parish, cost four thousand pesos. The ownership of this property clearly helped the couple's business endeavor, since they were not required to rent a space. Benítez appeared to have made more success in the company of her husband than without him, since she moved from a five-hundred-peso house to a four-thousand-peso house. It is difficult to determine how much of a role the pulpería had in the success and who was responsible for the daily operation of the store. The financial gains of the couple hint that Benítez herself ran the pulpería. A four-thousand-peso profit would have been quite a handsome gain for a pulpería business, even in busy Potosí, which suggests that Osorio may have profited from different businesses. Another clue comes from the words of Benítez herself. Even though her husband was still living, Benítez noted in her will that the store's wine inventory needed to be paid. Her attention to this detail in a will full of weighty clauses indicates that she ran the store and kept track of such orders.

Though African men controlled a much smaller share of economic resources than Spanish or even indigenous men, some African women received tangible benefits from their marriages. Enslaved African women who married freemen also counted on their legal and moral support in efforts to protect themselves from owners or gain their freedom. María Atienzo's husband Francisco Díaz protected both his wife's economic interests and their marriage. Atienzo kept chickens and rabbits in the home of her owner, with his permission, and used them to gain extra money. She probably sold them to street cooks or cooked meals herself. When her owner planned to sell her to a rural hacienda, it threatened both her marriage and her activities in the urban economy. Díaz sued his wife's owner to save her from being sold to the hacienda.[32] Though Africans, both free and enslaved, had the support of the church to marry in colonial Spanish America, obstacles such as the opposition of owners and separation by sale made it difficult to marry.[33] The scanty evidence on married African couples, free or enslaved, makes it much harder to argue that marital status helped African women in the urban economy. Atienzo's case points to the ways, other than large property bequests, in which this support was possible.

Married indigenous women who concentrated on other indigenous people as both creditors and customers found great rewards in a place like Potosí where the sizeable indigenous population offered both financial support and a market for commodities. In the case of most indigenous women merchants, there was little question as to who ran an urban enterprise. It was almost always the wife. Isabel Choquima, a native of Potosí, presided over the transport of goods like coca, corn, wool, and sheep by advancing money to indigenous men and women to bring the goods to Potosí for her. For example, she hired Tomás Quispe to bring coca in the amount of 130 pesos. In turn, she sold the goods to Potosinos like the nine pesos' worth of coca that Andrea Sisa purchased on credit.[34] In addition to using her wealth as a petty creditor, Choquima owned a small house in front of the San Sebastián church. Choquima's marriage to Lucas de Cuenca, a yanacona of the Santo Domingo convent, likely enhanced her standing in the urban economy because most Potosí yanaconas enjoyed distinct status.

Petty entrepreneur Juana Colquema was a married indigenous woman who achieved success by drawing on a variety of networks. Colquema, a native of the town of Colquemarca in the province of Carangas, ran a wax store, a chichería, and sold other goods like coca and ají as well as acting as a banker for indigenous neighbors. As discussed earlier, she began her career when a woman named Joana Colquema, who was not identified as a relative but who was also from the town of Colquemarca, offered her five hundred pesos to "seek her livelihood."[35] The investment proved to be an enormous help to Colquema. In contrast to many women who relied on elite family ties or Spanish men to start their businesses, Colquema found her sponsor in an indigenous woman, who probably earned her money as a successful petty trader. In time, Colquema returned the five hundred pesos, and even commissioned five wax statues as an interest payment. She also learned from the experience that her position as a trader could be reinforced if she acted as a lender to her community. In 1670, indigenous men and women owed her 850 pesos. While no debts equaled the five hundred pesos she had received to start her business, she clearly played a crucial role fulfilling the economic needs of her community.

Colquema's lending activities supported indigenous friends and customers, but she did not restrict her interactions exclusively to neighbors. As a trader, she also drew on the support of Spanish men for credit. Juan de Loyola offered her coca on credit, Captain Sebastián de Cassadebante gave her money to stock her store, and the licentiate don Suero Pelaez allowed her to fall behind some sixty pesos on the rent of her store. Colquema saw the advantages and, indeed, necessity of entering into financial relationships with men who monopolized the long-distance trade of coca and dominated the Potosí real estate market. Her relationship with men who bore titles, a captain and a licentiate, suggests an astute reckoning of business and politics in the market around her. Though she owed the three men a total of 631 pesos, she could easily pay that amount. She had over 150 pesos in cash in her possession as well as 300 pesos' worth of wax, twenty baskets of coca worth between 120 and 160 pesos, and 33 baskets of ají. Colquema ordered these goods, along with personal items like clothing and two pieces of property to be sold at an auction to gain money for her estate.

Colquema was married to an indigenous man, don Blas Quispe. Before her marriage, however, Colquema had started her business as well as purchased her home and store (two modest rooms in the San Lorenzo parish). She also had two daughters outside of marriage. When she married Quispe, she expanded her family with one son and likely expanded her trading circle. Quispe's honorific title, "don," suggests that he may have been a member of the native elite, or that he might have acted as a leader of the men reporting for mita duty from his district. In either case, Quispe's status could have had a residual effect for Colquema's businesses. She may have gained a new set of customers who used her as a vendor or a lender because of her husband's status.

Numerous married women engaged in urban trade. Some worked directly with husbands, from whom they gained direct legal, financial, or labor cooperation. Others worked independently of husbands but still enjoyed certain benefits of marriage. Doña María Osorio received legal help and access to credit networks from her husband. Benítez enjoyed ownership of her store thanks to the financial success of her husband. Atienzo received legal support. Choquima and Colquema gained access to elite indigenous networks through their husbands. In each instance, these women relied on their husbands for economic, legal, and social aid that helped their trading endeavors. Their husbands were important reasons, but not the only reason, behind the success of their work. These women simultaneously tapped other sources to support their trading efforts.

If married women in Potosí enjoyed financial and legal support from husbands to become petty entrepreneurs, how did widows fare with the potential financial support of inheritance and the legal freedom to represent themselves? Some women's historians have emphasized widowhood as a stage of life where, having gained control of their husband's estates, women managed to become active in economic transactions in ways they were unable to as wives.[36] This is especially true in the case of elite widows in parts of the English colonies who invested in business. In contrast, elite women in the Iberian context generally invested in sacred, not secular, enterprises.[37] Well-off Potosí widows, Spanish or indigenous, did not shun religious donations but they seemed more like their English counterparts than their Iberian ones to the extent that they bought stores and invested in urban businesses. Looking strictly at Potosí, widows were no more likely to engage in trade transactions than married women. Some put up their own dowries to celebrate a new marriage. Others entered the urban economy in a mere struggle to earn their subsistence. Widows from the complex colonial economy were a varied bunch who belied both the image of the stately widow calculating handsome profits earned from her husband's inheritance and the stereotype of the widow making donations exclusively to church or convent.

The amount of property and saleable goods left to widows by their late husbands had a significant effect on their ability, and incentive, to invest in small businesses. Spaniard Doña María de Salas owned a house and store in Potosí, a well-stocked farm called Chulchcani, and numerous silver pieces, furniture, and clothing. The few signs of personal economic activity in her will, however, suggest that she may have inherited much of her wealth from the estate of her deceased husband, Joan Díaz Talavera.[38] Most widows lived less comfortably. Elvira Sánchez, a Spanish widow who ran a pulpería, had only modest lifetime gains.[39] After receiving what little came from her husband's estate, she labored earnestly to acquire a home and a store. To supplement her income from the store, she rented out rooms on her property. In her will, she bequeathed the store to a niece, its furniture to a granddaughter, and half the proceeds from the sale of the house for the dowry of a girl she had raised as an orphan. The other half of the proceeds she designated for masses at the convent of Santo Domingo. Apart from the home, she was owed some 135 pesos for goods she sold on credit from her store. In turn, she had debts totaling 143 pesos.

Her resources dwindled after writing her first will, however, and she had to write a codicil to cancel the masses for her soul because, she lamented, "there is no money to be able to have them said."[40]

Sánchez's decision to rent rooms to generate income was a common option for widows fortunate enough to own property. The Potosí native and widow Petrona Beltrán owned two bakeries. In 1650 she rented one, located above the Plazuela del Rayo, to Gonzalo de Olivera.[41] Yet the rental of the properties was never guaranteed, and thus even propertied widows could find themselves in a precarious state. Recall Beatriz de Soto from chapter 2, who asked the council to forgive the taxes on her store because she was "a poor widow."[42]

In addition to garnering support from husbands' estates or from living male kin, widows who operated on a thin margin, like Sánchez, Beltrán, or Soto, used another strategy in the urban economy. They sent their slaves into the street to earn their keep and support the household. The widow doña Ines Vázquez had her slave Gregoria ply the various enterprises that she dreamed up. Though Gregoria allegedly spent the money she earned, Vázquez intended that it be used for the upkeep of the house. A slave named Madalena cooked meals in the plaza and sold them, along with chicha, all for the benefit of her mistress, the widow doña Rafaela Flores.[43] Thus, the labor of slave women was an important financial resource for Spanish women, who considered themselves too respectable to engage in street trade or to build up small business ventures. For the slave women who performed this street trade for them, any and all extra-curricular sales could be to their benefit—they had incentives to try and make extra earnings because at times they could buy their freedom in Potosí society. The African women who filled Potosí's main plaza cooking meat dishes were likely a mixture of slave women working for masters, like the above examples, and others who had gained their freedom.[44] Significantly, these African women were often a key ingredient in keeping afloat the petty enterprises of their widowed owners or employers.

At the opposite end of the entrepreneurial spectrum was widow María de Vargas. Widowhood spurred some women into productive economic activity beyond what their husbands had achieved, to the extent that these women could boast about their gains in the wake of their husbands' passing. Vargas, a *peninsular*, ran a bakery that supplied bread to thirteen pulperías in the city, the convent of Santo Domingo, and the royal mint—the Casa de la Moneda.[45] She had debts when she wrote her will in 1619, but the money owed her well exceeded the totals of her debts and left a surplus of 3,269 pesos.

In 1630, years after Vargas's death, her flour supplier, Francisco de Olmos, brought a civil suit against her descendants because he was unable to collect his money. In this case, the family could not resort to the common rhetorical strategy of the "poor miserable widow" to defend nonpayment. Olmos produced copies of Vargas's notarized will to prove that the bakery had been extremely profitable in her lifetime. Doña Teresa Chacón and doña Luciana de Vargas, the legitimate daughters of María de Vargas and Juan Rodríguez Chacón, received twenty-thousand-peso dowries from their mother. In Potosí, this was a sizable sum to offer to a betrothed daughter. Judging from the lack of personal property in her will, Vargas consolidated profits into the dowries. Other assets helped to pay to send a third child, her son, Diego de Vargas Chacón, to Lima to study in the Colegio de San Martín, also a prestigious "dowry."

The community considered Vargas herself to have shaped this successful destiny. A witness in the civil case brought by Olmos pointed specifically to Vargas's efforts, calling her a "woman of good judgment and dedicated to work."[46] The death of her husband appeared to have whetted her ambition to raise her children and marry her daughters properly. Focusing on the bakery, Olmos suggested that "in the time of her widowhood she acquired the rest of her wealth . . . which she could not have amassed with the goods of her [late] husband."[47] Vargas and her husband ran the bakery together during his lifetime. She expanded the business after his death and invested her profits, raising the standard of living for herself and her children. In her will, Vargas did not call herself a doña nor her husband a don, but she did use those titles of honor with her children, who achieved elevated social status as a result of their mother's enterprise. Clearly, numerous economic and social factors needed to align for a widow to achieve the success that Vargas did in the petty economy. She was no widow sitting atop a handsome inheritance.

Though widows, like Beatriz de Soto, might seek to inspire the pity and favor of magistrates by referring to themselves as "poor widows," they did find avenues for profit in petty trade. Some, like Salas, lived comfortably with property or financial support left behind by husbands and male relatives. Others, like Vargas, built on their husbands' estates to achieve a higher economic status. Still others, such as Sánchez or Flores, earned their subsistence by renting property or ordering slaves to engage in petty commerce. The economic gains that these single women achieved varied greatly. Overall, their examples reinforce the argument that to gain modest prosperity, a woman alone counted as much on the social and family networks at her disposal as on the assets inherited from her husband.

Though both single and widowed women were unmarried, the status of single women was distinct. Having never been married, they had no inheritance from husbands, nor had they experienced the legal representation, financial backing, or social clout of husbands as they started trading businesses. The cases of Potosí's *soltera* traders reveal that while such women may not have had these potential benefits, they did have important support networks comprised of males and females. Male friends, or sometimes partners, of women traders offered support in the absence of a husband. Brothers or fathers who enjoyed elevated social status could be creditors. In addition to immediate social networks, single women in particular found religious institutions, and their lay organizations called *cofradías*, to be critical locations for nurturing their urban connections. Through these different possibilities for support, single women found that urban petty commerce was open to them regardless of their marital status. These solteras had the best chance to access credit from urban networks if they created reputations for being "hardworking" and "trustworthy."

For some Spanish solteras, inheritance from parents provided them with homes, clothes, or jewelry. In the absence of a male provider, however, they needed to engage in some form of business to keep cash coming in. Chicha sales emerged as a way to supplement insufficient incomes from inheritance. Though Spanish women of means would never stoop to such a trade, the majority of Spanish women had to act more practically. The diminutive investment requirements needed to produce chicha meant that Spanish women did not need to purchase expensive equipment, and they could find cheap labor from among numerous indigenous women who needed cash in the urban market. Women who decided to enter the chicha trade had to form networks outside their families to survive. They sought backers to set up their stores, and they nurtured relationships with indigenous brewers, often with advances of money, to ensure the delivery of the products.

Though it was unusual, women could use female-only networks to run successful petty trade ventures. The Oruro native doña Juana de Urquizo, a chicha vendor, followed this strategy. Urquizo had one daughter, doña María Cavellero, but she was neither married nor close enough to the father to mention his name in her will. She drew upon connections with indigenous and Spanish women to run a successful chicha business and amass one thousand pesos and own numerous pieces of jewelry.[48] She hired five indigenous chicheras to help her with her business. For loans, she looked to fellow Spaniards doña Paula Núñez and doña Blasía Villena. Urquizo also approached a Spanish widow, clothing merchant doña Catalina de Caseres, to guard her one thousand pesos in savings. Her reliance on women solely for financial transactions shows that some single women gained enough power in the urban economy to operate independently of men.

Another soltera chicha seller, doña Juana de Figueroa, was more typical in her reliance on male financial support. Figueroa was an *hija natural*, a daughter born outside of marriage. She lived with her mother throughout her life. Though her father, Juan Fernández de Figueroa, was deceased, she acknowledged him in her testament. Many hijas naturales never knew their fathers, but Figueroa's recognition of hers in her will signifies that he may have made bequests to her at the time of his death. Either through his generosity or her own efforts, she was able to purchase a small house in the San Sebastián neighborhood.

At one point, Figueroa possessed enough capital to loan one thousand pesos to a La Plata merchant, don Alberto Bello Romero. The loan to Bello Romero was likely made at a more comfortable stage of her life, since she did not have many liquid assets at the time she dictated her will. Indeed by that point, she had been using pawn as a way to gain credit at a pulpería and cash at other venues.[49] And she began to sell chicha, having secured a brewer named Agustina as her supplier. When she could not recover her loan to Bello Romero, Figueroa turned to a male member of the community for sustained support. Her status as a single woman may well have contributed to her difficulty in collecting from Bello Romero. An anonymous man rescued her in the wake of these troubles with a donation that provided for her sustenance. Significantly, her chicha business did not garner enough profit to support both Figueroa and her mother over time.

Free African women generally stood in a less stable economic position than Spanish chicha sellers, but they too used expertise and trading skills to set up petty businesses for their own economic benefit. Dominga, a mulata slave, achieved renown for her cooking, washing, and sewing while she worked for the school master don Francisco Pérez de Morales.[50] An acquaintance of Pérez de Morales, doña María Ana Isabel de Morillo, admitted that Dominga was "very hardworking, [a] good cook and washerwoman." Morillo added further, "I always saw her cooking for her master . . . and making preserves and [saw] that she sewed any type of tailoring and [made] hand-sewn clothing and that she is very capable."[51]

Pérez de Morales offered freedom to Dominga when he died. Soon thereafter doctor don Manuel de Peñalosa y Mansilla claimed that he owned
Dominga, and he challenged her manumission. Peñalosa y Mansilla drew
on Dominga's reputation as a good worker to argue that he should be
compensated for losing her at eight hundred pesos, not at the typical five-
hundred-peso value of slaves. By the time the doctor filed his lawsuit,
Dominga was earning her living cooking for new arrivals to Potosí.

Single *pulperas*, whose situation in the hierarchy of petty trade generally placed them in a more comfortable position than chicha sellers or
street vendors, nonetheless needed to rely on male support for relief to
keep households going and for credit to keep their businesses going. Failing pulpera doña Luisa de Tres Palacios y Escando relied on her brother to
pay for the rental of the store that she operated on the Plaza de Mendiola.
Though doña Luisa was the owner of a small home adjoining the store, by
1685 she found herself forced to pawn numerous personal items for cash.[52]

Another pulpera, doña Lorenca de Salas y Rivera, turned to Spanish
men for help with a bit more success than Tres Palacios.[53] A native of Potosí, Salas y Rivera may have been a young woman, given that she had two
sisters whom she called "maidens" or *doncellas* (signifying that they had yet
to reach a suitable age for marriage). Whatever her age, Salas y Rivera ran
a successful petty business in a rented pulpería on a corner of Gerónimo
del Salto Street. She fostered relationships with two Spanish men for economic and legal guidance when she started the store. Cristóbal Gutiérrez
provided her with 112 pesos to guarantee her business, an act that suggests
she was considered a legitimate grocer, though no record of such recognition has survived. To buy goods for the store, she borrowed money from
Diego Sánchez de la Lano. Sánchez de la Lano also served as her representative for the rental agreement for the pulpería. At the writing of her
will, Salas y Rivera carried few debts and had managed to make a generous
loan of eight hundred pesos to an acquaintance named Martín de Quiñones. She specifically ordered that both her financiers be repaid with earnings from the pulpería. Moreover, she promised her bed, bedclothes, and
mattress to Sánchez de la Lano "in gratitude for how much he has encouraged and helped me."[54] Though it was Salas y Rivera who did the difficult
work of running her store, the assistance from Gutiérrez and Sánchez de
la Lano proved instrumental. Like many other single traders and grocers,
Salas y Rivera relied on male creditors to fund her petty enterprises.

Longstanding family ties to Potosí could also prove beneficial to soltera traders. Through various enterprises, Juana Payco amassed a sizeable estate during her lifetime.[55] She was a native Potosina whose parents

and grandparents were buried in the city. Despite the fact that Spanish and church officials described her as being of Spanish and indigenous ancestry (mestiza), she dressed in indigenous clothing and ate indigenous staples like corn and chuño. Most Potosinos who knew her considered her to be culturally Indian. She was an enterprising woman who owned a well-furnished house in the city center, down from the Tambo de San Agustín. Her efforts earned her savings of some 520 pesos that she secreted into various containers throughout her home. Payco was, by all accounts, equally devoted to spiritual enterprise. Between 1624 and 1627, she served as a prioress of the cofradía of Nuestra Señora de la Soledad, based in the convent of Our Lady of Mercy (Mercedes), during which time she oversaw the collection of 1,500 pesos' worth of alms.

Payco's personal assets were valuable enough that two different churches, which expected to be the beneficiaries of her estate, found themselves battling claims from her grandnephews. The inventory of her goods, conducted after her death, provides a few clues as to how she profited in Potosí. Her belongings point toward the possibility that she sold clothing, much like Leonor Sasytoma. Her home was filled with clothing and dress pins, stored in various trunks, well beyond the amounts necessary for the average person. Some pieces of clothing were likely taken as pawn items, given claims made on the estate.[56] Payco also owned thirty-three skeins of wool, from which she might have made or ordered special pieces of clothing. The other goods stockpiled in her home, including oregano, corn, and peanuts, suggest that she could have sold other sundry items along with clothing. Moreover, her niece Madalena Taquima admitted that she assisted Payco in the business of buying goods in the public plaza and reselling them (*regateando*).[57]

Payco built extensive social networks that helped her succeed in petty enterprises. At the time of her death in 1631, Payco had no husband and no children of her own, but she drew people into her household. She raised her two nephews, Thomas and Salvador Quispe, in the absence of their mother, and took orphan children into her home, some of whom worked for her as servants and spoke highly of her. Further, Payco was well-known among the indigenous population in her neighborhood. She served as a godmother for two of Juana Arnanca's daughters. During Payco's illness, Inés Titima, her next-door neighbor, attested to the numerous men and women who came and went from her home. And a group of indigenous women, including Gerónima de Salas, assisted Payco in her illness, helping her to "die well" (*bien morir*). Payco's ties to the indigenous community ran deep, but her good name extended to the

Spanish population of Potosí as well. When Pedro de Teves Talavera had to leave town for a lengthy stay in La Paz, he asked his wife to give a Cuzco-style (blue and white cumbe) bedspread and an elaborately decorated woman's blouse to Payco for safekeeping. He chose Payco, he asserted, "because she is a trustworthy and well-known person."[58]

As a single woman whose parents were long deceased, Payco did not rely on any single male provider for support. Instead, she created a far-reaching network in which her cofradía was very significant. Payco made the church and the cofradía a priority during her lifetime; she decorated her home with items bearing the cofradía's insignia and paid to construct a chapel for Indians in devotion to Our Lady of Grace. Cofradías, many of them sponsored by the Jesuits, quickly became important unifying groups for urban indigenous residents. The Jesuits proudly reported one thousand cofradía members in their Potosí institutions by 1600. By 1690, over one hundred indigenous cofradías existed in the city.[59] Disruptions posed to ayllu life by the impositions of colonial society forced many native Andeans, especially those in urban areas, to create or adapt new groups of social identity. They looked frequently to the lay religious structure of the cofradías for both social and financial support in a changing world.[60] And, interestingly, many of these groups drew women.

Fray Diego de Ocaña described in great detail the female members of the Jesuit cofradía of the Niño Jesus. As Ocaña watched the cofradía march in the Holy Week procession, he could not help but comment on their displays of wealth and their status as single women. The cofradas, he claimed, were all "very rich indias and pallas, with whom the soldiers are cohabitating."[61] Despite the disdainful tone, his claim had a kernel of truth. In the last decades of the sixteenth century, single women like vendor Catalina Palla, a cofrada in Nuestra Señora del Rosario, lived with Spanish men and had children with them. These relationships had social and economic implications in the urban world as the women often received donations of urban property from the Spanish men.[62] For Ocaña, and perhaps for other observers, the combination of what he perceived to be sexual impropriety and financial excess called attention to a unique identity of urban Andean women.

Clothing was an unmistakable part of their identity. The cofradas "dressed in very fine silk patterned with velvet, and underneath the azú [acsu] a skirt better than the Spaniards'. The 'liquidas' [llicllas]—which are what they wear over their shoulders like shawls—of velvet and damask; and the ñañaca, which is the clothing that they wear over the head, of the same; the chumbes, which are what cinches the waist, are of their wool of many colors."[63] The elaborate dress was but one indication that the cofradía was a place in which urban Andean women pooled their wealth. They did this as an act of not just devotion, but also identity formation. These women's urban Andean identity was linked to money and material goods through both earning and donation. As women pledged devotion to the cofradía, they also made connections to each other that served in addition to or in place of ayllu ties.[64] And, for single women who lacked the social and economic ties that came with marriage, the cofradía was a place to protect and perhaps even enhance their financial standing.

Women like Payco incorporated both trade earnings and religious devotion into their lives outside the convent. Women, both indigenous and Spanish, made important donations to religious institutions. The convent of Santo Domingo inherited a corner lot from Isabel Cayco Palla, for example.[65] She willed the lot to the convent of Santo Domingo in a chantry (or *capellanía*) in exchange for thirty-six masses for her soul. Cayco came into possession of the urban lot because her employer, don Juan de la Torre, appreciated her years of service; when she relinquished ownership, she did so with the request that other Spaniards (the Santo Domingo clergy) would offer services on her behalf. Within little time, the religious men at Santo Domingo had opted to develop the lot for maximum profit and built the Tambo de la Esquina (Corner tambo) on her former property. The urban economic activities of nuns, even those physically restricted to the cloisters of the convent, has been well documented for Cuzco.[66] While the case remains to be made for Potosí, examples emerge that suggest similar kinds of extension into urban finance by women in the convents. The nun doña Bernavela paid taxes on her pulpería, though presumably someone outside the convent staffed the store.[67] Single women, both inside or outside the convent, appear to have had particular inclination to link their financial networks to religious institutions.

Single women scanned the terrain of the urban world and came away with numerous sources of potential support in the absence of a husband. Male friends or fellow female traders proved to be important sources of credit. For Spanish women, the careers of fathers and brothers or inheritance from parents provided that assistance. African women like Dominga who ventured into petty trades might count on aid from a former employer or owner. Social ties led to multiplying wealth for indigenous women who came from elite families, such as those that headed mita regiments or those that had yanacona status. These single traders supported Potosí's economy, and the city's size and dynamic market sustained their trading ventures.

Of course, all women did not fall neatly into categories of wife, widow, and soltera. Women entered into relationships with men that did not equal marriage legally, even if they approximated it socially. Some marriages ended in a physical sense while they continued in a legal sense. One woman, labeled *soltera* at the beginning of her will, began to reveal information about a former marriage in the body of that same will without acknowledging a contradiction.[68] The label *soltera* might have been the work of the notary. Or she may have identified herself as soltera since, in her mind, the dissolution of her marriage left her single. The potential error in labeling reminds us that the importance officials attached to marital status likely differed from that perceived by neighbors and friends.[69] If women found themselves in a position where their marital status might be questioned, it was of utmost importance for them to clarify what economic gains they had achieved independently and what plans they had for those gains.

Women were careful to credit their own hard work for their success. For the indigenous Francisca Cachimbocllo, marriage to a Spanish man provided no path to fortune but rather erected roadblocks to happiness and success. Cachimbocllo amassed an estate including some two thousand pesos and houses in the Tiopampa neighborhood without the help of her husband, Juan de Obregón, to whom she was married for over thirty years. Cachimbocllo found she could not count on him. She sold many personal belongings early in the marriage, allegedly to pay costs to clear Obregón of a murder charge. Moreover, she lamented, "during the time of our marriage the said Juan de Obregón my husband has neither fed nor supported me in little or in great quantity. And when the said Juan de Obregón has come to this Villa he begged me and forced me to give him baskets of coca, silver, and other goods, all of which I did many times, and he had only lived with me as my husband for four years."[70]

Obregón fled alone to the town of Tarija, located 150 miles southwest of Potosí, and visited only when he needed to make trips to gather merchandise. The couple never had children. Instead of linking her trade to a relationship with a Spaniard, Cachimbocllo's ties to or wealth from her native Cuzco, the former Inca capital, may have been important to her ability to engage in urban enterprise. She entrusted two indigenous men, Antón Coro and Diego Gualpa Roca, with the administration of her estate. Her will ordered the men to give her money to the Church and to keep any of the estate from reaching the hands of her estranged husband.

While most women did not fear that their estranged husbands would collect their hard-earned pesos as inheritance, many women did make attempts similar to Cachimbocllo's to differentiate between what they brought to a marriage or earned on their own and what their husbands offered or earned. Doña Costansa de Sossa, a Potosí widow, listed a sizeable collection of silver in her will—all of which, she specified, "I have sought out and acquired with my personal work after the death of my husband."[71] María Poco, a widowed coca trader, declared that her husband Goncalo Capi brought no goods to the marriage and their estate "has not multiplied one bit." Moreover, she pointed out that she bought the house and store where she lived with "my money."[72] Chicha vendor doña María Rencifo's pleas were more desperate.[73] In 1683, she took action with the ecclesiastical court to obtain a legal separation from Marcos Joseph, an indigenous man she married in 1679. Rencifo claimed that her husband physically abused her, failed to provide for her nourishment, and, finally, left her. She insisted that, "if I had not sought [my sustenance] with my own enterprises I would have perished."[74]

The personal investment by these women in their urban businesses led them to pronounce profits as their own, especially if they did not feel supported by husbands—financially or otherwise. Factors beyond mere pride and satisfaction led women to make such declarations. Technically, married men stood to inherit a portion of their wives' estates. Indigenous women, like Francisca Cachimbocllo, who married a wayward Spanish man, tried earnestly to prevent this from happening. They suspected, with good reason, that Spanish men would have a better chance to fight for their money than an indigenous husband might. Despite leaving a will through a Spanish notary, Cachimbocllo chose two indigenous men as trustees of her estate and fought the notion that her husband deserved any inheritance. Another critical reason for some women traders to name their own earnings was that they had children outside of marriage. Under Spanish law these children, hijos naturales, did not automatically receive a portion of their parents' estates, as did children born to married parents. Pulpera María Benítez was married to Juan Osorio, but had a son and a daughter prior to her marriage. In her will, she asserted that the couple bought their house together "with money earned by both after our marriage even though when he married me he brought for his estate three hundred pesos in reales and one hundred in pawns."[75] For her part, Benítez owned a slave and a house worth five hundred pesos. She bequeathed the slave, the five hundred pesos, and half the value of the house and store purchased with Osorio to her daughter. The girl, ten-year-old Petrona Hernández, was to use the property as her dowry when she reached marriageable age. Both Cachimbocllo and Benítez emphasized their independent economic holdings in their wills so as to protect the use of their earnings after they died.

When these women declared independent profits, they revealed changing values about women, work, and money in the colonial city, where women could earn profits and claim them as their own. Women's desire to stake out what they earned with their enterprises is consistent in the statements of mestizas like doña María Rencifo, Spaniards like doña Costansa de Sossa, and indigenous women like María Poco. For women native to the Andes, this propensity toward delineating the individual and the private fits with a Spanish legal framework that weighed heavily in their last testaments. The wills of Spanish women also reveal a degree of independence toward economic endeavors. In Potosí's booming market, Spanish women had multiple chances to earn profits that might exceed their husbands' earnings. Though men might contest such assertions, it was easy to imagine how women could earn their livelihoods, and sometimes their fortunes, through trade.

CONCLUSION

Like other cities in colonial Spanish America, Potosí was home to many enterprising women. Indigenous women played a major role in street market commerce that dates almost to the foundation of the city. In the 1550s, when native kurakas and Spanish merchants sought urban dealers, the female relatives of mine laborers and indigenous elites staked out their commercial locations. In the latter decades of the sixteenth century, relationships with Spanish men provided a measure of financial security, generally in the form of property, that helped single indigenous women like Catalina Palla maintain stable positions in the urban economy. By the end of the sixteenth century, indigenous women's locations within the urban economy expanded, as did the cast of women traders. African women appear as regular participants in petty street trade. Spanish women began to make their mark by the 1600s, especially in the business of chicha. This expansion and diversity is directly related to the growth and ethnic diversification of Potosí's population during the same time span.

Whether married, widowed, or single, women in Potosí had both the opportunity and the necessity to carve out space in the growing num-
ber of trading places in the city. As the examples of María Vargas, Juana Colquema, and Juana Payco show, widows, wives, and solteras could all achieve a comfortable level of economic success. Though marriage affected women's legal and social status in the colonial world, these three examples reveal that many factors in addition to marriage influenced one's ability to enter and succeed in the urban economy. The relationship of marriage to women's trade differed somewhat for Spanish and indigenous women. Married Spanish women often ran businesses with their husbands and gained their husbands' representation for town council or legal matters. María Osorio could draw upon her husband's good credit reputation to buy goods for her store. Married indigenous women showed fewer direct ties between their businesses and their husbands. Juana Colquema relied instead on a skillfully crafted web of trade support with elite members of her native community and members who relocated to Potosí. Widows, who lost the benefit of their husbands' earnings, could gain freedom to maneuver in urban business, as did widow María Vargas, who dowered her children through profits from her bakery. But widowhood alone was not enough to move women into business prosperity; it forced other women into selling chicha. Single women had perhaps the most challenging task of gaining a foothold in the urban economy, especially single indigenous women. As an urban trader and avid cofrada, Juana Payco would seem to be of the same mold as Catalina Palla, yet donations from Spanish men diminished greatly from the late sixteenth century to the late seventeenth century, possibly because of the rise of Spanish women in the population. Instead, Payco invested in an elaborate network comprising relatives, neighbors, and cofradía connections.

If women's initiative is evident in this history of trade, it is equally clear that men were complicit in this development. Spanish men, in particular, made numerous loans to help start and maintain women's businesses. As entire families responded to the pressures of the colonial economy, fathers and husbands required the energy and earnings of wives and daughters who ran independent enterprises. The connection of women's activities to the needs of city markets and urban families produced a situation where Potosí's economy needed women traders. This critical element in the general social and economic development of the city provided certain women with significant economic power. Despite regulations that promoted men in urban groceries and laws that compelled women to transact economic transactions through male representatives, the climate in Potosí's market encouraged women's activities. After all, the trading roles of these enterprising women were intrinsic to the city's colonial economy.

The Urban Marketplace in the
Face of Decline, 1650–1700

6

If a sixteenth-century inhabitant of Potosí were to glimpse the city one
hundred years later, he or she still would be able to locate most of the
city's main sites of commerce. The Plaza de las Gallinas lost its home with
the construction of Nuestra Señora de la Misericordia in 1649. But the
centerpiece of urban trade, the Gato de las Indias, still dominated the large
plaza adjoining the main square. When an idea surged in 1660 to construct a new convent in the Gato, displacing the market, the town council
debated the matter, with the viceroy of Peru, the conde de Alba, adding
his weighty opinion. Town heads and the viceroy agreed that the market
should not be moved.[1] No one could think of another spot large enough
for the countless indigenous marketeers to sell all their comestibles. By
their reasoning, the town's main plaza was too small, especially since the
council feared the market would crowd onto the adjacent San Agustín
convent, the Jesuit church, and the Iglesia Mayor. Thus, despite a request
by the church, the town council refused to yield, and the hub of the urban
economy did not budge. The predominance of Potosí's Gato as an institution of economic and social exchange was legendary, and in the 1660s Potosinos were not prepared to sacrifice it. The customary sites of urban exchange attested to long-standing traditions in urban trade; yet, locations
aside, much about the late seventeenth-century city would be unfamiliar
to those who had known Potosí in its busiest days.

In contrast with the Potosí of the 1550s, when people and goods
flocked to the city, the city population dropped from the 1650s on. Further, silver production declined steadily. This chapter, in explicit contrast
to chapter 1's focus on the growth of the city, explores the reasons for
the decline and the decline's impact on urban trade and urban society.
The problem of dwindling silver production, viewed from the perspective of native Andean leaders as well as Crown and viceregal officials, is
the subject of the first part of this chapter. Ayllu Indians who owed service to the mita draft continued to try to escape it by fleeing or changing

identity. Given the intertwined nature of mita labor and Potosí history, the implications of this crisis reached not merely to the Cerro Rico, but more generally to the functioning of urban society. When Potosí became

a place of shrinking fortunes, people took any chance of wage labor, even when it meant breaking up a family or severing ties to an ayllu. Indigenous men and women increasingly sought labor on their own terms, not in Potosí but in cities like Oruro and La Paz or on haciendas.[2] Over time, the economic demands and opportunities of a city like Potosí had threatened the very identities (ayllu Indian vs. yanacona) through which the Crown organized its tribute and through which colonial kurakas gained their legitimacy.[3]

While viceroys pondered how to rescue the mita, and kurakas tried to maintain their ayllus, petty entrepreneurs in Potosí found it harder to profit as marketplaces and stores saw fewer customers. The dominance of the Gato reveals that Potosí's sites of trade were well established, and they still supported both indigenous and Spanish merchants in small enterprises. But, as the second portion of this chapter shows, tax records for pulperías suggest that the economic decline spurred by the mines affected urban trade. The official groceries were quick to close their doors in this era in order to avoid taxes. Thus the large-scale decline in silver production and its related effect on population did have a measurable negative impact on profits in the urban economy.

The extent to which the hard economic times affected city residents had much to do with social identity. The Crown had established theoretical divisions among people based on ethnic identity and, in response, most native Andeans devised methods to manipulate those identities when necessary. Yet the legal and economic status implied by colonial distinctions, such as yanacona or mita captain, did influence differentiation among the indigenous sector of Potosí. The seventeenth-century trade success of certain indigenous men and women is our focus in this chapter's third section, which explores the relationship between colonial identity, urban history, and economic opportunity. The interplay of personal and urban histories helped to determine how Potosinos weathered the silver collapse. By the late seventeenth century, the town was no longer filled with newcomers, but with residents who had personal and family histories linked to Potosí. While one sector of Potosí debated mita reforms, and poor mitayos fell into debt, Potosí hosted a core population of nonmitayo Indians and laboring Spaniards who defended property and economic interests. The seeds of differentiation had been planted in the sixteenth century; by the late seventeenth, the harvest was one of stark contrasts.

By the late seventeenth century, the mita had turned into a "money rent transaction" whereby mine owners received cash instead of able-bodied workers.[4] Silver production therefore slowed, since mine owners no longer had an incentive to invest in mining. For mine workers, the era of low yield meant it was more difficult to purloin choice nuggets of silver as a daily supplement to wages. Mita captain Diego Charca of Jesús de Machaca charged that in the time of Viceroy Toledo mitayos had many opportunities to retrieve silver, but "today the ores are very reduced."[5] Given these conditions, any Indian with the capital to buy his way out of the mita would hand over pesos instead of serving a turn. Some could earn such cash through wage labor, such as mining at Oruro, others drew on family wealth. The usual abuses of the mine labor in combination with falling profits increased incentives for men to flee the mining draft.

Thus the legendary treks to Potosí by mitayos and their families were smaller than they had been in the late sixteenth century. In 1661, mita captain Charca and his wife gathered for the start of the trip with fifteen llamas bearing cargo. Men gathered before him from various ayllus under his control. The Spanish corregidor of the region, don Antonio de Videante, compiled the roll call for the mita workers. The names of those men who failed to appear outnumbered the names of those who did. In the case of the ayllu Sullcatiti, three adult males appeared with their wives and their llamas laden with subsistence goods. Four additional men on the list, however, had fled their homes. Fellow ayllu members volunteered their supposed whereabouts: the valley of Quiyabaya, San Antonio de Esquilache, Chuquisaca, and the Valley of Pallca.[6]

For men like Charca, who were low-level leaders from the indigenous community, the absentees presented problems. During the sixteenth and early seventeenth centuries, these mita captains had enviable positions, as many were able to profit handsomely in Potosí's market. By the end of the seventeenth century, however, leading one's mitayos to Potosí became, in the words of one historian, "a source of displeasure and economic distress."[7] Tracking down the men who did not show up was a decades-old problem, but coupled with shrinking economic opportunities it was increasingly difficult. Low-level ayllu chiefs, known in Aymara as *hilacatas*, came to have the full-time job of seeking out these adult males from their urban and rural hideouts. If mitayos failed to show, the mita captains had to pay a fee, and many captains landed in debtors' prison. Some were unable to leave Potosí until they could satisfy their creditors. Nonpayment of mita rent also led to physical abuse, such as beatings and hanging by the hair, at the hands of Spanish officials.[8]

Maintaining control of mitayos who arrived in the city was a difficult task as well. In a well-known 1663 petition to powerful mining interests, don Gabriel Fernández Guarache, a kuraka from Pacajes, claimed that many mitayos fled the mines and in time, those who remained would "stray from natural origin."[9] Specifically, he meant that whole families shunned their communities for urban identities in the hopes of avoiding tribute payment and taxing mine labor. The misery spread beyond workers to their families as they felt compelled to enter the urban economy not from a position of strength, but as little more than indentured servants. "Not having any other recourse more respectable," he lamented, "they [the workers] sell and indenture their wives and children in private homes and in chicherías."[10] In the kuraka's telling, the poor conditions of Potosí mine labor coupled with the sector's struggling economy compelled male workers to become estranged from their wives and children.

This particular petition of Guarache's reached Spanish eyes during an era when miners' profits were down sharply, and kurakas combatted high levels of absenteeism. Given Guarache's position as a leader of native peoples, it was natural for him to complain to Spanish officials and miners about the effects of Spanish policy on the welfare of the community. He had to defend his inability to deliver the required number of workers. But Spaniards had heard complaints, very similar ones in fact, from leaders of mita contingents for over a century. The claim that mita abuses prompted ayllu members to abandon their home communities was not news. As early as 1575, don Juan Colque feared the undoing of community cohesiveness because his men on mita duty in Potosí strove to shed their ayllu identity to become yanaconas.[11] Likewise, evidence that economic forces pulled women into wage labor or into commerce could not have surprised Guarache or Spanish officials.[12]

The familiarity of these complaints obscured real differences between the 1570s and the 1660s. Colonial economic forces diminished native leaders' control over the mita. Moreover, the late seventeenth-century mita jurisdictions had shifted to zones based on the Spanish corregimiento instead of on native Andean regions.[13] Thus the sense of urgency that emerges in Guarache's descriptions is not merely the argument of a persuasive leader, but also evidence of Potosí's miserable state. Indeed, the ayllu experience of missing men and poor silver profits was emblematic of overall changes in population and silver production for Potosí.

By the 1650s and 1660s, Potosí entered a period of economic and population decline from which it would never fully recover (see table 10 in the appendix).[14] A decline in the population of the city accompanied the decline in silver production. The population height of 160,000 for the mid-century had dropped to 145,000 by 1660, and it fell between 15,000 and 20,000 persons per decade through the seventeenth century. By 1680 this number had dropped to 110,000. Only 73,000 people were said to live in Potosí in 1700. Though the population would experience a spike in the first decades of the eighteenth century—as high as 95,000—it dropped precipitously during a 1719–21 epidemic and never again reached 75,000 during the eighteenth century.[15]

In addition to the complaints of men like Guarache and Charca, the gravity of the Potosí situation weighed on the minds of viceregal officials. Assuming the solution to the problem was harnessing more laborers, King Philip IV aimed to revise current mita operations in order to boost production. He ordered a new mita charter and a *reducción general* for the sixteen mita provinces in 1650. This was, at heart, an indication that the Council of the Indies believed the mita could still function in its Toledan guise if only profits rose for the miners and abuses ended for native mineworkers.[16]

The viceroys in this era, Conde de Salvatierra, Conde de Alba, Conde de Lemos, and Conde de Castellar, were of a different mind—all stepped onto Peruvian soil convinced that the failing mita must be abandoned. Once they adjusted to their surroundings, however, the politics of silver and native labor either swayed their opinions or kept their hands tied. Most officials and miners in the Viceroyalty of Peru reacted to proposed innovations to the mita or attempts to count the native population with fear and anger. The result was a pattern of inaction or thwarted attempts at action over the next three decades. When Conde de Alba, viceroy between 1655 and 1661, appointed Fray Francisco de la Cruz to consider the possibility of a repartimiento in Potosí, de la Cruz's swift investigations discomforted the powerful mining interests. While in Potosí, de la Cruz died, allegedly poisoned by his enemies. The Conde de Lemos, during his rule (1667–72), declared successful reform of the mita to be impossible. Still, he refused to abolish the system without a royal cédula. His actions amounted to several orders, such as one 1669 decree that mita captains could not be held accountable for more mitayos than those with whom they had left their own province (thus they were not to pay fees for the absent ones). The corregidor of Potosí Luis Antonio de Oveido flatly refused to implement the viceroy's reforms. And, to the Conde's disappointment, Queen Mariana never produced the cédula he desired. By the 1670s, both the new king, Charles II, and the new viceroy, Conde de Castellar, determined to give new life to the flawed mita. Their plan increased the numbers of workers by extending the labor draft to new provinces. The spirit of Philip IV's 1650s cédula was alive.[17]

As the Crown had done with Toledo in the 1570s, it sought a great reformer to engineer a solution to the Potosí mita. And, indeed, in 1683 the viceroy of Peru, the duque de Palata, put himself to the task. As he mused over the mita problem, he observed that miners and officials had complained about the state of mita labor in Potosí for the previous fifty years, but their reactions only made a bad situation worse. The duque explained, "The decline of the Potosí mita became apparent; to fix it [they] tightened and repeated the demands against the poor Indians who suffered the duty; with the demand, more Indians went missing, and shrinking to such a small number that the mines of Potosí to whom señor don Francisco de Toledo had assigned four thousand mita Indians, came to have only 1,400."[18] Though miners had successfully lobbied the Crown for as much indigenous labor as possible, their efforts had precisely the result described by the duque de Palata and lamented by men like Charca and Guarache—the labor force of the mita had become a shadow of its former self.

The viceroy ordered a new census of thirty administrative divisions, the *corregimientos*, in Upper Peru to determine the exact number of men eligible for assignment to the mita at Potosí. Census takers carried out the population count between 1683 and 1688. The most shocking revelation of the census was the high population of nonayllu Indians known as *forasteros*, 75 percent in some districts.[19] Technically, forasteros were not eligible to serve in the Potosí mita. These findings made it plain for all to see that officially designated colonial identities had outgrown the Crown's plans for harnessing labor and production. Palata ordered an end to the legal distinction between regular tribute-paying ayllu Indians and those who did not pay regular tribute, such as forasteros and yanaconas. Protest about the new reform caused such uproar that the Crown refused to support the idea.[20] In the end, Palata could not repeat Toledo's achievement; the miraculous production of the 1580s and 1590s never materialized in the 1680s and 1690s. For their part, native leaders came away from these decades without concrete reforms to help meet tribute demands or renew community identity.

The stormy transatlantic debates about mita reform seemed far from sites of urban trade in Potosí. In the late seventeenth century, bakers like Juan de la Sierra and the widowed doña Mariana de Uzeda Zedillo turned out bread for the city's residents.[21] At Ana de Saldana's pulpería, customers could buy eggs at a price of two for one real, while a pound of cheese sold for two reales. Shoppers could also find oil and honey, each at one real per measuring cup.[22] Just like the market stalls in the Gato, these sites of trade dealt in necessities that people bought even in hard times. With their focus on subsistence goods, markets, pulperías, and chicherías stayed the course of the wavering silver economy.

But if daily trade continued, its pulse had weakened. Signals of the impact of economic decline on petty trade are visible in the value of store rentals during the late 1650s. In a 1657 dowry, the parents of doña Juana Antonia Hordones de la Marquina noted the significant decline. They had planned to dower their daughter with, among other things, a Potosí property on the Calle de las Mantas that consisted of a residence and five stores. At the time of doña Juana's marriage, they lamented, the entire property was only worth twenty-four thousand pesos "because the rents in said Villa are in decay."[23] Signs of economic pressure also appear in late seventeenth-century work agreements. The wives of mitayos, at least from Guarache's province, could no longer make money collecting valuable tailings for refining or running profitable trade enterprises. Instead they served chicha in drinking establishments that he nearly equated with houses of prostitution when he cited the women's exposure to the "sensual appetites of all classes of people."[24] Guarache's claim that mitayos indentured their wives in chicherías was not off the mark. As we saw in chapter 3, the chicha sector became profitable for female chichería owners but exploitative for chicha brewers.

An even more significant clue to the impact of falling silver production comes through pulpería tax records from the 1650s. Don Melchior de la Valgama served as a royal tax collector for pulperías in Potosí during the 1650s.[25] As part of his work, de la Valgama kept track of stores that had closed or changed hands, facts critical to clarifying that he was not responsible for the taxes on those particular stores. All eight reports that he submitted to the local government listed at least thirty stores that had closed.[26] In some instances, pulperías closed and reopened with new business. A store in the house of baker Joan Ruíz de Porras became a coca store. Alternately, a store was transformed into a residence, as was the case with the store next to the Recojidas convent.

It was more common for the stores simply to close, rather than transform into other businesses. For instance, de la Valgama visited the Crown pulpería owned by Juana Payco in the Tiopampa. She had closed her store during five of the eight visits.[27] The constant opening and shutting of Payco's stores between 1652 and 1654 likely reflected the rental market. If no one was renting her store, she "closed" to avoid paying its taxes. Another store that de la Valgama declared closed was the pulpería of the captain of the yanaconas, don Francisco Cusi Paucar. De la Valgama listed the same property as closed in October 1651, April 1654, October 1654, April 1655, and November 1655. The store apparently opened during 1652 and 1653. In all likelihood, Cusi Paucar himself rarely operated the store. For example, he and his brother, don Juan Cusi Paucar, rented the store to the licenciate Pedro de Zerbantes in February 1649, who then leased it to Diego de Mena Pizarro and doña Petronila de Guevara.[28] If business dropped off as mitayo contingents dwindled or neighborhood residents moved away, Cusi Paucar might not have been able to find a renter for the store. He, like other storeowners, reasoned that in the absence of a renter it was ill-advised to pay the tax, and he notified de la Valgama of his intention to close, maybe at the very time the collector approached the door to the store.

These closings appear to reflect shrinking trade at the middle level of commerce (not the lowest, such as street markets, or the highest, like merchandise stores). Other scholars of pulperías are careful to warn that the closing of these groceries, generally unstable economic enterprises, should not be read as signs of economic change.[29] Yet if a population of 160,000 dropped with each passing decade after 1650, one can imagine that the number of grocers needed to support the city would be in decline. Moreover, tax records from the 1650s indicate a significant degree of instability for individual storeowners as they responded to the beginnings of silver decline. At the very least, the closings offer a window on the increased uncertainty of this sector of trade in Potosí. Moreover, they suggest cunning on the part of the owners, who closed to avoid taxation during temporary periods of economic contraction, population decline, or neighborhood transition.

Pulperías, though perhaps in smaller numbers, continued to be fundamental sites of exchange for food, alcohol, and credit. Visitors who strolled through the city in the last decades of the seventeenth century would find Spaniards like Lucas de Botes running a pulpería on Shoemakers' Street in the city center.[30] Doña Ana Jacinta de Vargas ran a similar property in San Lorenzo. Vargas's tenure as the operator of the pulpería was fairly stable in 1666, when she was able to prepay fifty-six pesos of rent for 1667.[31] Moreover, she went on to purchase the property from Simón Paytan on 12 August 1687.[32] In 1681, Salvador de los Ríos, a free mulato, showed similar stability when he agreed to a four-year contract to rent two stores and a chichería from Joseph de Atienza at 150 pesos per year.[33] As a whole, the city needed the small groceries, so the cast of characters who ran official pulperías and range of locations where they could be found had expanded greatly since the early 1600s.

De la Valgama's lists reveal that by the late seventeenth century, ruling bodies (like the Crown and town council) had expanded their idea of who might run an official taxpaying pulpería. The lists include men and women, both Spaniards and Indians, who owned and operated these official pulperías. The lists also identify some surprising locations. Juana Payco's store in the area known as Tiopampa is an example of how predominantly indigenous areas of town, once off limit for official taxation, could now host official pulperías. This area had been on the periphery, both physical and social, of sixteenth-century Potosí. Seventeenth-century growth of the Spanish downtown, however, impinged on the space in San Bernardo parish. As a result, some of San Bernardo's indigenous population was pushed toward the Tiopampa making it into a regular city neighborhood.[34] The growing number of indigenous men and women in de la Valgama's tax lists for the 1650s, as well as the situation of a royal taxpaying pulpería in the Tio, suggests that the Crown acquiesced to organic changes in the operation of groceries so as to focus on collecting taxes.

Petty grocers enjoyed a reprieve from scrutiny in the latter half of the seventeenth century. After 1650, the council debated the nuisance and danger of taverns and stores on five occasions, while prior to 1650, they had discussed sites of trade more than twenty times.[35] Rather than read this difference in emphasis as a sign that prior council regulations had succeeded or that petty traders operated as the council rulers wished, the entrenched practices of the trading world suggest that the difference stemmed from the council itself. The specter of indigenous workers frittering away the workday by drinking, raised so prominently in chapter 2 by María Sissa's objection to the neighborhood pulpería in the 1630s, had become less threatening in times of economic decline. The emphasis in regulating these small urban operations shifted from concerns such as store location and alcohol consumption to tax collection. Owners could be Spanish or indigenous, male or female. And, the stores opened freely in areas once outlawed by regulation. This drastic change marked a determination, not to open commerce for the sake of stimulating urban trade, but to boost revenue.

When, in the final days of 1655, de la Valgama asked to be excused from his civic duty, he cited "illnesses and great lack of health." Though he spoke of personal afflictions, he could easily have been speaking of the urban economy. If the store closings show people's responses to immediate factors, other developments in the urban economy suggest a response to more entrenched economic realities. The contractions in the larger economy made for consolidation of urban resources among fewer people, and as we see in the final section of the chapter, identity within urban society signaled who had the best chance to take advantage of remaining economic resources.

"THE CONVENIENCE OF SETTING UP A PULPERÍA"
ETHNIC IDENTITY AND URBAN TRADE

The connection between identity and economic status became particularly marked among the indigenous population in Potosí in the mid- to late seventeenth century. Who owned property and was thus able to open a pulpería? Who had connections to rural suppliers in order to fill urban storehouses with grain or coca? Who had credit networks in the city that allowed them to invest in urban businesses? As in the sixteenth century, one's identity (man or woman, Indian or Spaniard, kuraka or mitayo) had a connection to success in the urban economy. The contrast between haves and have-nots had always been a characteristic of Potosí's urban society even during times of silver bonanza. The late seventeenth century was distinct in two ways. First, the absence of silver extras from which sixteenth-century laborers benefited made this divide more rigid. Second, the social transformation of the colonial city meant that the identities of Potosinos were more complex than they had been a century earlier.

Here we compare the economic position of non-elite indigenous women, mitayo captains, and yanaconas. Many regular tribute-paying Indians suffered the fate of Guarache's broken families with wives and children farmed out to spots in the urban economy. In time, the women sought to distance themselves from their tribute-paying status by taking on identities as urban yanaconas. In contrast, for certain mitayo contingents, and in particular their enteradores, it was important to emphasize their identity as labor tributaries of the Crown. The historical link between their communities and the labor of the Cerro Rico helped them preserve property and related income potential in the rancherías of Potosí. Finally, in the case of families who had nurtured ties to the city for decades, the urban economy of the late seventeenth century still afforded economic status.

The advantageous opportunities, both economic and social, of the 1550s or the 1580s and 1590s that helped even those on the lower rungs of the social hierarchy had all but disappeared. Indigenous women who previously gained quantities of silver through their proximity to the mining trades increasingly lost that chance. Stories like those of the guayra (smelter) named Isabel became rare, indeed.[36] Isabel had earned a tidy sum for herself in the early days of mining in Potosí and made a legal donation of three bars and one piece of silver to her son Francisco. Such donations by indigenous women were virtually nonexistent for the 1650 to 1700 period. A changing social climate in Potosí limited yet another channel through which indigenous women might gain a degree of economic status. In late sixteenth-century Potosí, many indigenous women labored for Spaniards, and subsequently married them or bore them children. In a representative example, Catalina Canicha and Luis de Murcia, though never married, had a son together. While their son, Gerónimo de Murcia, died at a young age, Luis de Murcia acknowledged his obligation and gratitude to Canicha through a legal donation of a plot of land and a small farm.[37] Similar economic benefits to non-Spanish women decreased in the seventeenth century as the population of Spanish women in the city grew.

Women who felt these economic pressures, especially the wives of poor mitayos or single or widowed women, had few options. Don Guarache's claims about women in chicherías and child servants are echoed in other historical records of this era. Women began to act independently to seek out urban labor opportunities for their children, especially boys. While this practice had happened through de facto, informal agreements in the past, after 1620 the number of contracts for young apprentices rose. In November 1659, Juana Colquema and her ten-year-old son Pedro Porras went before notary Juan Pérez with the master guitar maker Pasqual Guarache.[38] Colquema, born in the nearby village of Puna, was a servant in Potosí, a position that could have provided space and nourishment for a baby and infant, but not for a young boy. Colquema apprenticed her son for three years to Guarache, who in turn pledged to feed and clothe the boy and care for him when he was ill. Urban indigenous women commonly made contracts to hire out their children.[39]

If women were economic actors in these cases, they were also, as

Thierry Saignes has noted, "agents of change."[40] The Pacajes leader don Gabriel Fernández Guarache believed that women who sought out these contracts for their boys meant to abandon native ayllus as well as the labor and financial responsibility they owed them. He charged that "widowed and single indias go and take leave of their towns and provinces with their children, and they move away to populous places, *villas* and cities, where they become cofradas."[41] Once in the city, they changed their dress, spoke in Spanish, joined cofradías, and apprenticed their sons to one of three types of tradesmen—blacksmiths, tailors, or shoemakers. The Spanish artisans, eager to protect their labor, Guarache continued, taught the boys "to say they are sons of yanaconas, and they defend them and protect them."[42] Thus some indigenous women confronted economic challenges by taking the path Guarache described, and their response added to the social transformation of urban areas.

Claims by Guarache and other native leaders emphasized the loss of mitayo community and ayllu identity wrought by poor mining conditions. This is but a part of the total socioeconomic picture in a complex place like Potosí. Here the growing yanacona population coexisted with mita communities that had deep urban roots. Despite Potosí's large and ever-shifting population, the town was very much divided by people's identification with their pueblos of origin, or even with those of their parents and grandparents. Potosinos put into practice a double-sided identification system that allowed them to identify kindred spirits through neighborhood or regional origin and to distinguish outsiders, those from other sectors of Potosí or from other areas of the viceroyalty. Thus, social networks in the rancherías had a rural component that could help newcomers find places to stay, and stores where they might obtain goods on credit. The continued social renewal from rural areas contributed to a vital social dynamic in these mitayo communities.[43] The members and their leaders, the enteradores, had vested interests in both property and commerce in the city. Legal cases from the late seventeenth and early eighteenth centuries reveal how leaders consciously invoked their mita service to defend those interests.

In 1700, Santo Paredes inherited a ranchería property from his mother, the widowed india María Mullo.[44] It was a store located in San Lorenzo, commonly known as Munaypata. Situated near the Gato de las Indias, it clearly served as an important center of urban trade. In her will, Mullo stated that she had lent the store to mitayos from Guayllamarca as an act of kindness. Not only did they not pay rent, but Mullo hinted that they showed little gratitude, as they refused to do upkeep, such as repairing the walls and recovering the straw roof.[45]

The Guayllamarcas took exception to this version of events, made public when Santo Paredes attempted to take over the store. Don Andrés Navarro Marca, the governor and mita captain of the Guayllamarcas, challenged Paredes's ownership in court. In the late sixteenth century, Navarro related, mitayos from the villages of Totora and Guayllamarca, both located in the Carangas province, had received San Lorenzo property assignments from Viceroy Toledo.[46] Over time, they created a community of core residents who hosted visiting mitayo laborers as well as kin visiting the city for trade purposes. Navarro offered no evidence to prove his case, but he relied heavily on the historical place of the mitayo properties in Potosí history.

Paredes, in contrast, told a tale that acknowledged sixteenth-century land distributions but relayed them in terms of individual, not community, property. He traced the history of the store to his great-grandfather don Diego Guaguamollo, who he claimed received the lot during the sixteenth-century and constructed buildings on it.[47] Guaguamollo willed the property to his son don Pedro Caque, who in turn left it to his daughter María Mullo. Mullo's will was the only documentary evidence presented in the case. This written material convinced local judges to grant possession to Paredes, and forced Navarro to appeal.

The appeals stage brought new evidence—and new interest in the property. To Navarro's disappointment, the leaders of adjacent ranchería communities, the Totora and Curaguara, placed an additional claim on the property. These new complainants emphasized that a community-based sense of ownership was most appropriate for the property in question. As ninety-year-old Juan Mamani understood from his father and grandfather, "for many years the Indians from the village of Totora, along with those of Guayllamarca and Curaguara, who are all from one *repartimiento* generally lived and possessed the *ranchos*."[48] This view quashed Santo Paredes's individual claim to the property. But, it also disputed the supreme right of Navarro to the rooms and store.

As the head of mitayos from Guayllamarca, Navarro stood to gain the most from running a pulpería. Men in his position, or their wives, often controlled the seat of commerce for those mitayos in Potosí. Many teetered on the edge of financial ruin because they were responsible for fronting large sums of money to Spanish officials if their workers did not meet quotas. Profits from regional trade or from a general store or tavern often provided the difference between a successful and an unsuccessful tenure as a captain. Navarro himself called attention to the commercial potential of the property during the appeal process. He presented no evidence against the Totora and the Curaguara, except his impassioned charge that "the curacas and enteradores of Totora maliciously claim rights to the said three rooms in order to have the convenience of setting up a pulpería in the room on the street corner."[49]

Navarro did find additional evidence to argue against Santo Paredes. Witnesses in the appeal suggested that Paredes's mother, María Mullo, was not a Totora Indian because she had been born in the province of Cochabamba, and that she therefore had no claim to the property. This "foreign" birthplace would not always have been interpreted as a complete severing of ties to her family's ayllu. But, playing on fears that Indian Potosinos were being transformed into yanaconas, Navarro ignored Mullo's ancestral ties and made a winning case based on the power of a mitayo identity within Potosí's history. Navarro and his kurakas regained the cornerstone of their social and economic domain in Potosí as well as "the convenience of setting up a pulpería."

Navarro won the case, but who really owned the pulpería in San Lorenzo? The extant documents do not provide a wholly convincing answer. Instead they reveal that mitayos and their enteradores kept alive urban communities even after decades of struggle against the mita. And, their members felt compelled to fight for emblematic and economic pieces of those communities, such as the store. Moreover, the Paredes-Navarro case highlights the complexity of urban indigenous identity in property claims. Mitayo and ayllu identities were more legitimate than other, "outsider" indigenous identities. Though Mullo had clear ancestral ties to Guayllamarca, she had been born in Cochabamba. Paredes learned that despite his mother's claims to belong to an indigenous community, migratory choices had invalidated those claims before the high court.

The yanacona portion of Potosí's population offers equally compelling evidence that identity and historical connections to Potosí helped certain indigenous residents weather the failing economy. The industrious trading career of doña Sevastiana Cusi Paucar exemplifies both the crucial role of family networks in trade success and the role of the native elites in the local economy.[50] In the last decades of the seventeenth century, Cusi Paucar had contracts with indigenous brewers who provided her with chicha, she dealt in bulk amounts of coca with local vendors, and, late in her career, she set up a wax business with Baltasar de Lemos. Moreover, she was a creditor for people who wanted to start trades, like don Bartolomé

Choqui Guaman who took 263 pesos from her to set up a business transporting wine.[51] She likely had her hand in other business ventures as well, given the more than 1,900 pesos she was owed at her death.

Cusi Paucar's blood and marriage relatives situated her at the intersection of power in the Potosí indigenous and mining communities. She was born to the captain of the yanaconas, the cacique don Francisco Cusi Paucar, and eventually married the captain major of the mitayos, don Juan López del Portillos.[52] Her kin played a crucial role in the political life of the nonayllu indigenous elite in Potosí and parlayed this into commercial success over time. The Cusi Paucar family was prominent in Potosí from at least as early as the 1580s.[53] In 1611 don Fernando Cusi Paucar, brother of don Francisco, held the position of cacique and captain of the yanaconas.[54] In 1620, Diego Quispe, a Yauyo Indian, identified himself as a yanacona of the king, subject to the captain don Francisco Cusi Paucar.[55] The family's prominence lasted throughout the seventeenth century. For instance, when resident Isabel Choquima wanted to identify the location of her home in her 1695 will, she specified that the house sat in front of the San Sebastián church and next to the home of the Cusi Paucar family.[56] It was of no small significance that the family owned property in San Sebastián, otherwise known as *el acagato*, a busy site of commerce in the rancherías across the Ribera. The links between the family's social and political roles in Potosí and their economic ventures are clear.

For doña Sevastiana, this provided the foundation for her petty businesses. Cusi Paucar's career reflected the patterns of a successful female trader in seventeenth-century Potosí. She had important family connections to the city and its indigenous population, she fostered relationships through goodwill loans and brokered numerous pawns, and she diversified by dealing in traditionally indigenous products, like coca, as well as those with a multiethnic following, like chicha. Don Francisco Cusi Paucar's pulpería, oft-closed in the 1650s, had become one of many properties doña Sevastiana Cusi Paucar controlled. Independently, doña Sevastiana owned a large home on the Calle Larga, which she rented out. Furthermore, she lived and headquartered her trade endeavors in a house, a guitar store, and pulpería in the San Pedro parish (adjacent to the busy San Sebastián parish).

The estimable urban property holdings and trade ventures of Cusi Paucar show that indigenous families became institutionalized in Potosí's world of trade. This adds an important comparison to examples of Spanish families that dominate economies in urban areas. This is a case of a yanacona family, but it is important to note that a variety of indigenous men who served in positions of social or administrative power, such as kurakas and enteradores, had the chance to prosper and pass their wealth on to their children. Cusi Paucar, of course, also adds a female face to the multigenerational trading families. Given the latitude for women within Potosí's world of trade, the daughters of native elites drew on the inheritance of goods and of status to emerge as important traders.[57] The combination of elite native status and women's urban enterprising led to a legacy of trade that moved from one generation to the next.

Even in apparent decline, Potosí was a major metropolitan area whose markets continued to move goods in large, albeit lesser, quantities. A select few families transported goods, extended credit, and owned stores that kept trade in motion at its reduced pace. The sustained prosperity of the Cusi Paucar family reveals the critical link between elite ties, like the yanacona status of the Cusi Paucars and doña Sevastiana's marriage to a mita captain, and economic well-being throughout the seventeenth century. Mita captains, like Navarro, still stood a chance to gain a corner store and to profit through trade. Potosí did not, however, offer the economic opportunities it had in an earlier era, and its economy exhibited a sharp divide among indigenous residents. For mine laborers and their wives and for some single women, economic pressures forced them to offer their labor for the most meager of wages. Under these circumstances many strove to be excused from tribute by blending in with the shrinking but ever more diverse urban population.

CONCLUSION

By the late seventeenth century, the Spanish phrase for a thing of great value, "vale un Potosí" ("it is worth a Potosí"), no longer resonated with the force of earlier days. Potosí's worth to its elite merchants, mineowners, and the Crown declined steadily with the drop in silver production during the second half of the seventeenth century. Peru's viceroys pondered this problem, but they never managed to move past theoretical discussions of mita reform to acknowledge once and for all the full failure of the Toledan structure. As mita reform stalled and sputtered for decades, production stagnated and Potosí residents and markets experienced the deprivations of a shrinking economy. Overall, Potosí was no longer a city of great opportunity and growth but home to a declining population and fortunes. Pulperías, owned predominantly by Spaniards, lost their rental value in the shrinking economy. Town officials remained eager to collect taxes whenever possible, and so officials legitimized stores regardless of who owned them or where they were located. Given the falling profits, however, owners often closed the shops to avoid taxation.

A thin silver lining still shone around the dark cloud overhanging Potosí's urban economy. Those merchants and traders who had diversified their economic transactions in the urban market found continued demand for their products. Indigenous traders, especially those with elite status, drew on community and regional resources to foster highly successful businesses in their neighborhoods. These successful entrepreneurs, like doña Cusi Paucar, prove how sectors of the active urban economy that had grown to support the mining city survived the chaos of plummeting silver production. These traders, however, operated in a changed economy.

The new reality of the frail economy exaggerated the benefits of native elite status and long-standing ties to Potosí's world of trade. Declining silver deposits made it difficult for mine laborers to continue smuggling valuable silver pieces to family members and into the town's markets. Mita families thus turned to exploitative wage labor opportunities for women and apprentice contracts for children. In this era of little silver, native leaders experienced increasing difficulty filling their mita quotas and maintaining control of those men they had chaperoned to the city. Yet mita leaders remained focused on the potential for urban trade; some, like Navarro, touted historical ties to Potosí's bountiful mining days in order to control trading sites. Yanaconas and elites more generally drew on generations of trade expertise and custom to help them succeed. If some enteradores were locked up in debtor's prison, and some mitayos' wives were indentured in chicherías, other indigenous men profited from commerce while their wives and sisters owned chicherías. In the final equation, identity in the colonial system and within Potosí's urban history had significant consequences for trading roles during the city's economic decline.

CONCLUSIONS

An economic and social institution from the sixteenth century on, the Gato de las Indias successfully held off a challenge in the seventeenth century by nuns who wanted to put a convent there. People had gathered to exchange goods and silver in the Gato well before Viceroy Toledo imposed a sense of order on the space in the 1570s. The marketplace was the centerpiece of commerce for metal, coca, food, and cloth. It revealed the economic vitality of the burgeoning silver city—and a unique blend of local indigenous and Spanish trading customs that challenged Crown mandates. But the Gato did not survive to the end of the eighteenth century. In 1758 the vendors moved their stalls to make way for construction on a new Casa de la Moneda. When the workers finally put away their tools in 1773, the new mint completely covered the site of the former market. The vendors and their goods had been displaced onto the much smaller adjacent Plaza San Lázaro. The volume of trade had already declined remarkably in the seventeenth century; the late eighteenth-century exchange of the marketplace for the mint symbolically concluded an era of urban trade history in Potosí.

The silver mines, Potosí's raison d'être, brought to life one of the most dynamic colonial cities in the history of the world. It is these mines and their home, the Cerro Rico, that historically have held the attention of Potosí's observers. Here we have shifted our view from the mines to the markets in order to glimpse the process by which city residents created urban society through transactions of trade. Nonetheless, the mines remain both context and background. The labor and economic relationships of indigenous, African, and Spanish Potosinos in the center of town were unique because of mining and mita. The world of mining influenced working opportunities, conditions, and identities for men and women who labored outside the mines. In this historical context, the seemingly simple act of a Spaniard using pesos to buy bread from an Indian woman in the market plaza requires detailed analysis. Information about economic forces and social identity is revealed by where such transactions take place, who engages in them, what colonial rules govern them, and what objects exchange hands. Potosí's urban economy was a site in which indigenous vendors had come to sell products like bread that were originally known as Spanish. Moreover, they named prices in pesos and they based modes of exchange on practices becoming customary in the city market: cash or forms of credit. Colonial economic forces influenced this exchange—forces that compelled an indigenous woman to earn money, even forces that fostered the production of the bread. The transaction also reveals much about people's social identities and their place in the world of trade: while the Spanish man might run a grocery, market sales were the domain of indigenous women. To bring these urban trade exchanges in from the margins is to enhance our understanding of the urban colonial world.

This book has argued that the everyday trading of Potosí's residents reveals the interplay between colonial social hierarchies and economic practice. Trade practices in Potosí show that the combination of large amounts of silver with an extraordinarily high population made for some surprising economic realities in this colonial city. The diversity of ethnic identities and of fortunes were unique to the colonial era of Potosí's history. Because of the makeup of this urban economy, people fashioned links between certain ethnic and gender identities and roles of trade. In the silver-rich world of Potosí, traders drew upon these connections in order to make profits.

HISTORICAL LESSONS FROM THE URBAN ECONOMY OF THE MINING CITY

Potosí's markets and stores emerged in response to colonial economic demands. Spanish masters coerced native laborers in their quest for silver. The mines' bounty apparent, fortune seekers of all types appeared in the city: they included immigrants arriving from Europe, Spaniards from other parts of the Indies, and kurakas and their ayllu members looking for tribute payment. The population demanded market goods, and thus the business of trade became a source of profit parallel to that of the silver mines. Potosí's marketplace reveals the world of trade as one where familiar figures appear in unexpected guises: Spanish men as poor laborers, Spanish females as enterprising businesswomen, indigenous men and women as both propertied and empowered. These historical actors rarely met with the rigid hierarchies imagined for the colonial world because the size of the population and the intensity of market opportunities created flexibility.

In an ironic twist, the Spanish-imposed labor and economic demands gave rise to an urban population and practices that clashed with idealized Spanish hierarchies and Crown rules. Although the town council and

Crown officials regulated with a particular idea of urban society in mind, their plans were thwarted by traders and customers who sold prohibited products in illicit places for forbidden types of payment. Trade exhibited people's inclinations to create their own economic practices however they could, legal or not. These actions represent the attempts of local peoples to negotiate colonial rule in piecemeal fashion as they pursued personal, family, or community agendas in the face of colonial burdens.

In carrying out their entrepreneurial plans, the city's traders affected Iberian mandates for the social structure of the city. Trade and trading sites show the Spanish "center" of the city was also populated by mulatos and Indians. While Spanish men owned most property, the diversity of Potosí's population ensured that no steadfast rules existed about ownership and rental: a Spanish man might rent a pulpería to a mulato and an indigenous woman might rent to a Spanish man. Spaniards did not limit themselves, especially economically, to the central "Spanish" section of town. Nor did they manage to keep African slaves from forging social and economic relationships with indigenous Potosinos. Of course the reverse was also true—indigenous residents of the city not only dominated the rancherías, but they also bought property and set up shop in the so-called Spanish section. Many market women who lived in the rancherías worked daily in a town center that housed elite families and government officials. They sold their products to Spanish women or to their African slaves. Spanish storeowners relied heavily on the labor of indigenous women to carry out the day-to-day commerce of their businesses; and Spanish women who ran chicha taverns entered into economic agreements with indigenous women to obtain their supplies. This urban economy simply could not have functioned without indigenous and African laborers and traders in the very center of commercial activity.

Ethnic seepage across Spanish/indigenous residential borders indicated changing social relationships. The very populace of the city contradicted Crown and local Spanish imaginings. The Crown's regulations on where Indians were to live signified, in theory, that the indigenous population of Potosí would comprise a small sector of yanaconas and a larger sector of mitayos who would stay only long enough to fulfill their turn in the mines. Yet the nonmitayo indigenous population was large and continued to grow in the seventeenth century. Moreover, mitayos did not return to their native lands once their turn in the draft ended. To the disappointment of Crown and kurakas, they, along with female relatives, sought work in Potosí's urban economy. They then branched out into new social relationships that challenged native ayllu identities and the Spanish categories of ethnic identity through which labor and tribute were designated. If Spanish colonial law endeavored to make certain geographic locations and labor assignments a reality for ayllu Indians, then the latter responded by taking on new social identities for themselves or their children, in particular those of yanacona or forastero, when necessary and possible.

In Potosí's early decades, people could rise through the cracks in social and economic hierarchies. Despite the forces within colonial rule that privileged Spanish males and a few indigenous elites, the relationship between gender and economic activity or between ethnic identity and economic activity (or a combination of the two) is infinitely more varied than appears in urban histories not focused on trade. Generally, this urban economy shows initiative by people to use colonial circumstances — and, more specifically, the unique circumstances of silver-rich Potosí — to try to meet or exceed demands on them. Their success needs to be read as more than a story about upward social mobility. For, despite economic and material comforts, indigenous women traders in Potosí lived among other Indians, dressed like other Indians, and had success as traders because they were indigenous. They sought and achieved the best economic outcomes from their enterprises, but they did not seek to climb higher on what we think of as the colonial social ladder and take on Spanish identity. I will speak first of the special indigenous experience in Potosí, and indeed the range of indigenous experiences in Potosí. Then I will discuss Spaniards and women in this urban economy.

The first few decades of silver production in Potosí were both a golden era and a dark age for indigenous men and women. More opportunities for indigenous profit existed in the early era for kurakas and for their subjects, as well as for their female relatives. Many took advantage of urban opportunities and many examples of those who profited emerge. They utilized connections to rural suppliers that took advantage of native Andean sociopolitical custom. They turned these into trading profits in the city by selling coca, chuño, corn, and cloth. Yet being Indian in Potosí's marketplace in the sixteenth century was also a great burden. Some Indians came eagerly to Potosí, not because they wanted to live in the large city, but because therein they saw the chance to earn wages necessary to pay tribute. Others, like Indians from Lipes, served mita service not in the mines but in bakeries and quickly become trapped in urban debt servitude. There were mitayos in the city for whom the majority of economic transaction was negotiated through their ayllu leaders. Other migrants kept up ties to ayllus while engaged in individual economic endeavors. The variety of economic statuses among the urban indigenous population is remarkable; so is their degree of individual economic engagement.

The picture of urban life with trade at the center complicates our view of urban Spaniards. Although their overall economic status was much higher than that of native peoples, in Potosí they, too, evidence a range of experiences not normally associated with the city of silver. Only so much room existed in the mines for silver seekers. Many Spaniards, and other Europeans, who hoped to become rich in the Potosí mines ended up seeking their fortune, or merely their living, in the world of trade. Laboring Spaniards thus appear to battle with indigenous traders about locations of trade in a town where their superior social status did not guarantee a superior trading position vis-à-vis indigenous entrepreneurs, who had kin connections to important suppliers.

Furthermore, the number of Spanish women who labored in the urban economy confirms the needy situation of laboring Spanish men, and of Spanish families that did not bequeath valuable inheritances. Being a Spanish woman in Potosí could mean a variety of lifestyles. Some elite Spanish women had few cares for engaging in trade. Others, though not reduced to engaging in trade themselves, rented their property as spaces of urban trade. Spanish women who owned slaves contrived arrangements whereby their female slaves earned pesos for the household through petty trade in the streets. And, finally, many women took up work themselves, running petty businesses. Women from any of these socioeconomic levels might turn to pawn exchanges to seek credit from time to time. Potosí's Spanish women traders shattered entrenched images of cloistered females, owning and running pulperías, pawnshops, large bakeries, and chicha taverns. The integration of Spanish women into this urban market is both surprising and telling. Spanish women needed to earn their keep, and Potosí offered spaces where they could do so.

The prominence of indigenous women in certain sectors of this marketplace meets a more common expectation. In the 1970s Elinor Burkett laid out plainly the economic role of urban Indian women. Ann Zulawski complicated this picture by emphasizing the difficulties for Indian women to live above subsistence level in other colonial cities. But both scholars clearly placed women in the urban market as prominent laborers and economic actors. This book reveals extreme differentiation in women's economic comfort levels in Potosí. It cries out, though, for Indian women to be recognized as entrepreneurs who gained both economic and social capital in their urban workaday worlds. The significance of these activities cannot be overestimated: indigenous women ran businesses with multiple functions. They supplied the city with food, drink, clothing, and credit. A minority of successful Indian women and mestizas forged profitable links to Spanish men. Still more indigenous women made money in the market while maintaining close economic and social links to indigenous men and women from their native ayllus or regions. Indeed it was precisely these kin ties that smoothed their access to popular indigenous products like coca, wax, corn for chicha, and textiles. And, surely, thousands of women labored at lower levels of the urban economy, finding only the most meager of recompense and never being able to initiate independent economic activity. Of special note for Potosí is that these poor indigenous women might well find themselves laboring as servants or chicha makers for enterprising indigenous women as easily as for Spanish women.

Since most men in Potosí worked in mine-related labor or as long-distance traders, this left ample space for women to operate in the urban economy. They had both the chance and the need to do so. Men generally supported women's economic endeavors, offering them credit for businesses. Women who could count on start-up support from husbands or other male relatives made the biggest gains. The source of such assistance varied from the sixteenth to the seventeenth century, particularly for indigenous women, who received less and less aid from Spanish men.

Fieldwork from the late twentieth century in Peru suggests that men denigrate women's work as market sellers, claiming that it is not real work: it can be done sitting down and is a task that can be carried out by children.[1] Yet in Potosí's early colonial market few male objections to women's work surface, with the notable exception of don Guarache, who complained not of women's work per se but of the alienation caused by their work. Even the town council acknowledged the extensive role of women in this sector of the economy, when it directed most market rules at the women vendors who challenged elite sensibilities. Many women made independent economic decisions, especially when using pawn to seek credit, and some female traders even envisioned hard-earned profits as their own, independent of their husbands.

COLONIAL POTOSÍ IN COMPARATIVE PERSPECTIVE

Given this level of participation and influence of both Indians and women, it is little wonder that if we look at two significant contributions of this work (non-elite credit networks and the chicha sector), we find unofficial and often non-Spanish initiatives behind them.

The remarkable credit networks that existed in the non-elite trading places of Potosí greatly revise our understanding of the colonial urban experience throughout Latin America. Potosí forced upon all of its residents, particularly native Andeans, an accelerated process of insertion into the monetary economy. The propensity of people to rely on peso exchanges and credit transactions to meet the economic demands of urban life set the city apart from others.

Since many Potosinos had no access to elite banking channels, they devised their own methods to deal with their daily need and use of pesos. For most households in Potosí, obtaining credit was often easier and more crucial than obtaining money. While the town council voiced concern that robbery fueled the market for pawn goods, daily practice by Potosinos showed otherwise. Though some residents found their social connections were enough to obtain a loan or credit in stores and markets across town, many others found that personal belongings and household goods helped them gain access to credit or food. Lending occurred back and forth across racial lines, though native Andeans favored transactions with one another, as did Spaniards. Women were the majority of pawnbrokers and customers, revealing women's major role as vendors of subsistence goods as well as women's social responsibility for providing food to families and, thus, their need to pawn goods at stores and markets. The extensive networks of loan and pawnbroking among non-elites show the parallel world of economic practice that existed along with the more traditional sources of finance: churches and convents.

In terms of regional comparison, the patterns of petty credit activities confirm anecdotal evidence of small credit transactions in other colonial cities. It also fits with studies of women's credit needs in early modern Europe and nineteenth-century Mexico. The distinctions that emerge here include women's predominance as creditors or lenders. Women in Potosí did not merely ask for money. They gave it out, especially among the indigenous population. Furthermore, the sums of money coming from grocery or other small business proprietors was more than one would expect in less prosperous colonial cities. Here again, the dynamism of the market in Potosí made a difference: it likely strengthened the confidence of traders, who might extend up to several hundred pesos' worth of credit. The unique range of items that stood as collateral reflected the ethnic makeup of the city. The tens of thousands of indigenous residents affected the goods that moved in the urban markets as well as the value of indigenous items. In Potosí, valuable items included silver pieces, in indigenous as well as Spanish form, and textiles of local and European origin. Spaniards as well as Indians in Potosí trafficked in and valued chicha, coca, textiles, and even silver drinking vessels. And pawnbrokers accepted such items with a colonial market value in mind.

Potosí's sizeable indigenous population contributed to the increasing trade in indigenous products. The role of Potosí in the trade of coca has been well documented, but urban trade in Potosí also reveals the rise of chicha as a colonial business. As with coca, this reveals a mix of indigenous cultural influence with colonial economic forces. The chicha business began in the 1560s and intensified in decades that followed. It involved flour growers and millers, both indigenous and Spanish, and numerous urban participants. The role of Spanish women as employers of chicha brewers and proprietors of chicherías, as well as the two-tiered production system that emerged, made the brewing and sale of chicha in colonial Potosí distinct from those in other highland cities. Indigenous women continued to dominate sales of chicha from small taverns in the rancherías, but Spanish women acquired chicha from indigenous brewers to sell from stores located in the center of town.

Not only did benefits from the production and sale of chicha extend beyond indigenous residents, so too did the practice of drinking chicha, judging from the popularity of the drink and the innumerable sites to consume it. "This is the port where so many mestizos, *sambos*, mulattos, and even poor Spaniards, arrive," claimed Doctor don José de Suero Gonzales Andrade, the vicar of the San Bernardo parish, and chicha, he followed "is the bread of them all."[2] Gonzales Andrade was writing in 1767, an era when chicha was no longer a profitable venture, and his missive aimed to convince officials to be lenient when taxing corn flour, so that indigenous women and poor people could earn their livings selling chicha. As the vicar portrayed them, these chicha sellers were pathetic, barely able to sustain themselves.

The predominance of female merchants in the early decades of Potosí's history fades from view in most writing on the eighteenth century. Yet as if they had been hidden away for a generation, urban women reemerged in the second half of the nineteenth century as successful entrepreneurs. Like their colonial counterparts, these female republican entrepreneurs dominated the chicha industry. The market value of chicha was distinct in colonial Potosí, as was its cultural value. These both shifted, and, when chicha reemerged as an important commodity in nineteenth-century Bolivia, it was linked exclusively to women known as *cholas*, a label that set them apart from rural indigenous women. Potosí's chicha business had energetic participation from urban Spanish women who, along with some indigenous women, came to dominate a two-tiered system of chicha production and sale. Criollo women (republican counterparts to Potosí's Spanish chichería proprietors) were absent in the reemergence. Of course the reemergence of chicha serves as a reminder that the economic context of the Andes had shifted. The business of chicha in republican Bolivia took place not in Potosí, but in Cochabamba, the region where the grain was produced.

The presence of these profiteering traders in the republican marketplace brought back both the status and the accusations that women had experienced in colonial Potosí. Representations across time of non-Spanish women involved in trade are remarkable in their similarity. In particular, profits earn women the reputation of being aggressive. The charges of Mateos from 1620 that female traders were "ferocious" and "bold regatones" are quite similar to stereotypes of chola market women in the late nineteenth and early twentieth centuries.[3] In addition to a reputation for aggressiveness, the success of these traders earned them insinuations of inappropriate sexual behavior.[4] When female traders specialized in the sale of chicha, their profits stood to be greater, but so too did the risk of tarnishing their reputations, a danger to which they continued to be exposed in the late nineteenth and early twentieth centuries.[5]

In early Potosí, then, we witness the formation of a specifically female identity linked to urban economy. This is a significant colonial legacy to women traders of the republican era. The decades of the 1550s through the 1620s in Potosí gave birth to a female non-Spanish urban identity linked to commerce. While these traders had substantial success in the market, their rise in fortune differentiated them from other urban indigenous women, and men, in ways that could cause tension. In addition, their marketing was aggressive enough to capture the attention of Spanish men as well, who viewed this as a natural part of their culture, independent of colonial society.

A GLANCE INTO THE EIGHTEENTH CENTURY

Whereas sixteenth- and seventeenth-century visitors to Potosí commonly remarked on the dominance of the Gato de las Indias, it was not the market but the new Casa de la Moneda that caught the attention of the itinerant Concolorcorvo when he wrote of Potosí in the late eighteenth century. The mint was, in his opinion, the only "lavish building" in the city.[6]

The new Casa de la Moneda represented attempts by the Bourbons to put a new shine on administration in the viceroyalty of Peru. In comparison to the late seventeenth century, the early eighteenth was a sunny economic spell in Potosí. The War of Spanish Succession (1700–1713) between the Hapsburg and the Bourbon dynasties busied officials on the Iberian peninsula. In the meanwhile, British and French ships sailed up and down the coast of Peru. Their desire: Potosí silver. In exchange, they offered luxury goods that Spain had stopped supplying during the war. Between 1700 and 1730, these ships spawned a small but measurable increase in Potosí's silver production. Enrique Tandeter has proved that out of this era emerged significant indigenous agency in the mining sector.[7] Though a severe epidemic passed through the region between 1719 and 1721, the viceroyalty as a whole experienced an economic upturn.[8] This growth, coupled with an increasingly threatening international scene for the Spanish empire, prompted Charles III to increase both taxes and the efficiency of tax collection.

One of the many areas affected by increased taxation was the business done by indigenous traders, of particular interest in Potosí because of the extensive trafficking by native leaders in products such as coca. In 1779, Bourbon reformer José Antonio de Areche decreed an end to alcabala exemption for natives because of the grave need to raise revenues in the viceroyalty. His tax proposals included a 6 percent tax on coca. These proposals represented a blow to indigenous profits. Though the Council of Indies officially disagreed with Areche's suggestions in 1787, evidence exists that taxes were charged to native Andean merchants, and certainly in the case of Potosí.[9] Thus, despite economic difficulties at the end of the seventeenth century, indigenous merchants remained a vital component of the urban economy in late eighteenth-century Potosí and comprised a major portion of potential taxpayers to the Crown.

In the years leading up to Areche's ruling on the alcabala, a fight had been in the making between indigenous merchants and the head tax collector of Potosí, don Manuel Maruri. When the collectors visited indigenous merchants, the latter reported that their gobernador had told them not to pay. "They have resisted paying the said royal tax," don Maruri charged, and he began to mount a legal case to document their responsibility for the tax.[10] Don Maruri argued that kurakas and mita captains had to pay the alcabala for any merchandise that they bought from Spaniards, even if such merchandise fell under the category of native products. Don Maruri questioned a number of Spanish witnesses to prove his point that mita captains and their deputies sold coca, ají, cotton, and native textiles they had purchased from Spaniards on the coast, in La Paz, or in the

Yungas. His witnesses also suggested that the captains and their deputies monopolized the commerce of these goods in stores, plazas, and canchas to an extent that no others could enter the business. Thus, if these indigenous merchants did not pay the taxes, no one would pay them for the city of Potosí, and this would cost the Crown thousands of pesos. In 1770, the gobernador, real audiencia, and viceroy emphasized, in keeping with Areche's ruling, that Indians could only be exempt from taxes for "those goods that are product of their labor, like the merchandise that they personally breed, farm, or cultivate."[11] Indigenous merchants had to pay taxes on any products from Spain or from Peru that they purchased from Spaniards with the purpose of reselling. But the legal case brought by don Maruri suggests that the indigenous merchants also constituted a considerable threat to Spanish merchants in the trade of indigenous goods like coca. Crown officials in the city set their sights on additional profits for the Crown through increased taxation, and harassment, of indigenous merchants.

In conjunction with the evidence from Potosí's legal records, a group of scholars studying 1793 alcabala records for goods entering Potosí concluded that indigenous merchants continued heavy trade to Potosí, and had to pay taxes on items like coca and locally produced textiles.[12] They also cited the verdict of Spanish merchants of Potosí in an early nineteenth-century economic assessment, "The Spaniard never prospers in a trade in which the Indian takes part."[13] While Spaniards profited handsomely from trade in various goods, they might expect an easier profit with brandy, the popularity of which soared in the 1700s, than with coca, owing to the different degree of indigenous participation.[14] Existing studies do not suggest whether these transport merchants continued to supply women traders in the city.[15]

Thus, it was in the context of increased silver production and taxation and continued trade by indigenous merchants that the symbolism of the new Casa de la Moneda emerges. According to some scholars, the obliteration of the Gato by the new mint represented the loss of indigenous dominance in the Potosí market.[16] After all, the indigenous population in Potosí for 1779 is estimated at 12,886.[17] With this drop in population and economic decline in comparison to the 1545–1650 period, it is difficult to suggest anything other than a period of economic stagnation for the urban market. But the Maruri case and the evidence from Tandeter's study suggest continued relevance for a sector of indigenous traders well through the eighteenth century.

When we bear this in mind, the placement of the mint on top of the market becomes less a sign of indigenous decline in the market and more a concrete representation of the Crown clamping down on local trading practices that conflicted with economic designs from the metropole. Since the earliest era of trading in Potosí, urban entrepreneurs had defied Crown forces over their trade. The Gato had hosted lots of silver trading, especially in the sixteenth century, all of which escaped taxation. In the Bourbon era, when the Crown was keener than ever to tighten its fiscal screws, the construction of the mint over practices and profits that had slipped through the cracks for centuries bespoke the tensions of colonial urban economic activity in Potosí.

The grand Casa de la Moneda eventually became a museum to showcase Potosí's history. The market shrank in size as its home in the plaza of San Lorenzo was gradually chipped away. If one wants to visit Bolivian markets today, then La Paz or Cochabamba are the ideal destinations to see dynamic displays of goods and energetic women traders buying, selling, and bartering. Visitors to Potosí instead trek through the tunnels inside the Cerro Rico, still mined, not for silver riches, but for yields of tin and zinc. Or they tour the exhibits in the Casa de la Moneda, without ever suspecting that they are walking above a site that was as dramatic in the sixteenth century as the Cerro Rico itself. Adjacent to the museum, in the inner patio of the mint, one finds the Archivo Histórico de Potosí. So it was that the original Gato de las Indias sat buried in archeological layers beneath me as I studied urban trade in the historical layers of the archives. In the 1990s, economic vitality lived on in the aging folios that had come to rest in the mint. Potosí's bountiful days had created a dynamic urban economy that represented the meeting of economic incentive and social custom. During an era when people made the most of the great run of silver and the innumerable trading opportunities that went with it, trading roles were not set in stone. Instead, Potosinos of every identity shaped opportunities in the urban economy to give trading places and practices a colonial identity while earning tangible profits in the process.

APPENDIX

(R) denotes a location in a ranchería.
(C) denotes a location in the city center.

Location	Trader's Name
Copacabana (R)	Soto, Beatriz de–Pulpera
San Cristóbal (R)	Nieto, Francisca—Pulpera
San Lorenzo (Carangas) (R)	Chamorro, Francisco—Pulpero
	Colquema, Juana—Trader
	Mullo, María—Pulpera
	Sissa, María—Home of
	Vargas, doña Ana Jacinta de—Pulpera
San Pedro (R)	Cusi Paucar, doña Sevastiana—Trader
San Sebastián (Acagato or Akakjato) (R)	Choquima, Isabel—Trader
	Cusi Paucar—Trading Family
	Figueroa, doña Juana de—Chichera
	Layme, Lorenzo—Chichero
	Padilla Solórzano, Diego de—Pulpero
	Rodríguez de Quiroga, Licenciate Domingo—Pulpero
Tiopampa (R)	Benítez, María—Pulpera
	Cachimbocllo, Francisca—Trader
	Lorenzo Hernández, Juana—Trader
near San Agustín (C)	Almendras, Sra.—Pulpera
	Benítez de la Vega, Pedro—Pulpero
	Payco, Juana—Trader
near Hospital of San Juan de Dios (C)	León, doña Michaela de—Pulpera
near Juego de la Pelota (C)	Martínez, Francisca—Pulpera
near Church of San Francisco (C)	Segovia, María de—Chichera

TABLE 5: *Property Transactions for Stores and Taverns in Notarial Records, 1570–1700*

Type	Number
Rental	195
Sublet	48
Sale	42
Will	34
Dowry	6
Inventory	3
Donation	3
Total	331

Source: AHP–CNM.EN, 1570–1700, extant volumes for every fifth year.

TABLE 6: *Number and Type of Store Rentals, by Ethnicity and Gender of Landlord and Tenant, 1570–1700*

Landlords and tenants	Pulpería	Chichería	Pulpería/ Chichería	Tambo	Tienda de coca	Pandería	Pastelería	Tienda	Total
Spanish landlords									
Tenant: Spanish men	67	6	3	4	1	1	—	57	139
Spanish women	18	3	2	1	—	1	—	2	27
Spanish couples	3	—	—	—	—	—	—	—	3
Indigenous men	3	1	—	—	—	—	—	2	6
Indigenous women	—	1	—	1	1	—	—	—	3
Indigenous couples	—	1	—	—	—	—	—	—	1
Mestizo women	—	—	—	—	—	—	—	1	1
African men	—	1	—	—	—	—	—	—	1
Spanish landladies									
Tenant: Spanish men	10	—	1	—	—	1	1	5	18
Spanish women	4	—	—	—	—	1	—	2	7
Spanish couples	—	—	—	—	—	—	—	2	2
Indigenous couples	—	1	—	—	—	—	—	—	1
Spanish landlords (couples)									
Tenant: Spanish men	1	—	—	—	—	—	—	—	1
Spanish couples	1	—	—	—	—	—	—	1	2
Indigenous men	1	—	—	—	—	—	1	1	3
Indigenous landlords									
Tenant: Spanish men	3	—	—	—	—	—	1	3	7
Indigenous landladies									
Tenant: Spanish men	2	—	—	—	—	—	—	2	4
Spanish women	3	—	—	—	—	—	—	—	3
Total	116	14	6	6	2	4	3	78	229

Source: AHP–CNM.EN, 1570–1700, extant volumes for every fifth year.

TABLE 7: *Number of Loan Transactions, by Ethnicity and Gender of Lenders and Clients,* 1570–1700

| | Spanish | | | Indigenous | | | Mestizo | African |
	Women	Men	Married couples	Women	Men	Married couples	women	women
Lender								
Spanish								
Women	29	51	1	22	11	4	—	1
Men	39	62	9	11	6	—	8	2
Married couples	—	13	1	—	—	—	—	—
Indigenous								
Women	3	17	—	53	65	6	5	—
Men	2	3	—	4	18	—	2	—
Married couples	1	—	—	1	8	—	—	—
Mestizo women	—	10	—	6	3	—	—	1
African women	—	—	—	—	—	—	1	—

Source: AHP–CNM.EN, 1570–1700, extant volumes for every fifth year. Twenty loan transactions refer to neither ethnicity nor gender and are not entered here.

TABLE 8: *Number of Pawn Transactions, by Ethnicity and Gender of Participants, 1570–1700*

| | Spanish | | | Indigenous | | | Mestizo | African |
	Women	Men	Married couples	Women	Men	Married couples	women	women
Lender								
Spanish								
Women	24	12	—	6	3	—	3	1
Men	39	12	—	1	4	—	6	2
Married couples	—	—	—	—	—	—	—	—
Indigenous								
Women	4	6	—	11	8	—	—	—
Men	2	1	—	—	—	—	—	—
Married couples	—	—	—	—	—	—	—	—
Mestizo women	1	2	—	1	—	—	—	—
African women	—	—	—	—	—	—	1	—

Source: AHP–CNM.EN, 1570–1700, extant volumes for every fifth year. Fifteen pawn transactions refer to neither ethnicity nor gender and are not entered here.

TABLE 9: *Number of Taxpaying Pulperos and Bakers, by Gender, 1599–1601*

Vendor	1599 N and (%)	1600 N and (%)	1601 N and (%)
Pulpero			
Men	84 (90)	41 (85)	26 (76)
Women	9 (10)	7 (15)	8 (24)
Total	93 (100)	48 (100)	34 (100)
Baker			
Men	14 (78)	10 (91)	21 (87.5)
Women	4 (22)	1 (9)	3 (12.5)
Total	18 (100)	11 (100)	24 (100)

Source: ANB.CPLA.

TABLE 10: *Potosí Silver Production, by Decade, 1561–1710 (in Pesos of 272 Maravedís)*

Decade	Peso Amounts
1561–70	20,730,974
1571–80	28,461,500
1581–90	63,456,500
1591–1600	69,244,686
1601–10	66,812,143
1611–20	53,711,925
1621–30	51,177,606
1631–40	52,429,286
1641–50	45,082,740
1651–60	38,561,481
1661–70	30,671,421
1671–80	29,847,359
1681–90	32,087,727
1691–1700	23,676,514
1701–10	15,460,828

Source: Data compiled and provided by John J. TePaske.

NOTES

INTRODUCTION

1. Lizarraga, 86. Translations from the Spanish are by the author unless noted.

2. "Relación muy particular del cerro y minas de Potosí y de su calidad y labores, por Nicolas del Benino, dirigida a don Francisco de Toledo, Virrey del Perú, en 1573," 366.

3. Ocaña, 187–88.

4. Ibid., 201.

5. Pedro Cieza de León, *Primera parte de la crónica del Perú*, vol. 26 of Biblioteca de Autores Españoles (Madrid: Atlas, 1947), 449; cited by Murra, "Aymara Lords and Their European Agents at Potosí," 232.

6. "Descripción de la Villa y minas de Potosí," 380.

7. To date, the late colonial era dominates studies on petty trade, but two recent studies promise to help configure our understanding of urban trade in comparative perspective. See Gauderman, esp. chap. 5, as well as Garafalo. For the republican era, historian Marie Francois analyzes the role of petty shopkeepers in credit transactions in nineteenth-century Mexico City, and Gina Hames studies the role of chola chicha vendors in Bolivian national identity.

8. I use the terms *urban trade*, *petty trade*, and *trade* interchangeably in the text. To clarify the parameters of the study, *petty trade* is defined here as the local buying and selling of foodstuffs, alcohol, and some clothing in modest pulperías (general stores), bakeries, chicherías (taverns), and outdoor stalls or markets. Long-distance traders, artisans like carpenters or silversmiths, and high-end merchants are not the main focus here. One of the first studies devoted exclusively to petty trade was *Petty Capitalism in Spanish America* (1987), Jay Kinsbruner's analysis of petty capitalism in late colonial urban areas. For analysis of the role of grocers in urban society in late colonial Mexico, see Martin. My work does not focus on the practices of middling and elite Spanish merchants, a subject aptly explored for Argentina by Susan Migden Socolow (*The Merchants of Buenos Aires*), and for Mexico by Louisa Schell Hoberman and John Kicza.

9. Capoche, 160–61.

10. Early studies by Gwendolin Cobb ("Supply and Transportation for the Potosí Mines, 1545–1640") and Lewis Hanke (*The Imperial City of Potosí*) confirmed the value of researching Potosí's intriguing colonial era, though they did not necessarily challenge the portrayal of the Indian as victim.

11. Murra, "El control vertical de un máximo de pisos ecológicos en la economía de las sociedades andinas."

12. Murra, "Aymara Lords and Their European Agents at Potosí," 231–43.

13. Spalding, *Huarochirí*, 16, 21, 35. For discussion of the mindalaes (long-distance traders) in Ecuador and pre-Hispanic markets in Quito, respectively, see Ramírez, "Exchange and Markets in the Sixteenth Century," 140–42; and Salomon, *Native Lords of Quito in the Age of the Incas*, 97. Salomon draws on Hartmann.

14. Assadourian, *El sistema de la economía colonial*, 136, 140.

15. The work of Luis Miguel Glave is notable here because it followed Assadourian's establishment of economic circuits in the region with a detailed analysis of the structures used by native Andeans to provision cities like Potosí. See Assadourian, *El sistema de la economía colonial*; and Glave, *Trajinantes*.

16. Larson, "Andean Communities, Political Cultures, and Markets," 20.

17. Assadourian's thesis on regional economy and Potosí as its central force assumed an important role in Andean ethnohistory. Several scholars built on its premise, but they took great pains to search for indigenous agency in the local contexts they pursued. In particular, see Larson, *Colonialism and Agrarian Transformation in Bolivia*; Spalding, *Huarochirí*; Stern, *Peru's Indian Peoples and the Challenge of Conquest*; and Zulawski, *They Eat from Their Labor*.

18. Representative of this is Spalding, "Kurakas and Commerce," as well as Stern, *Peru's Indian Peoples and the Challenge of Conquest*.

19. Work on individual economic dealings by native elites in Potosí includes Murra, "Aymara Lords and Their European Agents," and Rivera Cusicanqui.

20. Saignes, *Caciques, Tribute, and Migration in the Southern Andes*. On Andean ethnic identity in the sixteenth century, see Saignes, *En busca del poblamiento étnico de los Andes bolivianos*.

21. On the urban development of Potosí's town center and rancherías, see Gisbert, as well as Sordo.

22. In the colonial cities of Huamanga and Oruro, for example, commodification of labor emerges in the seventeenth century, while Potosí shows evidence of the same pattern by the 1570s. On Huamanga, see Stern, *Peru's Indian Peoples and the Challenge of Conquest*, esp. 143–46. On Oruro, see Zulawski, *They Eat from Their Labor*, esp. chap. 2, 59–60.

23. On differentiation among the indigenous population of Potosí, see Escobari de Querejazu, "Migración multiétnica y mano de obra calificada en Potosí, siglo XVI."

24. Bakewell, *Miners of the Red Mountain*. Spanish society comes into view in *Silver and Entrepreneurship in Seventeenth-Century Potosí*, Bakewell's second book on Potosí, based on the life of the wealthy mine owner Antonio López de Quiroga. The other leading studies of Potosí's mines are Buechler, Cole, González Casasnovas, and Tandeter.

25. Tandeter.

26. For discussion of indigenous credit engagement through the tribute system, see Greenow, 10.

27. Martin Minchom's study of colonial Quito, *The People of Quito, 1690–1910*, brings together a discussion of urban indigenous identity and petty trade.

28. Pioneering studies of credit in Latin America include Martínez López-Cano; Martínez López-Cano and del Valle Pavón; Quiroz, *Deudas olvidadas*; and Quiroz, "Reassessing the Role of Credit in Late Colonial Peru."

29. Of particular interest for this study is Brooke Larson's "Producción doméstica y trabajo femenino indígena en la formación de una economía mercantil colonial," which notes women's potential for gain in the profitable silver sector of the sixteenth century.

30. Archivo Histórico de Potosí–Casa Nacional de la Moneda, Escrituras Notariales (hereafter AHP–CNM.EN) 4, Martín de Barrientos, cuaderno no. 6, fol. 31v, will of Catalina Palla, india, 3 Sept. 1572. *Palla* signified noble status among the Incas.

31. On women in street markets, see Karasch. A more general view of street trade in Peru, including male peddlers, is Iwasaki Cauti. In the case of Mexico, of course, the image of market women dates to the preconquest era.

32. See, for example, Seligmann, and Buechler and Buechler.

33. Burkett, "Indian Women and White Society," 117. See also Burkett, "In Dubious Sisterhood."

34. Burkett, "Indian Women and White Society," 113.

35. Silverblatt.

36. Larson, "Producción doméstica y trabajo femenino indígena en la formación de una economía mercantil colonial," 180, 184.

37. Glave, "Mujer indígena, trabajo doméstico y cambio social en el virreinato peruano del siglo XVII." On this debate, see also Salomon, "Indian Women of Early Colonial Quito as Seen through Their Testaments."

38. Zulawski, *They Eat from Their Labor*, 156. See also Zulawski, "Social Differentiation, Gender, and Ethnicity."

39. AHP–CNM.EN 123, Pedro Bellido, fol. 374–75v, will of Francisca Nieto, muger soltera, 8 Aug. 1670.

40. AHP–CNM.EN 4, Martín de Barrientos, cuaderno no. 9, fol. 30–34: will of Leonor Sasytoma, india, 16 Oct. 1572.

41. Larson's 1983 article on Potosí points to the saliency of the theme of female credit transactions. Larson, "La producción doméstica y trabajo femenino indígena."

42. AHP–CNM.EN 116, Baltasar de Barrionuevo, fol. 20–20v, will of María Vargas, 11 Jan. 1654.

43. This refutes Burkett's claims that indigenous men chose between fleeing the Spanish and obeying them. See Burkett, "Indian Women and White Society," 119.

44. An interesting monograph by Kimberly Gauderman (*Women's Lives in*

Colonial Quito) insists that patriarchy is not applicable for discussion of power structures in Spanish America. Her distinctions between the British case and the Spanish American case are convincing and important, yet the significant power of males in both official and family contexts in Potosí is compelling. Here the definition of patriarchy that I employ posits men as dominant in controlling power and resources, but allows women room to maneuver in both economic and legal contexts. In this I am influenced by Bennett, *Ale, Beer, and Brewsters in England*, 156–57.

45. Select works on gender norms and resistance include Arrom; Lavrin, *Sexuality and Marriage in Colonial Latin America*; Seed, *To Love, Honor, and Obey in Colonial Mexico*; Stern, *The Secret History of Gender*; and van Deusen. On indigenous women under colonial rule, see the seminal Silverblatt, as well as Graubart; on Mexico, see the various approaches in Schroeder, Wood, and Haskett.

46. For an example of the former, see Van Kirk. The most remarkable example of the latter trend is Burns.

47. Just as Latin American scholars have noted indigenous women's presence in markets, they have also noted Spanish women's presence in other locales of petty trade. See Kicza, which notes that women were heavily involved in retail trade except at the highest level (101).

48. On England, see Bennett, *Ale, Beer, and Brewsters in England*.

49. On pawn, see Hunt, Ross, Stansell, and Tebbutt.

50. Thus I hope this work will contribute to discussions of women's economic activity such as Larson, *Colonialism and Agrarian Transformation in Bolivia*, chap. 10, esp. 366; Gotkowitz; and Hames.

51. See, for instance, the explicit discussion of peasant *ferías* in the second edition of Larson, *Colonialism and Agrarian Transformation in Bolivia*, 360–66.

52. On the matter of the alcabala and petty traders in Mexico, see Kinsbruner, 78; and in Quito, see Gauderman, 98–101, and Minchom, *The People of Quito, 1690–1810*, 105–8. See also Minchom, "La economía subterránea y el mercado urbano."

53. Jay Kinsbruner (55) used the term *petty capitalism* to describe the small-scale retail operations he studied in late colonial and early republican Spanish America and determined that groceries "presented the most extensive opportunity for people of limited wealth to enter a nonartisan, fixed-store commercial venture." The extent to which such ventures were profitable, however, was debatable.

54. Again, the work of Thierry Saignes is particularly helpful for thinking about indigenous economic activities in the context of ayllu structures. See Saignes, *Caciques, Tribute, and Migration in the Southern Andes*.

55. See Burkett, "Indian Women and White Society," 117; and Larson, "La producción doméstica y trabajo femenino indígena en la formación de una economía mercantil colonial," 184. For the development of this identity in the

nineteenth century, see Larson, *Colonialism and Agrarian Transformation in Bolivia*, chap. 10, esp. 366; Gotkowitz; and Hames.

56. Cahill offers a compelling discussion of Andean ethnic identity.

57. Kuznesof, 155.

58. Ethnic and racial labels used to identify Potosinos in this study include *criollo/a* (Spanish descent born in the Americas); *español/a* (Spanish descent); *indio/a* (Indian or indigenous descent); *indio/a ladino/a* (Indian descent but Hispanicized in terms of dress and language); *moreno/a* (dark-skinned, generally free black); *mestizo/a* (Indian and Spanish descent); *mulato/a* (African and Spanish or African and Indian descent); *negro/a* (African or Afro-Peruvian descent); and *peninsular* (Spanish descent born on the Iberian peninsula). For a general discussion of mestizaje in the colonies, see Mörner. On race and cultural identification in the mature colonies, see Cope; and Seed, "Social Dimensions of Race."

59. AHP–CNM.EN 91, Francisco de Urbilla, fol. 3061–64v, will of María Benítez, 17 July 1635.

60. Tandeter et al., 220.

61. AHP–CNM.EN 8, Luis de la Torre, fol. 1346–48: will of María Poco, 12 Dec. 1577.

1. "LARGEST POPULATION, MOST COMMERCE"

1. Summary of events as described in Archivo General de Indias (hereafter AGI), Charcas 134, ms. no. 1, dated 1603, fol. 1r–v. For other variations of Potosí's discovery, see also Bakewell, *Miners of the Red Mountain*, 8; Cobb, "Potosí, a South American Mining Frontier," 39–40; Hanke, *The Imperial City of Potosí*, 1; Ocaña, 184. For a thorough discussion of several primary accounts, see Ballesteros Gaibrois, 11–21.

2. Garcilaso de la Vega, 536.

3. Cobb, *Potosí y Huancavelica*.

4. Bakewell, *Miners of the Red Mountain*, 8–9.

5. Rostworowski de Diez Canseco, 80–81; Barnadas, *Charcas*, 17–19.

6. Arzáns de Orsúa y Vela, part 1, book 1, chap. 5, 27. Arzáns recounts the report of Guayna Capac's explorers some eighty-three years before the Spaniards' arrival.

7. Rowe, esp. 97–102.

8. See Murra, "El control vertical de un máximo de pisos ecológicos en la economía de las sociedades andinas."

9. Stern, *Peru's Indian Peoples and the Challenge of Conquest*, 6.

10. For a thorough discussion of the founding and early history of La Plata see Presta, 54. The exhaustive history of colonial Charcas is Barnadas, *Charcas*.

11. Rowe, 98.

12. On colonial yanaconas, see Murra, "Aymara Lords and Their European Agents at Potosí," and Spalding, "Social Climbers."

13. Acosta, *Natural and Moral History of the Indies*, 175; Bakewell, *Miners of the Red Mountain*, 14. On yanaconas in the late sixteenth century, see Escobari de Querezaju, "Migración multiétnica y mano de obra calificada en Potosí, siglo XVI."

14. Ocaña, 206. On the intense cold, see also Lizarraga, 86.

15. Lizarraga, 91.

16. AGI Charcas 32, Alonso de Herrera to "muy poderoso señor," 29 Oct. 1565, fol. 3r. Juan de Matienzo reported twenty thousand Indians living there a full decade before Toledo's arrival, cited in Padden, xxi. Lewis Hanke comments on the unreliability of population estimates for Potosí in Hanke, Prologue, 14.

17. Acosta, *Natural and Moral History of the Indies*, 173.

18. On the growth of Potosí, see Bakewell, *Miners of the Red Mountain*, 10–12.

19. "Descripción de la Villa y minas de Potosí," 374.

20. The first chapter of Peter Bakewell's *Silver and Entrepreneurship in Seventeenth-Century Potosí*, "Beginnings," provides a detailed description of the urban setting in colonial Potosí. Bakewell analyzes the difference between the indigenous rancherías and the Spanish city, suggesting that while the rancherías remained more "Indian," Spanish influence, especially through the Church, prompted Hispanicization. Through my analysis of trade, I argue that cross-cultural influence (Hispanic) moved from city center to rancherías with regard to control of pulperías, but, in addition, cross-cultural influence (indigenous) moved from ranchería to city center, because numerous Indian women and men worked in the "Spanish" section of town. Another description of urban Potosí can be found in Escobari de Querejazu, "Conformación urbana y étnica en las ciudades de La Paz y Potosí durante la colonia," 43–77.

21. Arzáns de Orsúa y Vela, part 5, book 1, chap. 2, 149, citing Cieza de León.

22. "Descripción de la Villa y minas de Potosí," 373. On these market plazas, see also Arzáns de Orsúa y Vela, part 5, book 1, chap. 2, 148–49.

23. Lizarraga, 89.

24. Town council records and wills routinely referred to marketeers using the feminine, such as yndias gateras, yndias fruteras, or yndias vendedoras de pan. Secondary literature on street vendors elsewhere in the Americas and Europe includes Hanawalt; Beckles; Graham; Karasch; and Perry, 18–19.

25. For a thorough discussion of how markets operated in colonial Mexico City, see Mangan.

26. Arzáns de Orsúa y Vela, part 1, book 1, chap. 1, 5.

27. Andrien, *Andean Worlds*, 81.

28. On corn, ica, coca, and meat, see AGI Justicia 667, ramo 1, no. 1, 1550 Polo's comisión, fol. 243r–v. On wheat, corn, and chuño, see AGI Lima 313, Fray Domingo de Santo Tomás, 1550, fol. 4v.

29. See the example of the kuraka don Diego Caqui cited in Cummins, 206, n. 30.

30. Ocaña, 186.

31. Lizarraga, 91.

32. AGI Charcas 32, Diego Pacheco de Chávez, corregidor and justicia mayor of Potosí, to the king, 5 Sept. 1565, extant folio 3r (marked 29r).

33. Bakewell, *Miners of the Red Mountain*, 41.

34. On long-distance trade, see Glave, *Trajinantes*; and Ocaña, 205.

35. Andrien, *Andean Worlds*, 86–87.

36. For delivery of goods, see AHP–CNM.EN 19 Juan Gutiérrez Bernal, 1590, fol. 2123, contract between Juan de Jaramilla and Diego de Mendoza.

37. On circuits of commerce between Cuzco and Potosí, see Escobari de Querejazu, *Producción y comercio en el espacio sur andino, s. XVII*.

38. Details on the marketplace are from "Descripción de la Villa y minas de Potosí," 378–83; and Ocaña, 197, 200–201. See also Cobb, "Supply and Transportation for the Potosí Mines, 1545–1640."

39. Acosta, *Natural and Moral History of the Indies*, 228.

40. On wine production in the Cinti Valley of Pilaya y Paspaya, see Bakewell, *Silver and Entrepreneurship in Seventeenth-Century Potosí*, 143; and Zulawski, *They Eat from Their Labor*, 51.

41. Larson, *Colonialism and Agrarian Transformation in Bolivia*, 46.

42. See Parkerson, which argues that this was not the case.

43. On the ill-effects of forced labor in the coca valleys on the indigenous population, see AGI Indiferente General 1239 ramo 2, no. 1, "Sancho de Valencuela responde a los capitulos que se le mando que respondiese de Luis Osorio de Quniones," n.d, fol. 1r.

44. Coca leaves play both a historical and a contemporary role in nutrition, ritual, and social interactions among the people of the high Andes. To understand this role for the colonial period, one must suspend all connections between coca leaves and the drug cocaine. Indigenous Potosinos chewed coca to bring out juices that offer nutrients and chemicals to help the body function at high altitudes. For Spanish opinion on coca consumption in colonial Potosí, see the analysis in Saignes, "Capoche, Potosí y la coca."

45. Garcilaso de la Vega, 510–12.

46. Larson, *Colonialism and Agrarian Transformation in Bolivia*, 45. On the inflationary prices, see Garcilaso de la Vega, 536.

47. Acosta, *Natural and Moral History of the Indies*, 210.

48. AHP–CNM.EN 4, Martín de Barrientos, cuaderno no. 11, fol. 19, contract between Miguel Choloyla and Juan Carrasco, 10 Dec. 1572.

49. AHP–CNM.EN 4, Martín de Barrientos, fol. 13, work contract between Diego de Gómara and Ynés Taquima, 12 Dec. 1572. A comprehensive study of clothing in the colonial Andes is Money.

50. Yanaconas dominated the occupation of guayra (smelting). See Esco-

bari de Querezaju, "Migración multiétnica y mano de obra calificada en Potosí, siglo XVI." See also Assadourian, "La produccion de la mercancía dinero en la formación del mercado interno colonial."

51. Garcilaso de la Vega, 538–39.

52. Bakewell, *Miners of the Red Mountain*, 17, citing Capoche, 111.

53. Stern, *Peru's Indian Peoples and the Challenge of Conquest*, xxxv. Brooke Larson also argues for economic autonomy of the yanaconas in *Colonialism and Agrarian Transformation in Bolivia*, 45.

54. Garcilaso de la Vega, 539.

55. Ibid. Even when refining was in Indian hands, Spanish mineowners were pleased enough with the profits they garnered. Though they failed in attempts to overtake the smelting business by turning guayra refining into a large-scale operation, mine owners did not invest in the new techniques of mercury-based amalgamation that had been used in Mexico since the 1550s. Only in the 1570s, when rich-grade ores were depleted (low-grade ores were not easily processed in the guayras), did mine owners put up the capital to explore other methods. See Bakewell, *Miners of the Red Mountain*, 18; and on the process of refining, both guayra and amalgamation, 14–22.

56. Archivo Nacional de Bolivia, Escrituras Publicas (hereafter ANB.EP), Aguila, fol. 88, legal donation, 23 Jan. 1559.

57. See Larson, *Colonialism and Agrarian Transformation in Bolivia*, 59, citing Capoche, 154.

58. Cole, 14. By the eighteenth century this practice developed into well-organized groups of ore "thieves" known as the kajcha, who made up an independent sector of those working the mines, see Tandeter, *Coercion and Market*, esp. 89, 95.

59. Ocaña, 190, 202–3. See also Bakewell, *Miners of the Red Mountain*, 141; and Tandeter, 89.

60. Acosta, *Natural and Moral History of the Indies*, 177.

61. Josep Barnadas analyzes both sides of the debate on rescate in "Una polémica colonial." For town council debate on rescate in the 1590s, see ANB. Rück no. 2, 29 Nov. 1596, fol. 3–3v.

62. This description of ore trading draws on Capoche, esp. 156, 160–61.

63. Platt.

64. Ibid., 236, 240.

65. AGI Charcas 32, "sobre que los yndios que biben en esta Villa para el beneficio y labor de las minas biben sanos," 18 Sept. 1565, fol. 26v, extant folio 3v.

66. Bakewell, *Miners of the Red Mountain*, 44.

67. On kurakas, also spelled *curacas*, see Murra, "Aymara Lords and Their European Agents at Potosí"; and Karen Spalding, "Social climbers."

68. Díez de San Miguel, 19; Bakewell, *Miners of the Red Mountain*, 57.

69. Cieza de León, 449, cited in Murra, "Aymara Lords and Their European Agents at Potosí," 232.

70. Matienzo, 23; my translation.

71. On this point see the work of Saignes, who suggests that kurakas generally maintained more control over urban Indians than they might admit to Spanish officials. Saignes also gives definitive evidence that some urban indigenous residents paid tribute to native ayllus through at least the late seventeenth century. See Saignes, "Indian Migration and Social Change in Seventeenth-Century Charcas."

72. Stern suggests that women used gendered means to ease colonial burdens. See Stern, *Peru's Indian Peoples and the Challenge of Conquest*, 170. For property given to indigenous and mestiza women by Spanish men, see ANB.EP, Aguila, legal donation, 28 Aug. 1559, fol. 860; AHP–CNM.EN 4, Martín de Barrientos, cuaderno no. 6, fol. 31, will of Catalina Palla, 3 Sept. 1572; AHP–CNM.EN 4, Martín de Barrientos, cuaderno no. 7, fol. 6, legal donation, 11 Dec. 1572.

73. For instance, in his study of Huamanga, Stern has emphasized a shift in the wealth of indigenous communities between the late sixteenth century and the early seventeenth century. From 1580 to 1590, he notes, communities were able to put aside up to thousands of pesos. By 1620 to 1630, however, many had coffers which barely covered basic needs. See Stern, *Peru's Indian Peoples and the Challenge of Conquest*, 91. In Potosí, indigenous residents agreed to wage labor contracts by as early as the 1570s.

74. Bakewell, *Miners of the Red Mountain*, 36; Escobari de Querejazu, "Migración multiétnica y mano de obra calificada en Potosí, siglo XVI," 71.

75. AGI Lima 313, Fray Domingo de Santo Tomás to Council of Indies, 1 July 1550, fol. 5v. The letter by Fray Tomás was likely a response to Polo's rosy report on the well-being of indigenous laborers in Potosí. The question of indigenous labor in Potosí mines sparked vigorous debate because the 1542 New Laws had forbidden the use of indigenous laborers in large-scale mining. See discussion of the letter in Bakewell, *Miners of the Red Mountain*, 43.

76. Bakewell, *Miners of the Red Mountain*, 26.

77. Larson, *Colonialism and Agrarian Transformation in Bolivia*, 55, citing Capoche, 135.

78. Arzáns de Orsúa y Vela, part 5, book 1, chap. 2, 148.

79. Larson, *Colonialism and Agrarian Transformation in Bolivia*, 56–57. On the use of barter in postconquest markets in colonial Quito, see Minchom, *The People of Quito, 1690–1810*, 177.

80. ANB.EP, Aguila, sale of mines by Beatriz, india, to Vasco Valverde, 1 June 1559, fol. 473v.

81. Andrien, *Andean Worlds*, 85.

82. Acosta, *Natural and Moral History of the Indies*, 175.

83. Larson, *Colonialism and Agrarian Transformation in Bolivia*, 43–45; Bakewell, *Miners of the Red Mountain*, 60.

84. Bakewell, *Miners of the Red Mountain*, 26.

85. Ibid., 59–60, 67, 70; Cole, 18.

86. "Relación muy particular del cerro y minas de Potosí y de su calidad y labores, por Nicolas del Benino, dirigida a don Francisco de Toledo, Virrey del Perú, en 1573," 366. Both Bakewell and Cole discuss mitayos at length in their work; see Bakewell, *Miners of the Red Mountain*, 82–134; and Cole, 9–12.

87. Larson, *Colonialism and Agrarian Transformation in Bolivia*, 63.

88. ANB, Cabildo de Potosí Libros de Acuerdo (hereafter ANB.CPLA), vol. 14, council regulations for slaughter of llamas, 21 Jan. 1615, fol. 74v.

89. The number expanded to eleven by 1585. See Capoche, 135–39; and Bakewell, *Miners of the Red Mountain*, 93.

90. Saignes, *Caciques, Tribute, and Migration in the Southern Andes*, 4.

91. Murra, "Aymara Lords and Their European Agents at Potosí." The capitanes enteradores de mita were almost exclusively male; however, in some instances it appears that a widow filled in for her deceased husband. See ANB.EC, document 1667.43, fol. 4, reference to doña Francisca Orcoma, capitán enteradora de mita.

92. The strategies of capitán don Diego Chambilla are discussed at length in Murra, "Aymara Lords and Their European Agents at Potosí."

93. Padden, xxiii. On churches, see "Descripción de la Villa y minas de Potosí," 378. For a study of the complex process of physical, religious, and social development of the rancherías, see Sordo.

94. Ocaña, 191; Arzáns de Orsúa y Vela, part 1, book 2, chap. 4, 42–43.

95. Bakewell, *Miners of the Red Mountain*, 94–96. For specifics on mine labor and mita in the sixteenth century, see Bakewell, *Miners of the Red Mountain*, and Cole. For a different view on living quarters, see Escobari de Querejazu, "Migración multiétnica y mano de obra calificada en Potosí, siglo XVI," 74, which speculates that Spanish rulers may have assigned living quarters in such a manner as to separate Indians from their fellow ayllu members.

96. *Francisco de Toledo*, 1:39. Provision by Viceroy Toledo, "Para que los indios que acudieren a comerciar en Potosí vivan junto con sus paisanos," Potosí, 12 Feb. 1575.

97. Bakewell, *Miners of the Red Mountain*, 77; see also 67, 75.

98. Ibid., 79, 101.

99. Acosta, *Natural and Moral History of the Indies*, 173.

100. AHP–CNM.EN 19, Juan Gutiérrez Bernal, fol. 1536–40v, will of Antón de Miranda, indio ynga, and María Alcapulco, india, husband and wife, 10 March 1590.

101. Capoche, 140.

102. AHP–CNM.EN 4, Martín de Barrientos, fol. 20, work contract between María Carrillo and Juan Barba, 12 Dec. 1572.

103. For population figures, see Arzáns de Orsúa y Vela, part 1, book 1, chap.1, 9–10; Padden, xxi; and Hanke, *The Imperial City of Potosí*, 1.

104. Arzáns de Orsúa y Vela, part 1, book 5, chap.14, 192–93.

105. AGI Charcas 415, book 2, cédula to Audiencia of Charcas, 7 Oct. 1581, fol. 34r–v.

106. AGI Charcas 415, book 2, cédula to Pedro Coras de Ulloa, corregidor of Potosí, 5 Feb. 1589, fol. 66r.

107. Fears about urban instability rose after a 1586 protest by mestizo soldiers. See primary source appendix in Barnadas, *Charcas*, 593–94.

108. AHP–CNM.EN 4, Martín de Barrientos, fol. 31v, slave sale, 24 April 1572.

109. AHP–CNM.EN 8, Luis de la Torre, fol. 150, slave sale, 24 April 1577.

110. ANB.Minas, vol. 123, no. 4, fol. 330, letter from the Real Audiencia of La Plata to the king giving its opinion as to the convenience of bringing slaves to Potosí to assist the mita Indians, 1 Feb. 1610. For a general description of Africans in Potosí, see Hanke, *The Imperial City of Potosí*, 33.

111. AHP–CNM.EN 8, Luis de la Torre, fol. 1204, will of Luisa de Villalobos morena, 25 July 1577. Known as a piña, this piece of silver was not minted, and thus bypassed the legitimate channels through which it was subject to the royal tax. See Bakewell, *Miners of the Red Mountain*, 22, and Tandeter, 4.

112. Mary Money describes a type of pre-Hispanic *jubón*, but generally in the Potosí documents the term refers to Spanish clothing.

113. AHP–CNM.EN 8, Luis de la Torre, fol. 706v, legal donation from Andrés Vela to Antona, negra, 21 March 1577. Notary records revealed few Spaniards recognizing children with Africans. Numerous mulato or moreno identifications of people throughout Potosí records, however, suggest that such unions between Spaniards and Africans or between Indians and Africans occurred frequently.

114. AGI Charcas 415, book 1, recapitulation of order by Viceroy Toledo 1589, fol. 206r–v, 15 June 1589.

115. On the complex ethnic identities in Spanish American urban society, see Kuznesof; and on Mexico, see Cope; and Seed, "Social Dimensions of Race." On native Andeans and ethnic identity, see Cahill. For a general discussion of mestizaje in the colonies, see Mörner.

116. The classic work on mingayos, and the mineowners' increasing tendency to pocket payments (known as *indios de faltriquera*, "Indians in the pocket") is Bakewell, *Miners of the Red Mountain*.

117. I draw these seventeenth-century population estimates from "Descripción de la Villa y minas de Potosí," 377–78; Padden, xxiv; and Baquijano. See also Bakewell, *Miners of the Red Mountain*, 111–12; Bakewell, *Silver and Entrepreneurship in Seventeenth-Century Potosí*, 22; and Ocaña, 172–73; 175–76; on specific ranchería populations, see Ocaña, 196.

118. Murra, "Aymara Lords and Their European Agents at Potosí." The Lu-

paqas were also well-known for having profited in the sixteenth century from the sale of llamas to merchants in need of pack animals.

119. Ocaña, 198–99. Ocaña called this man, named Mondragón, an Indian and marveled at his manner of eating at ground level as opposed to using a table. However, he may have been mestizo, as a Pedro de Mondragón served on the town council in the same era.

120. Quoted in Murra, "Aymara Lords and Their European Agents at Potosí," 236, citing ANB.Minas 730, fol. 1211r.

121. Ocaña, 200.

122. Ibid., 187.

123. Acosta, *Natural and Moral History of the Indies*, 173.

124. Larson, *Colonialism and Agrarian Transformation in Bolivia*, 90.

125. AHP–CNM.EN 19, Juan Gutiérrez Bernal, fol. 1513v, work contract between Isabel Ycica and Pedro de Cavala, 30 April 1590.

126. AHP–CNM.EN 4, Martín de Barrientos, cuaderno no. 11, fol. 2, work contract of Elena, *chiriguana*, and Juan Pérez, 12 June 1571; AHP–CNM.EN 4, Martín de Barrientos, cuaderno no. 11, fol. 2v, work contract of Ana, mulata, and Sebastián de Palencia, 5 July 1571.

127. AHP–CNM.EN 4, Martín de Barrientos, cuaderno no. 11, fol. 5v, agreement to pay debt between Isabel Cayo and Luis Méndez, 30 July 1571.

128. ANB.CPLA, vol. 7, fol. 285–85v, council debate on quality of meats available in Potosí, 17 May 1594. AHP–CNM.EN 8, Luis de la Torre, fol. 1464v, work contract between Juan de Rojas and Baltasar Picón, 12 Nov. 1577. For references to African women's dominating outdoor market sales in the Americas, see Beckles, 72–90, and Karasch, 266–72.

129. AHP–CNM.EN 12, Pedro de Ochoa, fol. 38, bill of sale between Francisco and Gerónimo de la Cavallería and Francisco de Angulo, pulpero, 30 Jan. 1587.

130. AHP–CNM.EN 4, Martín de Barrientos, cuaderno no. 1, fol. 6v, sale of houses, 4 Jan. 1572. (Second Small Plaza of Corn); AHP–CNM.EN 19, Juan Gutiérrez Bernal, fol. 1536–40v, will of Antón de Miranda, indio ynga, and María Alcapulco, india, husband and wife, 10 March 1590. (Small Plaza of Flour).

131. AHP–CNM.EN 19, Juan Gutiérrez Bernal, fol. 1758v, bill of sale between don Francisco Martínez Ayra, don Francisco Yana, don Francisco Turumayo, and Felipe de Torres, 19 May 1590. Principal signifies a leader of a village. See also, AHP–CNM.EN 19, Juan Gutiérrez Bernal, fol. 1943v, bill of sale for wheat flour from Pedro Corvacho Paniagua, a Spaniard, to Francisco Domínguez, 30 May 1590.

132. AHP–CNM.EN 4, Martín de Barrientos, cuaderno no. 6, fol. 43, bill of sale between Lope Rodríguez Salgado and Diego Bravo for 270 bottles of Castilian wine, 19 Sept. 1572.

133. "Descripción de la Villa y minas de Potosí," 379.

2. MAKING ROOM TO SELL

1. ANB.CPLA, vol. 5, fol. 384v, council minutes on excessive number of pulperías, 14 April 1589.

2. Ibid.

3. An example is the pulpería run by husband and wife Juan Martínez Flores and Angela de Mendoza, described in ANB.EP 201, Salvador Gómez de Soto, fol. 276v–78, inventory of pulpería of Juan Martínez Flores, deceased, 16 Oct. 1680, and ANB.EP 201, Salvador Gómez de Soto, fol. 421v, will of Angela de Mendoza, 19 Jan. 1681.

4. ANB.CPLA, vol. 5, fol. 384v, council minutes on excessive number of pulperías, 14 April 1589.

5. *Azogue* is mercury; *pella* is the amalgam of silver and mercury produced in the silver refining process; a *piña* is refined silver that has not been minted. See Bakewell, *Miners of the Red Mountain*, 197–98.

6. One-sided Spanish documents are very revealing with regard to regulation of alcohol, but as Thierry Saignes discusses, the discourse about Indians and alcohol presents difficulties for analysis of indigenous drinking patterns. See Saignes, "Borracheras andinas."

7. Hanke, *The Imperial City of Potosí*, 31. On Spanish administration in the New World, see the classic Haring. For a detailed history of the town council, see Moore, *The Cabildo in Peru under the Hapsburgs*.

8. "Descripción de la Villa y minas de Potosí," 385, names positions sold in Potosí and lists their value.

9. See fears about disease and death caused by indigenous consumption of Peruvian wine (*bino nuevo*) in ANB.CPLA, vol. 6, fol. 66v, 15 Feb. 1592; ANB.Rück no. 2, fol. 181a, 3 Dec. 1596; ANB.CPLA, vol. 12, fol. 252, 30 Oct. 1609; ANB.CPLA, vol. 14, fol. 142, 25 Sept. 1615; ANB.CPLA, vol. 18, fol. 162v, 13 April 1627; ANB.CPLA, vol. 30, fol. 116v, 23 Aug. 1675; ANB.CPLA, vol. 31, fol. 228, 14 July 1679; ANB.CPLA, vol. 31, fol. 384v, 10 June 1681. On the sale of watered-down wine, see ANB.CPLA vol. 5, fol. 384v, 14 April 1589.

10. Wolff, 67–68.

11. ANB.EC, document 1667.2, don Pedro Benítez for the confirmation of an adjudication made to him of a lot in Potosí over which neighboring Indians claimed ownership, 1648–67. Information on Ana de Saldana contained within on fol. 11v–13v.

12. ANB.CPLA, vol. 24, fol. 370, council meeting on racial identity of pulperos, 8 April 1650. Here *zambahigo* signifies a person of mixed African and indigenous descent. For evidence of theft by slaves for exchanges with indigenous marketwomen in colonial Quito, see Minchom, *The People of Quito, 1690–1810*, 56.

13. ANB.EC, document 1667.2, fol. 11v–13v, Saldana in Benítez vs. neighboring Indians, 1659.

14. ANB.CPLA vol. 5, fol. 309, Viceroy don Fernando de Torres y Portugal

conde del Villar to Captain Juan Ortiz de Zárate justicia mayor y visitador del Cerro, 22 Nov. 1586. Ortiz de Zárate was later named corregidor of the Villa from 1592 to 1594. On long-distance supply and high prices, see Wolff, 65–67.

15. ANB.CPLA, vol. 14, fol. 75, council report on regatones, 21 Jan. 1615. *Regatones* translates in English as "regrater."

16. Murra, "Aymara Lords and Their European Agents at Potosí," 236.

17. Town council records highlight concerns over the sale of fruits and vegetables, eggs, poultry and meat, bread, candles, and chicha. See ANB.CPLA, vol. 7, fol. 285v, meeting on street sales of poultry and fish, 17 May 1594; ANB.CPLA, vol. 7, fol. 301, sale of bread in the plaza, not in pulperías, 5 June 1594; ANB.CPLA, vol. 14, fol. 9, excess and disorder by barley vendors, 23 July 1614; ANB.CPLA, vol. 14, fol. 75, high prices blamed on regatones of barley and yerba, 21 Jan. 1615; ANB.CPLA, vol. 16, fol. 31v–32, street sales of poultry and fish, 8 June 1618; ANB.CPLA, vol. 16, fol. 291v, street sale of fish, 15 May 1635; ANB.CPLA, vol. 20, fol. 287v, petition of Joan Lacaro de Sejas on high prices of fish and bacon, 19 Sept. 1635; ANB.CPLA, vol. 20, fol. 291v, petition of Joan Lacaro de Sejas on high prices of sugar, preserves, oil, and soles for shoes, 15 May 1635; ANB.CPLA, vol. 20, fol. 292v, sale of fish in the public plaza, 15 May 1635; ANB.CPLA, vol. 20, fol. 78–78v, sale of yerba in the Plaza de San Agustín, 18 Aug. 1634; ANB.CPLA, vol. 24, fol. 286v, scarcity of barley, 5 March 1649; ANB.CPLA, vol. 24, fol. 389, report on the weight of "two-" and "three-fer" bread (i.e., two or three pieces for one real) sold in the Gato de Fruta, 26 Aug. 1650; ANB.CPLA, vol. 24, fol. 447–48, sale and weight of "three-fer" bread, 17 May 1651; ANB.CPLA, vol. 31, fol. 2v, inspection of bread for sale in plazas, 9 Oct. 1676; ANB.CPLA, vol. 31, fol. 228, poor quality of bread for sale in the plaza, 14 July 1679; ANB.CPLA, vol. 31, fol. 385v, poor quality bread, 8 July 1681. Nonconsumable items like straw, candles, and firewood were also overpriced in street markets: ANB.CPLA, vol. 14, fol. 9, excess and disorder by straw vendors, 23 July 1614; ANB.CPLA, vol. 14, fol. 75, council report on high prices of straw and poultry, 21 Jan. 1615; ANB.CPLA, vol. 20, fol. 287v, price of candles, 19 Sept. 1635; ANB.CPLA, vol. 31, fol. 183, poor quality of candles for sale in the plaza, 20 Jan. 1679; ANB.CPLA, vol. 31, fol. 228, poor quality of candles for sale in the plaza, 14 July 1679; ANB.CPLA, vol. 31, fol. 271v, poor quality of candles that the indias sell in the plaza, 9 Jan. 1680; ANB.CPLA, vol. 31, fol. 396, poor quality of candles that the indias sell in the plaza, 22 Aug. 1681. On firewood, see AHP–CNM.EN 148, Pedro Bellido, fol. 192, rental agreement for property near the market where indias sell wood, 10 Dec. 1700. For quality concerns on noncomestibles, see discussion of a 1572 council-mandated test of the candlemakers in Wolff, 140–44.

18. ANB.CPLA, vol. 6, fol. 183v, provision from viceroy to Potosí council on pulperos, 30 July 1590, debated by council on 7 Aug. 1593.

19. ANB.CPLA, vol. 8, fol. 75, petition of Bastre Renglón on pulperías, 19 Aug. 1597.

20. ANB.Rück no. 575a, vol. 9 (*Cédulas y Provisiones del Superior Govierno*), fol. 121, provision against pulperías in the rancherías, 13 July 1618. Follow-up council provisions in 1619 and 1621 reiterated the ban on new pulperías and raised the punishment to four years' banishment from Potosí and a two-thousand-peso fine. See ANB.Rück no. 575a, vol. 9 (*Cédulas y Provisiones del Superior Govierno*), fol. 122, provision against pulperías in the rancherías, 5 Jan. 1619; and fol. 124v, provision against pulperías in the rancherías, 30 Aug. 1621.

21. ANB.CPLA, vol. 6, fol. 184, "Provisión del virrey que no aya mas de veinte y cuatro pulperos," 7 Aug. 1593.

22. ANB.CPLA, vol. 6, fol. 15v, minutes on demands to open pulperías, 30 July 1591. The Audiencia of Charcas, established in 1559, had jurisdiction over an expansive territory including parts of modern-day Peru, Bolivia, Argentina, and Chile. A general study of the audiencia in Spanish America is Burkholder and Chandler.

23. ANB.CPLA, vol. 6, fol. 176v, letter from the real audiencia to the corregidor and alcalde of Potosí, 16 June 1593. This prompted Viceroy García's August 1593 letter to limit licenses to twenty-four pulperos.

24. In 1559 mine owners in Potosí lobbied the Crown to gain status as a villa and, along with it, the right to limited local governance. The Crown granted the new status in 1561. For a comparative analysis of the formation of governing structures in La Plata and Potosí, see Wolff. Alberto Crespo Rodas reveals how conflicts between La Plata and Potosí that originated in the sixteenth century played out in the seventeenth-century war of the Vicuñas and the Basques.

25. ANB.CPLA, vol. 14, fol. 142v, petition of don Joan de Sandoval y Guzmán, 2 Jan. 1615.

26. Ibid. While the council did not spell out any reversal of pulpería rules in this particular meeting, they lightened up on prosecuting illegal pulperos, hence the need for the counterruling found in ANB.Rück no. 575a, vol. 9 (*Cédulas y Provisiones del Superior Govierno*), fol. 121, provision against pulperías in the rancherías, 13 July 1618.

27. AGI Escribanía 868a, legajo 1, no. 4, fol. 2r–v, Visitas de Potosí, 30 Feb. 1634.

28. AGI Escribanía 868a, legajo 1, no. 4, fol. 32r–v, Visitas de Potosí, Petition of Sevastian de la Torre Arenas, 30 Feb. 1634.

29. AGI Charcas 32, ms. 139, doctor don Sebastián de Sandoval y Guzmán procurador general de Potosí, to the Crown, 19 Feb. 1636, fol. 1r–v.

30. AHP–CNM.CGI, document 31, adjustment of the accounts of don Melchior de la Valgama from the time he was in charge of the collection for the pulperías of this villa belonging to the king, 1656.

31. ANB.CPLA, vol. 6, fol. 184, "Provisión del virrey que no aya mas de veinte y cuatro pulperos," 7 Aug. 1593.

32. Wolff, 180.

33. Crespo Rodas, 135–36.

34. ANB.CPLA, vol. 6, fol. 15v, council meeting on ban of pulperías in rancherías, 30 July 1591.

35. ANB.CPLA, vol. 5, fol. 384v, council meeting on excessive number of pulperías, 14 April 1589. Here *single* means that none of the women shared the pulpería license with a husband or other man.

36. Council provisions routinely specified punishments for both indio and india, español and española, etc. For example, ANB.CPLA, vol. 16, fol. 31v–32, petition of the protector general about fish market, 8 June 1618.

37. Examples of Spanish women appear in ANB.CPLA, vol. 9, fol. 93v, 94r, 94v, 95–1599 taxes. For Spanish females, indigenous males, and one moreno as pulperos see AGI Escribania 868a, legajo 1, no. 4, fol. 12r, 13v, 15v, 17v, 19v, 21r, 21v, 22v, 26r, 27r, 31r, Visitas de Potosí, 1 Feb. 1634. For Spanish women and indigenous men, see the tax lists of don Melchior de la Valgama in AHP–CNM.CGI 31, document 31, fol. 13, 13v, 14v, 15v, 16, 16v, 18, 19, 19v, accounts of don Melchior de la Valgama collection for the pulperías of this Villa belonging to the king, 1651–54.

38. ANB.CPLA, vol. 12, fol. 261, petition of Beatriz de Soto, widow of Domingo Díaz, 13 Nov. 1609.

39. For one that concentrated on wine, see ANB.EP 201, Salvador Gómez de Soto, fol. 421v, will of Angela de Mendoza, 19 Jan. 1681.This spectrum became more differentiated by the eighteenth century when small-scale groceries called *chagros* emerged in Quito, and *tiendas mixtas*, a bit more substantial than the average pulpería, appeared in late colonial Mexico City. See Minchom, *The People of Quito, 1690–1810*, 110; and Francois, 76.

40. The typical items found in pulperías are gathered from the following sources: AHP–CNM.EN 116, Baltasar de Barrionuevo, fol. 219, rental of pulpería by Magdalena Hernández to Juan de Canelas, 25 Feb. 1654; ANB.EP 145, Blas de Carvajal, fol. 535, rental of pulpería with marble counters by María López de Villacastín Montañez in avito de indias to Antonio de Fletes, 19 Feb. 1614; AHP–CNM.EN 112, Baltasar de Barrionuevo, fol. 95, rental of pulpería by Juan Gregorio Corco to Diego de Villalpando, 16 Jan. 1649; AHP–CNM.EN 118, Baltasar de Barrionuevo, fol. 84, rental of pulpería by Ursula Sisa to Francisca de la Reynaga, 28 Jan. 1659; AHP–CNM.EN 118, Baltasar de Barrionuevo, fol. 754, sale of pulpería by Juan Fajardo Paytan to Gerónima Picarro, 14 Sept. 1657.

41. ANB.EC, document 1667.2, fol. 11v–13v, Saldana in Benítez vs. neighboring Indians, 1659. For Crown concerns about measures in the New World, see Carrera Stampa.

42. ANB.EC, document 1618.9, civil suit Costanca de Almendras against Bartolomé Manuel over a house and store in Potosí, 1611–18; see fol. 131v and 166v for references to chicha.

43. AHP–CNM.EN 118, Baltasar de Barrionuevo, fol. 84, rental agreement between Ursula Sisa and Francisca de la Reynaga, 28 Jan. 1659.

44. AHP–CNM.EN 116, Baltasar de Barrionuevo, fol. 219, rental agreement between Magdalena Hernández and Juan de Canelas, 25 Feb. 1654.

45. AHP–CNM.EN 19, Juan Gutiérrez Bernal, fol. 1536–40v, will of Antón de Miranda, indio ynga, and María Alcapuco, india, husband and wife, 10 March 1590; AHP-CNM.EN 48, Pedro Venegas, fol. 1330–32v, will of María Payco, india, 1 June 1615.

46. Measurements were given as seven varas deep and fourteen varas wide. These details come from a property inspection in 1791. Despite the late date, the construction is noted to be "ancient," giving an approximate notion of the appearance of an earlier colonial chichería. See AHP–CNM.IYC, document 267, appraisal by don Antonio Yusta of the chicherías of Monaipata, property of the Animas cofradía appraised at 370 pesos, 1791.

47. Chicherías, housed in walled-in adobe buildings today, are still given away by the large earthenware jugs some two to three feet high sitting inside the door. A small white flag hangs outside the establishment when a new brew becomes available.

48. References to the Potosí tambos include: AHP–CNM.EN 32, Pedro Venegas, fol. 2323, rental agreement, 20 Sept. 1601; AHP–CNM.IYC, document 418, demand by Fray Fernando de Molina, procurador of the Predicadores, that Diego Martín Vello, rentor of the convent's tambo and pulpería, settle his account, 1632; AHP–CNM.EN 116, Baltasar de Barrionuevo, fol. 992, rental agreement, 7 Nov. 1654; ANB.EC, document 1659.15, fol. 10v, 12, acts by the steward of the Augustinian convent in the Villa de Potosí against the heirs of the royal lieutenant Domingo de Berasatigui and Clara Brava de Cartagena his wife, 1653; AHP–CNM.EN 118, Baltasar Barrionuevo, fol. 441, rental agreement, 27 Aug. 1659; AHP–CNM.EN 119A, Baltasar Barrionuevo, cuaderno no. 6, fol. 88, rental agreement, 15 Sept. 1663; AHP–CNM.EN 123, Antonio Domínguez, fol. 150, letter of debt, 29 March 1670; AHP–CNM.EN 123, Pedro Bellido, fol. 724, work contract, 27 June 1670; AHP–CNM.EN 133, Pedro Bellido, fol. 697, rental agreement, 28 Feb. 1681; AHP–CNM.IYC, document 417, register of properties and capellanías of the convent of Santo Domingo of this villa including the titles of the tambo of Mencia, 1642–1742.

49. AHP–CNM.IYC, document 417, register of properties and capellanías of the convent of Santo Domingo of this villa including the titles of the tambo of Mencia, 1642–72.

50. AHP–CNM.IYC, document 418, demand by Fray Fernando de Molina, procurador of the Predicadores, that Diego Martín Vello, rentor of the convent's tambo and pulpería, settle his account, 1632.

51. "Descripción de la Villa y minas de Potosí," 379.

52. AHP–CNM.EN 48, Juan Martín Menacho, fol. 48, rental agreement between Francisco de Oyanume and Joan Fernández, 21 Jan. 1615.

53. AHP–CNM.EN 48, Gaspar Esteban de Sagastegui, fol. 92, rental agreement between Bartolomé de Campelo and Diego de Quiroga, 17 Jan. 1615.

54. For example, AHP–CNM.EN 116, Baltasar de Barrionuevo, fol. 992, rental of tambo Los Melones for three years and four months, 7 Nov. 1654; AHP–CNM.EN 119A, Baltasar de Barrionuevo, cuaderno no. 6, fol. 88, rental of tambo Mencia la Chica for four years, rental agreement for Pedro Saabedra, 15 Sept. 1663; AHP–CNM.EN 133, Pedro Bellido, fol. 697, rental of tambo Santo Domingo for six years, 28 Feb. 1681.

55. ANB.CPLA, vol. 24, fol. 425v, provision against pulperías in the rancherías, 21 March 1651.

56. Ibid.

57. ANB.CPLA, vol. 26, fol. 305, council meeting on chichería closings, 28 April 1660.

58. AHP–CNM.EN 116, Baltasar de Barrionuevo, fol. 836v, rental agreement for Juan Quispe and Juana de la Cruz, 2 Sept. 1654; AHP–CNM.EN 116, Baltasar de Barrionuevo, fol. 992, renewal of rental agreement for doña Ana de Quintanilla, 7 Nov. 1654. For another example of this manner of renting urban tambos, see ANB.EP 195, Diego de Toledo, fol. 2v, rental agreement, 5 Jan. 1668.

59. Of 229 rental contracts for various types of stores, men or Potosí churches owned 187 of the properties, women owned 36, and married couples owned 6. The general analysis in this rental section comes from a sample of Potosí notary records, from 1570 to 1700 (see appendix, table 5). This sample provided 183 rental agreements and 46 sublet agreements that provide information on both the owners and renters of stores. I have used the 183 rental and 46 sublet agreements as the basis for representations of gender, ethnicity, and properties of petty trade (table 1). For further breakdown by gender and ethnicity, see appendix, table 6.

60. See AHP–CNM.IYC, document 417, register of properties and capellanías of the convent of Santo Domingo of this villa including the titles of the Tambo de Mencia show Indian women and Spanish men and women donating property, 1642–1742. Also, numerous wills reveal that members of the indigenous and Spanish populations gave houses, stores, and lots to churches in Potosí.

61. The rationale for making a division between tiendas and other stores is that references to pulperías and chicherías were used commonly, so that a tienda de pulpería or tienda de chichería was rented (and labeled) as an entirely different business than a simple tienda. Artisans and tradesman, generally male, occupied tiendas. One exception to this gender generalization was the indigenous woman Juana Cusi, a shoemaker who had her own store. See AHP–CNM.EN 118, Juan Pérez de Goynattivia, fol. 685, apprentice contract between Juana Cusi and Juana de Samadio for Andrés de Arosegui, apprentice, 3 Dec. 1659.

62. I address women's work being hidden from the record further in chapter 5. For the problem of invisible "partner-wives" elsewhere, see Kinsbruner, xvi.

63. AHP–CNM.EN 43, Pedro Venegas, fol. 1237v, contract between López and Sica, 27 July 1609. For additional examples, see AHP–CNM.EN 19, Juan Gutiérrez Bernal, fol. 1513v, contract between Isabel Ycica and Pedro de Cavala, 30 April 1590; AHP–CNM.EN 8, Luis de la Torre, fol. 1469v, contract between Juana Viscama and Francisco de Salazar de Mejía, 17 Dec. 1577; AHP–CNM.EN 4, Martín de Barrientos, cuaderno no. 12, fol. 29, contract between Isabel Guayro, india, and Joanes de Guzmán, 16 Oct. 1572; AHP–CNM.EN 4, Martín de Barrientos, cuaderno no. 11, fol. 14v, contract between Francisca, india, and Martín de Tineo, 20 Oct. 1572; AHP–CNM.EN 4, Martín de Barrientos, cuaderno no. 11, fol. 1, contract between Isabel Guayro, india, and Joan de Xexas, 23 May 1571; ANB.EC, document 1618.9, Costanca de Almendras against Bartolomé Manuel over a house and store in Potosí, 1611–18. Witness on fol. 166v says de Almendras had an Indian woman selling chicha for her from her store; ANB.EC, document 1657.35, complaint of Pablo d'Avila VillaVicencio against Pablo de la Torre for contempt of authority, 1657. Francisca Flores, a mulata slave, worked for de la Torre in his pulpería, see fol. 22–24v. Spanish women likely hired indigenous women to run stores that they owned, despite the absence of notarized work contracts to that effect. Evidence from a criminal trial from 1737 about a robbery from Spaniard María Barriga's pulpería shows that she had a female indigenous assistant, María, who opened and closed the store. See ANB.EC, document 1736.34, fol. 2–2v, criminal suit against Gil Bricielo for theft from María Barriga's store, La Plata, 1736. One example of a man being hired to sell goods for a Spaniard is in AHP–CNM.EN 4, Martín de Barrientos, cuaderno no. 12, fol. 2, contract between Alonso Carape and Albaro de Carrión, 17 June 1572.

64. Here my findings differ somewhat from Cheryl Martin's brief assessment of shopkeepers in eighteenth-century Chihuahua (135–39). Martin emphasizes the difference in social status between customers, mostly lower-class castas, and storekeepers, primarily Spaniards. She highlights the "social negotiation" between classes involved in these economic transactions. In Potosí, differences in social status between pulpería operators and customers varied in the different sections of the city. It is likely that in many instances, transactions would take place between people of closer social rank, especially in the rancherías, and thus did not involve the same degree of class antagonism. Those pulperías that sat in the city center, however, likely did witness a greater differentiation between pulperos and customers.

65. ANB.EC, document 1618.9, fol. 296–96v, Costanca de Almendras against Bartolomé Manuel over a house and store in Potosí, 1611–18.

66. Jay Kinsbruner reveals that pulperos in the late colonial era had little longevity (45). John Kicza notes a similar lack of advancement in colonial society by Mexican pulperos (111).

67. AHP–CNM.EN 32, Pedro Venegas, fol. 2323, rental agreement for Suárez, Albárez, and Francisco Moreno and María Gerónima, 20 Sept. 1601.

68. AHP–CNM.IYC, document 418, demand by Fray Fernando de Molina, procurador of the Predicadores, that Diego Martín Vello, rentor of the convent's tambo and pulpería, settle his account, 1632.

69. AHP–CNM.EN 133, Pedro Bellido, fol. 697, rental agreement for Sicilia Flores, 29 Feb. 1681.

70. AHP–CNM.CGI, document 31, fol. 13–22, adjustment of the accounts of don Melchior de la Valgama from the time he was in charge of the collection for the pulperías of this villa belonging to the king, 1656.

71. ANB.Minas, vol. 144, no. 4, Benítez vs. neighboring Indians, 1648–67. My analysis of the rental history of Padilla's property draws on the entire ninety-two-folio document.

72. ANB.CPLA, vol. 12, fol. 261v, petition of Roque de la Paz, pulpero, 13 Nov. 1609.

73. ANB.CPLA, vol. 20, fol. 209v–10v, petition of Lorenzo Layme, native of Chuquito, to open chichería, 24 April 1635.

74. ANB.CPLA, vol. 20, fol. 195v, council order to close chicherías, 7 March 1635.

75. ANB.CPLA, vol. 20, fol. 210, petition of Lorenzo Layme, native of Chuquito, 24 April 1635.

76. See ANB.CPLA, vol. 31, fol. 402v, petition of Lucas de Botes, pulpero, 3 Jan. 1681.

77. My research in both Sucre and Potosí archives revealed few examples of men involved in the chicha trade; Layme and one man from La Plata identified themselves as chicheros, but overall, women dominated the trade.

78. ANB.CPLA, vol. 20, fol. 210–10v, petition of Lorenzo Layme, native of Chuquito, 24 April 1635.

79. ANB.EC, document 1667.2, fol. 1v, don Pedro Benítez for the confirmation of an ajudication made to him of a lot in Potosí over which neighboring Indians claim ownership, 1648–67.

80. ANB.EC, document 1667.2, fol. 4–4v, Benítez vs. neighboring Indians, 1648–67.

81. AGI Escribanía 868a, legajo 1, no.4, fol. 17r, Visitas de Potosí, 30 Feb. 1634.

82. Incidently, Benítez did not keep the pulpería. At least as early as 1667, it was in the hands of Agustín Joseph Quispe, a yanacona Indian. See ANB.EC, document 1667.2, fol. 14.

83. In addition to the Rodríguez/Padilla and Sissa/Chamorro cases analyzed below, see ANB.CPLA, vol. 31, fol. 402, petition of Pablo de Paredes y Herrera, 25 Sept. 1681. In this incident, Pablo de Paredes y Herrera objected to the store doña María de Ampuero opened. Paredes y Herrera may have acted to stem the threat from Ampuero's location to his own business or he may have targeted Ampuero's husband, Lucas de Botes y Bedoya, a pulpero in Potosí, by attacking her.

84. ANB.CPLA, vol. 20, fol. 266, initial folio, petition of María Sissa, india, vs. Francisco Chamorro, pulpero, and neighbors, 31 Aug. 1635. Continued in ANB.CPLA, vol. 20, fol. 380, 389–93v, 407v–10v, 11 Jan. 1636.

85. ANB.CPLA, vol. 20, fol. 266, petition of María Sissa, 31 July 1635.

86. ANB.CPLA, vol. 20, fol. 392v, response of don Pablo Vázquez, protector general de los naturales, for María Sissa, india, 17 Jan. 1636.

87. AGI Charcas 416, Libro IV, fol. 98r–v, king to Viceroy Conde de Salbatierra, 23 Feb. 1648.

88. ANB.CPLA, vol. 20, fol. 410, response of don Pablo Vázquez, 17 Jan. 1636.

89. ANB.CPLA, vol. 20, fol. 380, petition in response to Sissa by Francisco Chamorro, Manuela Núñez, Antonio Ruiz, doña Felipa de Truxillo, Isabel del Arce, 11 Jan. 1636.

90. ANB.CPLA, vol. 20, fol. 380v, petition of Francisco Chamorro et al., 11 Jan. 1636.

91. Ibid.

92. AGI Escribanía 868a, Legajo 1, no. 4, fol. 13r, Visitas de Potosí, 30 Feb. 1634.

93. ANB.CPLA, vol. 20, fol. 389v–92v, response of don Pablo Vázquez, 17 Jan. 1636.

94. Ibid., fol. 391v.

95. Ibid., fol. 391v–92.

96. Ibid., fol. 392.

97. Ibid., fol. 392v–93.

98. ANB.Minas, vol. 144, no. 4, Diego de Padilla vs. Domingo de Quiroga clérigo de menores hordenes, about permission to open a pulpería in Los Arquillos de la Villa de Potosí, 1644. This Diego de Padilla should not be confused with the Diego de Padilla who served as an alcalde ordinario in Potosí in the 1630s and 1640s.

99. ANB.Minas, vol. 144, no. 4, fol. 10v–11, Diego de Padilla vs. Domingo de Quiroga, 1644. Incidentally, Rodríguez's second reference to María de Figueroa is misleading. María de Tena owned the property.

100. Ibid., fol. 1v.

101. Of the council rulings Padilla referred to, the 1605 one is not extant. The 1624 ruling is found in ANB.Rück no. 7, fol. 30, provision of the marqués de Guadalcazar viceroy to the corregidor of Potosí, prohibiting pulperías in rancherías, 30 Aug. 1624. This copy of the provision does not list the limits.

102. For a thorough study of the Pacajes and their mita service, see Cañedo-Argüelles Fábrega, *Potosí*.

103. Unfortunately, the legal suit between Padilla and the Pacajes has not survived, but the few references contained in the Rodríguez-Padilla suit spell out the determination of various parties, both Spanish and indigenous, to control the destiny of this piece of urban property. The native complainants in the

two lawsuits are referred to as both Callapas and Pacajes, the former term denoting the repartimiento of Callapas, and the latter name, a reference to a more specific community within the region. The Pacajes brought the initial suit and were then joined by other Callapas natives in the ongoing legal battle.

104. ANB.Minas, vol. 144, no. 4, fol. 42–43v, Diego de Padilla vs. Domingo de Quiroga, 1644.

105. Ibid., fol. 7v–8v. The name of the attorney is not listed in the petition; he was, in all likelihood, a Spaniard, and may have had ties to Rodríguez as well as to the indigenous population.

106. ANB.Minas, vol. 144, no. 4, Benítez vs. neighboring Indians, 1648–67.

107. See ibid. One witness on the history of the property claimed that a don Diego Ayra, indio, owned the place in 1618 and rented out its pulpería to a "fat woman." Given the documentation on the Tena to Hernández sale in conjunction with various assertations that Tena owned and ran the pulpería for approximately the first fifteen years of the seventeenth century, it is very unlikely that Ayra owned the property. It is likely, however, that Ayra rented the property directly from Tena or through Salguero and Hidalgo before Isabel de Torres rented it. Ayra, in turn, could easily have sublet it to a woman or hired a woman to run it for him, as was common for pulperías and chicherías. In addition, Isabel de Torres could have been the "fat woman" whom daily customers so associated with the store that most witnesses never linked it to Ayra.

108. ANB.Minas, vol. 144, no. 4, fol. 3–3v, Diego de Padilla vs. Domingo de Quiroga, 1644.

109. Ibid., fol. 11–11v.

110. ANB.Minas, vol. 144, no. 4, fol. 92, pronouncement from the real audiencia, in Diego de Padilla vs. Domingo de Quiroga, 13 April 1644.

111. Potosí was not unique in this regard. The 1680s cabildo of Quito debated unlicensed pulperías in private houses. See Minchom, *The People of Quito, 1690–1810*, 110, 112.

112. Ocaña, 191.

3. LIGHT ON CHICHA, HEAVY ON BREAD

1. AGI Charcas 32, Gaspar de Saldana "sobre la arina del maiz" [partial ms.], 10 March 1565, and royal provision of the Real Audiencia of Charcas, 7 May 1604. Lack of corn for chicha is credited with causing "gran mortandad de los yndios." See also ANB.Rück no. 575a, vol. 9, fol. 114, Pedro Vicente Cañete, "Apuntos sobre Potosí," ordinance of don Gaspar de Saldana, corregidor, 10 March 1565.

2. "Descripción de la Villa y minas de Potosí," 380.

3. AGI Charcas 32, fol. 92v, Gaspar de Saldana "sobre la arina del maiz" [partial ms.], 10 March 1565. See also Ballesteros Gaibrois, 67. *Acua*, from the Quechua term for corn beer *aka* or *aqha* and also spelled *azua*, is synonymous with chicha.

4. AGI Charcas 32, fol. 92v (extant folio IV), Gaspar de Saldana, "sobre la arina del maiz" [partial ms.], 10 March 1565.

5. Mining towns were renowned for their use of alcohol to keep workers docile and recover the workers' wages. Two factors made Potosí unique in this regard. First, Potosí mine workers did not need to rely on overpriced supplies from mine owners, because the large city boasted alternative markets and merchants. Instances did arise in the region of Potosí where workers bought chicha on the job. Mitayos at Cari Cari, a site outside Potosí proper, paid two reales per day to the "yndia chichera" for daily rations of chicha. See ANB.EC, document 1678.29 (also listed as ANB.Minas, vol. 125, no. 21), fol. 365, 366v, criminal trial against the captain major of the mita of Potosí, José Fernández Valerín for offenses against mita Indians, Potosí, 1677–78. But typically, Potosí's immense urban marketplace offered mine laborers numerous vendors of food and alcohol. Second, many of Potosí's mine workers relied on the traditional habit of chewing coca leaves to suppress their appetites. Thus, coca was not a vice associated with absenteeism from the mita; moreover, it was a major source of income for numerous Spaniards and native Andeans alike. If Potosí officials turned a blind eye to the coca trade, they were zealous in their regulation of chicha. For treatment of coca regulation in Cuzco and Lima, see Garafalo.

6. Acosta, *Natural and Moral History of the Indies*, 199. For other priests' and friars' opinions on chicha's negative effects on native Andeans in Potosí, see the entire AGI Charcas 32, Gaspar de Saldana, "sobre la arina del maiz" [partial ms.], 10 March 1565; as well as Ocaña, 190–92, 204–6. Analysis of these critiques of native Andean drinking appears in Saignes, *Borracheras y memoria*.

7. ANB.Rück no. 575a, vol. 9, fol. 113v–14, appeal by Sancho Berdugo Barba, protector de naturales, 9 March 1591; ANB.Rück no. 575a, vol. 9, fol. 114, ruling by don Pedro de Lodena, corregidor, 18 July 1610.

8. ANB.Rück no. 575a, vol. 9, fol. 113–13v, provision of don Fernando Torres y Portugal on excessive prices of corn flour, 22 Oct. 1586.

9. AGI Charcas 32, fol. 92v, Gaspar de Saldana, "sobre la arina del maiz" [partial ms.], 10 March 1565.

10. Ibid., fol. 95r.

11. Ibid., fol. 92v–93r.

12. ANB.Rück no. 575a, vol. 9, fol. 113, provision of Viceroy Toledo to limit drinking binges, 1 Sept. 1572. It is worth noting, however, that while the council monitored chicha consumption and sites of sale, the drink itself was not tested for quality, nor was its price regulated. Furthermore, the chicheras paid no taxes for their trade. This situation differs remarkably from the example of England, where alewives underwent checks of their brew and paid the assize. See Bennett, *Ale, Beer, and Brewsters in England*, esp. 98–121 and 158–86.

13. Capoche, 141.

14. ANB.Rück no. 575a, vol. 9, fol. 113, provision of don Martín Enriquez to uphold Toledo provision, 30 Dec. 1582; and ANB.Rück no. 575a, vol. 9, fol.

113–13v, provision of don Fernando Torres y Portugal on excessive prices of corn flour, 22 Oct. 1586. See also Larson, 89–90. A famous example of an elite indigenous mill owner is don Diego Caqui from Tacna; see Cummins, 206.

15. ANB.CPLA, vol. 5, fol. 309–9v, provision of the viceroy count of Villar to Captain Juan Ortiz de Zarate, justicia mayor y visitador del cerro, 22 Nov. 1586.

16. ANB.Rück no. 575a, vol. 9, fol. 113v, reversals of earlier provisions by Marques de Cañete don García Hurtado de Mendoza, 31 July 1590 and 4 April 1591.

17. ANB.Rück no. 575a, vol. 9, fol. 114, royal provision of don Pedro de Lodena providing for sale of flour at reasonable prices, 9 March 1591.

18. ANB.CPLA, vol. 7, fol. 442, letter from Secretary Juan de Losa of the real audiencia to Potosí cabildo on corn flour, 15 June 1596.

19. ANB.Rück no. 575a, vol. 9, fol. 114, royal provision from the Audiencia of Charcas granting permission for the sale of wheat and corn, 7 May 1604.

20. On the business of chicha in republican Bolivia, see Gotkowitz, 87, 92–94.

21. Llano Restrepo and Campuzano Cifuentes, 24. See also Garcilaso de la Vega, 499.

22. See Llano Restrepo and Campuzano Cifuentes, 24–25 and 55–56; as well as Acosta, *Natural and Moral History of the Indies*, 199–200, which compares the method for brewing chicha to the one for brewing Spanish and French beers described by Pliny.

23. Lizarraga, 89.

24. Ocaña, 206. The "Descripción de la Villa y minas de Potosí" states that fifty thousand fanegas of the corn flour that entered Potosí went to the production of chicha. See "Descripción," 380. The fanega equaled 1.5 bushels of dry corn or 130 pounds of flour. On these units of measure, see Ramírez, *Provincial Patriarchs*, 279–80.

25. Ocaña, 191.

26. On the origins of chicha, see Acosta, *Natural and Moral History of the Indies*, 198–99.

27. Ocaña, 204–5.

28. Garcilaso de la Vega, 499.

29. On the aclla, see Silverblatt, 80–85, 101–7. For analysis of the problematic colonial representations of productive *and* reproductive roles of the aclla, see Graubart, 213–35.

30. Llano Restrepo and Campuzano Cifuentes, 27.

31. On the supreme significance of drink and drinking vessels in pre-Columbian ritual, see Cummins, 39–40. Note also Cummins's argument that as chicha became a commodity in the colonial economy, so too did queros, 208. Production of a new kind of quero—the painted quero—began around 1600, and most such decorated queros have been found near mining towns.

32. Ibid., 42–43.

33. Ibid., 249.

34. Ocaña, 204–5.

35. "Descripción de la Villa y minas de Potosí," 380.

36. Assadourian, *El sistema de la economía colonial*, 161.

37. "Descripción de la Villa y minas de Potosí," 380; Ocaña, 204. See also ANB.EC, document 1708.35, fol. 2–2v, criminal charge against the indio Lope for murder of the brothers Melchor and Nicolas, sacristans of San Lázaro in the city of La Plata, 1708, where María Lupersia went out of her home to buy chicha for the household. For reference to male and female drinkers, see Ocaña, 190.

38. Cole, 31. For a mining example of routine daily consumption, see ANB.EC, document 1638.13, fol. 22v, 24v–25, proceedings on doña María Pacheco Altamirano, La Plata, 1630–38. Altamirano sold chicha to mine workers at the Carata refinery in the village of Macha. See also ANB.EC, document 1678.29 (also listed as ANB.Minas, vol. 125, no. 21), fol. 365, 366v, criminal trial against the captain major of the mita of Potosí, José Fernández Valerín, for offenses against mita Indians, Potosí, 1677–78. For a rural example, see ANB.EC, document 1598.2, fol. 7–8, Antonio de Salaz, executor of don Joan Albarado y Velasco, deceased, against Mateo Gutiérrez over a third of the estate of the Hacienda del Valle de Anquioma, 1597–98. A booklet attached to the file lists all expenses for calendar year 1597, including costs for chicha for indigenous workers.

39. Town council records document social drinking in chicherías by men and women. See, for example, ANB.CPLA, vol. 20, fol. 195v, council report on dangers of chicherías, 7 March 1635; and ANB.CPLA, vol. 26, fol. 237v, council report on inspection of city-center chicherías, 3 Oct. 1659. Numerous legal suits include witness testimony that refers to men, and occasionally women, drinking chicha together in social contexts. See ANB.EC, document 1707.32, fol. 5, criminal trial against Lorenzo de Alvarado for illicit affair with a servant of the Justicia Mayor of Potosí, 1707. Corroborative evidence of drinking patterns from nearby La Plata includes ANB.EC, document 1675.8, fol. 2, criminal trial against Juan Quispe and Bartolomé Guanca for robbery of another Indian, La Plata, 1674–75; ANB.EC, document 1627.4, fol. 8, constable vs. pulperos for infractions, La Plata, 1627; ANB.EC, document 1669.10, fol. 11v, Antonio de Tapia and Julian de Vaca for disturbances committed by their servants, La Plata, 1669.

40. ANB.EC, document 1623.10, fol. 7, 10v, actions of doña Juana Verdugo against Rafaela Flores concerning a female slave, May 1623; AHP–CNM.EN 116, Baltasar de Barrionuevo, fol. 7, will of Mariana de Oriola, 5 May 1654; AHP–CNM.EN 133, Pedro Bellido, fol. 17, rental agreement between Joseph de Atienza and Salvador de los Ríos, 29 Jan. 1681; AHP–CNM.EN 138, Pedro Bellido, fol. 262–64, will of Pedro Velásquez Rodero, 21 Nov. 1690.

41. Brandy became another favorite drink of the masses, but merchants did

not ship it to Potosí on a regular basis until the eighteenth century. See Tandeter et al., 209–11.

42. Cummins, 83, drawing on Betanzos's account.

43. Evidence of men's involvement in chichería property includes AHP–CNM.EN 112, Baltasar de Barrionuevo, fol. 756, rental agreeement between Fray Gabriel de Tovar and Andrés de Melgarexo, 21 Jan. 1649; AHP–CNM.EN 123, Pedro Bellido, fol. 710v, rental agreement between Fray Andres de Rueda and Joan Lube de Liscaymata, indio, 13 Nov. 1670; AHP–CNM.EN 133, Pedro Bellido, fol. 17, rental agreement between Joseph de Atienza and Salvador de los Ríos, mulato, 29 Jan. 1681. In contrast to numerous references, general and specific, to women selling and brewing chicha, I found only one record of a man hiring a woman to brew chicha for him to sell, and a single passing reference to a male "chichero" who brewed his own chicha. In preconquest times, women brewed chicha in the sierra, while men made the corn beer on the coast and in the north. For examples of the gender distinction, see Cummins, 91, 205; Minchom, *The People of Quito, 1690–1810*, 184; and Garafalo, 101–2.

44. On women's role as chicheras in nineteenth- and twentieth-century Bolivia, see Gotkowitz and Hames. For Peru, see references to women and chicha (in practice and in discourse) in Cadena, *Indigenous Mestizos*, 71, 199.

45. AHP–CNM.EN 118, Baltasar de Barrionuevo, fol. 257v–59, inventory of Juana Lorenzo Hernández, 7 Jan. 1658.

46. AHP–CNM.EN 19, Juan Gutiérrez Bernal, fol. 1536–40v, will of Antón de Miranda and María Alcapuco husband and wife, 10 March 1590.

47. AHP–CNM.EN 118, Juan Pérez Goynattivia, fol. 630v–33v, will of doña Juana Cayala, 13 Sept. 1659. See also AHP–CNM.EN 4, Martín Barrientos, fol. 22–23v, will of Madalena Carbayache, 6 Oct. 1572; AHP–CNM.EN 127, Pedro Bellido, fol. 785–87, will of Ana Mormo, 8 May 1675; AHP–CNM.EN 138, Pedro Bellido, fol. 362–64, inventory of doña Isabel Maldonado, 12 April 1690. Maldonado was not identified by ethnicity, but her belongings suggest she did not live as a Spanish woman in a cultural sense (clothes, language, etc.). For further evidence of indigenous women claiming chicha vessels in wills, see also ANB.Minas, vol. 148, no. 8, fol. 8–9v, lawsuit over property in the neighborhood of Munaypata, in Potosí, 1700–1709.

48. Cobo, 169.

49. Cummins argues that urpus and queros were not all targeted for destruction during idolatry campaigns because Spaniards recognized their quotidian value as typical (perhaps the most typical) components of the Andean household (200–201).

50. AHP–CNM.EN 118, Baltasar de Barrionuevo, fol. 257v–59, inventory of Juana Lorenzo Hernández, 7 Jan. 1658.

51. Cummins, 36, citing C. de Molina, *Relación de las fábulas y ritos de los Incas*, CLDRHP, 1st ser., I (1916 [1573]): 61–77.

52. The phrase used in the Potosí documents is "mandar hazer chicha."

53. "Descripción de la Villa y minas de Potosí," 374. Men always significantly outnumbered women among the European population. Women who did reside in the city were sent to lower-lying towns for the duration of pregnancy, childbirth, and recovery. See Lizarraga, 90. My notary sample shows no dowries for Spanish women for 1572 and 1577 and numerous dowries in years thereafter.

54. Glave, *Trajinantes*, 354–55.

55. AHP–CNM.EN 118, Juan Pérez Goynattivia, fol. 676–77, debt of Madalena Piqllana, yndia, to doña Petronila Camargo, 30 Dec. 1659. Other contracts, identical in format and compensation for chicha trips are AHP–CNM.EN 118, Juan Pérez Goynativia, fol. 721v–22, deposit between María Uscama and María Lorensa Gonsaga, 20 May 1659; AHP–CNM.EN 118, Juan Pérez Goynativia, fol. 779–80, agreement to supply chicha between María Cangua and Juana de Torres, mother and daughter, and Graviela de Toro, 24 March 1659; AHP–CNM.EN 118, Juan Pérez Goynativia, fol. 782, agreement to supply chicha between Agustín Cagyacona and María Sisa, husband and wife, and María de la Barrera, 26 March 1659; AHP–CNM.EN 118, Juan Pérez Goynativia, fol. 806, agreement to supply chicha between Miguel Ocampos and Esperanza, husband and wife, and María de la Cruz, 1 Aug. 1659. Contracts which list both husband and wife specify that the husband gives his permission for the wife to make the chicha.

56. AHP–CNM.EN 118, Juan Pérez Goynattivia, fol. 779–80, agreement to supply chicha between María Cangua and Juana de Torres, mother and daughter, and Graviela de Toro, 24 March 1659. María de la Barrera had chicha arrangements with women other than Cangua and Torres. Perhaps she had too much chicha to accept more from Cangua and Torres.

57. Additional evidence of chicha arrangements, AHP–CNM.EN 48, Juan Martín Menacho, fol. 974–75v, will of doña Luisa Pardo, 5 April 1615; AHP–CNM.EN 123, Pedro Bellido, fol. 374–75v, will of Francisca Nieto, 8 Aug. 1670; AHP–CNM.EN 123, Pedro Bellido, fol. 714–16v, will of Juana Colquema, 21 Aug. 1670; AHP–CNM.EN 133, Pedro Bellido, fol. 59–61, will of doña Juana de Urquizo, 4 Jan. 1681; AHP–CNM.EN 138, Pedro Bellido, fol. 24–25v, will of doña Juana de Espinosa, 11 Jan. 1690; AHP–CNM.EN 138, Pedro Bellido, fol. 262–64, will of Pedro Velásquez Rodero, 21 Nov. 1690; AHP–CNM.EN 143, Pedro Bellido, fol. 519–20v, will of doña María Rencifo, 21 Oct. 1695; AHP–CNM.EN 148, Pedro Bellido, fol. 155–57, will of doña Juana de Figueroa, 17 April 1700; AHP–CNM.EN 148, Pedro Bellido, fol. 460–62v, memoria of doña Sevastiana Cusi Paucar, 1700, and ANB.EC, document 1697.15, fol. 21, lawsuit between Gaspar de Avila and María and Blasia Miranda over the property of some rooms in Potosí, 1693–97.

58. AHP–CNM.EN 48, Juan Martín Menacho, fol. 974–75v, will of doña Luisa Pardo, legitimate wife of Luys de Padilla, 5 April 1615.

59. AHP–CNM.EN 118, Juan Pérez Goynativia, fol. 721v–22, deposit be-

tween María Uscama and María Lorensa Gonsaga, 20 May 1659. Another example of a chicha contract between two indigenous women is AHP–CNM.EN 123, Pedro Bellido, fol. 715v, will of Juana Colquema, 21 July 1670.

60. The only exception I have located is doña Sevastiana Cusi Paucar, who paid a chichera a mere two and a half reales for each chicha delivery. See AHP–CNM.EN 148, Pedro Bellido, fol. 460–62v, memoria of doña Sevastiana Cusi Paucar, 1700. For one cántaro of chicha selling at one and a half pesos, see ANB.EC, document 1623.10, fol. 7, actions filed by doña Juana Verdugo against Rafaela Flores concerning a female slave, May 1623. Additional price example is in ANB.EC, document 1697.15, fol. 21, lawsuit between Gaspar de Avila and María and Blasia Miranda over the property of some rooms in Potosí, 1693–97.

61. Ocaña, 204, 206. The "Descripción de la Villa y minas de Potosí," 380, lists the same price, although it claims one fanega of corn yielded thirty-two botijas.

62. ANB.EC, document 1697.15, fol. 21, lawsuit between Gaspar de Avila and María and Blasia Miranda over the property of some rooms in Potosí, 1693–97. Will of María de Guzmán is contained within the lawsuit.

63. AHP–CNM.EN 133, Pedro Bellido, fol. 59v, will of doña Juana de Urquizo, soltera natural de Oruro, 4 Jan. 1681. See also AHP–CNM.EN 123, Pedro Bellido, fol. 714–16v, will of Juana Colquema, india viuda, 21 Aug. 1670.

64. ANB.EC, document 1618.9, fol. 64, 66, 115, 131, civil suit of Costanca de Almendras against Bartolomé Manuel over a house and store in Potosí, 1611–18. For a similar characterization of a chichera, see ANB.EC, document 1642.6, fol. 23v, 26, 28, 45, Martín Pérez, indio, and Isabel Iscami against Inés Sisa and Isabel Mulli over the sale of houses, La Plata, 1640–42.

65. ANB.EC, document 1638.13, fol. 22v–25, doña María Pacheco Altamirano vs. Luis Altamirano, her cousin, over goods, 1638.

66. ANB.EC, document 1647.19, fol. 59v, Domingo Gutiérrez vs. Catalina de Goycos over quantity of pesos, Potosí, 1647–48.

67. ANB.EC, document 1697.15, example of María Guzmán in lawsuit between Gaspar de Avila and María and Blasia Miranda over the property of some rooms in Potosí, 1693–97.

68. AHP–CNM.EN 4, Martín Barrientos, fol. 22–23v, will of Madalena Carbayache, 6 Oct. 1572; AHP–CNM.EN 118, Baltasar de Barrionuevo, fol. 257v–59, inventory of Juana Lorenzo Hernández, hija natural de La Paz, yndia, 7 Jan. 1658. See also AHP–CNM.EN 123, Pedro Bellido, fol. 714–16v, will of Juana Colqueman, india, viuda, hija legitima, 21 Aug. 1670; AHP–CNM.EN 148, Pedro Bellido, fol. 460–62v, memoria of doña Sevastiana Cusi Paucar, 1700, and ANB.EC, document 1658.24, fol. 6–10v, Joseph de Baños guardian for the children of Sebastián Rencifo over the distribution of the estate of Isabel de Castilla, 1650–58.

69. ANB.EC, document 1707.43, fol. 9, criminal trial against don Juan and

don Pedro Balda implicated in the death of the negro Juan Antonio, slave of don Juan Antonio de la Vega, Potosí, 1707. Witness testimony from Jasinta Sisa reveals the time she closed her tavern.

70. For this argument, see Chambers, 112, 111–14.

71. AHP–CNM.EN 48, Pedro Venegas, fol. 1330–32v, will of María Payco, yndia natural del Pueblo de Macha, 1 June 1615. See also AHP–CHN.EN 19, Juan Gutiérrez Bernal, fol. 1536–40v, joint will of Anton de Miranda and María Alcapuco, husband and wife, 10 March 1590. For other ranchería taverns, see AHP–CNM.EN 106, Diego Pacheco de Chávez, fol. 3516v, rental agreement between doña Ursula Cano and Francisca de Arana, 3 Aug. 1649. AHP–CNM.EN 116, Baltazar de Barrionuevo, fol. 836v, rental agreement between doña Ana Quintanilla to Juan Quispe and Juana de la Cruz, husband and wife, 2 Sept. 1654.

72. Examples of large downtown houses with a chichería include: AHP–CNM.EN 106, Diego Pacheco de Chávez, fol. 4040v, sublease of property, Leonor García, viuda to Xpoval Gutiérrez, 6 Sept. 1649; ANB.EC, document 1642.6, fol. 23v, Martín Pérez, indio, and Isabel Iscami vs. Inés Sisa and Isabel Mulli over the sale of houses, La Plata, 1640–42; AHP–CNM.EN 116, Baltasar de Barrionuevo, fol. 225–28, will of Costanca de Cívicos, 24 March 1654; AHP–CNM.EN 116, Fernando de Hervas, fol. 496v, rental agreement between Francisco de Cisneros and Andrés del Olmo de la Celada, 15 June 1654; AHP–CNM.EN 116, Baltasar de Barrionuevo, fol. 762, rental agreement between Favián Sánchez Romero and doña Gregoria de Ybarra, 13 July 1654; ANB.EC, document 1658.24, fol. 10–10v, Joseph de Baños, guardian for the children of Sebastián Rencifo over the distribution of the estate of Isabel de Castilla, 1650–58; AHP–CNM.EN 118, Baltasar de Barrionuevo, fol. 390, rental agreement between Agustín de Ortega and Tomás Lopes de Alxibe, 1 July 1659; AHP–CNM.EN 123, Antonio Domínguez, fol. 81–82, will of doña María Pacheco de Chaves, 4 March 1670; AHP–CNM.EN 123, Pedro Bellido, fol. 431, rental agreement between Simon Sánchez de Silva and Joseph Linares, 23 Sept. 1670; AHP–CNM.EN 127, Pedro Bellido, fol. 610, rental agreement between Gonzalo Meto and Sebastián Pérez de los Arcos, 22 March 1675; AHP–CNM.EN 127, Pedro Bellido, fol. 635–35v, dowry of doña Juana de Eguilcor, 14 Aug. 1675; AHP–CNM.EN 133, Pedro Bellido, fol. 17, rental agreement between Joseph de Atienza and Salvador de los Ríos, 29 Jan. 1681; AHP–CNM.EN 133, Pedro Bellido, fol. 402, rental agreement between Fernando Encalada and doña Angela de Segovia, 3 June 1681; AHP–CNM.CGI, document 51, 1654, fol. 1, lawsuit over rental of the house of María Pacheco in Potosí to Joseph Martín Suárez for the annual fee of 320 pesos, 1670–73.

73. AHP–CNM.EN 116, Baltasar de Barrionuevo, fol. 579v, rental agreement between Fernando Velásquez and María de Segovia, 27 June 1654.

74. ANB.CPLA, vol. 26, fol. 237, petition of mayor Francisco de Gamboa to shut down chicherías, 19 Sept. 1659.

75. ANB.CPLA, vol. 26, fol. 237v–38, meeting on the inspection of chicherías, 3 Oct. 1659.

76. ANB.CPLA, vol. 20, fol. 195v, proposal to council by Diego Villa de Figueroa to close chicherías, 7 March 1635.

77. Ibid.; ANB.CPLA, vol. 20, fol. 209v, petition to council by Lorenzo Layme to open chichería, 24 June 1635; ANB.CPLA, vol. 26, fol. 237, proposal to the council by Francisco de Boada to close certain chicherías, 19 Sept. 1659; ANB.CPLA, vol. 26, fol. 237v–38, report to council by Francisco de Boada, Captain Francisco de Gamboa, and Fernando de Encalada on their inspection of chicherías, 3 Oct. 1659; ANB.CPLA, vol. 26, fol. 305, council minutes on the adverse affect of chichería closings for rental incomes of the church, 28 April 1660.

78. Acosta, *Natural and Moral History of the Indies*, 198. Though Acosta called chicha a wine, chicha is generally termed "corn beer" in English.

79. ANB.CPLA, vol. 31, fol. 275, council report on bread regulations, 26 Jan. 1680.

80. ANB.CPLA, vol. 31, fol. 146, report to the council by Juan de Rubar y Quevedo, 15 July 1678.

81. Examples of such requests for information include ANB.CPLA, vol. 7, fol. 440, council members Pedro de Mondragón and Joan Cano order bakery test, 5 July 1596; ANB.CPLA, vol. 12, fol. 341v, complaint to council on great excess of small breads, 24 Nov. 1610; ANB.CPLA, vol. 14, fol. 167v, council debate on prices of bread, 16 Dec. 1615; ANB.CPLA, vol. 20, fol. 78, council request for prices of flour, 18 Aug. 1634; ANB.CPLA, vol. 24, fol. 389, council debate on weight of two-fer and three-fer bread, 26 Aug. 1650.

82. ANB.CPLA, vol. 6, fol. 70v–71, council debate on excessive prices of wheat flour, 13 March 1592.

83. ANB.CPLA, vol. 6, fol. 173–73v, council debate on ounces per real of bread, 13 May 1592.

84. ANB.CPLA, vol. 6, fol. 180v, council debate on ounces per real of bread, 13 July 1593; and ANB.CPLA, vol. 6, fol. 186v, council debate on excessive prices of bread, 23 Aug. 1593.

85. Examples of punishments include ANB.CPLA, vol. 11, fol. 330v, council orders public announcement of weights for bread, 14 Feb. 1606; ANB.CPLA, vol. 12, fol. 18v–19, council mandates twenty ounces of bread for one real, 27 Jan. 1607; ANB.CPLA, vol. 14, fol. 3, council debate on price of wheat flour, 9 July 1614; ANB.CPLA, vol. 14, fol. 191v, council mandate on weight of bread, 29 Jan. 1616; ANB.CPLA, vol. 14, fol. 193, council mandate to lower weight of bread, 9 Feb. 1616; ANB.CPLA, vol. 9, fol. 38v, council mandate on price and weight of bread, 24 Sept. 1599; ANB.CPLA, vol. 9, fol. 199, council results of ensaye and mandate on price of bread, 11 Jan. 1602; ANB.CPLA, vol. 24, fol. 389, report on the weight of two- and three-fer bread sold in the Gato de Fruta, 26 Aug. 1650; ANB.CPLA, vol. 31, fol. 329, council reading of rules on bread and punishments for bakers, 17 Jan. 1681.

86. ANB.CPLA, vol. 12, fol. 18v–19, council mandates twenty ounces of bread for one real, 27 Jan. 1607.

87. For instance, ANB.CPLA, vol. 18, fol. 278, petition from bakers to council seeking a higher price for bread, 31 March 1628; ANB.CPLA, vol. 30, fol. 75, petition from bakers to council seeking reduction in ounces of bread per real, 22 March 1665; as well as other examples in this paragraph. See also ANB.EC, document 1722.11, fol. 2v, 22, procurador general and the bakers of La Plata with the goal of fixing the price of flour and weight of bread, 1714–22. ANB.CPLA, vol. 12, fol. 331–31v, petition of bakers to the council in response to ensaye, 24 Sept. 1610. For the initial cabildo ruling, see ANB.CPLA, vol. 14, fol. 3, council debate on price of wheat flour, 9 July 1614, and the response by bakers in ANB.CPLA, vol. 14, fol. 4–4v, petition of bakers to town council, 16 July 1614.

88. ANB.CPLA, vol. 7, fol. 440, council members Pedro de Mondragón and Joan Cano order bakery test, 5 July 1596. Tax records indicate Silvera was still running a bakery in 1599. For additional examples of ensayes, see bakers' request in ANB.CPLA, vol. 14, fol. 88v, petition by bakers to the council for a reduction in the ounces of bread per real, 27 March 1615; and cabildo response in ANB.CPLA, vol. 14, fol. 167v, council adjusts bread price based on ensaye, 16 Dec. 1615.

89. ANB.CPLA, vol. 14, fol. 191v, council mandate on weight of bread, 29 Jan. 1616; ANB.CPLA, vol. 14, fol. 193, council mandate to lower weight of bread, 9 Feb. 1616.

90. ANB.EC, document 1722.11, fol. 3, procurador general and the bakers of La Plata with the goal of fixing the prices of flour and weight of bread, 1714–22. Guilds were not uncommon in urban areas of Latin America. See, for example, references to bakers' guilds of eighteenth-century Chihuahua in Martin, 35, 112, 167. These guilds reportedly included women, but they gave them very little power. In early modern Spain, women were banned from such guilds and fined for selling bread or pastries that they baked in petty enterprises. See Perry, 18–19.

91. ANB.CPLA, vol. 20, fol. 103v, petition of Martín de Soles, representative of the bakers, to the council, 22 Oct. 1634; ANB.CPLA, vol. 20, fol. 113, petition of Martín de Soles, representative of the bakers, to the council, 24 Nov. 1634.

92. ANB.CPLA, vol. 24, fol. 447v–48, council report on the visit of Geronimo del Salto to the bread vendors, 17 May 1651. The name of the woman is not given in the report to the cabildo. R. Douglas Cope cites an example of a female vendor whose bread was taken away from her for being underweight (42–43). The bread was given to the poor, as mandated by the council. In this particular case, an irate man protested the council's senseless practice.

93. ANB.CPLA, vol. 24, fol. 447v–48, council report on the visit of Geronimo del Salto to the bread vendors, 17 May 1651. There are no surviving records of any punishment of Pacheco by the cabildo. After he had thrown his

tirade, they seemed satisfied just to be rid of him. It seems unlikely that his bakery operation, although illegal, was shut down.

94. ANB.CPLA, vol. 31, fol. 183, council debate on poor quality of bread for sale in plazas, 20 Jan. 1679. They specify a visit to the "bendederas" (in the feminine) of the bread to remedy the situation. Also see ANB.CPLA, vol. 31, fol. 228, council complaint on poor quality of bread for sale in plazas, 14 July 1679, and ANB.CPLA, vol. 31, fol. 385v, council order to visit bread vendors to control sale of poor quality bread, 8 July 1681.

95. Ibid., 198.

96. Garcilaso de la Vega, 594. He credits a Spanish woman, María de Escobar, with bringing the first wheat seeds to Peru, but he notes that several harvests went by before farmers gathered enough seed to replant and make bread. According to Acosta, "It has not been discovered that they had any sort of wheat"; *Natural and Moral History of the Indies*, 197. On the production of wheat in Peru, see Davies, 48–49; and Keith, esp. chap. 3.

97. The earliest reference I have located is AHP.CNM EN 4, Martín de Barrientos, cuaderno no. 6, fol. 31–32v, will of Catalina Palla, 3 Sept. 1572. Palla sold bread to Indian customers. Widespread consumption of bread by non-Spaniards produced the hierarchy of breads explained below. For additional references to widespread consumption, see ANB.CPLA, vol. 24, fol. 447v–48, council report on the visit of Geronimo del Salto to the bread vendors, 17 May 1651; ANB.EC, document 1722.11, fol. 2–3, procurador general and the bakers of La Plata with goal of fixing the prices of flour and weight of bread, 1714–22.

98. ANB.CPLA, vol. 24, fol. 389, report on the weight of two- and three-fer bread sold in the Gato de Fruta, 26 Aug. 1650.

99. ANB.CPLA, vol. 30, fol. 23v, council ruling on bakers' request for reduction, 14 Nov. 1674; ANB.CPLA, vol. 30, fol. 76v, council report on bakery inspection, 29 March 1675; ANB.CPLA, vol. 31, fol. 329, council reading of rules on bread and punishments for bakers, 17 Jan. 1681; ANB.EC, document 1700.7, fol. 7v, inspection of bakeries and decree against the baker Sebastián Córdova for baking bread with moldy flour, March 1700. On the distinction of breads in colonial Mexico City, see Super, 35.

100. ANB.CPLA, vol. 9, fol. 199, council report on ensaye of bread, 11 Jan. 1602; ANB.CPLA, vol. 12, fol. 342–42v, council order that no wheat bread be sold in the rancherías, 3 Dec. 1610.

101. On Lima bakeries staffed by runaway slaves and accused criminals, see Arrelucea Barrantes, Aguirre, and Flores Galindo. On Mexico City bakeries staffed by Indians in debt, see Cope, 94, 99–102.

102. ANB.Rück no. 575a, vol. 9, fol. 118v, Pedro Vicente Cañete, "Apuntes sobre Potosí," provisions for distributing Lipes Indians to Potosí bakeries, 16 Aug. 1603, 12 April 1612, 14 July 1655, 1 Dec. 1655.

103. Bakewell, *Miners of the Red Mountain*, 165.

104. AHP–CNM.EN 19, Juan Gutiérrez Bernal, fol. 2218v, work contract for Domingo Guanare to serve don Juan Pérez as a baker, 20 June 1590. For a seventeenth-century example from neighboring La Plata, see Pablo Bilca, indio hornero, in ANB.EC, document 1676.37, fol. 1, 5, lawsuit by doña Juana González against don Felipe de Arcienaga over the value of a bedspread worth 120 pesos, La Plata, 1666–76. For additional examples of indigenous workers in bakeries, see ANB.EC, document 1673.49, don Francisco Maldonado vs. don Diego Paez over responsibility for bakery ovens, 1673; ANB.EC, document 1699.49, fol. 4, 14v–15, Felipa Domínguez, widow of José de Uruquizu, vs. Diego de Bera for the death of her husband, 1698–99; ANB.EC, document 1649.19, fol. 1, 6, warrants and measures against pulperos who sell new wine (*vinos nuevos*) in violation of the ordinances, La Plata, 1649; ANB.CPLA, vol. 7, fol. 440, council report on bread inspection carried out in the house of baker Joana Silvera, 5 July 1596.

105. ANB.EC, document 1663.25, fol. 21v–22, lawsuit filed by Francisca Hermoso, daughter and heir of Martín Hermoso, against Diego Mejía over possession of houses left by her father in the Villa of Potosí, 1661–63. See also, María, negra in bakery of Joan de la Vega, AHP–CNM.EN 4, Martín de Barrientos, cuaderno no. 1, fol. 27, sale of house and store by Joan de la Vega to Sebastián de Cansero, 16 Jan. 1572.

106. For evidence that Indian workers in bakeries were also placed in shackles, see ANB.EC, document 1649.19, fol. 1, 6, warrants and measures against pulperos who sell Peruvian wine (*vinos nuevos*) in violation of the ordinances, La Plata, 1649.

107. ANB.EC, document 1670.25, complaint of Francisco Díaz against the sale of his wife, the mulata slave María Atienzo, July–Aug. 1670. For similar treatment of slaves, see also ANB.EC, document 1650.5, fol. 1, 13, demand of Alvaro Pinto, guardian of Clemente Francisca and Josepha de Rocha, for a slave, María, negra, 1650–61, and ANB.EC, document 1704.68, fol. 2v, doña Inés Vásquez against her slave Gregoria Vásquez, who petitioned to be sold alleging abuse, La Plata, Nov. 1704.

108. ANB.EC, document 1707.43, fol. 3, criminal trial against don Juan de Balda and don Pedro Balda, 1707.

109. ANB.EC, document 1722.11, fol. 9, procurador general and the bakers of La Plata with the goal of fixing the prices of flour and weight of bread, 1714–22. Doña Clara Varriga offers information on deliverymen in 1714.

110. AHP–CNM.CGI, document 102, lawsuit of the baker Juan de Soliz y Ulloa against his deliveryman Sebastián Picón over quantity of pesos, 1694.

111. ANB.EC, document 1609.15, fol. 128, doña Isabel de la Bandera, wife of Lucas de Aguirre, against Elvira de Aranda and Manuel Gorge Barreto, her husband, over houses in Potosí, 1604–9.

112. AHP–CNM.EN 4, Martín de Barrientos, fol. 14v, contract between

Francisco and Francisca, husband and wife, and Martín de Tineo, for Francisca to sell bread, 20 Oct. 1572. See also bread sales by Antonio Ximénez in AHP–CNM.EN 38, Pedro Venegas, fol. 719, will of Antonia Ximénez, 9 March 1604.

113. ANB.EC, document 1633.9, Francisco del Olmos vs. the heirs of María de Vargas over quantity of pesos, Potosí, 1619–33. Women ran bakeries in other parts of colonial Latin America, though few as large as these examples in Potosí. See several examples in Martin, 165–72.

114. ANB.EC, document 1633.9, fol. 9v–11, Francisco del Olmos vs. the heirs of María de Vargas over quantity of pesos, 1619–33.

115. These numbers do not fully reflect the financial gain Vargas took away from the bakery. See further discussion of her socioeconomic status in chapter 5.

116. This held true in other colonial contexts. John Kicza notes that Spaniards, including three women, owned all fifty-eight official bakeries in 1790s Mexico City (189–90).

117. AHP–CNM.EN 19, Juan Gutiérrez Bernal, fol. 1758v, bill of sale between don Francisco Martínez Ayra, don Francisco Yana, don Francisco Turumayo, and Felipe de Torres, 19 May 1590. *Principal* signifies a leader of a village. See also, AHP–CNM.EN 19, Juan Gutiérrez Bernal, fol. 1943v, bill of sale between Pedro Corvacho Paniagua, a Spaniard, and Francisco Domínguez for wheat flour, 30 May 1590.

118. ANB.EC, document 1609.15, fol. 128, doña Isabel de la Bandera against Elvira de Aranda and Manuel Gorge Barreto, her husband, over houses in Potosí, 1604–9.

119. ANB.EC, document 1592.7, Miguel Jorge vs. Leonor Rodríguez, morena, over ingredients for baking bread, La Plata, April 1592.

120. In addition to Vargas's example, see ANB.EC, document 1609.15, fol. 128, doña Isabel de la Bandera against Elvira de Aranda and Manuel Gorge Barreto, her husband, over houses in Potosí, 1604–9.

121. ANB.EC, document 1592.7, fol. 15, Miguel Jorge vs. Leonor Rodríguez, morena, over ingredients for baking bread, La Plata, April 1592. Witness refers to "the pulperos to whom [she] had given her bread and other things to sell."

122. Ibid., fol. 5v. On honesty and verbal contracts in colonial times, see Cope, 113.

123. ANB.EC, document 1609.15, fol. 307v, testimony of Andrés Bravo in doña Isabel de la Bandera against Elvira de Aranda and Manuel Gorge Barreto, her husband, over houses in Potosí, 1604–9. This is echoed on fol. 319, testimony of Sebastián de la Reynaga.

124. ANB.EC, document 1609.15, fol. 319v, doña Isabel de la Bandera against Elvira de Aranda and Manuel Gorge Barreto, her husband, over houses in Potosí, 1604–9.

125. See Gotkowitz and Hames.

1. AHP–CNM.EN 4, Martín de Barrientos, cuaderno no. 6, fol. 31v, will of Catalina Palla, india, 3 Sept. 1572. The collas were an Andean ethnic group located to the north of Lake Titicaca. The colla borrower was from the *urco*, or western, part of the region.

2. AHP–CNM.EN 4, Martín de Barrientos, cuaderno no. 4, fol. 2v–5v, will of Juan Bautista Jinobel, español, 24 June 1572.

3. Ocaña, 190, 192, 205.

4. On the Church as an economic institution in colonial Spanish America, see Schwaller. Pioneering studies of credit in Latin America include Greenow, and Quiroz, *Deudas olvidadas*.

5. On credit transactions, like pawn and loan, by non-elites in seventeenth- and eighteenth-century Mexico City, see the insightful discussion in Cope, 109–18.

6. The exception here is the role of nuns in extending credit as revealed in Burns, esp. 135–46.

7. Jay Kinsbruner has noted the social significance of grocers' extending credit for bread in urban centers during the late colonial era (93–94).

8. The marked role of women as providers, not just seekers, of credit stands in contrast to Marie Francois's findings for late colonial and early republican Mexico, where male grocers, obliged by the government to take pawn, made up the majority of pawnbrokers. Margaret Hunt provides clear evidence for a high number of women pawnbrokers in the English context. However, she links their practice of the trade to the rise in consumer culture in eighteenth-century England (42, 132–33, 145). Asunción Lavrin and Edith Couturier refer to women's important role as moneylenders in their study of elite Spanish women in colonial Guadalajara. Further, they suggest that clients often left pawn items with women lenders (302–3). Other studies that discuss women and the practice of pawn include Martin, 162; Ross; and Tebbutt.

9. AHP–CNM.EN 8, Luis de la Torre, fol. 35, sale of lot and enclosure by Catalina Maqui, yndia, to Francisco Ramirez, 22 Jan. 1577.

10. "Relación muy particular del cerro y minas de Potosí y de su calidad y labores, por Nicolas del Benino, dirigida a don Francisco de Toledo, Virrey del Perú, en 1573," 366.

11. Zulawski, *They Eat from Their Labor*, 69, based on Antonio de Ayans, "Breve relación de los agravios que reciben indios que ay desde cerca del Cuzco hasta Potosí," in *Pareceres jurídicos en asuntos de indios*, ed. Rubén Vargas Ugarte (Lima: 1951), 38.

12. AHP–CNM.EN 116, Baltasar de Barrionuevo, fol. 225–28, will of Costanca de Civicos, india viuda, 27 March 1654; ANB.EP 201, Salvador Gómez de Soto, fol. 390v, will of Juana de Medina, mestiza, 13 Nov. 1680.

13. AHP–CNM.EN 8, Luis de la Torre, fol. 1320v, contract between maestro Pedro Cabautista and Geronimo Leto, 6 Dec. 1577. See also AHP–CNM.EN 4,

Martín de Barrientos, cuaderno no. 12, fol. 9, work contract of Luisa, mulata, with Ana Flores, 5 July 1572.

14. AHP–CNM.EN 4, Martín de Barrientos, cuaderno no. 12, fol. 29, work contract of Isabel Guayro and Pedro Azque with Joan del Enzmán, 23 May 1572.

15. AHP–CNM.EN 38, Pedro Venegas, fol. 719, will of Antonia Ximénez, española, 9 March 1604. Other examples of goods given on credit by street vendor: ANB.EP 201, Salvador Gómez de Soto, fol. 390v, will of Juana de Medina, mestiza, 13 Nov. 1680; AHP–CNM.EN 4, Martín de Barrientos, cuaderno no. 9, fol. 30–34, will of Leonor Sasytoma, india, 16 Oct. 1572; AHP–CHM.EN 106, Diego Pacheco de Chávez, fol. 350v, codicil of Marcella de Peralta, 19 July 1640; AHP–CNM.EN 116, Baltasar de Barrionuevo, fol. 5–9, will of Mariana de Oriola, india or mestiza, 5 Jan. 1654; AHP–CNM.EN 143, Pedro Bellido, fol. 273–74, will of doña María de Aguilar, viuda, 30 July 1695. Examples of store debts include: AHP–CNM.EN 48, Pedro Venegas, fol. 1203–5v, will of Elvira Sánchez, española, 1 May 1615; AHP–CNM.EN 4, Martín de Barrientos, cuaderno no. 9, fol. 30–34, will of Leonor Sasytoma, india, 16 Oct. 1572; AHP–CNM.EN 61B, Baltasar de Barrionuevo, fol. 2157–62, will of doña María Monrroy, española, 2 June 1625; AHP–CNM.EN 61B, Baltasar de Barrionuevo, fol. 2078–80, will of Captain Luis Antonio Baldivieso, español preso, 8 May 1625; AHP–CNM.EN 116, Baltasar de Barrionuevo, fol. 313–14v, codicil of doña María Díaz de Orellana, 13 March 1654; AHP–CNM.EN 116, Baltasar de Barrionuevo, fol. 5–9, will of Mariana de Oriola, india or mestiza, 5 Jan. 1654; AHP–CNM.EN 123, Antonio Domínguez, fol. 682–84, will of don Juan Francisco Choqueticlla, 1 Feb. 1670; AHP–CNM.EN 123, Antonio Domínguez 1670, fol. 267–69v, will of doña Juana de Peralta, española, 1670; AHP–CNM.EN 127, Pedro Bellido, fol. 369–98v, will of dona Ana de Estrada, española, 9 July 1675; AHP–CNM.EN 135, Pedro Bellido, fol. 449–49v, will of doña Damiana Bohórquez, española, 15 Nov. 1685; AHP–CNM.EN 143, Pedro Bellido, fol. 122–23v, will of doña Isabel Lazo de la Bega, soltera española, 4 May 1695; AHP–CNM.EN 148, Pedro Bellido, fol. 397–98v, will of Ana María de Elorriaga, mestiza, 8 Dec. 1700.

16. AHP–CNM.EN 43, Pedro Venegas, fol. 2719–23v, will of Isabel del Benino, india, 23 Aug. 1601. Much of Benino's wealth probably came from Florentine miner Nicolás Benino, for whom she worked. Evidence from her will suggests that she had one daughter, by her employer.

17. ANB.EC, document 1675.8, fol. 2, criminal charge against Juan Quispe y Bartolomé Guanca, for robbery of another Indian, La Plata, 1674–75. For a similar case involving a Potosí chichería, see also AHP–CNM.CGI, document 187, fol. 5v, criminal complaint of doña Michaela Yncata against Juan Ramírez for theft of some jars of lard and colored wool, Feb.–March 1737. The thieves here took the stolen goods to a chichería to sell them.

18. ANB.EC, document 1667.2, fol. 11v–13v, don Pedro Benítez for the con-

firmation of an adjudication made to him of a lot in Potosí over which neighboring Indians claim ownership, 1648–67.

19. AHP–CNM.EN 32, Pedro Venegas, fol. 2724–26, inventory of María de Orduña, 22 Oct. 1601; AHP–CNM.EN 53, Sancho Ochoa, fol. 3606, will of Diego Quispe, 7 Dec. 1620; AHP–CNM.EN 48, Pedro Venegas, fol. 1203–5v, will of Elvira Sánchez, 1 May 1615. Other examples of store debts on pawn goods include: AHP–CNM.EN 53, Pedro Lopés Pallares, fol. 2845–47v, will of Ana de Cabrera, mestiza, 22 Sept. 1620; AHP–CNM.EN 61B, Baltasar de Barrionuevo, fol. 2157–62, will of dona María Monrroy, española, 2 June 1625; AHP–CNM.EN 116, Baltasar de Barrionuevo, fol. 5–9, will of Mariana de Oriola, india or mestiza, 5 Jan. 1654; AHP–CNM.EN 148, Pedro Bellido, fol. 155–57, will of doña Juana Figueroa, española, 17 March 1700.

20. See, for example, loans of 387 pesos and 500 pesos made by Joana Colquema in AHP–CNM.EN 123, Pedro Bellido, fol. 714–16v, will of Juana Colquema, india viuda, 21 Aug. 1670.

21. AHP–CNM.EN 123, Pedro Bellido, fol. 714–716v, will of Juana Colquema, viuda, 21 Aug. 1670. The will states that Colquema received the money so she might "buscasse su vida."

22. AHP–CNM.EN 123, Pedro Bellido, fol. 569–70v, will of doña Lorenca de Salas y Rivera, 23 Dec. 1670. See another example in AHP–CNM.EN 123, Antonio Domínguez, fol. 58–60, will of Salvador de Vega, español, 5 Feb. 1670.

23. ANB.EC, document 1618.9, fol. 296–96v, Costanca de Almendras against Bartolomé Manuel over a house and tienda in Potosí, 1611–18.

24. AHP–CNM.EN 91, Francisco de Urbilla, fol. 3061, will of María Benítez, mestiza (possibly india, discrepancy in will), 17 July 1635. Women shopkeepers in eighteenth-century America also purchased goods on credit. See Cleary, whose shopkeepers represent a more middling sector of the population than most of my examples.

25. For chicherías in debt, see AHP–CNM.EN 116, Baltasar de Barrionuevo, fol. 5–9, will of Mariana de Oriola, india or mestiza, 5 Jan. 1654; AHP–CNM.EN 128, Pedro Bellido, fol. 262–64, will of Pedro Velázquez Rodero, 21 Nov. 1690.

26. ANB.EC, document 1633.9, Francisco del Olmos vs. the heirs of María de Vargas over quantity of pesos, Potosí, 1619–33. Vargas listed several more substantial debts in her will, and while they likely stem from relationships to petty traders, she did not specify the trade of the other men and women who were indebted to her. Pulperos with debts to Vargas: María de León, 600 pesos; Hernando de la Paz, 490 pesos; Antonio de Ensinas, 600 pesos; Juan Bautista de Torres, 500 pesos; Juan Maldonado, 400 pesos and 300 pesos in rent for the house where he lived; Francisco de Torres, 700 pesos; Gregoria García, 300 patacones corrientes; Pedro Machado, 600 pesos; Miguel Moreno, 250 pesos; Francisco Pacheco, 960 pesos; Beatriz Sudino, 200 pesos; Leonor de Albarado, 260 pesos.

For additional debts owed on bread, see ANB.EC, document 1696.11, fol. 23,

Domingo Ramos de Torres, vecino of the Villa Ymperial of Potosí with the defense council of the Villa over the nullity of the sale of a bakery to Antonio de Carrión, 1696. Also, don Juan Quixano Benavides owed him more than 100 pesos for goods he gave him to sell, and the merchant Gaspar de Maríaca owed him more than 300 pesos for bread.

27. Murra, "Aymara Lords and Their European Agents at Potosí," 235–36.

28. AHP–CNM.EN 4, Martín de Barrientos, cuaderno no. 9, fol. 22–23v, will of Madalena Carbayache, 6 Oct. 1572. On the supply of coca to Potosí, see Glave, *Trajinantes*, esp. chap. 2, "La producción de los trajines: Coca y mercado interno colonial," 83–97.

29. AHP–CNM.EN 19, Juan Gutiérrez Bernal, receipt of goods and debt, Ysabel Cotaqui and doña Ysabel Pacheco, 4 June 1590.

30. AHP–CNM.EN 19, Juan Gutiérrez Bernal, fol. 1891–96, will of Isabel Cotaqui, india, 4 June 1590.

31. AHP–CNM.EN 148, Pedro Bellido, fol. 460–62v, memoria of doña Sevastiana Cusi Paucar, india, 1700. See also AHP–CNM.EN 143, Pedro Bellido, fol. 519, will of doña María Rencifo, viuda, 21 Oct. 1695 (María Ygnacia mortgaged her houses to obtain 200 pesos to buy coca).

32. ANB.Minas, vol. 148, no. 8, fol. 8–9v, will of María Mullo contained in acts before the Audiencia of Charcas by don Andrés Navarro Marca, 1 July 1700.

33. See ANB.EP 201, Salvador Gómez de Soto, fol. 390v, will of Juana de Medina, mestiza, 13 Nov. 1680.

34. AHP–CNM.EN 116, Baltasar de Barrionuevo, fol. 5–9, will of Mariana de Oriola, 5 Jan. 1654. See additional exoneration in AHP–CNM.EN 48, Pedro Venegas, fol. 1330–32v, will of María Payco, india, 1 June 1615.

35. To analyze how these transactions occurred within colonial social hierarchy, I studied the factors of gender and ethnicity through a database of wills and codicils for the period 1570 to 1700. I use the information in the database for all of the tables in this chapter, from which I then draw my analysis. The material in the database comes from my sample of extant notary records using approximately every five years between 1570 and 1700 with adjustments for years with missing data. One must consider, of course, that numerous transactions among people in this sector of the population were never recorded. This extant material provides a general idea of patterns. Specifically, a review of 165 codicils and wills from the notary archives at the Archivo Histórico de Potosí, Casa de la Moneda, shows 120 with evidence of loan or pawn activity. Of these 120, 97 record a total of 503 loan/debt transactions. Of these 503 transactions, 389 involved loans of pesos; 89 represented the sale of goods on credit; 10 were loans of material goods; 8 were loans of services on credit (the services of a lawyer, for example); 4 were loans of a combination of cash and goods; 3 consisted of cash and goods on credit; and 3 cases were goods on consignment. Of the 120 relevant records on pawn, no information exists on the identity of the pawn client in 5 cases; 10 cases did not identify the pawnbroker.

36. AHP-CNM.EN 118, Juan Pérez Goynattivia, fol. 46v, letter of debt between Tamayo and Mansilla, 22 Jan. 1659.

37. AHP-CNM.EN 123, Antonio Domínguez, fol. 68–69, will of dona Juana de Gamboa, española, 14 Feb. 1670.

38. AHP-CNM.EN 135, Pedro Bellido, fol. 449–49v, will of doña Damiana Bohórquez, española, 15 Nov. 1685. For an additional record showing debts to a street vendor for coca and to a pulpero for sweets, valued at a few pesos each, see AHP-CNM.EN 4, Martín de Barrientos, cuaderno no. 9, fol. 30–34, will of Leonor Sasytoma, india, 16 Oct. 1572.

39. ANB.EC, document 1633.4, fol. 113–17v, 121v–22, lawsuit between the convent of San Agustín and the convent of the Company of Jesus over the ownership of goods left by the soltera Juana Payco, also called La Lunareja, mestiza en abitos de india, 1631–33.

40. AHP-CNM.EN 53, Sancho Ochoa, fol. 3621, letter of debt between María Poco and Isabel Poco, 12 Dec. 1620.

41. AHP-CNM.EN 8, Luis de la Torre, fol. 1024–26v, will of Luisa de Villalobos, color morena, libre, 24 July 1577.

42. AHP-CNM.CGI, document 102, fol. 5–5v, "Memoria de las ditas que tengo," in lawsuit of the baker Juan de Soliz y Ulloa against his deliveryman Sebastián Picón over quantity of pesos, 1694.

43. Ibid.

44. Closest extant cabildo record to 1694 is ANB.CPLA, vol. 31, fol. 329, council report on bread prices, 17 Jan. 1681. In this meeting, the cabildo fixed prices at 24 ounces of table bread, 30 ounces of pan de a tres, or 60 ounces of molletes for one real.

45. AHP-CNM.CGI, document 102, fol. 5, memoria de las ditas que tengo, in lawsuit by the baker Juan de Soliz y Ulloa against his deliveryman Sebastián Picón over quantity of pesos, 1694.

46. ANB.EC, document 1652.29, fol. 29, doña María Beltrán with doña Bernabela Beltrán, doña Clara Beltrán and Martín Alonso Delgado over possession of goods of Petrona Beltrán, deceased, Potosí, 1650–52.

47. ANB.EC, document 1697.15, fol. 5v–18, 19v–21, lawsuit between Gaspar de Avila and María and Blasía Miranda over the property of some rooms in Potosí, containing will of María de Guzmán, 9 March 1693, and codicil of same, 2 May 1693.

48. For debates about whether the quipu were mnemonic devices or if they comprised a writing system, see Quilter and Urton. On the quipu as a form of writing, see also Mignolo, 234–37.

49. Tristan Platt analyzes one such case.

50. AHP-CNM.EN 4, Martín de Barrientos, cuaderno no. 9, fol. 30–34, will of Leonor Sasytoma, india, 16 Oct. 1572; AHP-CNM.EN 8, Luis de la Torre, fol. 1145–46v, 1147–48, will and inventory of Leonor Chumbo, 12 Oct. 1577 and 27 Oct. 1577; AHP-CNM.EN 8, Luis de la Torre, fol. 1346–48, will of María

Poco, india biuda, 12 Dec. 1577. For other strategies, see AHP–CNM.EN 61B, Baltasar de Barrionuevo, fol. 2078–80, will of Captain Luis Antonio Baldivieso, 8 May 1625; AHP–CNM.EN 4, Martín de Barrientos, cuaderno no. 6, fol. 31–32v, will of Catalina Palla, india, 3 Sept. 1572.

51. AHP–CNM.EN 133, Pedro Bellido, fol. 59–61, will of doña Juana de Urquiza, soltera, 4 Jan. 1681.

52. ANB.EC, document 1697.15, fol. 8v–9, lawsuit between Gaspar de Avila and María and Blasía de Miranda over property in Potosí containing will of María de Guzmán, 9 March 1693. Note that Guzmán did not specify Dorotea's last name in her will. See also remate in ANB.EC, document 1633.4, fol. 3v–5, 127v–33, lawsuit between the convent of San Agustín and the convent of the Company of Jesus over the ownership of the goods left by the soltera Juana Payco, also called La Lunareja, mestiza en abitos de india, 1631–33.

53. AHP–CNM.EN 53, Pedro Lopés Pallares, fol. 2845–47v, will of Ana de Cabrera, mestiza soltera, 22 Sept. 1620. Almendras is likely Costanca Almendras, the pulpera who operated a business around 1620.

54. AHP–CNM.EN 133, Pedro Bellido, fol. 51–53, dowry of Ana de Saldívar, 6 Feb. 1681. The dowry lists twenty marks of worked silver in pawn.

55. Frank Salomon describes the chichería of Francisca Vilcacabra in colonial Quito where customers left pawns as a promise to repay drinking debts. See Salomon, "Indian Women of Early Colonial Quito as Seen through Their Testaments," 337.

56. AHP–CNM.EN 123, Pedro Bellido, fol. 374–75v, will of Francisca Nieto, muger soltera hija natural, 8 Aug. 1670.

57. I found no complete inventories of Potosí pulperías; however, this example from nearby La Plata serves to illustrate what pawn items would likely be found on Potosí store shelves. ANB.EP 201, Salvador Gómez de Soto, fol. 276v–78, inventory of the pulpería of Juan Martínez Flores, deceased, 16 Oct. 1680. For an incomplete inventory of a Potosí pulpería that lists pawned items, see AHP–CNM.EN 123, Antonio Domínguez, fol. 58–60, will of Salvador de Vega, 5 Feb. 1670.

58. ANB.EC, document 1609.15, fol. 322, doña Isabel de la Bandera, wife of Lucas de Aguirre, against Elvira de Aranda and Manuel Gorge Barreto, her husband, over houses in Potosí, 1604–9.

59. For another example of a pawn client retrieving his belongings, see ANB.EC, document 1699.49, fol. 3, 5, 11v, Felipa Domínguez, widow of José de Uruquizu, vs. Diego de Bera for the death of her husband, 1698–99.

60. Throughout colonial Latin America, and Spain, interest charges were frowned upon because of association with the sin of usury. See Quiroz, *Deudas olvidadas*, 31.

61. ANB.EC, document 1676.37, lawsuit by doña Juana González against don Felipe de Arcienaga over the value of a bedspread worth 120 pesos, La Plata, 1666–76.

62. AHP–CNM.EN 48, Pedro Venegas, fol. 1301, will of doña María de Sala, 13 May 1615.

63. Clothing examples: AHP–CNM.EN 4, Martín de Barrientos, cuaderno no. 6, fol. 30–34, will of Leonor Sasytoma, 16 Oct. 1572; AHP–CNM.EN 53, Pedro Lopés Pallares, fol. 2822–23v, will of doña Catalina de Arraya, 14 Sept. 1620. See descriptions of colonial clothing in Money.

64. Jewelry examples: AHP–CNM.EN 116, Baltasar de Barrionuevo, fol. 20–20v, will of María de Vargas, 11 Jan. 1654; AHP–CNM.EN 133, Pedro Bellido, fol. 318–20v, will of Inés de Bargas, 24 May 1681; AHP–CNM.EN 116, Baltasar de Barrionuevo, fol. 5–9, will of Mariana de Oriola, 5 Jan. 1654.

65. Religious examples: AHP–CNM.EN 106, Diego Pacheco de Chávez, fol. 3094–95, inventory of doña Alfonsa Díaz, 26 June 1640; AHP–CNM.EN 133, Pedro Bellido, fol. 608, will of doña Ana María de Monnroz, 26 Nov. 1681.

66. Household examples: AHP–CNM.EN 143, Pedro Bellido, fol. 519, will of doña María Rencifo, 21 Oct. 1695; AHP–CNM.EN 127, Pedro Bellido, fol. 369–98v, will of doña Ana de Estrada, 9 July 1675.

67. The dowry wealth belonged to the wife according to Spanish law and was not to be used by her husband without her specific consent. On women's legal rights with regard to dowries, see Arrom, chap. 4; and Lavrin and Couturier. Very few examples of notarized dowries exist for indigenous women; the few extant dowries reveal lower overall values but similar material composition to those of Spanish women. Examples include ANB.EC, document 1702.48, fol. 29–33, dowry of Juana Payco, india, contained within lawsuit brought by María Fajardo, india, against the grandchildren of Juan Paytan over a pulpería in Potosí, 21 Feb. 1650; ANB.EC, document 1658.24, fol. 12, Joseph de Baños, tutor and curador for the children of Sebastián Rencifo, over the distribution of the estate of Isabel de Castilla, 1643–58; and from La Plata, ANB.EP 113, Antonio Herrera, fol. 228–29v, dowry of Gerónima Sisa, yndia natural palla, 13 March 1630. Gender analysis herein based on data from table 2.

68. Household examples of varying value: AHP–CNM.EN 135, Pedro Bellido, fol. 449–49v, will of Damiana Bohórquez, 15 Nov. 1685; AHP–CNM.EN 48, Pedro Venegas, fol. 1321–22v, will of Lucía de Baños, 28 May 1615.

69. ANB.EC, document 1697.15, fol. 5–8v, 19–21v, lawsuit between Gaspar de Avila and María and Blasía de Miranda over property in Potosí containing will of María de Guzmán, 9 March 1693, and codicil of same, 2 May 1693.

70. AHP–CNM.EN 123, Antonio Domínguez, fol. 678–80v, will of Ana Chuqui Cani, 8 Jan. 1670.

71. AHP–CNM.EN 123, Antonio Domínguez, fol. 678–80v, will of Ana Chuqui Cani, 8 Jan. 1670. The fiscal from Copacabana may also have had kin ties to Chuqui Cani. Most Indians residing in Copacabana hailed from towns around the shores of Lake Titicaca like Paucar Colla.

72. See the pawn transaction of don Alonso de Lisana in AHP–CNM.EN 48, Pedro Venegas, fol. 1301, will of doña María de Sala, 13 May 1615.

73. AHP–CNM.EN 148, Pedro Bellido, fol. 155–57, will of doña Juana de Figueroa, 17 March 1700.

74. Indigenous men pawned items for credit on fifteen occasions, eight of those (53%) to indigenous women. Remarkably, they never took a pawn to another indigenous man, whereas indigenous women chose to make eleven of seventeen pawn transactions (65%) with other indigenous women. Moreover, indigenous women did not choose any indigenous men as pawnbrokers.

75. Elinor Burkett opened serious inquiry into the history of native Andean women in an article that suggested that Indian men and women in urban settings barely interacted and that women gained more economic and social advantage in cities than did their male counterparts. See Burkett, "Indian Women and White Society." Another version of this argument appeared in Salomon, "Indian Women of Early Colonial Quito as Seen through Their Testaments."

76. Extensive documentation of indigenous men's long-distance trade roles is found in Glave, *Trajinantes*.

77. See, for example, AHP–CNM.EN 23, Juan Gutiérrez Bernal, fol. 1536–40v, will of Antón de Miranda, indio ynga, and María Alcapuco, husband and wife, 10 March 1590; AHP–CNM.EN 118, Baltasar de Barrionuevo, fol. 750–53, will of don Pedro Catacora, indio, 10 Sept. 1657; AHP–CNM.EN 123, fol. 682–84, will of don Juan Francisco Choqueticlla, indio, 1 Feb. 1670; ANB.EP 23, Cuaderno no. 4, fol. 335–37, will of Andres Poma, indio. Karen Spalding shows how kurakas negotiated labor contracts for men in sixteenth-century Huánuco. See Spalding, "Kurakas and Commerce." Evidence of the same practice in the seventeenth-century Andes appears in Cummins, 246–47.

78. Zulawski's study offered a firm critique of Elinor Burkett's theories about indigenous women's elevated status vis-à-vis indigenous men in the urban arena. See Zulawski, "Social Differentiation, Gender, and Ethnicity."

79. See, for example, AHP–CNM.EN 8, Luis de la Torre, fol. 1024–26v, will of Luisa Villalobos, color morena, libre, 24 July 1577. African women appear more frequently in notary records in the Caribbean, where they constituted a larger percentage of the population. For one discussion of their economic activities, see Socolow, "Economic Roles of the Free Women of Color of Cap Français."

80. Analysis based on database of materials in AHP–CNM.EN, 1570–1700 as explained in note 35 above.

81. See transactions for real estate worth three hundred pesos between doña Juana Sisa and Juana Payco in ANB.EC, document 1633.4, fol. 113–17v, 121v–22, lawsuit between the convent of San Agustín and the convent of the Company of Jesus over the ownership of goods left by the soltera Juana Payco, also called La Lunareja, mestiza en abitos de india, 1631–33.

82. ANB.EC, document 1697.15, fol. 5–8v, 19–21v, lawsuit between Gaspar de Avila and María and Blasía de Miranda over property in Potosí containing will of María de Guzmán, 9 March 1693, and codicil of same, 2 May 1693.

83. ANB.EC document 1658.24, Joseph de Baños, tutor and curador for the children of Sebastián Rencifo, over the distribution of the estate of Isabel de Castilla, 1643–58, fol. 12. Isabel de Castilla bequeathed to her daughter doña Maria Rencifo "un vestido acsso llillca, y nanaca de cumbe morado."

84. AHP–CNM.EN 123, Antonio Domínguez, fol. 58–60, will of Salvador de Vega, 5 Feb. 1670. Identity of his clients taken from statements in the will regarding debts owed him.

85. AHP–CNM.EN 48, Pedro Bellido, fol. 101, testamento de Ursula Poco natural del pueblo de Pulani, "cocos de plata," 3 Jan. 1615. Since aquillas and queros (also called cocos) were generally male objects, it is interesting that Poco had them. Her will shows numerous loans to indigenous men from Chayanta, so she may have received the cocos as pawn items herself. Queros are mentioned infrequently in the wills of indigenous women in comparison with textiles and other silver items, but for two additional examples, see AHP–CNM.EN 76B, Baltasar de Barrionuevo, fol. 462, will of Maria Payco, india, 20 Jan. 1630; and AHP–CNM.EN 8, Luis de la Torre, fol. 1147, inventory of Leonor Chumbo, yndia palla, 27 Oct. 1577.

86. On the meaning and worth of queros in the colonial market, see Cummins, 186, 195, 211, 267.

5. ENTERPRISING WOMEN

1. AHP–CNM.EN 4, Martín de Barrientos, cuaderno no. 9, fol. 30–34, will of Leonor Sasytoma, india, 16 Oct. 1572.

2. For descriptions of the use and meaning of indigenous clothing in this period, see Money, 170–93, and glossary. Money notes that the *acsu de cintura*, the acsu in the form of a skirt as it is worn today, first appeared in the mid-eighteenth century, at which time the use of the chumbe became unnecessary. The chuspa was a small pouch worn over the shoulders and used to carry coca. Mangas were sleeves adorned with silk and lace favored by elite Andeans.

3. Murra, "Aymara Lords and Their European Agents at Potosí," 236.

4. Kimberly Gauderman argues that in seventeenth-century Quito, Spanish law generally did not limit women's economic opportunities in ways that historians of women have commonly assumed (45–47). For my purposes here, the marital status of women traders did make a difference before local officials and tax collectors in Potosí.

5. See Kinsbruner, 14, 99; Bowser, 319; and Karasch, 271. Karasch draws her analysis from Flusche and Korth.

6. For two examples of European women's history that have used marital status as a helpful tool for analyzing women's lives, see Chojnacka; and Bennett and Froide.

7. ANB.CPLA, vol. 18, fol. 263, petition of doña Juana de Funes to the town council, 11 Feb. 1628.

8. Example of "Francisco López y su muger" is from ANB.EC, document

1633.9, fol. 11, Francisco del Olmos vs. the heirs of María de Vargas over quantity of pesos, Potosí, 1619–33. Cheryl Martin acknowledges the role of wives in the family business of shopkeeping in eighteenth-century Chihuahua and suggests that many women acted on their own to run the stores (161–62).

9. ANB.CPLA, vol. 18, fol. 147v, petition of the baker Diego de García de Villegas arguing against the removal of young, single pulperos from their stores per Crown orders because of debts they owed him, 10 Jan. 1627.

10. ANB.CPLA, vol. 9, fol. 92v–102, 105–12, 164–73v, three consecutive annual lists of taxes paid by Potosí merchants and businesses, 5 Aug. 1599, 1600, 24 July 1601.

11. ANB.CPLA, vol. 9, fol. 94, 105v, 165v, Diego de Penranda's name on three consecutive annual lists of taxes paid by Potosí merchants and businesses, 5 Aug. 1599, 1600, 24 July 1601. I should note that over the three years of these tax records, the number of pulperos who paid taxes dropped from ninety-three to thirty-four. The representation of women among these ranks rose during the same period, from 9.6% to 24%. For an insightful essay on reading male-centered records for clues to women's activities, see Bennett, *Ale, Beer, and Brewsters in England*, appendix "Interpreting Presentments under the Assize of Ale."

12. ANB.CPLA, vol. 9, fol. 165, list of taxes paid by Potosí merchants and businesses, 24 July 1601.

13. ANB.CPLA, vol. 5, fol. 387v, council minutes on license for Francisco Angulo, 15 May 1589; ANB.CPLA, vol. 9, fol. 94, 105v, 165, Elvira Angulo's name on three consecutive annual lists of taxes paid by Potosí merchants and businesses, 5 Aug. 1599, 1600, 24 July 1601.

14. Arrom discusses women's legal status, generally and for colonial Mexico City in particular (chap. 4). In addition to bequeathing shares of an estate to each child, the parent also could donate one fifth of his or her estate (called a *mejora*) to a single child above the others. Lavrin and Couturier provides a succinct overview of women's legal status.

15. ANB.Minas, vol. 144, no. 4, Diego de Padilla vs. Domingo de Quiroga clérigo de menores hordenes, about permission to open a pulpería in the Arquillos de la Villa de Potosí, 1644. The sources of the percentages of females referenced in tax and property records on the one hand and witness testimony and wills on the other are from my database of AHP–CNM.EN and ANB.EC.

16. On the issue of nonpayment of alcabalas by indigenous traders, see the extensive analysis by Gauderman, 92–116. See also Minchom, *The People of Quito, 1690–1810*, 62–63; and Minchom, "La economía subterránea y el mercado urbano," 175–86.

17. AHP–CNM.EN 123, Pedro Bellido, fol. 545v, dowry of doña Francisca Gómez, 6 Dec. 1670.

18. ANB.EC, document 1696.11, fol. 17–26v, Domingo Ramos de Torres

vecino of the Villa Ymperial of Potosí with the defense council of the Villa over the nullity of the sale of a bakery to Antonio de Carrión, 1696. He moved the bakery to buildings in Ollería Street for which he paid six thousand pesos, one thousand up front and the rest on loan from four men and women. Carrión chose this site because it was located next door to houses inherited by his wife from her mother, doña Juana Gomes.

19. For literature on women and the household economy, see, for instance, Hanawalt.

20. AHP.CNM EN 43, Pedro Venegas, fol. 1870–72, letter of debt between Juan de Medina Bonal and the couple Francisco Feijo and Juana de la Pérez, 29 Oct. 1609.

21. AHP–CNM.EN 148, Pedro Bellido, fol. 70–71, will of doña Michaela de León, 12 March 1700.

22. AHP–CNM.EN 148, Pedro Bellido, fol. 70v, will of doña Michaela de León, 12 March 1700.

23. ANB.EC, document 1609.15, doña Isabel de la Bandera, wife of Lucas de Aguirre, against Elvira de Aranda and Manuel Gorge Barreto, her husband, over houses in Potosí, 1604–9.

24. Ibid., fol. 307v, 391v.

25. Ibid., fol. 127v–30, 215v.

26. Ibid., fol. 128.

27. Also, when the couple married, it was de la Bandera who presented her own dowry, made up of houses, slaves, and other goods. No parents or other relatives made a donation of *bienes dotales* to her.

28. ANB.EC, document 1609.15, fol. 307v, 319, testimony of Andrés Bravo and Sebastián de la Reynaga in doña Isabel de la Bandera against Elvira de Aranda and Manuel Gorge Barreto, her husband, over houses in Potosí, 1604–9.

29. I draw out this example to contrast this situation with traditional wisdom and to suggest conceptual changes for historians of household economy to consider. I would like to emphasize that I am not suggesting this was always the case with female traders.

30. AHP–CNM.EN 106, Diego Pacheco de Chávez, fol. 3642–49, will of doña María Osorio, 29 July 1640.

31. AHP–CNM.EN 91, Francisco de Urbilla, fol. 3061–64v, will of María Benítez, 17 Aug. 1635. Benítez is alternately referred to as india and mestiza.

32. ANB.EC, document 1670.25, fol. 7–7v, Francisco Díaz against the sale of his wife, the mulata slave María Atienzo, La Plata, 1670. Though Díaz did not offer an explicit statement of economic assistance to Atienza, his legal entreaties would have cost money.

33. Frederick Bowser explains both the Church position on slave marriage and owner opposition to it (esp. 255–71). Herman Bennett has given an in-

sightful analysis of slave marriage in colonial Mexico. See also Seed, *To Love, Honor, and Obey in Colonial Mexico*, 58, 81–83.

34. AHP–CNM.EN 143, Pedro Bellido, fol. 613, will of Isabel Choquima, 8 Nov. 1695.

35. AHP–CNM.EN 123, Pedro Bellido, fol. 714–16v, will of Juana Colquema, 21 Aug. 1670.

36. See, for instance, Burnard; and Carr and Walsh.

37. See Bilinkoff.

38. AHP–CNM.EN 48, Pedro Venegas, fol. 1301–4v, will of María de Salas, 13 May 1615.

39. AHP–CNM.EN 48, Pedro Venegas, fol. 1203–5v, will of Elvira Sánchez, 1 May 1609.

40. AHP–CNM.EN 48, Pedro Venegas, fol. 1206, codicil of Elvira Sánchez, 2 May 1615.

41. ANB.EC, document 1652.29, fol. 29, doña María Beltrán with doña Bernabela Beltrán, doña Clara Beltrán, and Martín Alonso Delgado over possession of goods of Petrona Beltrán, deceased, Potosí, 1650–52.

42. ANB.CPLA, vol. 12, fol. 261, petition of Beatriz de Soto, widow of Domingo Díaz, 13 Nov. 1609. For the case of a widow trying to sell property to earn funds, see ANB.Minas, vol. 144, no. 4, Benítez vs. neighboring Indians, 1648–67, where María de Tena tried to sell property to Gonzalo Hernández Paniagua.

43. ANB.EC, document 1704.68, fol. 5, doña Ines Vázquez against her slave Gregoria Vázquez, who solicited sale, alleging abuse, La Plata, 1704; ANB.EC, document 1623.10, fol. 7, doña Juana Verdugo vs. Rafaela Flores over a female slave, 1623. For African slaves working to pay off their own debts, see AHP–CNM.EN 8, Luis de la Torre, fol. 1320v, contract between maestro Pedro Cabautista and Gerónimo Leto for Elvira, negra, 6 Dec. 1577. When owners loaned out male slaves it was not for work in the trade of food and alcohol, but for hard labor. See AHP–CNM.EN 12, Pedro Ochoa, fol. 866v, rental of slaves Gonzalo and Gaspar from Andrés Velos to Rodrigo Alonso blacksmith, 1 June 1587. See also, AHP–CNM.EN 32, Pedro Venegas, fol. 2590v, slave sale, 6 Nov. 1601.

44. For sites on African women cooking in plazas, see ANB.CPLA, vol. 7, fol. 285, council report on high prices of poultry and fish, 17 May 1594.

45. ANB.EC, document 1633.9, fol. 11, Francisco del Olmos vs. the heirs of María de Vargas over quantity of pesos, Potosí, 1619–33. She owed 5,000 patacones to a Spanish flour supplier and had two debts, of 250 pesos and 235 pesos, to Spanish men.

46. Ibid., fol. 116.

47. Ibid., fol. 116v.

48. AHP–CNM.EN 133, Pedro Bellido, fol. 59–61, will of doña Juana de Urquizo, 4 Jan. 1681.

49. AHP–CNM.EN 148, Pedro Bellido, fol. 155–57, will of doña Juana de Figueroa, 17 April 1700.

50. ANB.EC, document 1684.20, fol. 1v, Dean Manuel de Peñalosa y Mansilla and the mulata woman Dominga on the liberty demanded by Dominga, La Plata/Potosí, 1683–84. See other single women of African descent in trade in ANB.EC, document 1592.7, Miguel Jorge vs. Leonor Rodríguez, morena, over ingredients for baking bread, La Plata, April 1592; and ANB.EP 25, Juan Bravo, cuaderno no. 14, fol. xxiv–xxv, will of Elena, color moreno, horra, 4 Feb. 1578.

51. ANB.EC, document 1684.20, fol. 19v–20, witness testimony of doña María Ana Ysabel de Morillo in Dean Manuel de Peñalosa y Mansilla and the mulata woman Dominga on the liberty demanded by Dominga, La Plata/Potosí, 1683–84.

52. AHP–CNM.EN 135, Pedro Bellido, fol. 289–90, will of doña Luisa de Tres Palacios y Escando, 29 April 1685.

53. AHP–CNM.EN 123, Pedro Bellido, fol. 569–70v, will of doña Lorenca de Salas y Rivera, 23 Dec. 1670.

54. Ibid., fol. 570.

55. ANB.EC, document 1633.4, lawsuit between the convent of San Agustín and the convent of the Company of Jesus over the ownership of the goods left by the soltera Juana Payco, also called La Lunareja, mestiza en abitos de india, 1631–33.

56. ANB.EC, document 1633.4, fol. 67v, petition of Pedro de Teves Talavera to retrieve bedspread and blouse contained in lawsuit between the convent of San Agustín and the convent of the Company of Jesus over the ownership of the goods left by the soltera Juana Payco, also called La Lunareja, mestiza en abitos de india, 1631–33. Petition of Catalina Cussi to retrieve an acsu and lliclla on fol. 112 of same document.

57. ANB.EC, document 1633.4, fol. 36–36v, alleged memoria contained in lawsuit between the convent of San Agustín and the convent of the Company of Jesus over the ownership of the goods left by the soltera Juana Payco, also called La Lunareja, mestiza en abitos de india, 1631–33.

58. ANB.EC, document 1633.4, fol. 67v, lawsuit between the convent of San Agustín and the convent of the Company of Jesus over the ownership of the goods left by the soltera Juana Payco, also called La Lunareja, mestiza en abitos de india, 1631–33.

59. Sordo, 261, 283.

60. Celestino and Meyers, 106, 110. Paul Charney highlights the significance of the cofradía as a place for women to wield power, though argues that in Lima men held most cofradía leadership roles (esp. 383).

61. Ocaña, 199. Ocaña uses the term *pallas* to refer to mestizas.

62. AHP–CNM.EN 4, Martín de Barrientos, cuaderno no. 6, fol. 31–32v, will of Catalina Palla, india, 3 Sept. 1572.

63. Ocaña, 200.

64. Celestino and Meyers suggest that ayllus remained united in urban settings but their identity shifted to be one of barrios or cofradías (106). For additional examples of female donations to cofradías in Potosí, see Sordo, 276–77, 280.

65. AHP–CNM.IYC, document 417, register of properties and capellanías of the convent of Santo Domingo of this Villa including the titles of the tambo of Mencia show Indian women and Spanish men and women donating property, 1642–42. See fol. 4v for details on Isabel Cayco Palla, also called Isabel Sisa. Also, numerous wills reveal members of the indigenous and Spanish populations who gave houses, stores, and lots to churches in Potosí. Information on the bequests of propertied Africans is not readily available; however, it is reasonable to believe that some would have made similar donations.

66. Burns.

67. AHP–CNM.CGI, document 31, adjustment of the accounts of don Melchior de la Valgama from the time he was in charge of the collection for the pulperías of this Villa belonging to the king, 1656.

68. AHP–CNM.EN 123, Antonio Domínguez, fol. 51, will of Joana de Montoya, soltera mestiza, 4 Feb. 1670.

69. Chojnakca argues for this distinction between official and neighborly concerns about marital status for women in early modern Venice (66).

70. AHP–CNM.EN 38, Pedro Venegas, fol. 1111–15, will of Francisca Cachimbocllo, 30 March 1604.

71. AHP–CNM.EN 148, Pedro Bellido, fol. 424v, will of doña Costanssa Sossa, 26 Nov. 1700. She had forty-three new pieces of worked silver in addition to fifteen used pieces of silver. See also claims in case of María Vargas.

72. AHP–CNM.EN 8, Luis de la Torre, fol. 1346–48, will of María Poco, 12 Dec. 1577.

73. AHP–CNM.EN 143, Pedro Bellido, fol. 519–20v, will of doña María Rencifo, 21 Oct. 1695. Some married women—doña Luisa Pardo, for example—used the part-time sale of chicha to help with household costs. See AHP–CNM.EN 48, Juan Martín Menacho, fol. 974–75v, will of doña Luisa Pardo, legitimate wife of Luys de Padilla, 5 April 1615.

74. ABAS.Divorcios, legajo 4, no. 5319, fol. 2, demand for divorce by doña María Rencifo against Marcos Joseph, Potosí, Feb.–March 1683. Witnesses in the case attested to both the physical abuse, citing a scene where he threw a plate full of ají at Rencifo, and to his attempts to sell for his own benefit the house her mother had left to her. See also ANB.EC, document 1658.24, Joseph de Baños, tutor and curador for the children of Sebastián Rencifo, over the distribution of the estate of Isabel de Castilla, 1643–58. This contains will of Rencifo's mother, Isabel de Castilla, and the copy of a dowry from Rencifo's first marriage to Agustín Díaz de Amberes (whom she never mentions in her will).

75. AHP–CNM.EN 91, Francisco de Urbilla, fol. 3062v, will of María Benítez, 17 Aug. 1635.

6. ¿VALE UN POTOSÍ?

1. ANB.CPLA, vol. 26, fol. 291v–92, letter of señor conde de Alva viceroy to the town council, 18 March 1660.

2. On wage-labor options of indigenous men, in particular, for seventeenth-century Oruro, see Zulawski, *They Eat from Their Labor*.

3. On the changing nature of indigenous communities, both urban and rural, see Wightman and Powers.

4. Tandeter, 5. On this point and the mita debates of the seventeenth century, see also López Beltrán.

5. AGI Escribanía 868a, legajo 2, fol. 1, 5r, "Diego Charca capitan chico de la mita de Potosí de Jesús de Machaca ante séñor don Bartolomé de Salazar oidor de la Real Audiencia de los Reyes," dated 1664.

6. Ibid., fol. 11r–v. The ongoing nature of the problem of "absent Indians" for the province of Pacajes between 1594 and 1748 is analyzed in Choque Canqui. See also the attempt to bring Pacajes migrants home from the city of Arica to serve their tribute duty as discussed in Wightman, 30.

7. Tandeter, 69.

8. Cole, 92.

9. AGI, Escribanía 868a, legajo 1, fol. 12rv, petition presented by don Gabriel Fernández Guarache to the azogueros guild, Potosí, 1663. Guarache was a very influential native leader, a gobernador and kuraka of Jesús de Machaca, who served as capitán de mita for Pacajes twelve times between 1628 and 1662. He made use of his position and personal wealth to defend the interests of his community in Spanish courts. He figures prominently in many works on the seventeenth-century southern Andean region. Of particular importance is Saignes, *Caciques, Tribute, and Migration in the Southern Andes*, esp. 6–7, 22–26. Rivera Cusicanqui includes Guarache's last testament, 20–27.

10. AGI, Escribanía 868a, legajo 1, fol. 12r, petition presented by don Gabriel Fernández Guarache to the azogueros guild, Potosí, 1663; my emphasis. Zulawski draws attention to the example of women's indenture in the Guarache petition; *They Eat from Their Labor*, 70.

11. "Provision para que los indios que acudieren a comerciar en Potosí vivan junto con sus paisanos," in *Francisco de Toledo*, 1:31–32.

12. Both men and women turned to urban wage labor in the sixteenth century. And, despite assumptions that this signaled a break with the ayllu, Thierry Saignes has argued effectively that many urban laborers worked not for individual gain, but as part of a collective ayllu response to colonial economic demands. He further demonstrates that local conditions influenced these strategies as some native provinces pursued urban labor, while others found the means to pay tribute through alternative resources. See Saignes, *Caciques, Tribute, and Migration in the Southern Andes*.

13. Saignes, *En busca del poblamiento étnico de los Andes bolivianos*, 34.

14. Driven by French and English desire for silver, levels of silver produc-

tion would increase, though never to the highs of the sixteenth century, from the period between the 1730s and the 1790s. On this era, see Tandeter.

15. These population figures come from Tandeter, 77, citing Daniel J. Santa-maría, "Potosí entre la plata y el estaño," *Revista del Instituto Panamericano de Geografía de Historia* (Mexico City, 1973).

16. So argues Cole, 88.

17. For a detailed discussion of these administrations' actions on the mita, see Cole, 90–100.

18. ANB.Rück no. 575, vol. 4, fol. 301, letter from the duque de Palata to the corregidor of Potosí, 29 April 1689. For an earlier complaint about abuses against Indians assigned to the Potosí mita, see ANB.Minas, vol. 145, no. 5: Royal Cédula to the Audiencia de La Plata, 7 Oct. 1660. The late seventeenth-century complaints were distinct because concerns like the duke's took place against the backdrop of disappointing figures for silver production and visibly depleted mita rolls. On the mita in the era of Palata, see González Casasnovas; and Cole, 105–15.

19. The most complete investigation of the creation of the forastero sector of the population, which argues for its influential role on both rural and urban societies, is Wightman.

20. Andrien, *Andean Worlds*, 64.

21. AHP–CNM.EN 123, Pedro Bellido, fol. 93, rental of bakery by doña María de la Fuente to Sergeant Juan de la Sierra, 1 March 1670, and AHP–CNM.EN 127, Pedro Bellido, fol. 277, rental of bakery by doña María de la Fuente to doña Mariana de Uzeda Zedillo, 7 Nov. 1675.

22. ANB.EC, document 1667.2, fol. 11–13v, price list for Ana de Saldana's pulpería, within don Pedro Benítez for the confirmation of an adjudication made to him of a lot in Potosí over which neighboring Indians claim owner-ship, 1648–67.

23. ANB.EP Alonso Gutiérrez, vol. 184, cuaderno no. 7, fol. 1–1v, dowry of doña Juana Antonio Hordones de la Marquina, 29 July 1657.

24. AGI, Escribanía 868a, legajo 1, fol. 12r, petition presented by don Ga-briel Fernandez Guarache to the azogueros guild, Potosí, 1663.

25. AHP–CNM.CGI, document 31, fol. 23–24v, adjustment of the accounts of don Melchior de la Valgama from the time he was in charge of the collection for the pulperías of this Villa belonging to the king, 1656.

26. AHP–CNM. CGI, document 31, adjustment of the accounts of don Mel-chior de la Valgama from the time he was in charge of the collection for the pulperías of this Villa belonging to the king, 1656.

27. AHP–CNM.CGI, document 31, fol. 13, 14v., 15v, 16v, 18, Payco's store named in ibid. This Juana Payco is not the woman of the same name who ap-pears in chapter 5.

28. AHP–CNM.EN 112, Baltasar de Barrionuevo, fol. 271, rental agreement for pulpería, 10 Feb. 1649. Clearly the rental contract expired by October of

1651, when de la Valgama noted the store as closed, unless Cusi Paucar conspired with de la Valgama to not pay the taxes.

29. Minchom, *The People of Quito, 1690–1810,* 112–14; Kinsbruner, 45.

30. ANB.CPLA, vol. 31, fol. 402v, petition of Lucas de Botes, pulpero, 3 Jan. 1681.

31. ANB.EC, document 1702.48, fol. 7, lawsuit brought by María Fajardo, india, against the grandchildren of Juan Paytan, over a pulpería in Potosí, 21 June 1694.

32. Ibid., fol. 69.

33. AHP–CNM.EN 133, Pedro Bellido, fol. 17, rental agreement between Joseph de Atienza and Salvador de los Ríos, 29 Jan. 1681.

34. A good source for the growth of the city's neighborhoods and buildings is Sordo, 150–51, 196, 225. Two rancherías established in the seventeenth century were San Roque del Tio in 1637 and San Roque de Vilasirca in 1668.

35. Again, as is the case with the asiento records, the stark contrast between the more prosperous days of Potosí's mines and the post-1650 period suggests a change in council priorities, even taking into consideration any absences in the scope of extant material.

36. ANB.EP 3, Aguila, fol. 88, letter of donation, 1559. For a similar act of largesse, see the donation of mines by Beatriz to Vasco Valverde. ANB.EP 3, Aguila, fol. 473v, letter of donation, 1559.

37. AHP–CNM.EN 12, Pedro Ochoa, fol. 31–31v, donation by Luis de Murcia to Catalina Canicha, 1 Jan. 1587. For similar incidences of non-Spanish women receiving economic benefit from Spanish men in early Potosí, see AHP–CNM.EN 4, Martín de Barrientos, cuaderno no. 6, fol. 31, will of Catalina Palla, 3 Sept. 1572; AHP–CNM.EN 4, Martín de Barrientos, cuaderno no. 7, fol. 6, legal donation by Gamboa to Juana de Gamboa, 11 Dec. 1572; AHP–CNM.EN 8, Luis de la Torre, fol. 706v, legal donation from Andrés Vela to Antona, negra, 21 March 1577; AHP–CNM.EN 8, Luis de la Torre, fol. 1145–46v, will of Leonor Chumbo, 12 Oct. 1577; AHP–CNM.EN 61B, Baltasar de Barrionuevo, fol. 2332, letter of obligation by Mariana Dargos to Pedro Velez de Argos, 21 June 1625. Public acknowledgements and donations do not appear in the record in the later period. By highlighting some examples where women of color benefited in an economic sense through relationships with Spanish men, I do not want to suggest that relationships based on abuses did not occur as well. Moreover, I argue that ties to a Spanish man were merely a part, albeit an important one for some women, of advantage in the urban economy.

38. AHP–CNM.EN 118, Juan Pérez de Goynattivia, fol. 588v, apprentice contract, 4 Nov. 1659. Note that, given her birthplace and son's name, this is not the same Juana Colquema, trader, discussed in chapters 4 and 5. See also AHP–CNM.EN 123, Pedro Bellido, fol. 245, apprentice contract, 10 July 1670.

39. In a notary sample from AHP–CNM.EN 1570–1700, only four boys were apprenticed before a notary between 1570 and 1625, while fifteen appeared be-

tween 1625 and 1680. Remarkably, female relatives, mothers or aunts, accompanied fourteen of these seventeen boys, which suggests not only that master craftsmen wanted these negotiations on record, but that mothers and aunts, more than fathers and uncles, shouldered the responsibility of providing food and shelter for boys.

40. Saignes, "Indian Migration and Social Change in Seventeenth-Century Charcas," 184–85. Here Saignes draws on the Guarache petition.

41. AGI, Escribanía 868a, legajo 1, fol. 16r, petition presented by don Gabriel Fernandez Guarache to the azogueros guild, Potosí, 1663.

42. Ibid., fol. 16v.

43. For descriptions of community celebrations in the ranchería, see Ocaña, 204.

44. ANB.Minas, vol. 148, no. 8, acts before the Audiencia of Charcas by don Andrés Navarro Marca, governor and mita captain of Guayllamarca, Carangas province, over the restitution of a store and rooms that from time immemorial the Guayllamarcas have had in the Munaypata neighborhood of Potosí, 1705–7.

45. ANB.Minas, vol. 148, no. 8, fol. 9–9v, will of María Mullo contained in acts before the Audiencia of Charcas by don Andres Navarro Marca, 1 July 1700.

46. ANB.Minas, vol. 148, no. 8, acts before the Audiencia of Charcas by don Andres Navarro Marca, 1705–7. Interestingly, Carangas Indians debated ownership of a store in Munaypata, Potosí, in a 1762 lawsuit. See ANB.Minas, vol. 127, no. 18.

47. The surname Guaguamollo is most likely another rendering of Guayllamarca.

48. ANB.Minas, vol. 148, no. 8, fol. 51v, 67, witness testimony contained in acts before the Audiencia of Charcas by don Andres Navarro Marca, 14 Dec. 1706.

49. Ibid., fol. 67v.

50. AHP–CNM.EN 148, Pedro Bellido, fol. 456–59, 460–62v, will of doña Sevastiana Cusi Paucar, 28 Dec. 1700.

51. Ibid.

52. López held a new, and surely powerful, position in Potosí. During the last three decades of the seventeenth century, Spanish officials replaced the eleven capitanes general de mita with a single official, the capitán mayor de mita. See Tandeter, 22.

53. Luis Capoche related that in 1582 don Pedro Cusi Paucar, a native of Cuzco, served as "capitán y superior de todos los yanaconas" (140).

54. ANB.EP 79, Michel, fol. 585v, padrón for five *yanaconas*, 3 Sept. 1611.

55. AHP–CNM.EN 53, Sancho Ochoa, fol. 3606, will of Diego Quispe, 7 Dec. 1620.

56. AHP–CNM.EN 143, Pedro Bellido, fol. 615, will of Isabel Choquima, 8 Nov. 1695.

57. Less common, though possible, was the chance for successful female traders to use earnings to launch the career of another woman in trade. See the career of the married indigenous (but not yanacona) trader Juana Colquema, discussed in chapters 4 and 5.

CONCLUSIONS

1. Cadena, "'Women Are More Indian,'" 334.

2. ANB.CPLA, vol. 51, fol. 177–77v, report issued at the request of the Potosí council by doctor don José de Suero Gonzáles Andrade, priest and vicar of the parish of San Bernardo of Potosí, 21 July 1767.

3. Murra, "Aymara Lords and Their European Agents at Potosí," 236, citing ANB.Minas 730, fol. 1211r, translation mine. On chola market women, see Hames, as well as the discussion in chap. 10 of Larson, *Colonialism and Agrarian Transformation in Bolivia*.

4. For the colonial era, see Ocaña, 196. Laura Gotkowitz offers excellent comparative analysis of sexual insults associated with chola vs. india traders in the republican era (98).

5. Hames, and Gotkowitz, 97–100.

6. Concolorcorvo, 341.

7. On this increase in production, see Tandeter.

8. Tandeter, 32, and Andrien, *Andean Worlds*, 76.

9. Tandeter et al., 199. See also Andrien, *Andean Worlds*, 97.

10. ANB.Minas, vol. 151, no. 23, fol. 1v, don Manuel Maruri, regidor and receptor de alcabalas about the continuation of payment by those who are obliged: the enteradores and their seconds of the food and native clothing that they bring into the Villa for public dispense at stores, plazas, and canchas, 1770.

11. Ibid., fol. 57.

12. Tandeter et al., 220.

13. Quoted in ibid., 198.

14. Ibid., 211.

15. Tandeter et al. shows that while four hundred pulperías operated in Potosí in 1804, thirty-three merchants controlled the majority of commerce (8–12).

16. Gisbert, 72.

17. Chao, 173. Concolorcorvo also gives the figure twelve thousand (341).

GLOSSARY

(Q) denotes a term that comes from the Quechua;

(s) denotes a term that comes from the Spanish.

Acagato (Q): commercial center in the Potosí rancherías

Aclla (Q): select women chosen to live in communal settings and serve the
    Inca

Açua (Q) (also spelled *acua* and *azua*; also known as chicha): corn beer

Acsu (Q): tunic, part of typical native Andean female dress

Aguacil mayor (s): chief constable

Ají (s): chili pepper

Alcabala (s): a sales tax imposed by the Crown

Alcalde ordinario (s): magistrate

Alférez real (s): second lieutenant

Alto (s): second-story loft

Aquilla (s): ritual Andean drinking vessel made of silver or gold

Asiento (s): contract

Audiencia (s): colonial jurisdiction of the high court

Avasca (Q): native cotton

Ayllu (Q): kin-based unit

Azogue (s): mercury

Bachiller (s): licenciate

Basquiña (s): skirt, part of typical elite Spanish female dress

Birque (Q) (also virqqui): large earthenware vessel

Borrachera (s): drunken binge

Botija (s): earthen jug

Buhío (s): a modest round dwelling constructed of adobe and straw

Cabildo (s): town council

Caja de censos de indios (s): cash fund in indigenous communities

Caja real (s): treasury office

Calle Real (s): royal street

Callejoncillo (s): alley

Camyseta (s): Spanish colonial for the unku, a pre-Columbian version of the
    poncho

Cancha (s): enclosure

Cántaro (s): a small two-handled jug

Capitán enterador de mita (s/Q): man charged with overseeing mita
    contingents

Capitán general de mita (s/Q): regional leader or liaison between local Indian kurakas and Spanish officials

Carta de obligación (s): promissory note

Casa de la moneda (s): mint

Cédula (s): order, decree

Cerería (s): wax store

Charqui (Q): dried llama meat

Chicha (s) (also known as *acua*): corn beer

Chichero/a (s): a brewer of chicha

Chichería (s): chicha tavern

Chumbe (Q): woolen belt used to cinch native Andean female dress

Chuño (Q): traditional Andean dish of freeze-dried potatoes

Chuspa (Q): a small pouch for carrying coca

Cofradía (s): lay religious organization

Coleto (s): fancy doublet, typical part of Spanish male dress

Corregidor de indios (s): provincial Spanish magistrate

Corregimiento (s): the jurisdiction of the corregidor

Costal (s): sack

Criollo (s): Spaniard born in the New World

Cumbi (Q): finely woven native textile

Doncella (s): "maiden" who has yet to reach a suitable age for marriage

Encomendero (s): the holder of an encomienda

Encomienda (s): Crown grant of authority over a group of Indians to a Spanish colonial

Faldellina (s): a pleated skirt typical of female Spanish dress

Fanega (s): grain measure which equaled 1.5 bushels of dry corn or 130 pounds of flour

Gatera (s): merchant woman

Gato (s): market, from the Quechua *kjato*

Guasesillo (s): small hut

Guayra (Q): a native Andean smelting process using clay ovens

Guayrador (Q): a man who smelted silver

Hatunruna (Q): commoners of the Inca Empire

Hilacata (Q): low-level ayllu chief

Iglesia Mayor (s): Main Church

Joxota (s): sandal-like footwear, from the Quechua *usuta*

Jubón (s): tight blouse, typical of Spanish dress

Justicia mayor (s): official chief justice of a local colonial

Kajcha (s): a man who illicitly took silver from Potosí mines

Kuraka (Q) (also called a "cacique"): indigenous chieftain, usually hereditary

Llautu (Q): head covering typical of native Andean male dress

Lliclla (Q): shawl typical of native Andean female dress

Mangas (s): sleeves adorned with silk and lace favored by elite Andeans

Maravedí (s): an old Spanish coin of rather small value

Mayordomo (s): a special official appointed by the Crown for important occasions

Mercader de plata (s): silver merchant

Mestizo/a (s): of mixed Indian and Spanish descent

Mingayo (Q): in colonial usage, wage laborer in Potosí's silver mines

Mita (Q): in colonial usage, the forced labor draft of indigenous workers who mined at Potosí

Mitayo (Q): mita laborer

Mollete (s): low-quality bread roll

Moreno/a (s): a dark-skinned person; in Potosí, generally denoted free person of African descent

Mote (s): corn gruel

Muk'u (Q): the startup for corn beer

Mulato (s): of mixed African and Spanish or African and Indian descent

Ñañaca (Q): head covering, part of typical native Andean female dress

Negro/a (s): of African or Afro-Peruvian descent

Oca (Q): tuber, common part of highland Andean diet

Oidor (s): judge

Ollería (s): pottery workshop

Palla (Q): Inca noblewoman or older woman

Panadería (s): bakery

Patacón (s): a silver coin worth 8 reales

Pella (s): the amalgam of silver and mercury produced in the silver refining process

Peninsular (s): of Spanish descent born on the Iberian peninsula

Peso corriente (s): a silver coin of small value

Peso de a ocho (s): a silver coin equal to eight reales

Peso de oro (s): a gold coin, worth 480 maravedís in the sixteenth century

Piña (s): unminted cone of refined silver

Prenda (s): pawned item

Protector de naturales (s): Spanish official charged with defending indigenous population

Pulpería (s): colonial general or corner store

Pulpero/a (s): the owner or employee of a pulpería

Quero (Q): native Andean drinking vessel, typically made of wood

Quinoa (Q): a high-protein grain cultivated in the Andes

Quinto (s): in colonial usage, refers to the one-fifth of total silver production which was property of the Crown

Quipu (Q): a device which used pieces of colored wool woven into strands and knots to record data such as population figures and crop production

Ranchería (s): indigenous neighborhood

Real (s): a silver coin usually worth about 34 maravedís; there were 8 reales
to a peso

Regatear (s): to resell goods

Regatón (s): regrater, or urban vendor

Rescate (s): in colonial Potosí, indigenous appropriation of and trade in
unrefined silver ore

Retablo: altarpiece

Ropa de la tierra: clothing produced regionally in the Andes, and not
imported from Europe

Tambo (s): inn

Tinaja (s): large earthenware vessel

Tomyn (s): a silver coin equivalent to the real in the sixteenth century

Topo (also tupu) (Q): silver pin used in typical native Andean female dress to
attach the lliclla to the acsu

Trajín (s): transport system using llama trains

Traspaso (s): subleasing agreements

Unku (Q): see Camyseta

Urpu (Q): ceramic vessel for chicha

Vincha (Q): head covering

Viñapu (Q): sprouted grains

Virqqui (Q): see Birque

Vizcacha (Q): Andean hare

Yanacona (Q): in colonial usage, a nonayllu Indian responsible to a Spanish
master

BIBLIOGRAPHY

ARCHIVAL SOURCES

Archivo Histórico de Potosí–Casa Nacional de la Moneda (AHP–CNM), Potosí
> Cabildo, Gobierno e Intendencia (AHP–CNM.CGI)
> Iglesias y Conventos (AHP–CNM.IYC)
> Escrituras Notariales (AHP–CNM.EN)
> *Notaries*
>> Martín de Barrientos (1572)
>> Luis de la Torre (1577)
>> Pedro Ochoa (1587)
>> Juan Gutiérrez Bernal (1590)
>> Pedro Venegas (1595; 1601; 1604; 1609; 1615)
>> Baltazar Ayllón (1609)
>> Juan Martín Menacho (1615)
>> Gaspar Esteban de Sagastegui (1615)
>> Pedro Lopés Pallares (1620)
>> Sancho Ochoa (1620)
>> Baltasar de Barrionuevo (1625; 1630; 1635; 1643; 1645; 1648; 1649; 1652; 1653; 1654)
>> Diego Pacheco de Chávez (1640)
>> Diego de Quiñones (1652; 1653; 1654)
>> Juan de Barrionuevo (1661; 1662; 1663)
>> Luis Maldonado (1663)
>> Juan de Barrionuevo (1663)
>> Antonio Domínguez (1670)
>> Pedro Bellido (1670; 1675; 1681; 1685; 1690; 1695; 1700)

Archivo General de Indias (AGI), Seville
> Charcas 32, 40, 47, 80, 134, 415, 416, 418
> Escribanía 868
> Indiferente General 1239
> Justicia 667
> Lima 313

Archivo Nacional de Bolivia (ANB), Sucre
  Cabildo de Potosí, Libro de Actas (ANB.CPLA)
    Extant Volumes:
      Vol. 5: 1585, 1586, 1587, 1588, 1589, 1590
      Vol. 6: 1591, 1592, 1593
      Vol. 7: 1593, 1594, 1595
      Vol. 8: 1596, 1597, 1598, 1599
      Vol. 9: 1600
      Vol. 10: 1602, 1603, 1604
      Vol. 11: 1605, 1606
      Vol. 12: 1606, 1607, 1608, 1609, 1610, 1611
      Vol. 14: 1614, 1615, 1616
      Vol. 15: 1616, 1617
      Vol. 16: 1618, 1619, 1620, 1621, 1622
      Vol. 18: 1626, 1627, 1628
      Vol. 20: 1634, 1635, 1636
      Vol. 24: 1649, 1650, 1651
      Vol. 26: 1658, 1659, 1660, 1661
      Vol. 30: 1674, 1675, 1676
      Vol. 31: 1676, 1677, 1678, 1679, 1680, 1681
  Correspondencia, Audiencia de Charcas (ANB.CACH)
  Expedientes Coloniales (ANB.EC)
  Escrituras Públicas (ANB.EP)
    Notaries:
      Juan Bravo (1576; 1577; 1578)
      Alonso Fernández Michel (1602)
      Blas de Carvajal (1614)
      Antonio Herrera (1630)
      Pedro Alvarez de Espinosa (1643)
      Francisco Ortiz Gallo (1659; 1660)
      Diego de Toledo (1668; 1669; 1670; 1671; 1672; 1673)
      Salvador Gómez de Soto (1680; 1681)
  Libros de Acuerdo, Audiencia de Charcas (ANB.LAACH)
  Minas (ANB.Minas)
  Rück (ANB.Rück)

Archivo-Biblioteca Arquidiocesano "Mons. Taborga" (ABAS), Sucre
  Causas y Acusaciones de y contra Eclesiásticos
  Causas Matrimoniales
  Causas Matrimoniales y Dispensas
  Divorcios

Acosta, José de. *Natural and Moral History of the Indies*. Edited by Jane E. Mangan, with introduction and commentary by Walter D. Mignolo, translated by Frances M. López-Morillas. Durham, N.C.: Duke University Press, 2002.

Arzáns de Orsúa y Vela, Bartolomé. *Historia de la villa imperial de Potosí*. Edited by Lewis Hanke and Gunnar Mendoza. 3 vols. Providence, R.I.: Brown University Press, 1965.

Capoche, Luis. *Relación general de la villa imperial de Potosí*. In *Relaciones histórico-literarias de la América Meridional*. Vol. 122 of *Biblioteca de autores españoles desde la formación del lenguaje hasta nuestros días*. Madrid: Atlas, 1959.

Cobo, Father Bernabé. *Historia del nuevo mundo*. Edited by D. Marcos Jiménez de la Espada. Seville: E. Rasco, 1893.

Concolorcorvo. *El Lazarillo de Ciegos Caminantes*. In *Relaciones histórico-literarias de la América Meridional*. Vol. 122 of *Biblioteca de autores españoles desde la formación del lenguaje hasta nuestros días*. Madrid: Atlas, 1959.

"Descripción de la Villa y minas de Potosí: Año de 1603." In *Relaciones geográficas de Indias: Perú*, edited by Marcos Jiménez de la Espada. Vols. 183–85 of *Biblioteca de autores españoles desde la formación del lenguaje hasta nuestros días*. Madrid: Atlas, 1965.

Diez de San Miguel, Garci. *Visita hecha a la provincia de Chucuito por Garci Díez de San Miguel en el año 1567*. Lima: Casa de la Cultura, 1964.

Francisco de Toledo: Disposiciones gubernativas para el virreinato del Perú, 1575–1580. Introduction by Guillermo Lohmann Villena and transcription by María Justina Sarabía Viejo. Seville: Escuela de Estudios Hispano-Americanos, 1989.

Garcilaso de la Vega, El Inca. *Royal Commentaries of the Incas and General History of Peru*. Translated by Harold V. Livermore. Austin: University of Texas Press, 1970.

Lizarraga, Fray Reginaldo de. *Descripción breve de toda la tierra del Perú, Tucumán, Río de la Plata y Chile*. Vol. 216 of *Biblioteca de autores españoles desde la formación del lenguaje hasta nuestros días*. Madrid: Atlas, 1968.

Matienzo, Juan de. *Gobierno del Perú*. Edited by Guillermo Lohmann Villena. Lima: Institut Français d'Etudes Andines, 1967 [1567].

Mercado, Melchor María. *Album de paisajes: Tipos humanos y costumbres de Bolivia*. La Paz: Archivo y Biblioteca Nacionales de Bolivia, Banco Central de Bolivia, 1991 [1841–1869].

Ocaña, Fray Diego de. *Un viaje fascinante por la América hispana del siglo XVI*. Edited by Fray Arturo Alvarez. Madrid: STVDIVM, 1996.

"Relación muy particular del cerro y minas de Potosí y de su calidad y labores, por Nicolas del Benino, dirigida a don Francisco de Toledo,

Virrey del Perú, en 1573." In *Relaciones geográficas de Indias: Perú*, edited by
Marcos Jiménez de la Espada. Vols. 183–85 of *Biblioteca de autores españoles
desde la formación del lenguaje hasta nuestros días*. Madrid: Atlas, 1965.

SECONDARY SOURCES

Aguirre, Carlos. "Violencia, castigo y control social: Esclavos y panaderías en
   Lima, siglo XIX." *Pasado y presente* 1 (1988): 27–37.
Andrien, Kenneth. *Crisis and Decline: The Viceroyalty of Peru in the Seventeenth
   Century*. Albuquerque: University of New Mexico Press, 1985.
———. *Andean Worlds: Indigenous History, Culture and Consciousness under
   Spanish Rule, 1532-1825*. Albuquerque: University of New Mexico Press,
   2001.
Arrelucea Barrantes, Maribel. "Conducta y control social colonial: Estudio
   de las panaderías limeñas en el siglo XVIII." *Revista del Archivo General de
   la Nación* 16 (1994): 133–51.
Arrom, Silvia Marina. *The Women of Mexico City, 1790–1857*. Stanford, Calif.:
   Stanford University Press, 1985.
Assadourian, Carlos Sempat. "La producción de la mercancía dinero en la
   formación del mercado interno colonial." In *Ensayos sobre el desarrollo
   económico de México y América Latina (1500–1975)*, edited by Enrique
   Florescano. Mexico City: Fondo de Cultura Económica, 1979.
———. *El sistema de la economía colonial: Mercado interno, regiones y espacio
   económico*. Lima: Instituto de Estudios Peruanos, 1982.
Bakewell, Peter. *Miners of the Red Mountain: Indian Labor in Potosí, 1545-1650*.
   Albuquerque: University of New Mexico Press, 1984.
———. *Silver and Entrepreneurship in Seventeenth-Century Potosí: The Life and
   Times of Antonio López de Quiroga*. Albuquerque: University of New
   Mexico Press, 1988.
Ballesteros Gaibrois, Manuel. *Descubrimiento y fundación del Potosí*. Zaragoza,
   Spain: Delegación de Distrito de Educación Nacional, 1950.
Baquijano, Joseph. "Historia del descubrimiento del Cerro de Potosí."
   Mercurio peruano 7 (Jan.–April 1793): 28–48.
Barnadas, Josep María. "Una polémica colonial: Potosí, 1579–1684." *Jahrbuch
   fur Geschichte von Staat, Wirtshaft und Gesellchaft Lateinamerikas* (Colonia)
   10 (1973): 16–70.
———. *Charcas: Orígenes históricos de una sociedad colonial*. La Paz: Centro de
   Investigación y Promoción del Campesinado, 1973.
Beckles, Hilary McDowell. *Natural Rebels: A Social History of Enslaved Black
   Women in Barbados*. New Brunswick, N.J.: Rutgers University Press, 1989.
Bennett, Herman. "Lovers, Family, and Friends: The Formation of Afro-
   Mexico, 1580–1810." Ph.D. diss., Duke University, 1993.

Bennett, Judith. "Feminism and History." *Gender and History* 1.3 (1989): 251–72.

———. *Ale, Beer, and Brewsters in England: Women's Work in a Changing World, 1300–1600*. New York: Oxford University Press, 1996.

Bennett, Judith, and Amy Froide, eds. *Singlewomen in the European Past, 1250–1800*. Philadelphia: University of Pennsylvania Press, 1999.

Bilinkoff, Jodi. "Elite Widows and Religions Expression in Early Modern Spain: The View from Avila." In *Widowhood in Medieval and Early Modern Europe*, edited by Sandra Cavallo and Lyndan Warner. New York: Pearson Education, 1999.

Bowser, Frederick. *The African Slave in Colonial Peru, 1524–1650*. Stanford, Calif.: Stanford University Press, 1974.

Buechler, Hans, and Judith-Maria Buechler. *The World of Sofía Velázquez: The Autobiography of a Bolivian Market Woman*. New York: Columbia University Press, 1996.

Buechler, Rose Marie. *The Mining Society of Potosí, 1776–1810*. Ann Arbor, Mich.: published for the Department of Geography, Syracuse University, by University Microfilms International, 1981.

Burkett, Elinor. "In Dubious Sisterhood: Class and Sex in Spanish Colonial South America." *Latin American Perspectives* 4 (1977): 18–26.

———. "Indian Women and White Society: The Case of Sixteenth-Century Peru." In *Latin American Women: Historical Perspectives*, edited by Asunción Lavrin. Westport, Conn.: Greenwood, 1978.

Burkholder, Mark A., and D. S. Chandler. *From Impotence to Authority: The Spanish Crown and the American Audiencias, 1687–1808*. Columbia: University of Missouri Press, 1977.

Burnard, Trevor. "Inheritance and Independence: Women's Status in Early Colonial Jamaica." *William and Mary Quarterly* 48 (1991): 93–116.

Burns, Kathryn. *Colonial Habits: Convents and the Spiritual Economy of Cuzco, Peru*. Durham, N.C.: Duke University Press, 1999.

Cadena, Marisol de la. "'Women Are More Indian': Ethnicity and Gender in a Community near Cuzco." In Larson, Harris, and Tandeter 1995.

———. *Indigenous Mestizos: The Politics of Race and Culture in Cuzco, Peru, 1919–1991*. Durham, N.C.: Duke University Press, 2000.

Cahill, David, "Colour by Numbers: Racial and Ethnic Categories in the Viceroyalty of Peru, 1532–1824." *Journal of Latin American Studies* 26.2 (1994): 325–46.

Cañedo-Argüelles Fábrega, Teresa. *Potosí: La versión aymara de un mito europeo: La minería y sus efectos en las sociedades andinas del siglo XVII. La provincia de Pacajes*. Madrid: Catriel, 1993.

Carr, Lois, and Lorena Walsh. "The Planter's Wife: Colonial Women in the Chesapeake." *William and Mary Quarterly* 34 (1977): 542–72.

Carrera Stampa, Manuel. "The Evolution of Weights and Measures in New Spain." *Hispanic American Historical Review* 29.1 (1949): 2–24.

Celestino, Olinda, and Albert Meyers. *Las cofradías en el Perú: Región central.* Frankfurt a.M.: Klaus Dieter Vervuert, 1981.

Chao, María del Pilar. "La población de Potosí en 1779." *Anuario del Instituto de Investigaciones Históricas* (Rosario, Argentina) 8 (1965): 171–80.

Choque Canqui, Roberto. "El papel de los capitanes de indios de la provincia de Pacajes en el entero de la mita de Potosí." *Revista andina* 1.1 (1983): 117–24.

Chambers, Sarah C. *From Subjects to Citizens: Honor, Culture and Politics in Arequipa, Peru, 1780–1854.* University Park: Penn State University Press, 1999.

Charney, Paul. "A Sense of Belonging: Colonial Indian Cofradías and Ethnicity in the Valley of Lima, Peru." *Americas* 54.3 (1988): 379–407.

Chojnacka, Monica. *Working Women of Early Modern Venice.* Baltimore: Johns Hopkins University Press, 2001.

Cieza de León, Pedro. *Primera parte de la crónica del Perú.* Vol. 26 of *Biblioteca de autores españoles desde la formación del lenguaje hasta nuestros días.* Madrid: Atlas, 1947.

Cleary, Patricia. "'She Will Be in the Shop': Women's Sphere of Trade in Eighteenth-Century Philadelphia and New York." *Pennsylvania Magazine of History and Biography* 119.3 (1995): 181–202.

Cobb, Gwendolin B. "Potosí, a South American Mining Frontier." In *Greater American: Essays in Honor of Herbert Eugene Bolton.* Berkeley: University of California Press, 1945.

———. "Supply and Transportation for the Potosí Mines, 1545–1640." *Hispanic American Historical Review* 29.1 (1949): 25–45.

———. *Potosí y Huancavelica: Bases económicas, 1545–1640.* Translated by Ing. Jorge Muñoz Reyes. La Paz: Banco Minero de Bolivia, Biblioteca Bamin, 1977.

Cole, Jeffrey. *The Potosí Mita, 1573–1700: Compulsory Indian Labor in the Andes.* Stanford, Calif.: Stanford University Press, 1985.

Cope, R. Douglas. *The Limits of Racial Domination: Plebeian Society in Colonial Mexico City, 1660–1720.* Madison: University of Wisconsin Press, 1994.

Crespo Rodas, Alberto. *La guerra entre vicuñas y vascongados: Potosí, 1622–1625.* La Paz: Colección Popular, 1969.

Cummins, Thomas B. F. *Toasts with the Inca: Andean Abstraction and Colonial Images on Quero Vessels.* Ann Arbor: University of Michigan Press, 2002.

Davies, Keith. *Landowners in Colonial Peru.* Austin: University of Texas Press, 1984.

Escobari de Querejazu, Laura. *Producción y comercio en el espacio sur andino, s. XVII.* La Paz: Embajada de España en Bolivia, 1985.

———. "Conformación urbana y étnica en las ciudades de La Paz y Potosí durante la colonia." *Historia y cultura* 18 (1990): 43–77.

———. "Migración multiétnica y mano de obra calificada en Potosí, siglo XVI." In *Etnicidad, economía y simbolismo en los Andes*, edited by Silvia Arze, Rossana Barragan, Laura Escobari, and Ximena Medinaceli. La Paz: Hisbol, 1992.

Flores Galindo, Alberto. *Aristocracia y plebe: Lima, 1760–1830 (Estructura de clases y sociedad colonial)*. Lima: Mosca Azul, 1984.

Flusche, Della, and Eugene Korth. *Forgotten Females: Women of African and Indian Descent in Colonial Chile, 1535–1800*. Detroit: B. Ethridge, 1983.

Francois, Marie. "When Pawnshops Talk: Popular Credit and Material Culture in Mexico City, 1775–1916." Ph.D. diss., University of Arizona, 1998.

Garafalo, Leo. "The Ethno-economy of Food, Drink, and Stimulants: The Making of Race in Colonial Lima and Cuzco." Ph.D. diss., University of Wisconsin-Madison, 2001.

Gauderman, Kimberly. *Women's Lives in Colonial Quito: Gender, Law, and Economy in Spanish America*. Austin: University of Texas Press, 2003.

Gisbert, Teresa. *Historia de la vivienda y los conjuntos urbanos en Bolivia*. Mexico City: Instituto Panamericano de Geografía e Historia, 1991.

Glave, Luis Miguel. "Mujer indígena, trabajo doméstico y cambio social en el virreinato peruano del siglo XVII: La ciudad de La Paz y el sur andino en 1684." *Boletín del Instituto Francés de Estudios Andinos* 16: 3–4 (1987): 339–69.

———. *Trajinantes: Caminos indígenas en la sociedad colonial, siglos XVI/XVII*. Lima: Instituto de Apoyo Agrario, 1989.

González Casasnovas, Ignacio. *Las dudas de la corona: La política de repartimientos para la minería de Potosí (1680–1732)*. Madrid: Consejo Superior de Investigaciones Científicas, Centro de Estudios Históricos, 2000.

González Sánchez, Carlos Alberto. *Dineros de ventura: La varia fortuna de la emigración a Indias (siglos XVI–XVII)*. Seville: Universidad de Sevilla, 1995.

Gotkowitz, Laura. "Trading Insults: Honor, Violence, and the Gendered Culture of Commerce in Cochabamba, Bolivia, 1870s–1950s." *Hispanic American Historical Review* 83: 1 (2003): 83–118.

Graham, Sandra Lauderdale. *House and Street: The Domestic World of Servants and Masters in Nineteenth-Century Rio de Janeiro*. Austin: University of Texas Press, 1992.

Graubart, Karen B. "Indecent Living: Indigenous Women and the Politics of Representation in Early Colonial Peru." *Colonial Latin American Review* 9: 2 (2000): 213–35.

Greenow, Linda. *Credit and Socioeconomic Change in Colonial Mexico: Loans and Mortgages in Guadalajara*. Boulder, Colo.: Westview, 1983.

Hames, Gina. "Honor, Alcohol and Sexuality: Women and the Creation of Ethnic Identity in Bolivia, 1870–1930." Ph.D. diss., Carnegie Mellon University, 1996.

Hanawalt, Barbara, ed. *Women and Work in Preindustrial Europe*. Bloomington: Indiana University Press, 1986.

Hanke, Lewis. *The Imperial City of Potosí: An Unwritten Chapter in the History of Spanish America*. The Hague: Martinus Nijoff, 1956.

———. Prologue to Capoche, *Relación General*.

Haring, C. H. *The Spanish Empire in America*. New York: Oxford University Press, 1947.

Hartmann, Roswith. "Mercados y ferias prehispánicos en el área andina." *Boletín de la Academia Nacional de Historia* (Quito) 54 (118): 214–35.

Hoberman, Louis-Schell. *Mexico's Merchant Elite, 1590–1660: Silver, State and Society*. Durham, N.C.: Duke University Press, 1991.

Hunt, Margaret. *The Middling Sort: Commerce, Gender, and the Family in England, 1680–1780*. Berkeley: University of California Press, 1996.

Iwasaki Cauti, Fernando. "Ambulantes y comercio colonial, iniciativas mercantiles en el Virreinato Peruano." *Jahrbuch für Geschichte* 24 (1987): 179–211.

Karasch, Mary. "Suppliers, Sellers, Servants, and Slaves." In *Cities and Society in Colonial Latin America*, edited by Louisa Schell Hoberman and Susan M. Socolow. Albuquerque: University of New Mexico Press, 1986.

Keith, Robert G. *Conquest and Agrarian Change: The Emergence of the Hacienda System on the Peruvian Coast*. Cambridge, Mass.: Harvard University Press, 1976.

Kicza, John E. *Colonial Entrepreneurs: Families and Business in Bourbon Mexico City*. Albuquerque: University of New Mexico Press, 1983.

Kinsbruner, Jay. *Petty Capitalism in Spanish America: The Pulperos of Puebla, Mexico City, Caracas, and Buenos Aires*. Greenwood, Conn.: Westview, 1987.

Kuznesof, Elizabeth. "Ethnic and Gender Influences on 'Spanish' Creole Society in Colonial Spanish America." *Colonial Latin American Review* 4.1 (1995): 153–76.

Larson, Brooke. "La producción doméstica y trabajo femenino indígena en la formación de una economía mercantil colonial." *Historia boliviana* 3.2 (1983): 173–85.

———. "Andean Communities, Political Cultures, and Markets: The Changing Contours of a Field." In Larson, Harris, and Tandeter 1995.

———. *Colonialism and Agrarian Transformation in Bolivia: Cochabamba, 1550–1900*. Durham, N.C.: Duke University Press, 1998 [1988].

Larson, Brooke, and Olivia Harris, with Enrique Tandeter, eds. *Ethnicity,*

Markets, and Migration in the Andes: At the Crossroads of History and Anthropology. Durham, N.C.: Duke University Press, 1995.

Lavrin, Asunción, ed. *Sexuality and Marriage in Colonial Latin America*. Lincoln: University of Nebraska Press, 1989.

Lavrin, Asunción, and Edith Couturier. "Dowries and Wills: A View of Women's Socioeconomic Role in Colonial Guadalajara and Puebla, 1640–1790." *Hispanic American Historical Review* 59.2 (1979): 280–304.

Llano Restrepo, María Clara, and Marcela Campuzano Cifuentes. *La chicha: Una bebida fermentada a través de la historia*. Bogotá: CEREC, 1994.

López Beltrán, Clara. "La mina gasta muchos indios: Mineros y campesinos del siglo XVII en las minas de Potosí." *Cuadernos hispanoamericanos: Los complementarios* (Madrid) 7–8 (1991): 59–86.

Lowry, Lyn Brandon. "Forging an Indian Nation: Urban Indians under Spanish Colonial Control (Lima, Peru, 1535–1765)." Ph.D. diss., University of California, Berkeley, 1991.

Mangan, Jane E. "To Market and Home Again: The Path to Autonomy of Colonial Mexican Pulqueras." Master's thesis, Duke University, 1995.

Martin, Cheryl English. *Governance and Society in Colonial Mexico: Chihuahua in the Eighteenth Century*. Stanford, Calif.: Stanford University Press, 1996.

Martínez López-Cano, María del Pilar. *El crédito a largo plazo en el siglo XVI*. Mexico City: Universidad Autónoma de México, 1995.

Martínez López-Cano, Maria del Pilar, and Guillermina del Valle Pavón, eds. *El crédito en Nueva España*. Mexico City: Instituto Mora, 1998.

Mignolo, Walter D. "Signs and Their Transmission: The Question of the Book in the New World." In *Writing without Words: Alternative Literacies in Mesoamerica and the Andes*, edited by Elizabeth Boone and Walter D. Mignolo. Durham, N.C.: Duke University Press, 1994.

Minchom, Martin. "La economía subterránea y el mercado urbano: Pulperos, 'indias gateras' y 'recatonas' del Quito colonial (siglos XVI–XVII)." In *Memorias del Primer Simposio Europeo sobre Antropología del Ecuador*, comp. Segundo E. Moreno Yánez. Quito: Abya-Yala, 1985.

———. *The People of Quito, 1690–1810: Change and Unrest in the Underclass*. Greenwood, Conn.: Westview, 1994.

Money, Mary. *Los obrajes, el traje y el comercio de ropa en la audiencia de Charcas*. La Paz: Taller Don Bosco, 1983.

Moore, John Preston. *The Cabildo in Peru under the Hapsburgs: A Study in the Origins and Powers of the Town Council in the Viceroyalty of Peru, 1530–1700*. Durham, N.C.: Duke University Press, 1954.

Mörner, Magnus. *Race Mixture in the History of the Americas*. Boston: Little Brown, 1967.

Murra, John V. *The Economic Organization of the Inca State*. Greenwich, Conn.: Westview, 1955.

Murra, John V. "El control vertical de un máximo de pisos ecológicos en la economía de las sociedades andinas." In *Formaciones económicas y políticas del mundo andino*. Lima: Instituto de Estudios Peruanos, 1975.

———. "Aymara Lords and Their European Agents at Potosí." *Nova Americana* 1 (1978): 231–43.

Padden, R. C., ed. *Tales of Potosí*. Based on Bartolomé Arzáns de Orsúa y Vela and translated by Frances M. López-Morillas. Providence, R.I.: Brown University Press, 1975.

Parkerson, Phillip T. "The Inca Coca Monopoly: Fact or Legal Fiction?" *Proceedings of the American Philosophical Society* 127.1 (1983): 107–23.

Perry, Mary Elizabeth. *Gender and Disorder in Early Modern Seville*. Princeton, N.J.: Princeton University Press, 1990.

Platt, Tristan. "'Without Deceit or Lies': Variable *Chinu* Readings during a Sixteenth-Century Tribute-Restitution Trial." In Quilter and Urton 2002.

Powers, Karen. *Andean Journeys: Migration, Ethnogenesis, and the State in Colonial Quito*. Albuquerque: University of New Mexico Press, 1995.

Presta, Ana María. *Los encomenderos de La Plata, 1550–1600: Encomienda, familia y negocios en Charcas colonial*. Lima: Instituto de Estudios Peruanos, 2000.

Quilter, Jeffrey, and Gary Urton, eds. *Narrative Threads: Accounting and Recounting in Andean Khipu*. Austin: University of Texas Press, 2002.

Quiroz, Alfonso W. *Deudas olvidadas: Instrumentos de crédito en la economía colonial peruana, 1750–1820*. Lima: Pontifica Universidad Católica del Perú, Fondo Editorial, 1993.

———. "Reassessing the Role of Credit in Late Colonial Peru: *Censos, Escrituras*, and *Imposiciones*." *Hispanic American Historical Review* 74.2 (1994): 193–230.

Ramírez, Susan Elizabeth. *Provincial Patriarchs: Land Tenure and the Economics of Power in Colonial Peru*. Albuquerque: University of New Mexico Press, 1986.

———. "Exchange and Markets in the Sixteenth Century: A View from the North." In Larson, Harris, and Tandeter 1995.

Rivera Cusicanqui, Silvia. "El Mallku y la sociedad colonial en el siglo XVII: El caso de Jesús de Machaca." *Avances* (La Paz) 1 (1978): 7–27.

Ross, Ellen. *Love and Toil: Motherhood in Outcast London, 1870–1918*. New York: Oxford University Press, 1993.

Rowe, John Howland. "Inca Policies and Institutions Relating to the Cultural Unification of the Empire." In *The Inca and Aztec States, 1400–1800: Anthropology and History*, edited by George Collier, Renato Rosaldo, and John Wirth. New York: Academic, 1982.

Rostworowski, María de Diez Canseco. *History of the Inca Realm*. Translated by Harry B. Iceland. New York: Cambridge University Press, 1999.

Saignes, Thierry. *Caciques, Tribute, and Migration in the Southern Andes:*

Indian Society and the Seventeenth-Century Colonial Order. Translated by
Paul Garner with revisions by Tristan Platt. London: Institute of Latin
American Studies, 1985.

———. *En busca del poblamiento étnico de los Andes bolivianos*. La Paz: Museo
Nacional de Etnografía y Folklore, 1986.

———. "Capoche, Potosí y la coca: El consumo popular de estimulantes en
el siglo XVII." *Revista de Indias* 48.182–83 (1988): 207–35.

———. "Borracheras andinas: ¿Por qué los indios ebrios hablan en español?"
with commentary by Roberto Choque Canqui, Teresa Gisbert, Penelope
Harvey, Dwight B. Heath, Jorge Hidalgo L., and Carmen Salazar-Soler.
Revista andina 7.1 (1989): 83–127.

———, ed. *Borracheras y memoria: La experiencia de lo sagrado en los Andes*.
Lima: HISBOL, Instituto Francés de Estudios Andinos, 1993.

———. "Indian Migration and Social Change in Seventeenth-Century
Charcas." In Larson, Harris, and Tandeter 1995.

Salomon, Frank. *Native Lords of Quito in the Age of the Incas: The Political
Economy of North Andean Chiefdoms*. Cambridge: Cambridge University
Press, 1986.

———. "Indian Women of Early Colonial Quito as Seen through Their
Testaments." *Americas* 44.3 (1988): 325–41.

Schroeder, Susan, Stephanie Wood, and Robert Haskett, eds. *Indian Women
of Early Mexico*. Norman: University of Oklahoma Press, 1997.

Schwaller, John Frederick. *Origins of Church Wealth in Mexico: Ecclesiastical
Revenues and Church Finances, 1523-1600*. Albuquerque: University of New
Mexico Press, 1985.

Seed, Patricia. "Social Dimensions of Race: Mexico City, 1753." *Hispanic
American Historical Review* 62 (1982): 559–606.

———. *To Love, Honor, and Obey in Colonial Mexico: Conflicts over Marriage
Choice, 1574-1821*. Stanford, Calif.: Stanford University Press, 1988.

Seligmann, Linda. "Market Places, Social Spaces, in Cuzco, Peru." *Urban
Anthropology* 29.1 (2000): 1–68.

Silverblatt, Irene. *Moon, Sun, and Witches: Gender Ideologies and Class in Inca
and Colonial Peru*. Princeton, N.J.: Princeton University Press, 1987.

Socolow, Susan M. *The Merchants of Buenos Aires, 1778-1810: Family and
Commerce*. Cambridge: Cambridge University Press, 1978.

———. "Economic Roles of the Free Women of Color of Cap Français." In
More than Chattel: Black Women and Slavery in the Americas, edited by
Barry Gaspar and Darlene Clark Hine. Bloomington: Indiana University
Press, 1997.

Sordo, Emma María. "Civilizational Designs: The Architecture of
Colonialism in the Native Parishes of Potosí." Ph.D. diss., University of
Miami, 2000.

Spalding, Karen. "Social Climbers: Changing Patterns of Mobility among the Indians of Colonial Peru." *Hispanic American Historical Review* 50.4 (1970): 645–64.

———. "Kurakas and Commerce: A Chapter in the Evolution of Andean Society." *Hispanic American Historical Review* 53.4 (1973): 581–99.

———. *Huarochirí: An Andean Society under Inca and Spanish Rule*. Stanford, Calif.: Stanford University Press, 1984.

Stansell, Christine. *City of Women: Sex and Class in New York, 1789–1860*. Urbana: University of Illinois Press, 1986.

Stern, Steve J. *Peru's Indian Peoples and the Challenge of Conquest: Huamanga to 1640*. Madison: University of Wisconsin Press, 1982.

———. "Feudalism, Capitalism, and the World-System in the Perspective of Latin America and the Caribbean." *American Historical Review* 93.4 (1988): 829–97.

———. *The Secret History of Gender*. Chapel Hill: University of North Carolina Press, 1995.

Super, John C. *Food, Conquest, and Colonization in Sixteenth-Century Spanish America*. Albuquerque: University of New Mexico Press, 1988.

Tandeter, Enrique. *Coercion and Market: Silver Mining in Colonial Potosí, 1692–1826*. Albuquerque: University of New Mexico Press, 1993.

Tandeter, Enrique, Vilma Milletich, María Matilde Ollier, and Beatríz Ruibal. "Indians in Late Colonial Markets: Sources and Numbers." In Larson, Harris, and Tandeter 1995.

Tebbutt, Melanie. *Making Ends Meet: Pawnbroking and Working-Class Credit*. New York: St. Martin's, 1983.

TePaske, John J., and Herbert S. Klein, eds. *The Royal Treasuries of the Spanish Empire in America*. Durham, N.C.: Duke University Press, 1982.

van Deusen, Nancy. *Between the Sacred and the Worldly: The Institutional and Cultural Practice of Recogimiento in Colonial Lima*. Stanford, Calif.: Stanford University Press, 2001.

Van Kirk, Sylvia. *Many Tender Ties: Women in Fur-Trade Society, 1670–1870*. Norman: University of Oklahoma Press, 1980.

Wightman, Ann M. *Indigenous Migration and Social Change: The Forasteros of Cuzco, 1570–1720*. Durham, N.C.: Duke University Press, 1990.

Wolff, Inge. *Regierung und Verwaltung der kolonialspanischen Städte in Hochperu, 1538–1650*. Cologne: Böhlau, 1970.

Zulawski, Ann. "Social Differentiation, Gender, and Ethnicity: Urban Indian Women in Colonial Bolivia, 1640–1725." *Latin American Research Review* 25.2 (1990): 93–113.

———. *They Eat from Their Labor: Work and Social Change in Colonial Bolivia*. Pittsburgh, Penn.: University of Pittsburgh Press, 1995.

INDEX

An f with a page number indicates a figure; m, a map; n., a note; t, a table.

Acosta, José de, 32, 40, 45, 81

Acua. *See* Chicha

Africans: alcohol consumption by, 51; chicha production and, 83; credit transactions of, 52, 111; as labor for bread production, 96–98; mixed unions with, 207 n.113; pawn transactions of, 111; property transactions of, 51, 52, 111, 193t; rancherías residency of, 71; as slave laborers, 18, 41–42, 83, 97–98, 151–52; zambahigos, 52, 209 n.12

African women: as bakery owners, 99–100; credit transactions of, 100–101, 128–29, 238 n.79; domestic service and, 151; loan transactions of, 194t7, t8; marriage of, 144–45, 241 n.33; as owners' agents, 148; as slaves, 151–52; as store clerks, 61

Ají, 27, 29, 37

Alcabala, 13, 39, 51, 139, 187, 200 n.52

Alcohol: consumption of, 51, 56, 69, 104, 209 n.6, 221 nn.39, 41; pulpería sales of, 49; regulations on, 18, 76; stolen goods as payment for, 107. *See also* Chicha; Chicha production; Wine

Aquillas and queros, 82, 85, 133, 220 n.31, 222 n.49, 239 n.85

Areche, José Antonio de, 187–88

Arequipa, 10, 30

Arrom, Silvia Marina, 200 n.45, 240 n.14

Assadourian, Carlos Sempat, 6, 7, 83, 198 nn.15, 17

Auction (remate), 118–19, 132

Audiencia of Charcas, 40–41, 53, 211 nn.22, 24

Ayllus: apprenticeships for sons and, 171–72, 247 n.39; cofradías and, 155, 172; communal identity and, 164, 245 n.9; forasteros (nonayllu Indians) and, 166; hatunruna and, 26; impact of market transactions on, 7; loan transactions and, 131; mita labor and, 37, 39, 44, 163–64, 164; reciprocity in, 25; ritual chicha drinking in queros and, 82, 83; urban migration and, 7, 10; vertical archipelagos and, 6, 25; wage labor, 162, 245 n.12. *See also* Kinship networks; Mita labor; Tribute system; Yanaconas

Bakeries: flour supplies for, 99–100; indigenous workers in, 97–98; marital status in ownership of, 140–41, 142–43, 148–49; price regulation of, 94, 227 n.88; profits of, 94, 99, 102; requests for town council action, 93–94, 226 n.81, n.85, 227 nn.87, 88, 90, 91; taxation of, 195t9. *See also* Bakers

Bakers: autonomy of, 94–95; social status of, 101, 102, 104; women as, 99–101, 142–43, 148–49, 227 n.90, 230 n.116. *See also* Bakeries

Hoberman, Louisa Schell, 197 n.8
Hunt, Margaret, 231 n.8

Inca period, 24
Indigenous men: loan transactions and, 115, 126–28, 127t, 128t, 194t7; pawn transactions of, 194t8, 238 n.74; wills of, 128; work contracts for, 128. *See also* Marriage; Mita labor
Indigenous peoples: kurakas on, 34, 164, 205 n.71; loan transactions of, 126–28, 127t, 128t, 194t7; mercury amalgamation and, 37; pawn transactions of, 111, 194t8; silver refining and, 31–32; subsistence goods trade and, 33; tavern ownership by, 51; taxation of, 39, 139; tribute system and, 33, 164; unrefined ore trade (rescate) and, 8, 32–33, 42, 204 n.58; wine consumption of, 60. *See also* Chicha; Indigenous men; Indigenous women; Kurakas; Rancherías
Indigenous women: apprenticeships for sons of, 171–72, 247 n.39; as bread vendors, 94–95, 228 n.94; in chicha industry, 84–85, 103, 185; collateral items, 113, 132; corn flour sales by, 80; credit activity between, 126, 130, 238 n.74; dress of, 134; entrepreneurship of, 145, 156–57, 182–83; loan transactions and, 87, 126–28, 127t, 128t, 194t7; marriages of, 145; neighborhood development and, 66–69; patriarchal authority and, 12, 199 n.44; pawn transactions of, 11, 123; prices inflated by, 52–53; property transactions of, 66–69, 193t; as regatones, 49, 52–53, 153; relations of, with Spanish

men, 61–62, 171, 205 n.72, 215 n.63, n.64, 247 n.37; in silver trade, 32, 171; Spanish women in Potosí and, 86–87, 223 nn.55, 56; as store clerks, 61–62, 215 n.64; urban economic spaces of, 14–15; wills, 114. *See also* Chicha
Iwasaki Cauti, Fernando, 199 n.31

Jesuits, 154

Karasch, Mary, 199 n.31
Kicza, John, 197 n.8, 200 n.47, 215 n.66, 230 n.116
Kinsbruner, Jay, 197 n.8, 200 n.53, 215 n.66, 231 n.7
Kinship networks: as credit sources, 113, 124–25; hija/o natural (child born outside marriage) and, 151; loan transactions and, 110–11, 131; market transactions and, 7; reciprocity and, 25; of single women, 152–53; urban migration and, 10; in vertical archipelagos, 6, 25
Kurakas: alcabala and, 187; capitanes general de mita and, 37; on chicha consumption, 79; trade agreements between European merchants and, 33; on indigenous presence in Potosí, 34, 164, 205 n.71; leadership roles of, 245 n.9; loan transactions of, 124–25; ritual offerings of chicha and, 82–83
Kuznesof, Elizabeth, 15

La Paz, 10, 30
La Plata, 25, 53, 211 n.24, 221 n.39
Larson, Brooke, 10, 30, 45, 198 n.17, 199 nn.29, 41
Lavrin, Asunción, 200 n.45, 231 n.8
Lipes Indians, 97, 103, 181

JANE E. MANGAN is an
assistant professor of history
at Davidson College.

Library of Congress
Cataloging-in-Publication Data
Mangan, Jane E.
Trading roles : gender, ethnicity, and the
urban economy in colonial Potosí /
Jane E. Mangan.
p. cm. — (Latin America otherwise)
Includes bibliographical references (p.)
and index.
ISBN 0-8223-3458-5 (cloth : alk. paper) —
ISBN 0-8223-3470-4 (pbk. : alk. paper)
1. Potosí (Bolivia) — Commerce — History —
16th century. 2. Potosí (Bolivia) —
Commerce — History — 17th century.
3. Potosí (Bolivia) — Ethnic relations —
History — 16th century. 4. Potosí (Bolivia) —
Ethnic relations — History — 17th century.
5. Sex role — Economic aspects — Bolivia —
Potosí — History — 16th century. 6. Sex
role — Economic aspects — Bolivia — Potosí —
History — 17th century. I. Title. II. Series.
HF3400.P68M36 2005
381'.0984'14 — dc22   2004026186